Garden Gate

The YEAR IN GARDENING

— VOLUME 14 —

SPECIAL PUBLICATIONS

Garden Gate

Please contact us to find out about other *Garden Gate* products and services:

By Phone: 1-800-341-4769
By Mail: 2200 Grand Avenue, Des Moines, IA 50312
By E-mail: GardenGate@GardenGateMagazine.com

OR VISIT OUR
Web Sites: www.GardenGateMagazine.com
or www.GardenGateStore.com
or www.GardenGateSpecials.com

Copyright 2008 August Home Publishing Co.

"*Surprise* is the greatest gift
which life can grant us."
— Boris Pasternak

Welcome

You hold in your hands a wealth of information from the pages of *Garden Gate* magazine 2008. Each year the editors bring you great stories about the plants you love, design ideas for your garden and basic how-to information from our test garden, along with tips and questions from our readers, before and after gardens and plans straight from our drawing board. We're here to help you create a beautiful place of your own!

In this new book, not only are all of the year's stories at your fingertips, but we've organized them in an easy-to-access format. Whether you're looking for inspiration from gardens we've photographed or how to plant and care for garden phlox, you'll be able to find the information quickly and easily. It's like having the editors of *Garden Gate* in your own back yard.

Each section has its own contents and in the back of the book you'll find an index for the entire book along with zone maps.

So sit back and enjoy a full year of gardening!

Garden Gate®
The Illustrated Guide to Home Gardening and Design®

PUBLISHER **Donald B. Peschke**
EDITOR **Steven M. Nordmeyer**
MANAGING EDITOR **Kristin Beane Sullivan**
ART DIRECTOR **Eric Flynn**
ASSOCIATE ART DIRECTOR **Carrie Topp**
SENIOR EDITOR **Stephanie Polsley Bruner**

ASSOCIATE EDITORS
**Jim Childs, Deborah Gruca,
Sherri Ribbey, Amanda Wurzinger**

SENIOR GRAPHIC DESIGNER
Kevin Venhaus

ILLUSTRATOR **Carlie Hamilton**
SENIOR PHOTOGRAPHER **David C. McClure**
CORPORATE GARDENER **Marcia Leeper**
VIDEOGRAPHERS **Mark A. Hayes, Jr.**
ELECTRONIC IMAGE SPECIALIST **Troy Clark**
EDITORIAL INTERN **Tigon Woline**

Garden Gate® (ISBN 978-0-9801046-6-0) Garden Gate® is a registered trademark of August Home Publishing Co., 2200 Grand Avenue, Des Moines, IA 50312. © Copyright 2008, August Home Publishing Company. All rights reserved. **PRINTED IN CHINA.**

TO ORDER ADDITIONAL COPIES
OF THIS BOOK
VISIT, WRITE OR CALL

www.GardenGateStore.com

Customer Service
P.O. Box 842, Des Moines, IA
50304-9961

800-341-4769
(Weekdays 8 a.m. to 5 p.m. CT)

To learn more about
Garden Gate magazine visit

www.GardenGateMagazine.com

Garden Gate contents

The YEAR IN GARDENING VOLUME 14

great plants — p. 8

Calibrachoa	10
Camellias	12
'Ville de Lyon' Clematis	16
Colchicums	18
Coreopsis	20
Cosmos	24
'Illustris' Elephant Ear	28
Foxglove	30
Hardy Hibiscus	32
Bigleaf Hydrangeas	36
Acapulco Salmon & Pink Hyssop	40
Native Plant Gardening	42
'Empress Wu's Yellow' Peony	44
Garden Phlox	46
'Henry Eilers' Sweet Coneflower	48
'Becky' Shasta Daisy	50
Siberian Iris	52
5 Plants That Live Up to Their Promise	56
Did You Know	58

top picks — p. 66

New Plants for 2008	68
Fragrant Flowers	76
Readers' Favorite Flowering Shrubs	82
Drought-Tolerant Perennials	86
Back-of-the-Border Perennials	92
Classic Lilies	98

before and after — p. 104

Starting from Scratch	106
From 'Oh, Dear' to 'Oh, Boy!'	110
Shade Garden Makeover	114
Midsummer Makeover	118
7 Tips for a Wonderful Water Garden	120
Sunny Side of the Street	124
Keep the Color Coming!	128

garden design — p. 132

Restful Retreat	134
Quick & Easy Shade Border	140
Small and Sensational	142
Best of Both Worlds	148
Inviting Spaces	154
Small-Space Secrets	158
Design on a Budget	160
Think Big	164
Create Great Island Beds	170
Vegetable Medley	176
Combine Bulbs and Perennials Like a Pro	180
Fall Splendor	182
Bring on the Blue	186
Color That Won't Quit!	190
Nine Tips for Season-Long Color	196
Winter Wonders	198
Did You Know	200

design challenge drawing board p. 204

Show Me the Door	**206**
Windowbox Wonders	**208**
Take Back Your Bed!	**210**
Flower Garden Makeover	**212**
Peace and Quiet	**214**
Patio Perfection	**216**
Weedy to Wonderful	**218**
As Easy as You Please	**220**
Divide and Disguise	**222**
One Hot Planting	**224**
A Change of Scenery	**226**
Room to Grow	**228**
Building Blocks of Design	**231**

COVER CREDITS:
Nuthatch photo © Jay Gilliam;
All others © Garden Gate.

all about containers p. 232

Choosing Containers	**234**
Double Delight	**236**
Dark and Dramatic	**238**
Garden Gems	**239**
First-Class Containers	**240**
Tropical Flair	**244**
Bold Combinations	**245**
Watering	**246**
Gold Rush	**248**
Holiday Packages	**249**
Condense Your Garden	**250**
Did You Know	**252**

WEB extras

Throughout the book, you'll find this icon indicating additional tips, videos and information on our Web site. Visit www.GardenGateMagazine.com, click the Web Extras button and look for this information in issues 79-84 of *Garden Gate* magazine. And while you're there, be sure to browse the rest of our helpful online content!

gardening basics p. 256

Go Green!	**258**
Compost Q&A	**260**
Save Plants, Save Money	**262**
Garden Myths?	**264**
Seed-Starting Solutions	**266**
Woody Weeds	**268**
Fight Tough Weeds and Win (Eventually)	**272**
7 Common Diseases	**274**
Too Big? Time To Dig!	**278**
Mail-Order Tips	**280**
How to Buy a Healthy Tree	**282**
Garden Gadgets	**284**
Tool Trellis	**286**
Feed Birds What They Love	**288**
One-Of-A-Kind Birdbath	**290**
Did You Know	**292**
Beneficials You Should Know	**304**
Pests to Watch For	**305**
Weeds You Should Know	**306**
Know Your Zones	**308**

index p. 310

great plants *for* your garden

YOUR OWN PERSONAL GARDEN COACH is what you'll find here. Great job dividing that Siberian iris! Prune your coreopsis here to get them to rebloom. Next year, buy a foxglove that looks like this. Answers to your questions, guidance and encouragement, inspiring photos. It'll all help you grow a winning garden this year!

Calibrachoa	10
Camellias	12
'Ville de Lyon' Clematis	16
Colchicums	18
Coreopsis	20
Cosmos	24
'Illustris' Elephant Ear	28
Foxglove	30
Hardy Hibiscus	32
Bigleaf Hydrangeas	36
Acapulco Salmon & Pink Hyssop	40
Gardening With Native Plants	42
'Empress Wu's Yellow' Peony	44
Garden Phlox	46
'Henry Eilers' Sweet Coneflower	48
'Becky' Shasta Daisy	50
Siberian Iris	52
5 Plants That Live Up to Their Promise	56
Did You Know	58

PLANTS | ANNUAL

Cover your containers in cascades of flowers!

Calibrachoa

CALIBRACHOA
Calibrachoa hybrids

*6 to 10 in. tall,
18 to 24 in. wide*
*Flowers in shades of blue, violet,
white, yellow, red, orange, peach,
bronze or pink from spring to frost*
Full sun to light shade
Moist, well-drained, slightly acid soil
No serious pests
Cold-hardy in USDA zones 9 to 11
Heat-tolerant in AHS zones 12 to 1

If there ever was a perfect container plant, calibrachoa is it. A trailing habit makes it great for hanging baskets, and a single plant can cover a container, like the ones at right. Or mix calibrachoa with other more upright or spiky annuals.

LOTS TO LIKE Just like petunias, this slightly fragrant annual blooms all summer and attracts hummingbirds. (Well, technically, it's a tender perennial, but most gardeners treat it as an annual.) But calibrachoa flowers hold up to rain better, don't need deadheading and don't form seeds that detract from the display. Even though the billowy flowers may slow a bit during the hottest part of summer, they come barreling back as the weather cools. With consistent moisture, they'll bloom right up until a hard frost or the days grow short.

A relative newcomer to the garden scene in North America, calibrachoa doesn't really have a common name yet. You may have heard it called mini petunia or million bells, which is actually a brand name. It does look like a smaller version of petunias, but with finer foliage and 1-inch flowers. Lots of series are on the market. Superbells®, Callie™, Million Bells® and Cabaret™ are some of the most popular ones. The colors you see in the photos at right are just a few of the dozens available at garden centers and nurseries.

HOW TO GROW IT With its blanket of flowers and trailing habit, calibrachoa really shines in containers and hanging baskets. In fact, it grows much better in containers than in the ground because it prefers the loose, slightly acid (pH of 5.5 to 6.5) soil in most potting mixes. When it's in alkaline soil, new growth will have a yellow tinge and the plant will be stunted and bloom poorly. Feed it monthly with a quarter-strength acid fertilizer, such as Miracid®, to keep the plant green and producing the most flowers.

And speaking of flowers, calibrachoa blooms best in full sun except in extreme heat, when some afternoon shade will prevent scorching. It'll flower with a little shade, but not as enthusiastically. Your plants may start to get lanky by midsummer. Check out "A quick perk-up" to learn how to remedy this.

Calibrachoa also likes even moisture, drooping a bit if it gets too dry. Usually a good soaking revives it, but don't overwater, either. If your plant stays droopy even after you water it, the roots have probably rotted and you'll need to replace the plant with another.

But calibrachoa's pretty undemanding. Just let the top inch of soil dry out between waterings and your plant will thrive and bloom happily. And you'll have color cascading down your favorite containers all season long!

— *Deborah Gruca*

A quick perk-up

By mid- to late summer, calibrachoa may start to look a bit tired, with some brown stems and foliage mixed in among the newer growth.

To undercut, lift the stems and pinch out any with dead foliage. Don't worry — you won't hurt the plant if you take some green, too.

The plant responds with a flush of new growth and flowers within a couple of weeks, especially if you give it a shot of fertilizer, too.

You can see where Superbells® gets its name. It's available in many colors, including the Tequila Sunrise, Red and Plum you see here.

Superbells® Plum

Callie™ Rose Star

Million Bells® Trailing Blue

Cabaret™ Yellow

www.GardenGateMagazine.com   *the* YEAR IN GARDENING

PLANTS | SHRUB

Think you can't grow these beautiful shrubs? Take another look!

Camellias

Camellia japonica

CAMELLIA
Camellia spp.

- 3 to 20 ft. tall, 3 to 10 ft. wide
- Showy flowers in early spring or late fall
- Part shade
- Moist, well drained, acid soil
- Scale as well as several other insects can become pests
- Cold-hardy in USDA zones 6 to 8
- Heat-tolerant in AHS zones 8 to 1

Botanical Names

False cypress
Chamaecyparis spp.
Japanese camellia
Camellia japonica
Sasanqua camellia
Camellia sasanqua
Yew *Taxus* spp.

PHOTOS: Courtesy of Monrovia Nursery

Almost everything about camellias is appealing. Glossy evergreen leaves and beautiful flowers make this a shrub that gardeners covet. But camellias are usually considered a Southern shrub with a reputation for being hard to grow. To me, the hardest thing about growing camellias is choosing a cultivar. Just look at some of the flower forms and colors available! And that's only a fraction of what you'll find when you shop.

I'll admit camellias do deserve at least part of their reputation for being tricky. Much of the problem stems from gardeners choosing the wrong spot or planting incorrectly. First I show you some of the gorgeous cultivars available. I'll help you get your plants off to a great start by sharing information about what they need, as well as the best planting technique. And if you're still thinking this is a shrub that only grows in USDA zones 7 to 8 — in other words, Southern gardens — I have a surprise for you on the next pages.

UNIQUE BLOOM TIMES Camellias arrived in North America some time in the late 18th century and have been a hit ever since. There are lots of beautiful species and hybrids in this large family of shrubs. But when you start to shop you'll discover there are mainly two popular species to choose from: Japanese or Sasanqua. And then there are lots of hybrids of these two species, as well.

The biggest difference between Japanese and Sasanqua camellias is their bloom time. Depending on the cultivar and where you live, Japanese camellias bloom in very early spring. Sasanquas bloom in late fall. Both are times when all gardeners could use some color in their landscape.

TAKE A LOOK AT THESE FLOWERS In the photos to the right you'll find five forms and a range of colors. Probably the most popular flower form, and the one that many of us start with when we buy our first camellia plant, is the formal double. You can see why with bright red 'Colonel Firey', a Japanese hybrid. Peony-form camellias have fewer petals and a center that's not quite so full as a formal camellia. Pink-and-white-streaked 'Jordan's Pride', another Japanese hybrid, is a colorful example. When it comes to unusual form and color, semi-double, creamy yellow 'Buttermint' steals the show. It's an early spring bloomer that's a hybrid of several different species. And it has a light carnationlike fragrance, rare among camellias. Anemone-form camellias have large petals surrounding a cluster of tightly curled ones in the center, like this pink Japanese hybrid, 'Elegans Splendor'. Last but not least, white 'Setsugekka' is a single-form Sasanqua camellia. Single flowers are often more weather resistant and hold up better during hard rains.

SHOW THEM OFF All camellias bloom when few other flowers are open. So these upright to oval-shaped shrubs combine well with other evergreens. And the flowers really show best against a contrasting background. For example, dark blooms show best against pale green or even yellow foliage, such as a golden false cypress. Place pale-colored varieties where they will shine in front of dark green yews.

If you're saying "They still won't grow in my zone," the truth is, they might. On the next pages I'll share some of the new hybrids that are inching their way north. Then I'll show you the perfect planting technique to get any camellia off to a great start.

12 *the* YEAR IN GARDENING www.GardenGateMagazine.com

COLD-CLIMATE CAMELLIAS

'Winter's Snowman'

'Winter's Interlude'

'April Remembere[d]'

Sources

Fairweather Gardens
www.fairweathergardens.com
856-451-6261
Catalog $5

Monrovia Nursery
At www.monrovia.com you'll be able to find a retailer near you. Go to "About Our Plants" and click on "Where to Buy."

Yes, camellias have journeyed as far north as USDA zone 6, and with thick mulch over their roots and a burlap wrap, even southern zone 5.

Many folks seem to think that the flowers of these new hybrids aren't quite as showy as some of their parents. But look at the three photos above — I don't think you'll be disappointed. There are many cultivars, both late fall and early spring bloomers, to choose from. To help you get started, I've selected three that are easy to find. Between the two sources on this page you'll be able to find all of the camellias I've shown you in this story.

'Winter's Snowman' and 'Winter's Interlude', above, are fall bloomers. Planted in zones 6 or 7, they'll bloom from early October until late December.

Fall bloomers are great in cold areas because the flower buds don't have to survive the roughest part of winter. Even if a cold snap blackens the flowers that are open, they'll be replaced as more of the hardy buds open. Eventually, long periods of bitter weather will reduce the blooms. And once the weather gets very cold and stays that way, the last few buds may not open.

'April Remembered' is one of the hardiest Japanese hybrids, flowering in late winter to early spring. While these hybrids are more temperamental when it comes to temperature changes, they still take much of zone 6 in stride — much colder than ordinary Japanese camellias. If you want to try them further north, it's a good idea to wrap the entire shrub in early winter with a layer of burlap. That helps protect the buds in northern zone 6, even into parts of zone 5. Be sure to unwrap the plant in late winter, after the coldest weather is over, so you can enjoy the flowers.

Are you intrigued and want to try a hardy camellia in your garden? To grow any of these beauties you'll need to know a few specific tips. I'll share those with you next.

Camellia corner

Since this camellia blooms in fall, I've planned a small garden featuring other plants to complement it. A bed close to the foundation, such as this northeast corner shaded from early morning light by a large tree, is a good spot.

- **A** Hybrid camellia *Camellia* 'Winter's Interlude'
- **B** Azalea *Rhododendron* 'Girard's Rose'
- **C** False Solomon's seal *Maianthemum racemosum*
- **D** Galax *Galax urceolata*

PLANTING SECRETS

It's true, camellias can be prima donnas. But like a true prima donna, when a camellia has what it wants, it'll be happy. Here's what a happy plant needs:

THE PERFECT SPOT Find a spot that's protected from bitter, dry winter winds. A southern or eastern exposure is good. Or you can screen camellias in winter from the windiest direction with sheets of burlap pinned to posts.

In summer, camellias need shade. Dappled light is best, as all-day sun will burn the foliage and dry the buds. Avoid planting close to a sunny wall, or where full morning sun warms the flower buds. That triggers them to open early in the day when air temperatures are still too cold for open flowers to survive.

THE BEST SOIL Like azaleas and rhododendrons, camellias prefer a low, or acid, pH, around 5 to 6. And at all cost, avoid both sandy soil that drains too quickly and clay that stays too wet. A well-drained, humus-enriched soil is a necessity for healthy camellias.

Camellia roots are shallow and won't tolerate extreme temperature fluctuations. A 2- to 4-inch-thick layer of pine needles or composted leaf mulch will help.

WATER DEEPLY When camellias are growing and setting buds in summer, they need steady moisture. If they get too dry, the buds drop and the foliage is stunted. So, water deeply but infrequently.

However, in winter, camellias like it dry, so you won't have to worry about watering.

A LEAN DIET A light feeding at the end of March or in early April and again in mid- to late June will keep all camellias blooming. Use a fertilizer specially blended for acid-loving shrubs.

MINIMAL PRUNING Since this is a slow-growing shrub, there's really not much pruning to do. However, if you need to shape the plant, do it after the flowers fade. Cut before new growth starts in spring so the plant has time to form next year's buds.

Below are specific and easy-to-do tips on planting. Once your camellia is established, it's quite carefree. When the flowers start opening, by all means pick a few to bring indoors. Most camellias make excellent cut flowers. □

—*Jim Childs*

Botanical Names

Azalea
Rhododendron spp.
Japanese camellia
Camellia japonica
Rhododendron
Rhododendron spp.

Off to a great start

Camellias are best planted in spring so their roots will have time to fully establish before winter. When you remove the pot, if the roots are circling, use a stream of water to help loosen the roots so you can tease some of them out from the tangled mass. Follow the instructions here for digging a hole and setting the plant in. After planting, build a reservoir around the plant and fill it with water. Then let the soil dry out before watering again. For the first year, if you don't receive an inch of rain each week, you'll need to water. But don't keep the soil too wet; camellias do best in well-drained conditions.

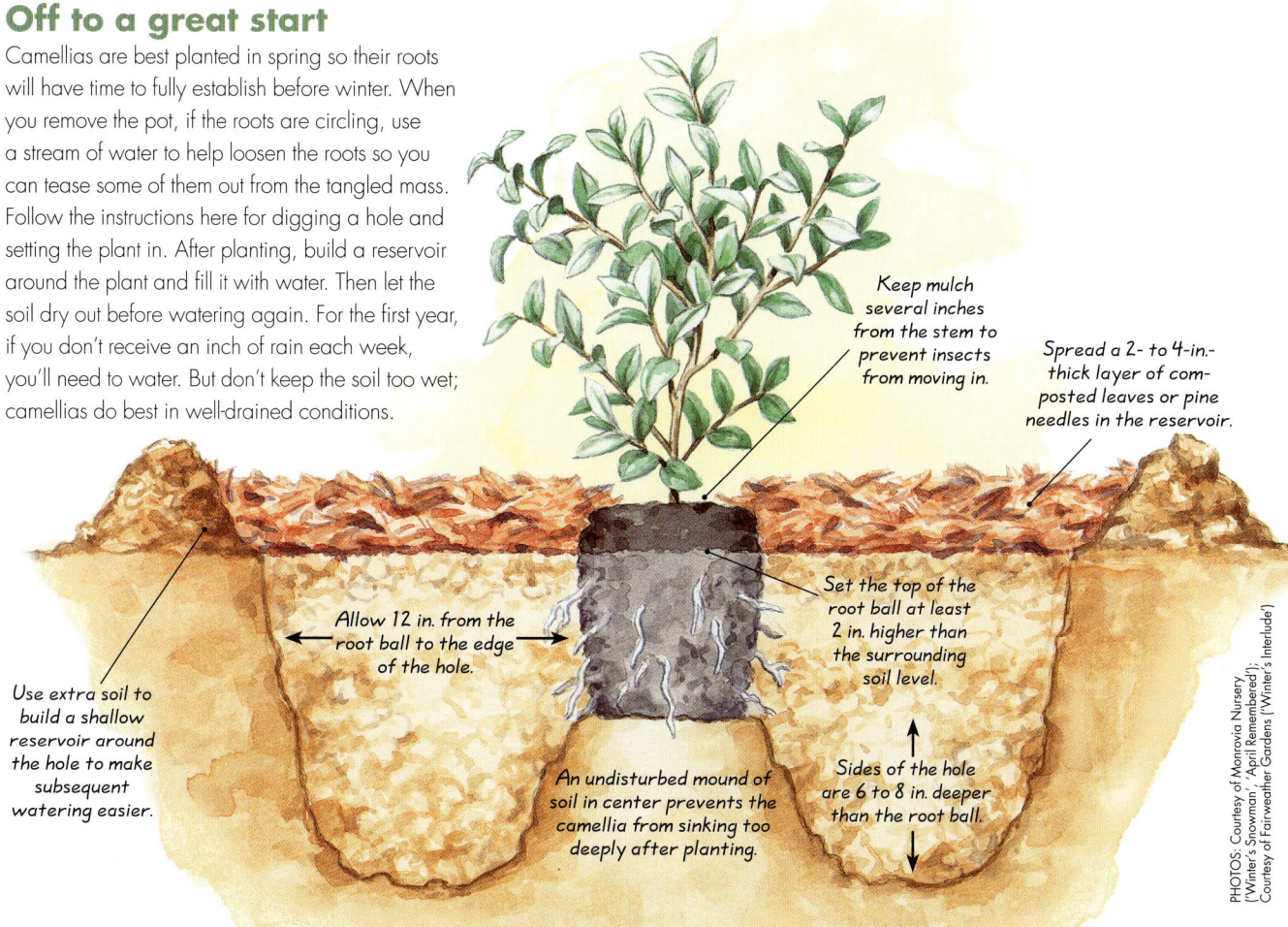

Keep mulch several inches from the stem to prevent insects from moving in.

Spread a 2- to 4-in.-thick layer of composted leaves or pine needles in the reservoir.

Set the top of the root ball at least 2 in. higher than the surrounding soil level.

Allow 12 in. from the root ball to the edge of the hole.

Use extra soil to build a shallow reservoir around the hole to make subsequent watering easier.

An undisturbed mound of soil in center prevents the camellia from sinking too deeply after planting.

Sides of the hole are 6 to 8 in. deeper than the root ball.

PLANTS | EDITOR'S CHOICE

'Ville de Lyon' Clematis

***Clematis* 'Ville de Lyon'**

Size	10 to 12 ft. tall by 3 ft. wide
Habit	Vine
Bloom	Carmine-red flowers from mid- to late summer, lighter rebloom in fall
Soil	Moist, fertile, slightly alkaline to neutral, well-drained soil
Light	Full sun to part shade
Pests	No serious pests or diseases
Hardiness	Cold: USDA zones 4 to 9 Heat: AHS zones 9 to 1

WEB extra Our *video* shows you how to cut with confidence!

They don't call clematis the "Queen of Vines" for nothing. Gardeners just love the big, gorgeous flowers, a long season of bloom and vines that reach to 12 feet tall. And with its mass of 5-inch-diameter carmine-red flowers, 'Ville de Lyon' is one of my favorites. Bright-yellow anthers highlight the intense color of the petals, and later, interesting airy seed heads decorate the foliage well into fall.

VINE DESIGN Clambering up and over arbors, trellises and pergolas is where 'Ville de Lyon' is at its best. Make sure your structure is sturdy; a mature plant in full bloom can be hefty. To train it on a fence or wall, supply small structures for the twining leaf stems to wrap around, like the bird netting at right.

'Ville de Lyon' is also terrific for twining up into a larger shrub or small tree. The clematis flowers will beautifully extend the blooming of a favorite lilac or shrub rose without smothering or damaging it.

CARE AND FEEDING Like many clematis, 'Ville de Lyon' is a long-lived vine that thrives in any moist, well-drained soil. To grow more stems and get a fuller plant, set the crowns of young plants 3 to 4 inches below the soil's surface when you plant. Six hours of sun a day is ideal, although 'Ville de Lyon' is more tolerant of shade than a lot of other clematis. The roots need to stay cool and moist, so grow shorter plants at the base to shade the soil. (Check out our combination below for some "cool" companions.) Or provide a 4-inch layer of organic mulch over the soil, but keep it a few inches from the crown to prevent rot.

A well-fed clematis is a healthy one, so I give my plants a dose of a balanced 20-20-20 granular food in early spring and again in early summer to keep the flowers coming.

It used to be thought that minimal pruning in early spring was best for 'Ville de Lyon' to get the largest and earliest flowers. This is true for areas with mild winters (USDA zone 8 to 10). Everywhere else the lower leaves tend to turn brown and fall off in late summer (its one shortcoming). So because this clematis blooms on new wood, pruning it is easy. I just cut mine back to 6 to 8 inches from the ground after flowering is finished in late fall to get rid of the brown leaves. Or you can wait and do it in early spring, if you prefer. Watch our Web extra video to find out how it's done.

Pruning this way gives the plant a nice, fresh start in spring and yet another opportunity to wind its way into your affections. ◻

Over the wall Combining 'Ville de Lyon' with the right part-sun companions plays up its colorful flowers. Here, the large leaves of the hostas and the tiny ones of the winter creeper contrast with those of the clematis. The reblooming iris provides another flower color while disguising the vine's bare knees.

- **A** Hosta *Hosta* 'Frances Williams'
- **B** Hosta *Hosta* 'Blue Wedgewood'
- **C** Bearded iris *Iris* 'Immortality'
- **D** Winter creeper *Euonymus fortunei* 'Emerald Gaiety'
- **E** Clematis *Clematis* 'Ville de Lyon'

PLANTS | FALL BULB

Colchicum agrippinum

COLCHICUM
Colchicum spp. and hybrids

3 to 10 in. tall, 3 to 8 in. wide

Flowers of white, pink, lavender or purple in fall

Full sun to part shade

Moist, humus-rich, well-drained soil

No serious pests or diseases

Cold-hardy in USDA zones 4 to 9

Heat-tolerant in AHS zones 9 to 1

Mail-order sources

Brent and Becky's Bulbs
www.brentandbeckysbulbs.com
877-661-2852. Catalog free

McClure and Zimmerman
www.mzbulb.com
800-546-4053. Catalog $3

No soil needed!
To force colchicum corms, set them in a dish or shallow tray filled with pebbles and a little water. Bring it out into the light and stand back! The flowers will emerge and open in days and last for a couple of weeks.

Add a splash of surprising fall color!
Colchicums

When you think of fall color, you usually envision blazing maples or bright mums and asters. But there's also a handful of fall-blooming bulbs that can contribute a colorful surprise just when lots of other plants are settling down for winter.

Most colchicums (KOL-chi-kums) bloom in fall. Though they're sometimes called "autumn crocus," they aren't actually related to crocuses. The flowers look similar but, at 3 to 10 inches, colchicums are a little taller. And their leaves show up in spring and are long gone by fall when they bloom.

If you're very lucky, you may see, down in the center of the whorl of leaves, the seed pod from the flowers of the previous fall. Seeds showing earlier in the year than the flowers like this explains another common name you might hear for colchicums: "sons-before-the-fathers."

In fall, everything you see above the ground is a part of the flower. Even the flower stalk isn't really a stem. It's actually the *perianth*, an extension of the flower itself. And all colchicum flowers open a white or pale color. As they age, their colors and patterns get more intense. *C. agrippinum*, at right, has fascinating checked petals.

COOL DESIGN IDEAS Grow colchicums, like the 'Waterlily' you see in the sunny border at right, under deciduous shrubs and trees or among other small-statured plants. (Mark them so you'll remember their location in summer.) Use a fine-textured mulch, like the pine needles around 'Lilac Wonder', at right, or the dark-colored wood mulch in the photo of 'Alboplenum', to make the flowers stand out from their surroundings. The mulch will also serve to keep the low-growing blooms clear of splashing mud.

Colchicums also look pretty lining a path or grown among ground covers. The ferns around the *C. speciosum* at right camouflage the fading foliage in summer.

GROW GORGEOUS COLCHICUMS Plant colchicum corms as soon as they're available in fall, as they can dry out quickly. Fresh ones will feel heavy and firm. Place them 3 to 4 inches deep and about 4 to 6 inches apart in humusy, moist, but well-drained soil. (Wear gloves, as they're very poisonous. Colchicine, the same chemical that keeps squirrels from digging them up and makes them distasteful to rabbits and deer, can irritate your skin.) The flowers bloom in just a few weeks and the corms multiply and spread to form a large mass of plants within several years.

You can also buy corms and grow them indoors — they're ridiculously easy to force. Many garden centers don't carry the corms because they bloom so readily while they're in the store, without soil, moisture or even light. So I've included some mail-order companies that carry colchicums. They're available for sale and shipped earlier than spring-blooming bulbs. So order them in summer and get them planted as soon as you can.

Summer is also a good time to dig and divide older clumps that aren't blooming as they once were. Work some grit and compost into the soil to improve drainage and replant the corms about 4 inches deep and apart in a random pattern. That way you're sure to get color to enjoy for many autumns to come. ☐

— *Deborah Gruca*

C. agrippinum

'Lilac Wonder'

'Alboplenum'

'Waterlily'

C. speciosum

PHOTOS: © Joseph G. Strauch, Jr. (C. speciosum) LOCATION: Jane Platt Garden ('Waterlily')

www.GardenGateMagazine.com　*the* YEAR IN GARDENING　**19**

PLANTS | SUMMER PERENNIAL

Wow! A garden full of flowers from spring to fall
Coreopsis

C. verticillata

C. grandiflora

COREOPSIS
Coreopsis spp.

6 in. to 8 ft. tall,
6 in. to 3 ft. wide

Flowers spring to summer

Yellow, pink, cream, bicolor;
double, single, fluted

Full sun

Average, well-drained soil

*Cold-hardy in
USDA zones 3 to 9*

Heat-tolerant in
AHS zones 9 to 1

Mail-order sources

Bluestone Perennials
www.bluestoneperennials.com
800-852-5243. Catalog free

Busse Gardens
www.bussegardens.com
800-544-3192. Catalog $3

Check out our online **slide show** for more great coreopsis!

PHOTO: Courtesy Walters Gardens, Inc. ('Full Moon')

When you're shopping at the garden center, what do you look for in a plant? Easy to grow, hardy, disease-resistant, lots of flowers over a long bloom time, butterfly magnet, different sizes and shapes? If you said "yes" to any or even all of these questions, you need to get yourself some coreopsis.

Coreopsis can grow practically anywhere in North America. Fortunately, most hybrids of this native wildflower are just as tough and hardy as their wild cousins. There are many species, including some annuals, but I'll focus on perennial coreopsis here. And for simplicity, I'll divide them into two groups: big-leaf and threadleaf. Big-leaf types include *Coreopsis auriculata*, *C. lanceolata* and *C. grandiflora*; and threadleaf types include *C. verticillata* and *C. rosea*. Threadleaf foliage is so fine that it's hard to see from a distance. Look closely at the last two insets and you'll see what I mean. Big-leaf types such as 'Jethro Tull', in the large photo at right, have bigger, coarser-looking leaves.

FLOWER POWER You'll have flowers from spring to fall by planting both groups of coreopsis. Big-leaf varieties start sending up blooms in late spring and bloom for several weeks. Threadleaf types begin flowering in early summer and slow down in the heat. After you deadhead, you'll get a second, smaller flush of blooms.

The classic coreopsis flower is a single yellow daisy shape. But that's not the only color or shape you'll find these days. 'Jethro Tull', at right, puts a little zing into this basic shape with fluted petals. Add more color with burgundy and yellow 'Sunfire' in the first inset. It's a big-leaf type that blooms the first year from seed. Bright yellow too much for you? Switch to pink with tough but pretty 'Heaven's Gate' in the middle inset. Or try the classic creamy yellow 'Moonbeam'. There's a brand-new threadleaf called 'Full Moon' in the last inset that has larger 3-inch soft-yellow flowers; Crème Brûlée is another popular threadleaf with buttery yellow flowers that bloom like crazy. Don't forget the doubles! Big-leaf types 'Early Sunrise' or 'Sunray' have twice as many petals. With all the varieties available, I couldn't possibly fit them all into these pages. Visit our Web extra for photos of 10 more great coreopsis.

HARDY OR NOT? Coreopsis has a well-earned reputation for hardiness. But check the plant tag before you buy. While some varieties easily survive winters in USDA zone 3, others are more tender. 'Limerock Ruby' and 'Dreamcatcher' are only hardy to zone 6. But that doesn't mean you should deprive yourself of these beauties if you live in colder areas. Just be aware they may not return every year. Or overwinter them somewhere cool that doesn't freeze, such as an unheated basement or attached garage.

Once you've chosen a few coreopsis for your garden, you're going to want to know where to put them and how to grow them. Turn the page and you'll find out just what to do with your new finds.

'Jethro Tull'
Big-leaf

'Sunfire'
Big-leaf

'Heaven's Gate'
Threadleaf

'Full Moon'
Threadleaf

GROW A GREAT-LOOKING GARDEN

Botanical Names

Beardtongue
Penstemon hybrid
Black-eyed Susan
Rudbeckia fulgida
Blazing star
Liatris spicata
Dahlia *Dahlia* hybrid
Oriental lily
Lilium hybrid
Shasta daisy
*Leucanthemum
xsuperbum*

Coreopsis is a carefree, versatile plant that looks great in mass plantings, cottage gardens, butterfly gardens and perennial borders. Whatever your style, you can fit in a coreopsis or two, or more! Don't settle for ones and twos of this versatile plant when you're shopping. Get at least five or six of one variety so you have plenty of flowers to bring inside for bouquets and still leave an enticing buffet for the butterflies.

SHAPE IT UP These perky daisy-shaped flowers look good in just about any garden. They're casual, cheery and natural-looking. Use them to create the feel of a wildflower meadow with other daisy shapes like Shasta daisies or black-eyed Susans. Add a few ornamental grasses and spike-shaped flowers like blazing star and beardtongue. The contrasting forms provide added interest.

Shape isn't limited to just the flower, either. The two groups of coreopsis have very different habits. Big-leaf coreopsis forms an upright clump like the 'Jethro Tull' that I mentioned earlier. Threadleaf coreopsis, on the other hand, forms a low mound.

TERRIFIC TEXTURE Coreopsis leaves bring more than color and shape to the garden. They're also useful for creating dramatic texture combos. Compared to many plants, big-leaf coreopsis is still pretty fine-textured. But threadleaf coreopsis foliage is so fine, it's almost needlelike.

Usually you can pair one type of foliage with its opposite for good results. In photo 1, the fine foliage of 'Heaven's Gate' is a great contrast to the wide bergenia behind it. Planting a drift of threadleaf varieties increases the impact. These 12 plants were planted in spring and covered in blooms by midsummer.

SMALL TO TALL Whether you're looking for a plant to edge a border, fill in the middle or stand tall in the back, coreopsis can do the job. Try big-leaf 'Nana' along the edge of a path — it only grows 6 to 8 inches tall. Most varieties are mid-sized, growing somewhere between 12 and 24 inches tall. See the 'Zagreb' in photo 2? Its 12- to 15-inch-tall, mounded form is accentuated against the upright lilies behind it. The finer coreopsis foliage offers plenty of contrast with the larger lily leaves, so this area is interesting even without blooms. If you need something for the back of the border, look for *Coreopsis tripteris*, a big-leaf that can get up to 8 feet tall! This species tolerates a wide range of conditions, but for the tallest, fullest plants, give it well-drained soil and consistent moisture.

(2) Coreopsis fits in anywhere. The sunny yellow flowers of 'Zagreb' really light up this mixed border. Cut a few stems and enjoy them in a vase, too.

(1) Small flowers make a big splash when you plant drifts of threadleafs, such as 'Heaven's Gate', above.

(3) Fill up containers with coreopsis. 'Sundancer' is a compact variety that keeps blooming all summer.

COOL CONTAINERS Have you ever thought of showing off your favorite coreopsis in containers? With its long bloom time and easy-care attributes, coreopsis fits in well with annuals and tender perennials of all kinds. In fact, containers are a great place to grow those varieties I mentioned that might not be hardy in your area. Or try the big-leaf 'Sundancer' in photo 3. The double yellow flowers are a bright spot of color near the dark foliage of the dahlia. This variety has a nice compact shape, growing only 10 to 12 inches tall so it won't take over the whole planting. 'Sundancer' isn't picky about deadheading, either. It will rebloom more quickly if you do, but if you forget, no problem. In fall, you can either throw plants on the compost pile or plant them in the ground. Plant three to four weeks before your area's first expected frost so the plants have time to get roots established.

When it comes right down to it, coreopsis looks good in any garden. No wonder this easy-going plant has been so popular over the years! □

— *Sherri Ribbey*

CAREFREE COREOPSIS

SUN AND SOIL Coreopsis is easy to grow and does best in full sun and well-drained soil. It tolerates shade but won't flower quite as much there. If you've had trouble with plants that only live 2 or 3 years, it could be the soil. Coreopsis doesn't last long in heavy clay — it tends to rot. To help plants live longer, plant the crown high, or about an inch above the soil line to help drain the water away.

Once established, coreopsis is quite drought-tolerant. The only exception is pink-flowered *C. rosea* and its cultivars. This threadleaf group needs regular moisture.

Don't worry about fertilizing coreopsis — plants will just get floppy in soil that's too rich.

MORE FLOWERS! Most coreopsis bloom for several weeks at a time. Deadheading after the first flush of blooms is finished will keep them going until frost, though flowering may be sparser on some varieties. If you have a lot of big-leaf coreopsis to deadhead, grab a handful of spent stems like the ones at right. Then cut them off as close to the foliage as you can.

As you can tell from the illustration below, threadleaf plants are even easier to deadhead. Just cut them back by half with your garden shears. For mass plantings, get out your string trimmer and cut them all down to just above the ground. It may seem drastic, but these tough plants will grow back with ease.

After threadleaf plants bloom, cut them back by half for more flowers.

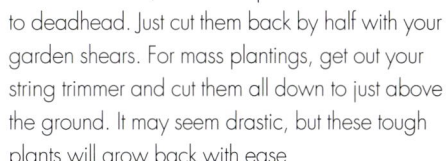

GET MORE PLANTS The easiest way to get more coreopsis is by division. This can help rejuvenate a tired plant, too. To divide plants, dig coreopsis in spring as new growth emerges. (If you forget, don't worry, you can still divide coreopsis in fall.) When the plant is out of the ground, cut it into smaller pieces with a sharp spade. Replant them and water well.

Some varieties reseed, but all the seedlings may not look like the parent plant. It's easy enough to pull seedlings you don't want. *C. rosea* and *C. verticillata* can reseed so much when they're grown in fertile soil and moist conditions that they become invasive.

ALMOST PROBLEM-FREE Aphids may take up residence on your coreopsis in summer. Get rid of them with a spray of water from the hose.

Powdery mildew shows up sometimes, too. To keep this fungus away, give plants space so air can circulate. And look for resistant varieties, such as 'Full Moon', 'Moonbeam' and 'Mayfield Giant'.

It doesn't take a lot to make coreopsis happy. With plenty of sun and well-drained soil, coreopsis will reward you with flowers for years to come.

PLANTS | ANNUAL

Sulphur cosmos
C. sulphureus

Tall cosmos
C. bipinnatus

Season-long blooms in spots where nothing else will grow!

Cosmos

COSMOS
Cosmos spp.

*Flowers in summer to fall
Full sun
Well-drained, poor soil
Annual*
Tall:
*3 to 6 ft. tall,
  1 to 2 ft. wide
Rose, pink, white
  or wine flowers*
Sulphur:
*1 to 5 ft. tall,
  1 to 2 ft. wide
Yellow, red or orange flowers*

A hot, dry area with poor soil is not usually ideal for growing flowers. But that's exactly the kind of place where cosmos thrive. Cosmos are some of those old-fashioned annuals that put me in mind of cottage gardens. But lots of newer cultivars with double flowers or rolled or color-banded petals put a new spin on these old favorites.

COSMOS QUALITIES Cosmos, like many other annuals, are pretty easy to grow. They don't require a lot of special care, so they're perfect for the novice gardener. But because they have so much more going for them, even experienced gardeners appreciate them. Aside from easy care, cosmos offer an almost constant supply of cheery flowers that reseed themselves and they attract butterflies and birds, to boot. And with plants that range from 1 to 6 feet tall, they can fit in almost anywhere.

The cosmos family has several species, but most often you'll find the hybrids of two species: sulphur cosmos and tall cosmos. Sulphurs come in warm colors, usually yellow, red or orange. 'Cosmic Orange' and 'Polidor', below, show how the colors can be plain or streaked.

Tall cosmos have flowers in shades of rose, pink, wine and white. And, as the name implies, they're generally taller than sulphurs. Most are in the 3- to 4-foot range. Even the 2- to 3-foot "dwarf" 'Sensation' is taller than most of the sulphur hybrids that usually top out around 2 feet.

But the biggest difference between tall and sulphur cosmos is the foliage. The thin, feathery foliage of tall cosmos is more delicate than the wider, lobed leaves of sulphurs. I love the bright flowers of this plant, but I'd probably grow cosmos just for those soft, lacy leaves.

You can see why sulphur cosmos is also called "orange cosmos." The vigorous plants reseed around your garden more readily than tall cosmos do.

'Cosmic Orange'

'Polidor'

FLOWER FEATURES The 2½- to 3-inch-wide flowers of both species are cup-shaped or daisylike. There are doubles and singles, such as 'Sonata Carmine' at right. Newer hybrids, especially of tall cosmos, include the very double blooms that you see on 'Double Click', below. Pink-edged 'Picotee' and the crazy petal arrangement of 'Psyche' are a sampling of other flower forms. You'll also find blooms with fluted petals, fringed edges and colorful streaks or rings around the center.

Now, I know you'll want some of these easy-to-grow favorites. Turn the page and I'll share different ways you can use cosmos in your garden. Also, I'll include simple tips for keeping them looking their best.

Dozens of tall cosmos hybrids provide lots of different flower forms. Long, wiry stems make them work well in cut arrangements.

'Sonata Carmine'

'Double Click'

'Picotee'

'Psyche'

www.GardenGateMagazine.com   *the* YEAR IN GARDENING   **25**

COSMOS DESIGN TIPS

Botanical Names

Evening primrose
Oenothera speciosa
Lobelia *Lobelia erinus*
Salvia *Salvia* spp.
Sulphur cosmos
Cosmos sulphureus
Tall cosmos
Cosmos bipinnatus
Variegated loosestrife
Lysimachia punctata

With their wide range of sizes, cosmos have lots of design uses. The tallest ones make airy, see-through backgrounds and screens for the back of a border. Tall cosmos look especially pretty in front of a wall or fence. And a structure like that will keep strong winds from knocking them flat. Surrounded by sturdy companions, they're also perfect in the center of an island bed. If you have moist, fertile garden soil, cosmos can grow a little lanky. I'll talk about staking in "Grow gorgeous flowers."

HAPPY MEDIUM Because cosmos have nearly constant blooms, midsized ones provide all-season color at the middle or edge of a bed, especially in very visible areas like along sidewalks or driveways. And it's a snap to snip the faded blooms of 'Sonata Pink' along the sidewalk in photo 2 on your way into the house. The mass of cosmos, especially with the white picket fence in back, creates an informal, friendly cottage garden welcome for your visitors.

Or plant a few cosmos among perennials in a mixed border to fill in the gaps between their bloom periods. 'Sonata White' in photo 3 started blooming about the same time as the purple salvia and pink evening primrose. But the cosmos will keep a constant supply of flowers coming even after the buds of the yellow variegated loosestrife have opened. And fresh blooms will still be going strong later when most of the perennials have finished blooming.

(2) Grow cosmos in full sun and they'll bloom like mad through late summer, with a little deadheading.

(3) Start cosmos from seed for loads of plants to repeat splashes of color through the garden.

(4) No need to feed. Cosmos thrive in poor soil. Once established in a well-drained site, they handle dry conditions, too.

HOT SPOTS Another ideal place? Rock gardens or raised beds provide the sharp drainage that cosmos thrive in. You can easily toss a few cosmos seeds into nooks and crannies that might be too rugged for a wimpier plant. Several cosmos, including 'Cosmic Orange' and 'Cosmic Yellow', soak up the heat from the stones in the rocky slope in photo 4. The warm soil there jump-starts germination and blooming.

More compact plants, such as 12-inch-tall Ladybird hybrids or 'Bright Lights' at 24 inches tall, are perfect in containers. They add lots of bright orange color without demanding a lot of elbow room. And they're very forgiving if you don't remember to water every day. Blue or purple annual lobelias and salvias make great container companions for these cosmos. The orange and blue complement each other, and all of the plants will be a big hit with the neighborhood butterflies.

Long, wiry stems make cosmos good cut flowers, too. Remove any leaves below the vase's water line to keep them from rotting. Flowers last just four or five days in a bouquet, but fortunately, you'll have loads of fresh new flowers opening in your garden all summer long! □

— *Deborah Gruca*

GROW GORGEOUS FLOWERS

You can buy cosmos plants at most garden centers. But they're also easy to start from seed and you'll get more for your money by sowing seed directly in the garden. Wait until the danger of frost has passed and the soil temperature is at least 65 degrees. Seeds germinate in seven to 10 days, with blooms opening in about 60. Thin the plants to 6 in. apart when they get 2 to 3 in. tall.

Fertilizer isn't necessary; in fact, it makes plants develop more foliage than flowers or grow tall and lanky.

STAKING If your cosmos grow out in the open and tend to tilt a bit, a well-placed section of edging or a few bamboo stakes pushed into the soil around the plants is all you need to keep them upstanding. And the billowing foliage soon covers any stakes.

DEADHEADING To keep cosmos blooming the longest, deadhead them. With lots of buds opening each day, this can be an ongoing task. I usually carry small pruners or scissors when I'm out in the garden. So whenever I think about it, I grab three or four stems of spent blooms at a time and snip them off. The stems are usually too tough to pinch with your fingers. You can see how far down in the foliage I cut in the photo — otherwise you'll be left with dozens of brown stems sticking up. It takes just a few minutes if you do it every three or four days. But what if, by midsummer, the deadheading has gotten away from you and there are too many faded blooms to snip? Simply cut the plants back to about 12 to 18 in. tall, letting the dried seeds fall to the ground. In a few weeks, the plants will rally and bloom again and the seeds will sprout in the warm soil, giving you even more flowers for the rest of the summer.

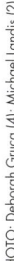

PLANTS | EDITOR'S CHOICE

'Illustris' Elephant Ear

Colocasia esculenta 'Illustris'

Size	2 to 5 ft. tall, 2 to 3 ft. wide
Soil	Wet to well-drained, slightly acid soil
Light	Full sun to part shade
Pests	None serious
Hardiness	Cold: USDA zones 8 to 11 Heat: AHS zones 12 to 1

If you've ever dreamed of warm tropical nights, I have the perfect plant for you. With its dark dramatic look, 'Illustris' may be as close to an island vacation as you'll get without leaving your own garden.

And junglelike lushness is exactly what this plant delivers. In moist areas, such as by a pond or stream, the bold heart-shaped leaves can grow to two feet long! It will handle full sun with even moisture, but in drier areas it needs some afternoon shade. The purple-black color will be more intense in sun, while in deep shade the leaves will be more green.

PLANT IT UP You can buy 'Illustris' as tubers or plants. The larger the tuber, the older it is and the larger the plant will get. Plant so the tuber's a couple of inches below the soil surface, water it in well and keep it moist. After the weather warms into the 70s, the plant will start growing. Leaves will emerge from the tuber in three to eight weeks, depending on the temperature. If you plant your elephant ear in a lightweight container, you might want to put a couple of bricks in the bottom first, so you're not constantly setting the pot back up. Those giant leaves act just like sails in a strong breeze, and wind-tattered is not a good look for them.

Give each 'Illustris' plant a big pot, at least 16 inches across. That's room enough for a few moist shade companions. Any good potting mix will do, but adding some water crystals to the mix or setting the pot in a saucer will cut down on watering chores. The combo bed below shows a few more plant partners.

CARE AND FEEDING Once elephant ear is up and growing, feed it with half-strength balanced 20-20-20 water-soluble fertilizer once a month to get it to really take off. Place it in that low spot in your garden that tends to stay damp. Next to or in a pond or water feature is also ideal. If you try to grow it in sharply drained soil, you'll be hard-pressed to keep the plant moist enough, and it won't reach its full size, either.

TAKE IT INSIDE After frost kills the top growth, lift the tubers. Shake off the soil and leave the tubers and any foliage in the shade to dry for a couple of days. Cut off the leaves, bring the tubers indoors for the winter and store them in a dry, dark, cool (between 35 and 50 degrees) area, keeping them in a cardboard box until spring. (Check the tubers during the winter and mist them lightly if they look shriveled.)

Think of this time as your chance to start dreaming of your next tropical vacation! □

Cool shady corner It can be tricky to choose plants dramatic enough to hold their own compared to 'Illustris'. But the spiky blue flowers of monkshood will rise above those big leaves. Meanwhile, the smaller impatiens and sedge play the perfect supporting cast to this blockbuster part-shade show.

A Monkshood *Aconitum* 'Stainless Steel'
B Elephant's ear *Colocasia esculenta* 'Illustris'
C New Guinea impatiens *Impatiens* Paradise® White
D Variegated Japanese sedge *Carex morrowii* 'Aurea-variegata'

Mail-order sources

Brent and Becky's Bulbs
www.brentandbeckysbulbs.com
877-661-2852. Catalog free

Logee's Tropical Plants
www.logees.com
888-330-8038. Catalog $4.95
(Includes a coupon worth $4.95 on your next order.)

PLANTS | BIENNIAL

These head-turning flowers always grab the spotlight.

Foxglove

COMMON FOXGLOVE
Digitalis purpurea

3 to 6 ft. tall, 2 ft. wide

Pink, yellow, lavender or white with spotted throats in early summer

Sun to part shade

Well-drained

No serious pests or diseases

Cold-hardy in USDA zones 4 to 8

Heat-tolerant in AHS zones 8 to 1

All parts of the plant are poisonous if ingested.

It's not hard to see why foxglove has been a favorite of gardeners over the years. Those tall, elegant spires add excitement to any mixed border.

There are many species of foxglove, but common foxglove, as you'll guess by the name, is the easiest to find. That doesn't mean it's boring, though — just look at all the colors and hybrids in the photos at right.

GOOD FOR ANY GARDEN Bright purple spikes poking up through the exuberant mass of flowers in the lead photo show classic cottage garden style. These upright flowers add structure and help lead your eye along the brick path. That same neat, architectural habit makes foxglove a good choice for formal gardens, too.

Think your garden is too small for foxglove? Think again. With its low rosette of foliage and narrow flower spike, foxglove is easy to squeeze in among other plants. If all you have is a patio or deck, add a few of the smaller varieties to a container.

GROWING KNOW-HOW Before we get started, you need to know that foxglove has a few quirks. It's usually found with the perennials at the garden center, but technically, common foxglove is a *biennial*. That means the first year there's just a rosette of foliage. The plant flowers the second year, sets seed and then dies. There are a few exceptions, though. The varieties 'Camelot' and 'Foxy' usually bloom the first year and like an annual, don't return the next. But to add to the confusion, sometimes even these varieties have been known to come back a second year. I usually play it safe and start seeds or get a few ready-to-bloom plants each year so I don't miss out on having plenty of those fantastic flowers for my garden. Check out the photos below left for what to look for when you go shopping.

Foxglove isn't hard to grow but it is particular. It needs sun to bloom well but doesn't like to get too hot or dry. You'll still get good results if you plant in dappled shade. In fact, afternoon shade is a must for foxglove in areas where summers get hot.

If your foxglove is in perfect light but you have trouble getting it through the winter, join the club. It's usually a matter of drainage. The gardeners I know that grow it in abundance have well-drained soil. Clay holds water around the crown, causing plants to rot. To help my foxglove survive, I made a small berm — it's only about 8 inches tall — with better soil on top of the clay. Once the plants are in the ground, top off the soil with an inch of chicken grit as mulch. This helps keep the crown and foliage dry. You can find grit at some garden centers or feed stores.

SEED-STARTING SAVVY Plants that are growing happily in your garden will more than likely reseed. But they may not come true, or look like the parent plant. If you're not picky about what color the flowers are, cut stems with brown, papery seed pods and shake them where you want more plants. Deadheading prevents reseeding and encourages a second, smaller set of blooms in some varieties.

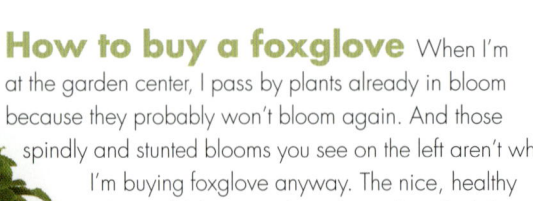

How to buy a foxglove When I'm at the garden center, I pass by plants already in bloom because they probably won't bloom again. And those spindly and stunted blooms you see on the left aren't why I'm buying foxglove anyway. The nice, healthy clump of foliage on the right is what I look for. Then I peer down into the leaves to see if I can see any buds forming. Buds let me know that if I get it home and in the ground, it should have decent blooms this year. If that foliage has no buds, I know that it'll either bloom later in the year or next year.

PHOTOS: Craig Anderson (plants in containers)

Mail-order sources

Thompson & Morgan
www.thompson-morgan.com
800-274-7333, *Seeds.*

Annie's Annuals & Perennials
www.anniesannuals.com
888-266-4370, *Plants.*

Starting foxglove from seed is easy. (For a specific cultivar, check out the sources above.) Sow seed outside in spring after all danger of frost is past. The seeds need light to germinate so don't cover them with soil. Plants should sprout in 14 to 21 days.

You can even start plants inside, where you have control over light and temperature, as late as July. Once the seedlings have two sets of true leaves (leaves that actually look like foxglove), move them to 4-inch pots. Plants can go in the garden by fall and as long as they have at least eight weeks before frost to get roots going, you should have blooms next year.

Foxglove may take a little extra care in some gardens but flowers like these are well worth the effort. □

— *Sherri Ribbey*

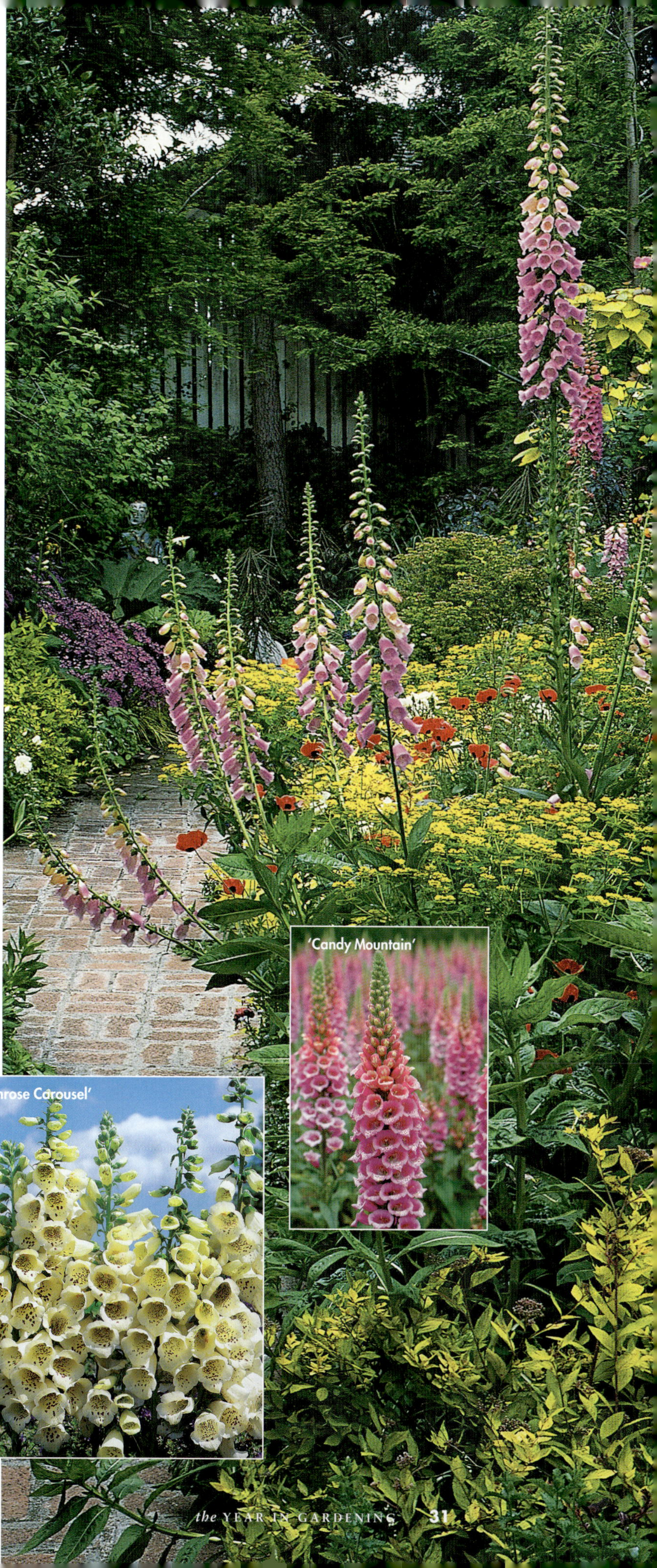

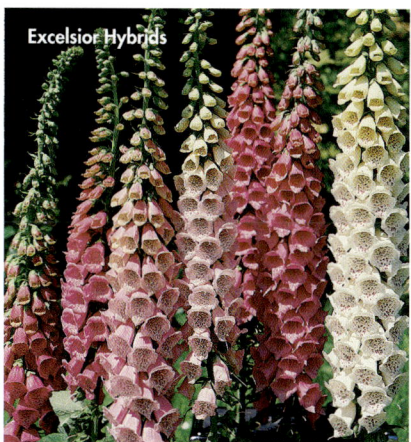

Flower spikes in many colors Tall and stately common foxglove in the large photo grows up to 6 ft. tall, with flowers on one side of the stem. At up to 5 ft. tall, the Excelsior Hybrids have been favorites for years. 'Primrose Carousel' grows to 30 in. so it's a good size for containers, too. The upward-facing pink flowers of 'Candy Mountain' go all the way around the stem.

PHOTOS: Michael Landis (lead image), Thompson & Morgan (Excelsior Hybrids, 'Primrose Carousel', 'Candy Mountain')

PLANTS | SUMMER PERENNIAL

Hardy Hibiscus

Add no-fuss tropical flair to any garden

'Lady Baltimore'

HARDY HIBISCUS
Hibiscus moscheutos

- 2 to 12 feet tall, 2 to 4 feet wide
- 6- to 12-in.-diameter flowers of white, pink or red from midsummer to frost
- Sun to part shade
- Moist, well-drained soil
- Occasional problems with Japanese beetles
- Cold-hardy in USDA zones 4 to 10
- Heat-tolerant in AHS zones 12 to 1

PHOTOS: Deborah Gruca ('Turn of the Century'); Courtesy Walters Gardens, Inc. ('Pink Elephant')

Mail-order sources

Carroll Gardens, Inc.
www.carrollgardens.com
800-638-6334. *Catalog free*

Garden Crossings
www.gardencrossings.com
616-875-6355. *Online catalog only*

Adding bright colors is a good way to inject excitement anywhere, including your garden. If yours could stand a little shot of stunning, consider growing hardy hibiscus. Large, lush flowers bloom continuously from midsummer to fall in shades of pink, red or white.

It used to be if you wanted the flamboyant flowers of hibiscus, you had to have enough space for big plants, like 4- to 7-foot-tall 'Lady Baltimore' in the illustration at left. But thanks to the efforts of plant breeders, newer ones are more compact — perfect for smaller gardens. The hardy hibiscus I'll talk about here are *Hibiscus moscheutos*, not to be confused with the smaller-flowered *H. syriacus*, commonly called rose-of-Sharon.

FANTASTIC FLOWERS Hardy hibiscus flowers are limited to white, pink and red, but a glance at the photos at right shows that they can really knock your socks off. Blooms range from quilted to smooth, and solid-colored to veined or striped. My favorite, 'Turn of the Century', at right, has flowers that fade from dark to light pink from one side of the petal to the other, giving it a pinwheel look. Others, such as 'Pink Elephant,' sport a contrasting throat. A few hybrids are described as yellow, plum and rose (though I'd call the yellow more of a creamy white). Each velvety, 6- to 12-inch-wide flower lasts just one day, but the plant is covered with enough buds to give you constant color from midsummer to frost.

LUSCIOUS LEAVES In addition to fabulous flowers, some hardy hibiscus hybrids also have dramatic foliage colors. The maple-leaf-shaped leaves of 'Kopper King' are copper-red. 'Cherry Brandy' foliage is big and bronze-red with tinges of purple and green. (See their flowers in the insets at right.) Other cultivars sport burgundy or purple leaves ranging from triangle-shaped to deeply cut.

SMALL TO TALL As I mentioned, lots of newer hybrids are easier to fit into mixed borders, with habits that are more compact than the species. They're designed to branch more, for a shorter, fuller form. The multiple branches of 'Luna Red' in the big photo hold dozens of blooms and the plant stays a tidy 2 to 3 feet tall.

Looking for a taller plant? Try 'Turn of the Century'. It really grabs attention anywhere as it reaches a respectable 6 to 8 feet. Or if you want an even bigger plant, you can always grow 'Red Flyer', at a whopping 12 feet tall!

You may think hardy hibiscus, with their exotic looks, are fussy. But they're surprisingly easy to grow — you can read about that on the next pages. And if you're wondering how to design with such showy plants, I'll share some tips on working them beautifully into your garden, along with a short list of my favorites.

DESIGN WITH HARDY HIBISCUS

WEB extra
Want more? See our **plan and plant list** for this pretty patio border.

With such a wide range of sizes, hardy hibiscus can be used lots of different ways in the garden. Their late bloom season gives any garden a dash of tropical color just when many other perennials are starting to lag.

Here are some design tips that work well with hibiscus, no matter what size they are. But I'll also give you specific tips for the smaller and the taller members of this colorful clan. Plus, I'll share some of my favorites in "Try these!"

— *Deborah Gruca*

FRONT OF THE BORDER Newer, more compact hibiscus fit perfectly near the front edge of a bed along a path or deck. If you surround your hibiscus with plants that have interesting foliage, you'll ensure visual appeal here even before the hibiscus begins to bloom.

AROUND A WATER FEATURE Hibiscus prefer moist soil, so they thrive in damp areas near ponds or water features, such as fountains.

IN CONTAINERS Smaller hardy hibiscus are naturals in containers. Pair them with plants that have contrasting forms — tall and spiky, as well as trailing. And use plants with very different leaf shapes to really pack a punch.

AS A SPECIMEN Place a single hibiscus, such as this 'Pinot Noir', in a pot as an effective (and portable!) focal point or specimen plant. A single tall hibiscus acts as a focal point wherever you use it.

TRY THESE!

Not that many years ago, hardy hibiscus were all large and lanky. Now there are more sizes and shapes than you can shake a stick at. Here are some of my favorites, arranged from smallest to tallest.

Cranberry Punch™ 24 to 30 in.; 4- to 5-in. dark red flowers and dark green leaves with red veins

'Pinot Grigio' (Splash series) 2½ ft.; white flowers edged with pink

'Fantasia' 2½ to 3 ft.; 8-in. ruffled pink to lavender flowers

'Disco Belle Mix' 3 ft.; 8- to 10-in. flowers in a mix of colors from white to dark red

'Robert Fleming' 3 ft.; 10-in., dark red, almost black, flowers

'Cherry Brandy' (Cordials collection) 3½ ft.; red flowers on red stems

'Plum Crazy' 4 ft.; 10-in. purple flowers and purple, maplelike leaves

'Blue River II' 4 ft.; 10-in. white flowers with light green foliage

'Old Yella' 4½ ft.; 8- to 10-in. quilted, creamy white flowers

'Kopper King' 4 to 5 ft.; 10- to 12-in. white flowers with burgundy eye; coppery red, deeply cut leaves

'Pink Elephant' 5 to 6 ft.; 12-in. ruffled, pink flowers with dark red eye

BACK OF THE BORDER Tuck several tall hibiscus behind shorter companions with contrasting forms, such as barberry, for eye-catching combinations. Choose a few plants for early-summer interest, like iris or perennial geranium. Later, the hibiscus will provide flower color from midsummer into fall.

Companions with a more dense look, such as these barberries and spireas, accent the open branching form of the hibiscus while deftly hiding hibiscus' bare knees.

PLANTED IN A MASS Another way to show off hibiscus is planting them in a mass. Taller hybrids create a flowering hedge that can screen a distracting view. Plant several compact ones along a patio to bring a touch of tropical color up close.

COMBINED WITH GRASSES Ornamental grasses make great companions for hardy hibiscus of any size. Simply choose a grass that's slightly taller than the hibiscus and plant them close enough for the leaves of the two plants to weave together. Interplant a few spring bulbs to provide a little early color until the hibiscus and grass emerge in late spring to summer. And in late fall, after the hibiscus stops blooming, the grasses will continue to look beautiful.

Like this border? Check out the plan and plant list online at our Web extra.

GROWING GREAT HIBISCUS

Though hardy hibiscus grabs attention, it's no prima donna that needs lots of pampering. Here are some simple growing tips.

PLANTING Hardy hibiscus can be started from seed or as small plants from about the end of May until late summer. If you start the seed indoors in late winter, for most cultivars you'll have a blooming plant the first season. (The hard seed coat needs to be soaked for 24 hours before planting.) When you sow seed directly into the garden after the weather warms, don't expect flowers until the following year.

Young starts bought and set out later than Labor Day will use more energy blooming than developing a strong root system. They might not survive the winter without a 2- to 3-in. layer of organic mulch. You can pinch off the buds when you plant, but in fact, in zones 6 and colder, you might want to mulch the plant the first winter anyway to give the roots some extra protection.

CUTTING BACK In areas with cold winters (zones 7 and colder), hardy hibiscus dies back to the ground. Cut the dead stems back in fall or spring. In zones 8 and warmer, plants may not die back, but it's a good idea to prune back and shape the stems in late spring before new growth starts. Be patient — these plants are very slow to emerge.

DIVIDING Spring is the best time to divide hardy hibiscus. Lift the root ball and split the clump with a knife or sharp spade. You may also take stem cuttings, which root quickly, in early summer. (Cut 3- to 4-in.-long pieces from stem tips and keep them in moist potting mix until rooted.)

CONTROLLING HEIGHT Make tall hibiscus shorter and more bushy with the method shown here. Cut the plant back by one-third to one-half in June. This will delay the start of flowering by a couple of weeks, but will eliminate the need for staking.

PLANTS | SHRUB

Our guide to the best and brightest
Bigleaf Hydrangeas

'Nikko Blue'

HYDRANGEA
Hydrangea macrophylla

1 to 6 feet tall,
3 to 6 feet wide

White, red, pink, lavender or blue mophead or lacecap flowers in midsummer

Sun to part shade

Moist, humus-rich, well-drained soil

Cold-hardy in USDA zones 4 to 9

Heat-tolerant in AHS zones 9 to 1

Mail-order sources

Carroll Gardens
www.carrollgardens.com
800-638-6334
Online catalog only

White Flower Farm
www.whiteflowerfarm.com
800-503-9624. Catalog free

Joy Creek Nursery
www.joycreek.com
503-543-7474. Catalog $3

PHOTOS: © Joseph G. Strauch Jr. (1); © Marilynn McAra (2); Courtesy of Hines Nursery (3); Courtesy of McCorkle Nurseries (4); Courtesy of Bailey Nurseries (7)

Lush, billowing mophead blooms or frilly lacecap flowers in shades of white, pink or blue on sturdy stems. What more could you want in a shrub? How about lustrous green or variegated foliage on a cold-hardy, compact plant? The bigleaf hydrangea group (*H. macrophylla*) is made up of dozens of cultivars that bloom heavily and live for many years in the garden. Many of the newest cultivars rebloom more reliably and have tidy, compact habits. You'll also find more colorful foliage and stems, bicolor flowers and earlier bloom periods. I'll introduce you to seven cultivars here, from old to new, with a variety of wonderful traits.

1 'BLUE BILLOW' The delicate, light-blue lacecap blooms of 'Blue Billow' are some of the most cold-tolerant (to USDA zone 4), which makes them a treasure in any garden. But this 4-foot-tall cultivar is also one of the first hydrangeas to bloom — in early summer. And it flowers happily in full shade.

2 'LEUCHTFEUER' is also sold as 'Firelight' or 'Lighthouse'. This cultivar blooms a dark rose-red, a rare color for hydrangeas, and stays red even in acid-soil conditions. (I'll talk more about this on p. 38.) The large 8-inch-diameter mophead flowers open in midsummer on 4-foot plants.

3 HALO HYDRANGEAS™ These cultivars sport picoteed deep pink, purple (like Angel Song in the photo) or blue mophead or lacecap flowers in early summer. The 7- to 8-inch-diameter blooms (many are also ruffled) open on sturdy stems. But the plants stay compact enough — at 3 to 5 feet tall — to look great in larger containers. Halo hydrangeas are easy to find and cold-hardy in USDA zones 6 to 9.

4 'LADY IN RED' First, red-veined green leaves emerge in spring. In late spring to summer, stunning lacecap flowers open pink and mature to red. Then in fall, the leaves turn a rich red-purple. This 3-foot-tall cultivar is mildew-resistant so it's great for areas with hot, humid summers, but is cold-hardy only to USDA zone 6.

5 ENDLESS SUMMER® BLUSHING BRIDE Like the first plant in this series, Blushing Bride blooms on both old and new wood, to ensure repeat blooms. But instead of being pink or blue, these semidouble flowers open a pure white, aging to lovely soft pink. The dark-green leaves on this 3- to 5-foot-tall plant are resistant to mildew. Even moisture is best, so mulch around the plant, especially the first season.

6 CITYLINE™ SERIES With names including Cityline Berlin, Paris and Venice (shown at right), these plants stay a diminutive 1 to 3 feet tall. They're perfect in very small beds or in containers, on decks and patios, in sun or part shade. And though the plants are small, the pink or blue mophead flowers are just as large as those of taller relatives.

7 LIGHT-O'-DAY™ ('BAILDAY') Bright green leaves edged in white sparkle on this 3- to 5-foot-tall plant in either sun or part shade. In addition to pretty foliage, Light-O'-Day has lovely two-tone lacecap flowers that bloom in either pink or blue, depending on your soil type.

Ready to learn more? Turn the page to see how to care for and use these stunning shrubs in the garden.

www.GardenGateMagazine.com

the YEAR IN GARDENING 37

CARE AND FEEDING

Bigleaf hydrangeas are not only beautiful but among the easiest flowering shrubs you can plant.

THE BEST SOIL AND LIGHT Ideal conditions for the most flowers and healthiest foliage include a moist, humusy, well-drained soil in full sun to part shade. In areas with very hot summers (USDA zones 7 and warmer), a little afternoon shade will keep the foliage from scorching. Apply a couple doses of a balanced, 10-10-10 fertilizer (one in spring and again after flowering) for the most and best flowers.

AMPLE MOISTURE Hydrangeas like consistent moisture and often have drooping leaves when they get overly dry. An inch or two of water each week, along with a 2- to 3-inch layer of organic mulch will keep the plants healthy. At times when temps soar into the upper 80s and above, foliage will flag even with ample moisture. If the soil feels moist, leave the plant alone. Once things cool later in the day, the leaves recover quickly.

CHANGING FLOWER COLOR Another neat feature of these plants? You can change the color of the flowers. Except for white-flowered ones and a few others, most can range from bright pink to true blue depending on your soil's pH and the presence of aluminum.

Below, "Blue or pink?" shows you what color flowers you'll get in soils of different pH. Do a soil test to find out what you have. If your soil is acid to neutral, and your flowers are pink but you'd like blue, apply some granular aluminum sulfate, sulfur or iron sulfate to acidify the soil. Ask at your local garden center what works best in your area. Always follow package directions carefully, as too much can stunt or kill your plant. Give this several months to work. Two or three lighter applications are better than one heavy one. Once you've lowered the pH, feed the plant Miracid® to help maintain the soil acidity. Try grouping plants together, as in photo 8, so you only have to change the pH in one area.

If your soil is alkaline, you can try to acidify it by working in lots of organic material and adding elemental sulfur gradually over several years. But if your pH is 7 or higher, this probably won't work. Of course, you can always grow blue-flowered ones in containers. With just that small amount of soil, you can more easily control the pH.

(8) A hedge of several hydrangeas provides long-lasting, colorful flowers along a lawn area, but doesn't need much pruning to keep looking beautiful.

Blue or pink? For your hydrangea flowers to be blue, aluminum (which is present in most soils) must be available to the plant. In acid to neutral soils this isn't a problem. But in alkaline soils, the roots can't take up the aluminum and the flowers will be pink.

Acid soil (pH 5.0 to 5.5)

Less acid soil (pH 5.5 to 6.5)

Neutral to alkaline soil (pH 6.5 and higher)

PRUNING Except for the Endless Summer series, most bigleaf hydrangeas bloom on mature wood. That means the plant actually forms the buds for the following year's flowers in late summer to early fall. You don't want to cut off the flower buds and miss out on the beautiful blooms! So a little light trimming in early spring is generally all that's required: Just cut back any old flower heads to the closest leaf nodes.

In especially bitter winters, the tips of the stems may be killed by the cold. Go ahead and remove what's died back. Although you'll have lost the flower buds at the tips of the stems, this pruning sometimes stimulates the dormant side buds to develop and bloom. Should the entire plant die back in a severe winter, cut it down to the ground in early spring. The roots of an established plant will usually survive and send up new growth as the weather warms.

THE RIGHT PLANTS If you garden where temperatures tend to fluctuate wildly in spring, the emerging flower buds may be killed by cold snaps in late spring. For most bigleafs, this results in no blooms for the season. Planting in a northern or eastern exposure makes them less likely to break dormancy too early in the season and be nipped by a late frost. You might also try growing more cold-hardy cultivars, such as 'Nikko Blue' or 'Blue Billow'. And newer cultivars that bloom on both old and new wood, such as Endless Summer, are other good choices. Even if the flower buds are winter-killed on these plants, more buds will form on the new growth and you'll still enjoy the midsummer flowers.

So, whether it's a hydrangea with large, blowsy mopheads or delicate, frilly lacecaps, the story's the same: It's bound to make a big impression on all your visitors! ◻

— *Deborah Gruca*

DESIGN WITH DYNAMITE!

After seeing the seven beautiful hydrangeas I shared on the previous pages, you may be wondering how to use them in the garden. Well, this versatile group is easy to use in lots of ways. Here are just a few of my favorites.

THE MAIN ACT A single hydrangea, covered in big, voluptuous flowers, creates a stunning focal point in any garden. Your eye is drawn to the plant, even in late summer, when the flowers turn an interesting papery brown.

HEDGE YOUR BEST Used as hedges, hydrangeas make a high-impact, low-maintenance way to line a path or fence. Mophead and lacecap blooms fit perfectly into informal settings and a mix of cultivars guarantees bountiful blooms for much of the summer. Or for a more traditional or formal-looking hedge, plant a line of a single cultivar.

MIX IT UP All but the tallest cultivars are a good fit for mixed borders. Unlike the blooms of many shrubs that are long gone by summer, midsummer hydrangea flowers combine well with those of surrounding perennials and annuals. And hydrangeas' tidy habit won't overwhelm their shorter neighbors. Use shade-tolerant cultivars, like 'Blue Billow' or the 'Mariesii' in photo A, to bring color to part-shade beds.

PERFECT IN POTS Many new, more compact cultivars, like the Cityline series or Endless Summer in photo B, are perfect for containers on the deck or patio. Placing them in pots makes it easy to bring them right up close, where you can enjoy the luscious blooms all summer.

PLANTS | EDITOR'S CHOICE

Acapulco Salmon & Pink Hyssop

Agastache mexicana **'Kiegabi' (Acapulco™ Salmon & Pink)**

Size 24 to 30 in. tall, 15 to 18 in. wide
Habit Upright
Bloom Summer to frost
Soil Well-drained, lean
Light Full sun to part shade
Pests None serious
Hardiness Cold: USDA zones 5 to 10
Heat: AHS zones 10 to 1

PHOTO: Deborah Gruca

Botanical Names

Blanket flower
  Gaillardia xgrandiflora
Cardoon
  Cynara cardunculus
Hydrangea *Hydrangea* spp.
Sweet potato vine
  Ipomoea batatas

Foot-long spikes of densely packed pink and orange tubular flowers catch your eye first. Acapulco Salmon & Pink hyssop sports hundreds of tiny flowers that entice butterflies and hummingbirds, as well as people.

But beautiful flowers aren't the only things Acapulco has going for it. Drought-tolerance and deer-resistance make it easy to have in the garden. And crush a few leaves with your fingers — you'll be rewarded with a yummy citrus scent.

At about 2 feet tall, Acapulco is slightly shorter than other hyssops. This compact size makes an eye-catching statement in a container design. Try it with a blanket flower and a burgundy sweet potato vine.

It also tucks right into a mixed border. A hydrangea or a giant-leafed cardoon contrasts nicely with the fine-textured flowers and leaves. Woody-stemmed neighbors will also offer support if very rich soil makes Acapulco flop a bit. (Placing it in full sun will help keep it growing upright and producing the most flowers for you.)

CARE TIPS Acapulco Salmon & Pink is tolerant of both heat and drought. But you'd do well to give it a little moisture for several weeks after planting to help the roots get established. It prefers lean to average garden soil, but also grows in humusy soil, as long as it's very well-drained. (If you're concerned about drainage, try planting it in a raised bed.) Water infrequently but deeply, and let the soil dry out between waterings. An inch of gravel mulch will help moisture drain quickly. If you see yellowing foliage, you're overwatering.

Acapulco starts blooming in midsummer and, with deadheading, keeps it up well into fall. Removing the faded blooms also discourages reseeding. Or just let it reseed — you can always pull or transplant the seedlings. (They probably won't look like the original plant anyway.)

Your plant will stop blooming after a hard frost in fall. To help the plant survive winter cold and moisture, wait to cut it back until spring. When you see new growth emerge, cut the stems back by about two thirds. Then you'll know that the hummingbirds can't be far behind! ☐

Low maintenance, high impact

A hot, sunny spot next to steps is perfect for this waterwise combination. Even lean, nutrient-poor soil doesn't faze these plants. The key for all of them is well-drained soil. In summer, the deep-violet salvia and dark-pink coneflower highlight the bright, clear colors of Acapulco. Meanwhile, the soft gray foliage of the lamb's ear and artemisia complement and soften the overall effect.

A Hyssop *Agastache mexicana* 'Kiegabi' (Acapulco Salmon & Pink)
B Coneflower *Echinacea purpurea* 'Kim's Knee High'
C Artemisia *Artemisia* 'Powis Castle'
D Salvia *Salvia xsylvestris* 'Blaühugel' (Blue Hill)
E Lamb's ear *Stachys byzantina* 'Big Ears'

Mail-order source

High Country Gardens
www.highcountrygardens.com
800-925-9387. Catalog free

PLANTS | HOW-TO

Native Plant Gardening
with Alan Branhagen

This end of the border is dry, so plants here need to tolerate this condition.

Native plants don't have to look wild and weedy! The truth is, anyone can work a few natives into an existing garden. Check out the garden at right. At first glance, I bet you can't tell that it's planted entirely with natives — it's looks just as tidy as one filled with more "civilized" varieties.

There are a couple of advantages to growing native plants, those that occur naturally in a certain region. They're adapted to your regional climate, so you won't have to bring in loads of topsoil, run a sprinkler all summer or baby them with extra winter protection. And wildlife will appreciate finding foods they already know.

But to get the full benefit, you can't buy just any old plant labeled "native." That's why I spoke with Alan Branhagen, director of horticulture at Powell Gardens, near Kansas City. He specializes in natives and had great tips on how to choose and use them.

START WITH THE RIGHT CHOICES
Just because a plant is native doesn't mean it grows anywhere in its region. A tree that naturally grows near a stream won't do well next to a hot concrete driveway. So make sure you know a plant's natural habitat. It'll look healthier and you'll be happier with your choice.

Try to find natives that were propagated from plants growing in your region. Sugar maple is native in both Vermont and Missouri, but a seedling grown from a tree in Vermont may not tolerate Missouri's hot summers. A Missouri gardener should look for one started in the Midwest. Ask your retailer for information, or check out regional plant societies for suppliers of plants propagated in your area.

And don't feel like you have to be a purist. Named cultivars of natives still count! They've just been selected for a specific trait, such as heat or cold tolerance.

CUSTOMIZE YOUR OWN BORDER
Now, check out the border at right for helpful tips on designing with natives. Here we've shown it filled with Midwestern plants, but if you like the look, find your region and use the corresponding plant list. Check out our Web extra to find complete plans, as well as lists of lots more plants for all of the regions. □

— *Jim Childs*

PHOTO: Courtesy of Alan Branhagen

Midwest

Hot, humid summers are common until you reach the cooler northern parts of this region. Winter brings snow to the north but rain and ice to the southern sections. Soils are often deep, rich and alkaline. The plants in our plan are hardy in USDA zones 4 to 7.

A Eastern redbud
Cercis canadensis
Tree; vivid pink flowers in spring; sun to part shade; well-drained soil

B Buttonbush
Cephalanthus occidentalis
Shrub; white buttonlike flowers in midsummer; sun to part shade; moist to wet soil

C Michigan lily
Lilium michiganense
Bulb; orange flowers with red speckles in midsummer; sun; moist to wet soil

D Black-eyed Susan
Rudbeckia hirta
Annual; yellow and gold flowers from midsummer to frost; sun; well-drained soil

E Canada columbine
Aquilegia canadensis
Perennial; red and yellow flowers in spring; sun to part shade; well-drained soil

WEB extra

Wonder what the rest of the plants are in our design? You can see the complete *plan* online.

Plant perennials and shrubs in groups for a natural look.

This side of the garden is lower and stays damp, perfect for moisture-loving plants.

Northwest

Summers are warm and humid along the coast; further north and inland it's cooler. Winters are often wet and rainy, with only occasional snow in some parts. Soils vary, but usually have an acid pH. These plants are hardy in USDA zones 6 to 9.

A Bitter cherry
Prunus emarginata mollis
Shrubby tree; small fragrant white flowers in spring; sun to part shade; well-drained soil

B Pink flowering currant
Ribes sanguineum
Shrub; pink to red flowers in spring; sun to part shade; moist soil

C Columbia lily
Lilium columbianum
Bulb; spotted orange flowers in midsummer; sun to part shade; moist, acid soil

D Globe gilia
Gilia capitata
Annual; blue flowers most of the summer; sun; tolerates dry soil; reseeds easily

E Western columbine
Aquilegia formosa
Perennial; red and yellow flowers in early summer; sun to light shade; moist soil

New England

Winters are cold here, as well as up into Canada, with snow cover to insulate plants. Summers can be hot, but generally not humid. Soils are variable, often shallow and rocky, usually with an acid pH. Plants in this plan are hardy in USDA zones 4 to 7.

A Serviceberry
Amelanchier laevis
Tree; white flowers in early spring; sun to part shade; well-drained soil

B Highbush blueberry
Vaccinium corymbosum
Shrub; white flowers in spring; edible blue fruit; sun to part shade; moist, acid soil

C Canada lily
Lilium canadensis
Bulb; orange flowers in midsummer; sun to part shade; moist, well-drained, acid soil

D Black-eyed Susan
Rudbeckia hirta
Annual; yellow and gold flowers from midsummer to frost; sun; well-drained soil

E Canada columbine
Aquilegia canadensis
Perennial; red and yellow flowers in spring; sun to part shade; well-drained soil

Southwest

Hot, dry summers are normal. Winters are cold and windy, but often not bitter. And depending on the elevation, there may be rain instead of snow in winter. Sandy or gritty soils are often alkaline. Our plant choices are hardy in USDA zones 6 to 9.

A Desert willow
Chilopsis linearis
Tree; fragrant white to pale lavender flowers in midsummer; sun; well-drained to dry soil

B Red-berry mahonia
Mahonia haematocarpa
Shrub; fragrant yellow flowers in late spring; evergreen; sun; well-drained soil

C Sago lily
Calochortus spp.
Bulb; tulip-like flowers in spring to early summer; sun; sandy, well-drained soil

D Chocolate flower
Berlandiera lyrata
Annual; light yellow chocolate-scented flowers all summer; sun; well-drained soil

E Arizona columbine
Aquilegia desertorum
Perennial; orange-yellow flowers in summer; sun to shade; moist, well-drained soil

Southeast

Southeast summers are hot and humid while winters are cool and often wet. It might snow occasionally, but it usually doesn't last long. Many of the plants native to this area like acid soil. These plant choices are hardy in USDA zones 7 to 9.

A Sweetbay magnolia
Magnolia virginiana
Tree; creamy white, lemon-scented flowers in late spring; part shade; moist, acid soil

B Red chokeberry
Aronia arbutifolia
Shrub; white flowers in May; sun to part shade; well-drained to wet soil

C Turk's cap lily
Lilium superbum
Bulb; spotted orange flowers in midsummer; sun to part shade; moist to wet soil

D Black-eyed Susan
Rudbeckia hirta
Annual; yellow and gold flowers from midsummer to frost; sun; well-drained soil

E Canada columbine
Aquilegia canadensis
Perennial; red and yellow flowers in spring; sun to part shade; well-drained soil

PLANTS | EDITOR'S CHOICE

'Empress Wu's Yellow' Peony

Paeonia 'Empress Wu's Yellow'

Size	3 to 4 ft. tall and wide
Bloom	Pale- to medium-yellow single flowers with bright gold stamens
Soil	Well-drained
Light	Full sun
Pests	None serious
Hardiness	Cold: USDA zones 4 to 8 Heat: AHS zones 8 to 1

For many gardeners, spring means peonies, with those big, fluffy pink, red, white and yellow (yes, yellow!) blooms.

Just like Grandma's peonies, 'Empress Wu's Yellow' is tough and fragrant. But it's pale yellow, with bright gold stamens. And the single flowers aren't heavy, so they don't usually need to be staked.

This plant is a splurge, at more than $100. You may not want to plant a whole row of them, but one or two really make a statement. (Peonies are long-lived, so it's a good "investment.")

You'll find this beauty can bloom as much as two weeks earlier than most other herbaceous (nonwoody) peonies. Choose companions that flower at the same time, like the columbines in "Spring has sprung" below. And a few plants that bloom later will keep this area interesting when the peonies are done.

GET GROWING Like other peonies, 'Empress Wu's Yellow' doesn't need much work if it's planted properly. Choose a spot with at least six hours of sun and well-drained soil. Make sure there's room for the plant to reach its full size. Peonies are often sold bare-root in late summer or fall, so you'll get a fleshy root with several pink buds. Plant the root with the buds pointing up and no more than 2 inches below the surface of the soil when you're done. Peonies don't bloom well if they're planted too deeply. Water after you plant to get rid of air pockets in the soil.

After the ground freezes, add 5 inches of mulch to protect the new plant over the winter. (You only need to do this the first year.)

Sprinkle all-purpose fertilizer around your peony in the spring when you feed your other perennials. If you have several hot, dry weeks the first summer it's in the ground, water it deeply now and then. You may see a few blooms the first spring, but a peony takes several years to get established.

Go on, indulge yourself. Settle 'Empress Wu's Yellow' in, then enjoy the show. ◻

Spring has sprung Pink and yellow — it's the perfect color mix for spring. Early bloomers, like columbine and creeping phlox, are great companions for this early-flowering yellow peony. And the variegated weigela has tinges of pink in the leaves to keep the theme going strong. Later in spring, the weigela will add some pink blooms of its own, and it doesn't get too big, so it won't take over the entire planting.

A	Peony	*Paeonia* 'Empress Wu's Yellow'
B	Weigela	*Weigela florida* 'Verweig' (My Monet®)
C	Columbine	*Aquilegia* 'Nora Barlow'
D	Columbine	*Aquilegia chrysantha* 'Yellow Queen'
E	Creeping phlox	*Phlox subulata* 'White Delight'

the YEAR IN GARDENING   www.GardenGateMagazine.com

Mail-order source

Cricket Hill Garden
www.treepeony.com
860-283-1042. Catalog free

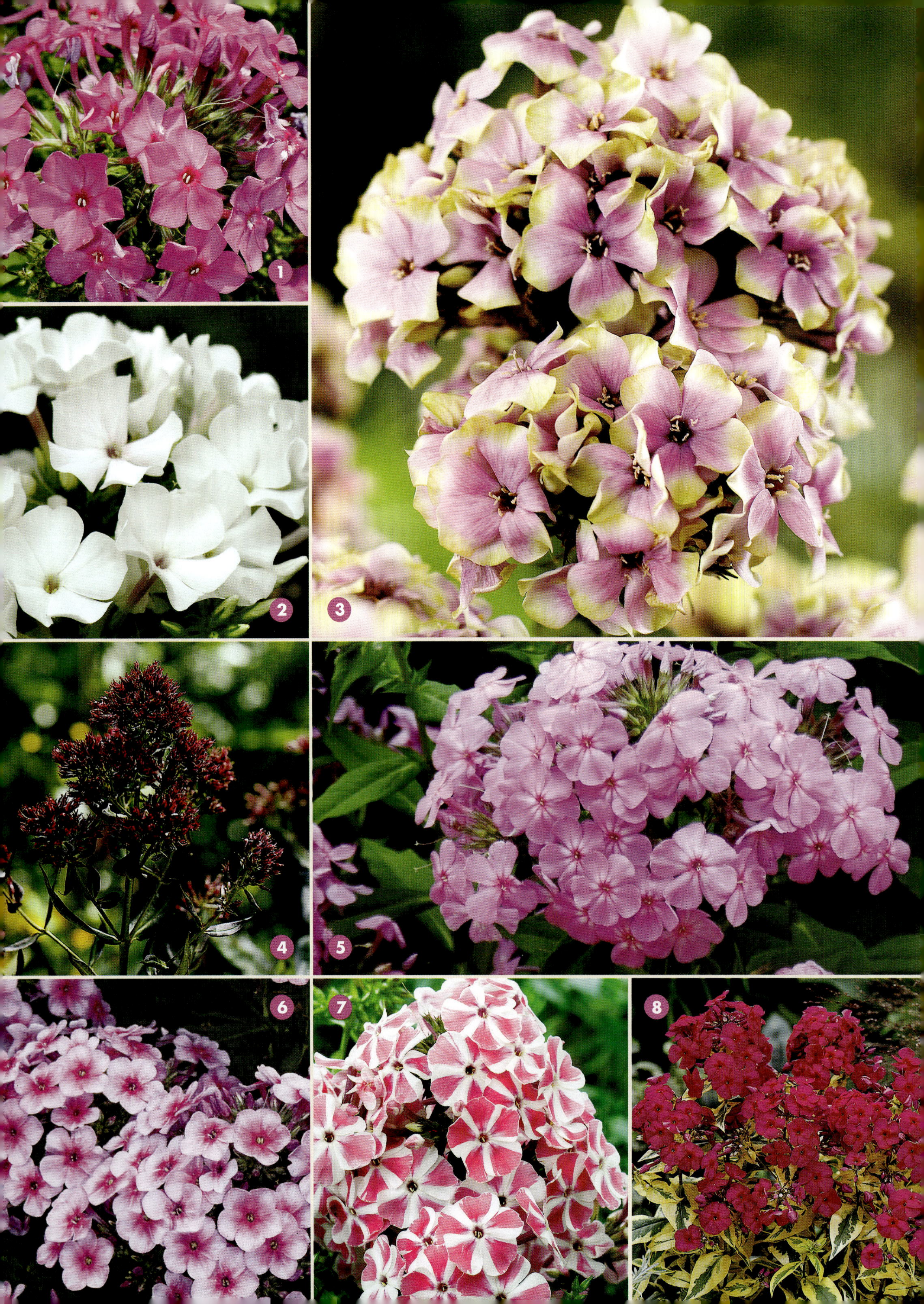
1
2
3
4
5
6
7
8

PLANTS | SUMMER PERENNIAL

8 new looks for an old garden favorite
Garden Phlox

'Eva Cullum'

When you hear that something is new and improved, are you a bit skeptical? I certainly was when I first heard about improved garden phlox cultivars. I assumed that to get rid of the mildew problem, they must have sacrificed that wonderful fragrance. Surprise, they didn't! It's still there!

Because of the fragrance, and its popularity with butterflies and hummingbirds, phlox has always been a much-loved perennial. You just had to tuck old favorites like 'Eva Cullum', in the illustration, behind a shorter perennial to hide the mildewed foliage. Now, I do have to warn you, even these new cultivars aren't totally immune to the disease — only resistant. Poor air circulation and high humidity can still trigger an attack. But these newer phlox are moving front and center in the summer garden. Let me introduce you to some of my favorites.

1 'JUNIOR DREAM' Many 2-foot-tall stems growing from the base of the clump and a short space between leaves means heavier branching up top. That translates to more of the gorgeous red-purple flowers. Try one of these in a container with annuals for some striking summer color.

2 'BARTWENTYNINE' Move this 15-inch-tall garden phlox, also sold under the name White Flame, to the front of the border. Or, it's a perfect size to grow with other plants in a container. And since it's extremely mildew resistant, you don't have to worry about hiding any ugly leaves.

3 'SHERBET COCKTAIL' A 28-inch-tall hybrid with yellow buds will make you take a second look. When the blooms open, they're pink and white with a yellow-green edge. To keep the color from looking "muddy," pair this phlox with a rich burgundy or dark blue-purple neighbor.

4 'RED FEELINGS' Narrow petals make this 24-inch-tall phlox unique. Plus, the bracts holding the petals are also colorful, so the heads will look like they're still in bloom even after the petals drop.

5 'DAVID'S LAVENDER' A sport of the white cultivar 'David', this phlox has exceptional mildew resistance. At 4 feet tall, it's great at the back of a border. Or pinch the tips out of any of these garden phlox when they're a foot tall to keep the plant shorter and get more flowering side branches.

6 'JOHN FANICK' Garden phlox in hot areas are rarely happy plants. But this 3-foot-tall cultivar was discovered growing just fine in San Antonio, Texas, where it can get very hot. However, if you like the light pink flowers with darker pink eyes, it'll do great in cooler areas, too.

7 'PEPPERMINT TWIST' There's nothing shy about this fluorescent pink-and-white-striped cultivar. Even the sweet fragrance reaches out to greet you when you enter the garden. At just 16 inches tall, with sturdy stems, this cultivar rarely needs staking, even in a windy spot.

8 'GOLDMINE' Once upon a time, all variegated garden phlox had leaves edged with creamy white. And the plants were often weak, even short-lived. But leaves with bright gold edges, combined with magenta-red flowers, make this robust 28-inch-tall cultivar sparkle in front of a dark-green background.

Try a couple of these phlox yourself. You'll get the best of old *and* new! □

— *Jim Childs*

GARDEN PHLOX
Phlox paniculata

12 to 48 in. tall, 12 to 36 in. wide

Flowers from white to many shades of lavender, pink and red; more than 10 weeks of blooms from mid- to late summer

Full sun

Well-drained soil

Powdery mildew, root rot

Cold-hardy in USDA zones 3 to 9

Heat-tolerant in AHS zones 9 to 1

Mail-order sources

Fieldstone Gardens
www.fieldstonegardens.com
207-923-3836. *Catalog $2.50*

Plant Delights Nursery, Inc.
www.plantdelights.com
919-772-4794. *Catalog free*

Roots & Rhizomes
www.rootsrhizomes.com
800-374-5035. *Catalog $3*

PLANTS | EDITOR'S CHOICE

'Henry Eilers' Sweet Coneflower

Sweet coneflower
Rudbeckia subtomentosa 'Henry Eilers'

Size	4 to 5 ft. tall, 18 to 24 in. wide
Habit	Upright
Bloom	Late summer to autumn
Soil	Moist, well-drained
Light	Full sun to part shade
Pests	Occasionally powdery mildew
Hardiness	Cold: USDA zones 4 to 8 Heat: AHS zones 8 to 1

If you like to show off your garden and have something that makes visitors ask questions, here's the plant for you. When I planted 'Henry Eilers', everyone — and I do mean everyone — had to know what this perennial was. That is, everyone except the deer — they weren't even interested!

You may pick up the scent of vanilla or anise coming from the stems and foliage on warm summer evenings. It's subtle, not strong, but a great addition to this unique perennial.

SHOW IT OFF! At 4 to 5 feet tall, 'Henry Eilers' is perfect for the middle or back of the border. Keep it in full sun and the stems won't flop. Or, if you're planting 'Henry Eilers' in a windy spot, crowd it between tall plants, such as maiden grasses, for support.

Don't have room in your garden for that much height? As with many late-summer perennials, you can pinch or prune it. Pinching gives you a plant that will stay about two-thirds its true height. And it'll be bushier with more of those gorgeous flowers that you, and lots of butterflies, can enjoy.

How do you pinch it back? When the plant is roughly half its ultimate height, usually around early to mid-June, cut all of the stems back by up to half. Make sure not to cut it back after early July or you may lose some of the flowers. Rather than giving 'Henry Eilers' a flat top, I like to cut the stems around the edge just a bit shorter than the center ones. That gives the plant a more natural dome shape when it blooms.

The clear yellow color is easy to pair with blue, like the bluebeard in the photo. And it goes beautifully with shades of pink. Try it with fall asters, such as 'Harrington's Pink', or 'September Charm' Japanese anemone.

KEEP IT HEALTHY Give 'Henry Eilers' a spot in full sun, or at least afternoon sun. Average to moist, well-drained soil's fine, but avoid rich soil or too much fertilizer. You're likely to end up with plants that have weak stems and fewer flowers.

'Henry Eilers' will tolerate short periods of summer drought after it's established. In fact, avoid wet areas or it could die of root rot.

You may spot some mildew on the leaves in late summer. It's not a serious problem that will kill the plant. But if you live where summers are hot and humid, plant 'Henry Eilers' in a spot with good air circulation to keep it healthy.

I know you'll eventually want more of this plant, or your friends will want starts. Make them wait at least three or four years before you divide your clump. Since it blooms late, early spring is an ideal time to divide and share this great perennial. ☐

Autumn pastels Fall gardens don't have to be filled with dark, somber colors. Why not try a pastel color scheme like this one? This gate is framed with 'Henry Eilers' sweet coneflower and several other late-blooming plants — mums, bluebeard and feathery grasses. All these plants are hardy to at least USDA zone 5 and prefer a spot in full sun.

- **A** Sweet coneflower *Rudbeckia subtomentosa* 'Henry Eilers'
- **B** Mum *Chrysanthemum koreana* 'Sheffield'
- **C** Bluebeard *Caryopteris xclandonensis* 'Heavenly Blue'
- **D** Korean feather reed grass *Calamagrostis brachytricha*

Mail-order sources

Great Garden Plants
www.greatgardenplants.com
877-447-4769
Online catalog only

Garden Crossings
www.gardencrossings.com
616-875-6355
Online catalog only

PLANTS | EDITOR'S CHOICE

'Becky' Shasta Daisy

Leucanthemum ×superbum 'Becky'

Size	3 to 4 ft. tall, 2 to 3 ft. wide
Type	Perennial
Bloom	White flowers with yellow centers from mid- to late summer
Soil	Well-drained
Light	Full sun to part shade
Pests	None serious
Hardiness	Cold: USDA zones 4 to 9 Heat: AHS zones 9 to 1

Think "garden" and I bet your mind's eye sees daisies! These perky blooms are at home anywhere.

EASY TO LOVE 'Becky' is one of the best of the Shasta daisies, with stiff stems that don't flop, and a long bloom time. With regular deadheading, it'll flower from early July into September.

A long season of bloom isn't all this daisy offers. Plants form nice clumps 2 or 3 feet across, but they don't take over your garden. My 'Becky' daisies are planted just outside my front door. The tidy plants don't block the sidewalk, and there's something blooming by the steps most of the summer.

I especially like the fact that 'Becky' flowers in midsummer, when the rest of the garden is looking a little forlorn. For a cool summer look, combine it with other light-colored plants, like the white blazing star, dusty miller and variegated maiden grass in "White on white" below.

EASY TO GROW This daisy is as easy to grow as it is to love. It prefers full sun, but tolerates part shade, particularly in the South. 'Becky' does need well-drained soil. Too much moisture, especially in the winter, can cause the roots to rot.

Speaking of winter, this is one of the most cold-hardy daisies available. And it's also one of the most heat- and humidity-tolerant, so it's a great choice wherever you garden.

As long as you have 'Becky' in the right place, there's not much to growing it. Spread a little all-purpose fertilizer around it when you feed your other perennials every spring. Otherwise, topdressing with compost is all it needs to thrive.

Divide your plants every two or three years, in early spring or early fall, to keep them going strong. It's time to divide when the center of the clump starts to die out. Cut a few chunks out of the edge, or lift the whole clump and divide it. Compost the woody, dead centers.

Then use the new plants to spread more happy-go-lucky cheer in your garden. ❑

White on white Whites and grays, in both foliage and flower, will shine in your evening garden. And the strong, contrasting shapes of the four plants keep this monochromatic look exciting. This planting peaks in mid- to late summer, just in time to keep your garden from giving in to the midsummer blahs.

A Shasta daisy *Leucanthemum ×superbum* 'Becky'
B Maiden grass *Miscanthus sinensis* 'Morning Light'
C Blazing star *Liatris spicata* 'Floristan Weiss' ('Floristan White')
D Dusty miller *Senecio cineraria*

Sources

Lazy S'S Farm Nursery
www.lazyssfarm.com
Online catalog only

'Becky' Shasta daisy is also available at most nurseries and garden centers.

PLANTS | SPRING PERENNIAL

Bright flowers and fabulous foliage add up to one great plant
Siberian Iris

SIBERIAN IRIS
Iris sibirica

*2 to 4 ft. tall,
18 to 24 in. wide*

Flowers in shades of blue, violet, white, maroon, yellow and pink in late spring to early summer

Full sun to part shade

Moist to wet, well-drained, acid soil

No serious pests

Cold-hardy in USDA zones 3 to 9

Heat-tolerant in AHS zones 9 to 1

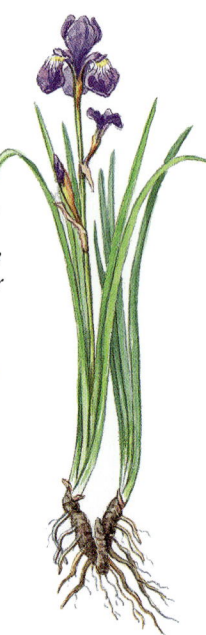

If you're looking for some elegant, graceful plants that don't need a lot of fussing, you'll love Siberian irises. Siberians can take nearly all soil conditions from moist and well-drained to boggy. In fact, you can grow Siberians in most areas, except the deep South, hot, arid areas, or, ironically, Siberia.

Give the plants a spot with at least six hours of sun and they readily form large, dramatic clumps like the 'Caesar's Brother' in photo 1. (In areas with very hot summers — USDA zones 8 and warmer — they prefer a little shade to prevent the foliage from scorching.) Then, when they bloom in late spring, the effect is enough to knock your socks off!

EASY ELEGANCE As well as being more tolerant of different soil types, Siberians are every bit as long-lived as their bearded cousins and are even more winter hardy. Not only that, but their graceful, grasslike foliage never gets tattered and stays green and upright all season long.

Actually, about the only downside with these tough perennials is their relatively short period of bloom that leaves gardeners wanting more. Breeders are working on ones that bloom for longer than the average one to two weeks. Also, breeders are developing earlier- or later-flowering plants and more repeat bloomers. Lavender-purple 'Springs Brook', photo 2, is one of the most reliable

1) 'Caesar's Brother' 40 in. tall; an established clump squeezes out any weeds

2) 'Springs Brook' 40 in. tall; a rebloomer that can flower up to six weeks in late spring

3) 'White Swirl' 30 in. tall; one of the first white cultivars; flared falls

4) 'Butter and Sugar' 27 in. tall; standards are a paler shade of the bright yellow falls

5) 'Pink Haze' 38 in. tall; introduced in 1969, it's still a very popular pink

rebloomers. The second flush of blooms is a little lighter and follows the first after just a short rest. But even the best Siberian rebloomers tend to be pretty erratic.

COLORFUL CULTIVARS Most of the newer Siberian cultivars came from crossing two species, *Iris sibirica* and *Iris sanguinea*. And almost all modern cultivars can point to 'White Swirl' somewhere in their family tree. Introduced in 1957, it was the first Siberian iris with flaring falls. Photo 3 shows why it's still one of the best white Siberians available.

Purple, lavender and blue are the most common colors. A favorite hybrid, 'Butter and Sugar' (photo 4) was the first strong yellow to hold its color in bright sun. If you want a good, nonfading pink hybrid, grow 'Pink Haze', in photo 5.

Flowers come in single colors, bitones (standards and falls of different colors), speckled, striped or edged with a contrasting color. Most have a striking patch of brighter color at the base of the falls called a "signal." Petals are upright, droopy, flared, ruffled or even curved under. "Petals and parts" at right points out different flower features. There's little variation in the foliage; all have similar upright, grasslike leaves that stay green all season.

Turn the page to see how to use these beauties in your garden and how to keep them growing great.

Petals and parts

Siberian iris descriptions in catalogs can be confusing. Basically, the flowers are made up of three standards, three falls and three styles. Here are a few flower terms you may come across when ordering.

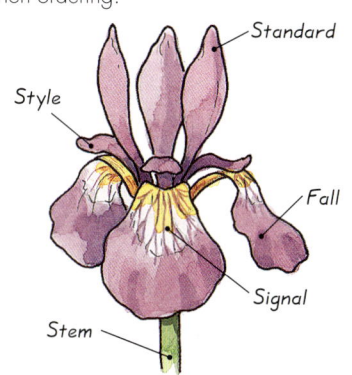

DYNAMITE DESIGN TIPS

Botanical Names

Goat's beard *Aruncus dioicus*
Joe-pye weed *Eupatorium purpureum*
Lady's mantle *Alchemilla mollis*
Marsh marigold *Caltha palustris*
Pink *Dianthus* spp.
Spiderwort *Tradescantia virginiana*
Spirea *Spiraea* spp.

In just a few years, a small planting of Siberian irises will fill in and create an impressive mass of color. You'll get a lot of impact from a sweeping bed of blooms. And when you plant cultivars with different bloom times, you can extend the overall bloom period to several weeks.

MIX IT UP But what if you don't have space to devote to one type of plant? Mix in a few Siberians among other perennials and flowering shrubs. Siberians are vigorous enough to compete with other plants without getting squeezed out. And they bloom early, then provide a green background for later-blooming neighbors.

In photo 6, the magenta spiderwort and pink dianthus bloom around the same time as the irises to make a bright spring combination. And later, when the spiderwort looks rough and you cut it back hard, spiky green iris leaves will still look good. Meanwhile, the mounded chartreuse spirea foliage will provide a nice shape contrast and carry color through to fall.

Because the iris leaves are what you'll be looking at for most of the season, choose plant companions with contrasting foliage shapes to play up the very vertical look. Goat's beard or lady's mantle are two good choices. "Stylish iris," below, gives you another option for a colorful spring

Stylish iris
The fresh look of this colorful part-shade combination spans the seasons. Spring kicks off with the 'Dreaming Yellow' Siberian iris and pink bleeding heart blooms. Soft blue flowers of the geranium continue the color into summer. And later, the iris foliage provides a beautiful contrast with the broad green and chartreuse hosta leaves.

A Siberian iris *Iris sibirica* 'Dreaming Yellow'
B Bleeding heart *Dicentra spectabilis*
C Geranium *Geranium* 'Johnson's Blue'
D Hosta *Hosta* 'Golden Tiara'

GROW GREAT SIBERIAN IRISES

Siberians thrive on lots of moisture and prefer a slightly acid soil pH between 5.5 and 6.5. They can tolerate standing water for short periods except when they're dormant. Rhizomes that stay wet in winter will rot. But, on the other hand, once established, these plants can also handle short periods of drought.

PLANTING Plant the rhizomes in spring if you garden in USDA zones 6 and colder, in fall in warmer zones. Dig a hole 10 in. deep and put well-rotted compost and a mound of soil in the bottom. Place the rhizome on the mound and fill the hole with more compost-amended soil so the crown ends up 1½ to 2 in. deep. Water the plant well and keep the soil moist with a 1- to 2-in. layer of mulch. Don't be discouraged — even in ideal conditions, Siberians often won't bloom the first year after planting.

FERTILIZING Siberian irises aren't heavy feeders, but you can give older clumps a boost with a 5-10-10 fertilizer or some compost sprinkled around the bed in early spring. Give rebloomers an extra shot right after the first flush of blooms is finished.

DEADHEADING Once flowers fade, cut the flower stems down at their base. Then the plant will use energy to build up its rhizomes. If you don't deadhead, you'll get interesting seed pods later. Let them dry for winter interest

Clean up foliage in fall.

combination that continues to look good for multiple seasons.

WATER COLORS Pair Siberians with other plants that thrive in moist areas near water, such as marsh marigold and Joe-pye weed. Though Siberians can take standing water while they're actively growing and blooming, just up the slope from a pond or stream is an ideal location. There, the roots stay moist, but the rhizomes aren't under water.

A LITTLE BACKGROUND With its grassy look, the tidy foliage is also perfect as a background for hardscaping, such as the bird bath in photo 6 or a garden ornament. Once the flowers fade, the garden art will grab more attention for itself against a backdrop of vivid green. Learn how to keep these versatile plants looking good in "Grow great Siberian irises" below.

What's the bottom line? Siberian irises will look gorgeous in just about any style garden, with almost no work. They help you add a lot of elegance to your garden without even really trying!

— *Deborah Gruca*

(6) The slender, grasslike foliage of Siberian iris echoes that of the clump of pink spiderwort in the foreground.

or cut them to include in dried arrangements. If left on the plant, they'll make lots of little seedlings that look different from the parent and may end up replacing it.

FALL CLEANUP Siberian irises aren't bothered by iris borer or bacterial soft rot like bearded irises are. Instead, they're almost disease- and pest-free. You can keep them that way by cleaning up the foliage where pests can overwinter after the plants die back in late fall. Make quick work of a big clump by grabbing a handful of brown foliage with one hand. Give it a couple of quick twists, as I'm doing at left. Then, with your other hand, cut off the bunch at the ground using pruners. Picking up the twisted bundles is much easier than raking up lots of loose leaves. If you don't get around to doing this in fall, it's not the end of the world — you can also wait and clean up the debris in spring.

DIVIDING Unlike their bearded cousins, Siberians don't require frequent dividing. Some cultivars can grow quite happily in the same spot for a decade. It's time to divide your clump when, in early spring, you notice the center dying out, as in the photo to the right. You can divide the plants any time after they bloom in the North (USDA zones 3 to 6), and in fall in Southern zones. When you dig the clump, cut the root ball into sections and throw away any dried or brown rhizomes. If you can't replant the rhizomes within several hours, soak them in a pail of water so they don't dry out. Check out our Web extra video to see how to divide.

Divide when the center dies out.

WEB extra

Need to divide your Siberians? Watch our *video* to see how.

PLANTS | EDITOR'S CHOICE

5 Plants That Live Up To Their Promise

Plant breeders are always crossing this with that, trying to create something new. And with every plant that's released, there's a lot of publicity, making all kinds of claims about how great the plant is. But how well do they really perform? Let's take a look at a few recent introductions that have stood the test of time in our garden.

Most of these plants have been around at least a couple of years, long enough that you can find them at a local garden center, but I've included some mail-order sources, just in case. ◻

— *Marcia Leeper*

Hollyhock *Alcea rosea* 'Queeny Purple'

HEIGHT 24 to 36 in. **WIDTH** 24 in. **LIGHT** Full sun **SOIL** Moist, well-drained **COLD-HARDY** USDA zones 3 to 11 **HEAT-TOLERANT** AHS zones 11 to 1 **BEST FEATURES** Compact plant; magenta-purple flowers **WHERE TO FIND IT** Territorial Seed Company, 800-626-0866, www.territorialseed.com

Put away the stakes — this hollyhock doesn't need them. 'Queeny Purple' is a dwarf variety with lots of branches to hold flowers. We started it from seed, and it bloomed the very first year.

Hollyhocks are actually biennials. They do reseed easily, and you can let the seedlings grow, but they may not look like the parent plants. If you want to keep them looking the same, deadhead to prevent self-seeding, and start a few new purchased seeds every year.

Tall sedum *Sedum telephium* 'Xenox'

HEIGHT 10 to 18 in. **WIDTH** 18 in. **LIGHT** Full sun **SOIL** Well-drained **COLD-HARDY** USDA zones 3 to 9 **HEAT-TOLERANT** AHS zones 9 to 1 **BEST FEATURES** Constantly changing foliage, upright habit **WHERE TO FIND IT** Garden Crossings, 616-875-6355, www.gardencrossings.com

This upright sedum puts on a gorgeous foliage show. The leaves start out dark chocolate-brown and lighten as the summer progresses. Leaf color is darkest when the plant's in full sun, but even in part shade, as it is in the photo, it has a burgundy tinge. Pink flower clusters show up in midsummer through fall. These smaller flower heads aren't as heavy and floppy as some tall sedums, so we haven't had to worry about it splitting apart in the middle as many sedums do.

Primrose *Primula sieboldii* 'Pink Snowflake'

HEIGHT 8 in., 12 in. with flower **WIDTH** 12 in. **LIGHT** Part shade to shade **SOIL** Moist, acid, well-drained **COLD-HARDY** USDA zones 5 to 8 **HEAT-TOLERANT** AHS zones 8 to 1 **BEST FEATURES** Deeply textured foliage and snowflake blooms **WHERE TO FIND IT** Big Dipper Farm, 360-886-8133, www.bigdipperfarm.com

'Pink Snowflake' graces the garden in early spring with crinkled leaves and frilly pink flowers. But like most primroses, the foliage goes dormant in summer, so plant it with later-blooming plants to cover the bare spot. Or just set a summer container directly over it — that won't hurt the primrose.

We grew this in a container at our test garden the first spring, then planted it in the ground after the leaves faded. It prefers soil that's evenly moist, especially while it's getting established.

Astilbe *Astilbe xarendsii* ColorFlash®

HEIGHT 10 in. **WIDTH** 12 to 18 in. **LIGHT** Part shade **SOIL** Moist **COLD-HARDY** USDA zones 4 to 8 **HEAT-TOLERANT** AHS zones 8 to 1 **BEST FEATURES** Colorful foliage all summer long **WHERE TO FIND IT** Widely available at local garden centers

Most astilbes have showy flowers, but this one has gorgeous foliage! It starts bright green, matures to burgundy with touches of purple and turns gold and orange in fall. (The small pink flowers show up in early summer.) All that color makes it a great, long-lasting container plant, too.

Our favorite thing about this astilbe? Unlike most others, it tolerates slightly dry soils and a little more sun without getting crispy. Of course, it'll be happiest with consistently moist, cool soil and part shade, though.

Jacob's ladder *Polemonium yezoense hidakanum* 'Purple Rain'

HEIGHT 18 to 24 in. **WIDTH** 12 to 18 in. **LIGHT** Full sun to part shade **SOIL** Moist, well-drained **COLD-HARDY** USDA zones 5 to 7 **HEAT-TOLERANT** AHS zones 7 to 1 **BEST FEATURES** Purple-blue flowers; deep purple foliage and stems **WHERE TO FIND IT** Fieldstone Gardens, 207-923-3836, www.fieldstonegardens.com

You *can* have it all — or at least this Jacob's ladder does. First you notice the large, purple-blue flowers in midspring, then you see the bronze-tinged foliage and dark-purple stems. In the test garden, the foliage color wasn't very noticeable until the second year.

'Purple Rain' needs even soil moisture, especially the first year. Extra-thick mulch will help it through the first winter, but pull most of the mulch away in early spring so the plant can get going quickly.

did you know...

Abnormal rose growth
Anna Edwards, Tennessee

Q One of my roses has dense clumps of branches and more thorns than usual. What's wrong with it?

A Those symptoms sound like rose rosette disease. Although you usually find it in weedy multiflora rose, all roses are susceptible. And it's becoming more common in cultivated ones. Symptoms include increased thorniness, small red or purple leaves and rapid, dense growth of the shoots in "witches' brooms."

Rose rosette is caused by an organism similar to a virus that's transmitted by mites. Unfortunately, there's no cure for it. If you think your rose has rose rosette, remove and send it away in the trash to prevent infecting others. Get rid of any nearby stands of multiflora rose, as well.

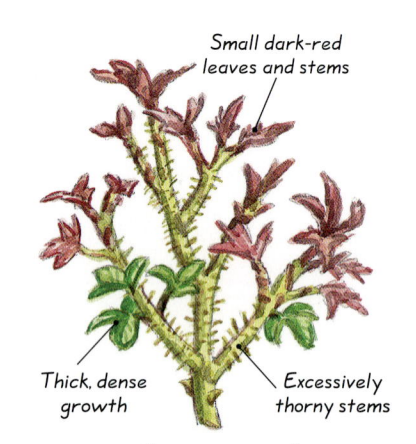

Small dark-red leaves and stems
Thick, dense growth
Excessively thorny stems

Rose with rose rosette disease

Normal leaf and thorn formation

Healthy rose

Glass wall
Jill Gross, Washington

Glass blocks like these look good in the house and the garden, too! Jill used some that had been discarded after a remodeling job to make a raised bed.

She dug a shallow trench and set the blocks into the ground, edge to edge. This made a short wall — no adhesive needed. By leaving a little room between some blocks Jill could plant hen and chicks.

The next spring, while checking on her garden for signs of life she had a little surprise. Those double glass walls worked as insulators, trapping warmth from the sun to heat the soil. Perennial plants growing in this bed emerged weeks before her other raised beds. Watch out for spring freezes, as they can damage early plants. Protect new growth with an old sheet.

How to store canna rhizomes
Madeline Alba, Missouri

Q Whenever I try to store my cannas over winter, they rot. What am I doing wrong?

A Chances are your cannas are too wet when you box them up to store. Even the slightest amount of moisture can cause your canna rhizomes to rot.

Cannas are cold-hardy in USDA zones 8 to 10. If gardeners in colder zones don't want to buy new ones each year, they need to dig and store them over winter. After the foliage has been killed by a frost, dig up the rhizomes and shake off most of the soil — don't wash them. Cut the stems back to 3 inches and set the roots outside for a few days to dry. Pack them loosely in a paper sack or cardboard box — you don't need any packing material. Store them in a basement or garage that stays between 50 and 60 degrees. Cannas don't need many special accommodations for the winter. Just check on them once in a while and toss any that have started to rot.

Six to eight weeks before the last frost date, pot them up to get a head start on the season.

Cleaning up evergreens

Creeping evergreens are great additions to any garden — they're easy to grow and adaptable to most soil conditions, and they bring year-round color and interest, even during the coldest winters. But, just like any other plant, if left to their own devices too long, they can start to look a little wild.

You can see in the illustration below how to cut back the lower branches of a juniper. Evergreens don't grow new foliage on old wood, and new growth can often form a thick mat that blocks sun from reaching lower branches, killing them. The easiest way to clean up shrubs, then, is to undercut them.

To undercut, lift a handful of foliage-laden branches, and take a look at what's growing underneath. If you see dead limbs, or limbs with sparse, struggling foliage, they're candidates for cutting back. But first, take the time to evaluate — with this branch gone, will the top side of the shrub still look OK? If the answer is yes, cut off the branch at the trunk with pruners or loppers. If the answer is no, leave the branch as it is.

Finally, to keep the juniper looking healthy and encourage a bit more growth, lightly trim up the tips of branches with new foliage.

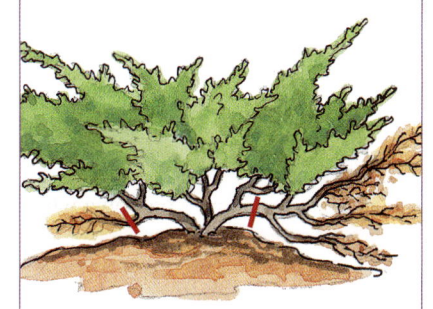

Undercutting evergreens gives them a fresh, healthy look.

in the news

Fresh from the field to you

Brent and Becky's Bulbs grows bulbs to sell. And now the company wants to share the lovely flowers from its bulb fields with you! Get fresh tulips, daffodils, gladiolas and other flowers shipped directly to your door. Check out www.brentandbeckysbulbs.com to order a bouquet of whatever is blooming in their fieldsthat week. We received this beautiful bunch of flowers in just a couple of days. Orders areaccepted March 15 through October 15.

Gardening = lower lung cancer risk

Lung cancer is the leading cause of cancer death in both men and women. But early results from an ongoing study have found that gardening and a good diet may help lower that risk. Researchers at the University of Texas M.D. Anderson Cancer Center are comparing the data of 3,800 smokers, nonsmokers and former smokers. They found that people who ate four or more servings of green salad each week and got out in the garden once or twice a week had a reduced risk of getting lung cancer compared to people who don't garden or eat their veggies.

Do daffodils change color?
Virginia Fugate, Virginia

Q *Last spring I had one white daffodil with a yellow cup bloom in the center of an established bed of all-yellow ones. How did it change color?*

A Individual plants don't change the color of their blooms, but there are a couple possible explanations. A bee may have fertilized one daffodil, crossing it with one of another color. The resulting plant grew from seed and bloomed with a different-colored flower. But more likely, there was an undersized bulb of a different cultivar in with the other, older bulbs that you originally planted. After a couple of years, it grew large enough to bloom.

did you know... (CONTINUED)

Moving trumpet vine plants
Pat Zens, South Dakota

Q *I'd like to move a trumpet vine to my new house to attract hummingbirds. What is the best way to move this plant?*

A Trumpet vine has a massive root system, so moving the whole plant might be more trouble than it's worth. But, at right, see how the vine sends out suckers from underground runners? Just dig up one of the "baby" trumpet vines and plant it. A sharp spade makes it easy to cut through the runner as you dig out the plant.

Another option is to take a cutting. The best time is in spring or early summer. Cut a 3- to 5-inch-long piece of the vine and plant the cut end in a pot of moist potting mix.

Trumpet vine can be invasive. Plant it away from any buildings so the aggressive roots don't damage the foundations.

Use a sharp spade to cut through the runner from the mother plant.

Trumpet vine suckers readily from the root.

Hold your (baby's) breath
Linda Grieve, Iowa

Perennial baby's breath (*Gypsophila paniculata*) is beautiful but sometimes its wiry stems can lean with the weight of that mass of white flowers. Linda found that a few Asiatic lilies, planted among the baby's breath, help hold it up. The baby's breath is open enough for the lilies to grow through and the lily stems are sturdy enough to act as stakes.

When your bougainvilleas won't bloom...
Ed Godfrey, Tennessee

Q *I bought two potted bougainvilleas several months ago. They've only had a couple of flowers since then, even though I fertilize them weekly and water them every other day. They get morning sun. How do I get them to bloom again?*

A Even happy bougainvilleas can have short rest periods between flushes of bloom. But a few hours of morning sun are probably just not enough for these plants to bloom. Try putting them in full sun — the more, the better.

Also, cut back on watering — an overwatered bougainvillea won't flower. Wait until the soil surface is dry and the plant just starts to wilt before you water, then do it deeply (until it runs out the bottom holes if in a pot). And feed your plants with a water-soluble high-potassium fertilizer, such as 12-4-18, once a month during the growing season to encourage flowering.

Finally, in late summer to fall, cut back a third to half of the oldest growth on the plant. Bougainvilleas bloom on new wood, and pruning will stimulate one to put out new growth and flowers.

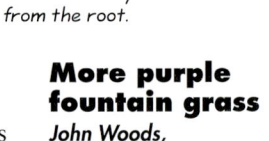

More purple fountain grass
John Woods, North Carolina

Q *I'd like to grow purple fountain grass from seed. Can I?*

A Unfortunately, the seed it produces is sterile, so in USDA zones 7 and colder, you'll need to buy new plants each year or bring yours inside over the winter. To do this, cut purple fountain grass (*Pennisetum setaceum*) back in late fall, divide it if it's large enough (12 inches in diameter or larger), and pot up the divisions. Overwinter them indoors under lights in a cool room that stays above freezing. Water the plants just enough to keep them from drying out. When nighttime temps are consistently above 60 degrees, plant them back outside.

the YEAR IN GARDENING   www.GardenGateMagazine.com

Grow clematis from seed
John McGill, Iowa

Q *Can you grow clematis using seed that you collect from the plant?*

A The short answer is yes. Seeds of small-flowered species, such as *Clematis macro-petala*, at right, are the easiest to start. And the plants will look like the parent plant.

To save seed, wait for a dry fall day when the seed heads are completely dry and have turned brown. Place the seed heads, including the attached plumes, in a paper bag (never plastic) and store them in a cool, dry place until it's time to plant.

C. tangutica, *C. alpina* and *C. serati-folia* will also germinate fairly easily and quickly. But large-flowered hybrids will try the patience of the most seasoned seed-starter. These seeds are often more difficult to start and may take as long as three years to sprout! And even if you succeed, the resulting flowers often look nothing like the ones on the original plant.

Fluffy plumes help the wind carry ripe seeds aloft.

Pool time for cardinal flower
Cynthia Gray, Pennsylvania

Q *Every time I've tried to grow cardinal flower, the plant dies. What can I do?*

A Cardinal flower (*Lobelia cardinalis*) thrives in rich, moist soils — almost bog-like conditions. If your garden doesn't have that kind of soil, you can create it by sinking a hard plastic wading pool in the garden. Dig a hole wide enough for the pool and slightly deeper, usually about 12 inches. Sinking the pool like this will hide the edge.

Tip the pool on edge and hammer a nail through the side in several places to create drainage holes. Set the pool in the hole and fill it with a mix of equal parts compost and soil. Plant your cardinal flower and add other bog plants like ligularias in the illustration below. Scarlet sage, queen-of-the-meadow and miniature cattails are other good bog plants to use. Water well and mulch to help keep in the moisture.

Fill with mix of compost and soil.

Punch holes in sides 5 in. from the bottom.

Weeping mulberry: What to cut
Linda Cerutti, Missouri

Q *We have a small weeping mulberry tree that's sending out lots of branches growing straight up. Should we cut these off?*

A You should remove the water sprouts, or branches growing straight up, as soon as they sprout. Cut them as close to the stem as possible and continue to cut them as new ones appear. Weeping mulberries are top-grafted onto a standard, or non-weeping trunk. If you leave the vertical sprouts, they'll sap energy from the plant and spoil its graceful, arching form. Don't worry; mulberries tolerate heavy pruning.

You should also always cut off any suckers, or shoots coming from the ground at the base of the tree or from the straight trunk. These are growing from the rootstock and if left, will eventually take over the grafted portion of the tree.

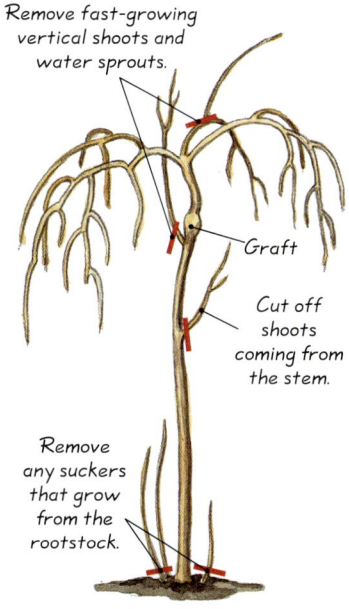

Remove fast-growing vertical shoots and water sprouts.

Graft

Cut off shoots coming from the stem.

Remove any suckers that grow from the rootstock.

did you know... (CONTINUED)

Hot pepper hang up
Edward H. Gasiecki, New York

Q We grow hot peppers in our garden every summer. Is there a good way to dry them?

A There are a few different ways to dry hot peppers so you'll have some to use in winter. You can use an oven or a food dehydrator or air-dry them. Wear rubber gloves when handling them — the chemical capsicum causes a burning pain on skin.

The fastest way to dry peppers is in the oven. Cut the peppers into 1-inch-thick pieces, and place them on the oven rack or a baking sheet in a 125-degree oven with the door open a bit. Dry peppers until they are crisp, turning them frequently. This may take 15 minutes to a few hours, depending on the size of the pieces and their moisture content.

To use a dehydrator, place it in a well-ventilated area while the peppers are drying because the fumes might make your eyes water. This may take several days, depending on the dehydrator. Consult the manual for specific instructions on drying peppers.

If you're not in a hurry, air-dry peppers whole by carefully threading them on a strong thread or fishing line with a sharp needle. Hang the string in a warm, dry place for three to four weeks; thicker-walled peppers may take longer. Air-dried peppers retain their color and spice better than those done in a dehydrator or oven.

When the peppers are ready, store them in an air-tight container or plastic bag in a cool, dry place.

Use a sharp needle and strong thread or fishing line to hang peppers.

Don't worry if peppers slide together on the thread. They'll dry just fine.

in the news

Fescue to the rescue
Did you know that some varieties of common fescue make their own natural broad-spectrum "herbicide" to fight lawn weeds? Scientists first discovered that fescues were able to inhibit plants from growing around them. Further research found that an amino acid called meta-tyrosine, or m-tyrosine, which is exuded from the roots of these lawn grasses, is the cause. M-tyrosine is toxic to plants but not to fungi, bacteria or mammals. It's too water-soluble to be used as an herbicide by itself but with this research as a starting point, scientists hope to develop new varieties of fescue that will suppress weeds even better.

Chia seeds are good for you
Researchers are rediscovering what the ancient Aztecs knew a long time ago. The tiny seeds of chia (*Salvia hispanica*) are packed with nutrition and lots of it. But don't go out and eat the stuff growing on your Chia Pet® just yet. It's the seeds that contain protein, fiber, calcium, phosphorus and many other nutrients, not the plants. On top of that, chia seeds have even more omega-3 fatty acids than flax seed and they won't turn rancid when stored, as flax does. To grow your own chia in the garden (not on your Chia Pet), visit Bountiful Gardens online at www.bountifulgardens.org or call 707-459-6410 to order.

Which plant to choose?
Are you having a terrible time figuring out which plants will work in your garden? Go to www.premiumplants.net and click on the Plant Selection Wizard. This site is operated by Hortech, a wholesale nursery, and home gardeners can use it to figure out which plants will work in their garden conditions. You can look for plants by keyword, flower color, leaf color and plant size. Or check boxes to indicate characteristics, such as light requirements, bloom time, deer resistance and many others. You'll get a list of plants that meet your criteria, then you can click on the name of the plant for more specific details.

Chock-full of rhubarb stalks
James R. Jones, Nebraska

Q *What fertilizer does rhubarb need? Nothing seems to make mine grow very well and the stalks are small.*

A Sounds as if your plants are in lean or poorly drained soil. Rhubarb (*Rheum* hybrid) needs full sun and very fertile, well-drained soil to produce lots of edible stalks. It can grow in part shade, but won't tolerate heavy clay or sandy soils.

If your plants are young (two years or less), you could amend the soil in a new spot and move the plants there. Work lots of compost or well-rotted manure into the soil to a depth of 12 inches.

With established plants, you could try transplanting them to a better spot, but they may not survive the move. Instead, try digging out a little soil around the plant and top-dressing twice a year with 3 inches of compost or well-rotted manure. In early March before plants emerge, and again in fall, place a layer around the plant about 12 inches out from the crown. This'll gradually improve the fertility of your soil.

Calcium = healthy tomatoes
Jerry Zoon, Pennsylvania

Q *My tomatoes have blossom-end rot. What can I do to prevent this in the future?*

A Blossom-end rot in tomatoes is caused by a calcium deficiency as the fruit develops. The illustrations at right show the soft, discolored, sunken area on the bottom of the young fruit that expands and darkens as it grows.

A plant's ability to absorb calcium is most commonly affected by wide swings in moisture. Make sure your plant receives an inch of water per week and apply a 2- to 3-inch layer of mulch to help conserve the moisture. Another thing you can do to prevent blossom-end rot is to amend your garden soil in spring with plenty of organic matter. This replaces calcium and other nutrients that are leached out of the soil, and helps the soil hold moisture. Your plants will be more vigorous and produce lots of healthy fruit.

Lastly, don't set out tomato plants too early in the season. Wait until nighttime temperatures stay above 55 degrees. Cold soil stunts root growth, making plants more likely to develop blossom-end rot.

Blossom-end rot appears on young fruit as a dark patch and grows darker and larger as the fruit matures.

Types of tomatoes

When it comes to tomatoes, there are lots of options. Do you want small, sweet, cherry-sized fruits, or huge, softball-sized ones? Here are four types of tomatoes and their best culinary uses.

- **Cherry** Cherry tomatoes grow in grapelike clusters, with each fruit weighing up to 1 oz. They're perfect for snacking, tossing in salads or sautéing whole.

- **Paste** These fruits are usually pear- or plum-shaped, and weigh between 2 and 6 oz. They've got thick walls and a meaty interior, without much liquid. They're ideal for sauces.

- **Standard** This is probably what you picture when you think of a tomato. Classic, globe-shaped fruits reach between 4 and 8 oz. each. Use them for just about anything — slice fresh for sandwiches, make them into soup or use in canning.

- **Beefsteak** These tomato giants have large lobes, making them look like squished pumpkins. They reach anywhere from 10 oz. to 2 lbs. They're great for eating fresh on burgers, or for tossing in baked dishes.

in the news

Save the cypress trees

Cypress mulch is a common sight at the garden center but you may not be seeing as much of it in the future. Starting this year, Wal-Mart will not sell cypress mulch that's harvested, bagged or manufactured in Louisiana. In the past, the mulch was made only from lumber scraps. But with the growing demand, forests are now being cut just for mulch. Because cypress is difficult to germinate, land is often not reforested. Want to know more about this growing problem? Visit www.saveourcypress.org for more details on the vital role these stately trees play in protecting southern states from tropical storms.

did you know... (CONTINUED)

Two staples hold the sandwich bag in place around

Use plastic bags instead of chemicals to keep fruit pest-free.

If condensation forms in the bag, clip off the lower corners.

Bags of perfect apples
Wayne Thuleen, California

Q I've read about sealing apples in plastic bags while the fruit is still growing on the tree to protect them from insects. Doesn't this cause problems with rot and fungus?

A Surprisingly, no. You can bag fruit on a tree when the fruit is between nickel and quarter size instead of spraying it with pesticide. Bags protect the developing fruit from codling moth worms, apple maggots and diseases like fire blight and apple scab. The illustration above shows how to put clear plastic sandwich bags (either the zip top or the fold-in flap kind) on the apples and staple them in place. It's so easy, you can do a whole tree in a few hours.

It seems as if the apples would "cook" inside the plastic, but they grow and develop just fine. If condensation forms inside the bag, clip the two lower corners for ventilation. Luckily, bugs and disease rarely enter through the openings

Help for hail-damaged hosta
Margaret Cullen, Minnesota

Q My hosta garden was hit by a bad hail storm. How can I help my severely damaged plants?

A As long as the hostas have been growing there for a few years, they'll most likely come back next spring, though they may be a little smaller or have fewer flowers. But you need to cut the most damaged leaves down to the ground.

The shredded leaves won't do the plant any good, and if you leave them on the plant, they'll just rot anyway. Leave any slightly damaged foliage (even if it doesn't look very nice) on the plant to help it produce the food it needs.

If the plants have flowers, remove them and the stalks, as well. That way, the plant won't waste any of its energy blooming.

Plants hit in late summer may simply go dormant for the rest of the season. If the damage happens early in the summer, your hostas may send up fresh new growth within a week. To help your plant bounce back, after you remove the leaves, give it a shot of a sea-based fertilizer, such as Neptune's Harvest, and be patient.

---

in the news

No more emerald ash borer?
Since its discovery in 2002, emerald ash borer (*Agrilus planipennis fairmaire*), or EAB, has destroyed more than 30 million trees in Michigan. Other U.S. states and Ontario have lost trees, too. Adult EABs don't do much damage. But the larvae tunnel into the bark, disrupting the flow of nutrients and killing the tree.

Last year, scientists at Michigan State University had great success with emamectin benzoate. Trees treated with this pesticide had 99 percent fewer larvae than untreated trees. Sold as Tree-äge™ at www.arborjet.com, it can only be applied by certified professionals every other year or annually, if needed. For more on EAB, visit www.emeraldashborer.info.

Get dirty, be happy
Gardeners know how important soil is to plants, but studies are now finding out that it's good for people, too. Researchers at Bristol University and University College London discovered that the soil bacteria *Mycobacterium vaccae* helps elevate your mood. Originally used to treat cancer patients' pain, scientists found the bacterium also increased feelings of well-being. Studies with mice found that *M. vaccae* affects the brain in a similar way to antidepressants. So get out in the garden and get dirty — it's good for you.

Damaged buds open into smaller, badly shaped flowers.

Aphids can cause buds to be bumpy and deformed.

Foliage has yellow and brown streaks.

Seed-sharing photos
Janet Maulick, Pennsylvania

When Janet's friends ask for seeds from her garden, she gets out her digital camera. She takes pictures of the requested plants, then prints out the pictures and glues them to envelopes. She makes notes on size, cultural needs and any helpful growing tips on the back. When the seeds are ready, Janet puts them in the envelopes and seals them up. Now when her friends look through their seeds, they'll know exactly what plant the seeds are from, how big the plant gets and what it'll look like when it blooms.

Spotty lungwort
Pat Bruegmann, Minnesota

Q *The past two years my 'Majeste' lungwort sent up a few leaves that were green and spotted. What causes this and what should I do about it?*

A The silver leaves of 'Majeste' lungwort (*Pulmonaria* hybrid) are caused by a genetic mutation. Plants like this are a little weaker than most lungworts that have more green on the leaves. Because the foliage doesn't have as much chlorophyll, the plant can't collect as much energy from the sun to make food. Sometimes cultivars like 'Majeste' will revert and send up greener shoots.

Lungwort is made up of many small plants connected by rhizomes. You can cut off the greener leaves, but to really stop the reversion, get rid of both the leaves and roots of the reverted section.

Otherwise, you can leave the plant be and just enjoy the mysteries of plant genetics.

Cultivars sometimes send up new growth that has reverted.

Bumpy buds and flawed flowers
Betsy Viall, Massachusetts

Q *Some of my daylily buds are shrunken and bumpy and produce small and distorted flowers. What's going on?*

A The damage you describe sounds like aphids, which feed on young buds, as well as the tips of the emerging leaves. Often, the affected leaves and buds will turn yellow or brown and the buds will become bumpy and deformed. And once buds open, the flowers can be damaged, as well. Aphids can also transmit viruses from other infected plants.

If the damage isn't too noticeable, wash the plants off with a strong stream of water from the hose. Spraying the plants with soapy water also works well. Do this in early morning or very late in the day, particularly in spring and fall, when aphids are most active. And don't worry — unlike most plants, daylilies don't mind overhead watering. If the infestation is very bad, treat the plants with malathion in early spring before the bugs have taken over.

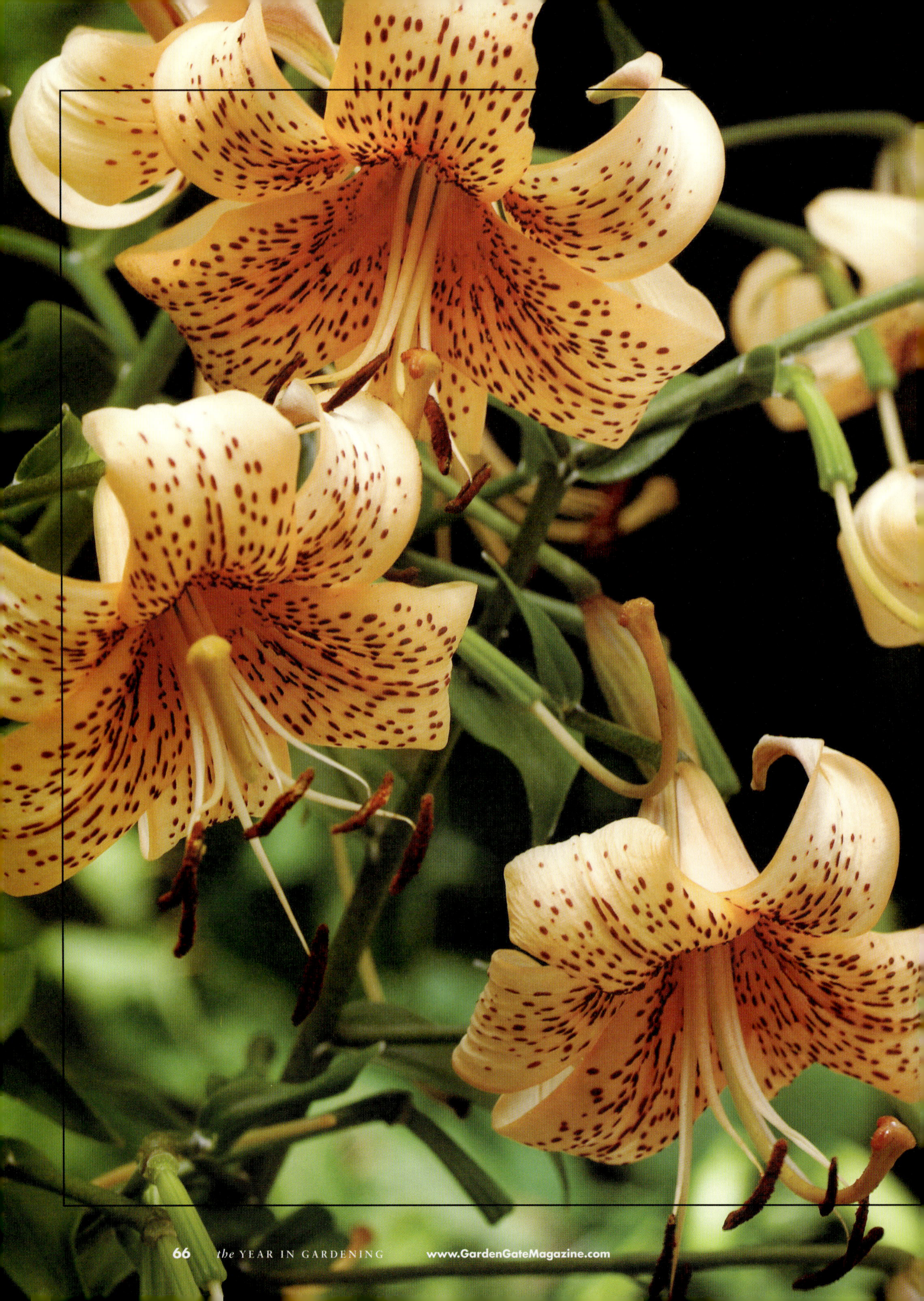

top picks

our favorite perennials, *your* favorite shrubs and more!

LET US TELL YOU WHAT WE THINK are great plants. The best new plants. Flowers whose fragrance will make you swoon. Perennials that won't beg for water when July rolls around. And more. Finally, enough about us — what are *your* favorites? We'll share the results of our readers' poll on best-loved flowering shrubs.

New Plants for 2008	68
Fragrant Flowers	76
Readers' Favorite Flowering Shrubs	82
Drought-Tolerant Perennials	86
Back-of-the-Border Perennials	92
Classic Lilies	98

top annuals

new plants 2008

It's that time of year again — time for another crop of new plants! It doesn't seem possible that a whole year has gone by since the last batch. But plant hybridizers have been working hard to get more exciting new introductions, like the ones you'll read about here, ready to show off. It's tough to narrow the field, however, I think we've found something for everyone.

Unfortunately, we can't grow everything. Trees and shrubs, for example, take a long time to evaluate, so it's hard to share our personal experience with you. But several sounded so good that we thought you'd want to know about them. Can't get enough new plants? Check out our Web extra.

One more thing before we get started. You'll notice that there are several *sports* among the new plants this year. In case you haven't heard this term before, a sport is a shoot that's different in some way from the typical growth of the "parent" plant. If you separate that piece, grow it and propagate it so that it comes back the same every year, you have a new plant!

And don't forget, as with anything new, it may be hard to find some of these plants at first. We've provided sources for you so be sure to get your order in early.

Now you can sit back, relax and start reading to find your new favorite plant. □

— *Sherri Ribbey*

WEB extra

Find more new plants and a few "almost new" ones in our online **video**

Our reader named this coleus!

'Piñata' coleus
***Solenostemon* hybrid**

It's no wonder coleus is so popular. It's easy to grow and comes in lots of colors. This new introduction is no exception — who wouldn't look twice at these festive colors? What makes this one extra special is that *Garden Gate* reader Norma Dellorto of Pennsylvania came up with the name!

Although some coleus prefer shade, others, such as 'Piñata', don't mind a little extra light. Protection from the hot late-afternoon sun prevents crispy leaves.

If you like to take coleus cuttings to overwinter, don't be surprised if the leaf color becomes less intense. This happens with a lot of varieties. But don't worry, they'll be back to eye-popping next spring.

Type Tender perennial
Size 24 in. tall and wide
Bloom N/A
Soil Moist, well-drained
Light Sun to part shade
Hardiness
  Cold: USDA zones 10 to 12
  Heat: AHS zones 12 to 1
Introducer Color Farm
Source Color Farm
  1604 W. Richway Drive
  Albert Lea, MN 56007
  www.colorfarm.com
What's new? Vibrant new variegation

Goldahlia™ Scarlet dahlia
Dahlia hybrid

These cheery flowers may be small, but they give big results. At only 12 inches tall, Goldahlia Scarlet is perfect for lining a path, edging a border or perking up a patio. We really liked Scarlet in containers in our garden. Summer heat caused some dieback but we cut off the affected parts of the plant and they bounced right back.

To keep Scarlet blooming, remove spent flowers and feed it weekly with a high phosphorus formula, such as Miracle Gro® Bloom Buster® Plant Food.

Like most dahlias, Scarlet does produce a tuber but it's small and doesn't overwinter well.

Type Tender perennial
Size 10 to 12 in. tall, 12 in. wide
Bloom Summer
Soil Well-drained
Light Full sun
Hardiness
  Cold: USDA zones 8 to 11
  Heat: AHS zones 12 to 1
Introducer Fischer USA
Source Local garden centers
What's new? New color in the series

Shock Wave™ petunia
Petunia hybrid

You've probably heard of Wave™ petunias. But now there's a new series on the horizon — Shock Wave. It looked great in our garden covered in blooms from spring to frost. The flowers are about 2 inches across and smaller than other petunias. But that's OK. There are so many of them, it makes a big show. This photo shows a mix of the three colors we planted — Ivory, Pink Vein and Purple. Rose and Pink Shades are also available. The soft, creamy Ivory color was the favorite of many staff members here.

Planted in the ground as they are here, Shock Wave petunias make a great ground cover.

Type Annual
Size 7 to 10 in. tall, 24 to 36 in. wide
Bloom Summer
Soil Well-drained
Light Full sun
Hardiness
  Cold: Annual
  Heat: AHS zones 12 to 1
Introducer Ball Horticultural Company
Source Local garden centers
What's new? Smaller flowers than the usual Wave petunias, same great habit.

PHOTO: Courtesy Color Farm ('Piñata')

top perennials

Festival Grass™ cordyline
Cordyline 'JURred'

Festival Grass is such a nice foliage plant, it even looks good by itself. I like the way the leaves sway in the slightest breeze. It's not stiff and formal like most cordylines. Those strappy leaves make a great backdrop for other plants.

Festival Grass is easy to care for. Just remove tattered looking leaves as needed and apply a balanced, slow-release fertilizer in spring.

This plant doesn't like to have its roots disturbed. Where it's not hardy, sink the pot in the ground so you can take it inside in the fall. Once inside, don't water it too much or it'll rot.

Type Tender perennial
Size 30 to 36 in. tall, 36 in. wide
Bloom Inconspicuous
Soil Well-drained with organic matter
Light Full sun to part shade
Hardiness
Cold: USDA zones 8 to 10
Heat: AHS zones 12 to 1
Introducer Anthony Tesselaar Plants USA, Inc.
Source Local garden centers
What's new? Casual arching burgundy foliage

'Heaven Scent' Jacob's ladder
Polemonium hybrid

Deer-resistant, shade-tolerant and pest and disease free, Jacob's ladder is a garden favorite. 'Heaven Scent' adds even more to this list of good qualities. In late spring flowers open with a light grape scent and new foliage emerges tinted red. As the season progresses, the leaves change to green. This new Jacob's ladder can take more sun than other varieties, too. If you plan on growing it in a sunny location, make sure to water regularly. That way, the leaves won't get crispy.

There's a limited supply of 'Heaven Scent' this year. Be sure to get your order in early.

Type Perennial
Size 18 to 24 in. tall, 24 in. wide
Bloom Spring
Soil Well-drained
Light Full sun to part shade
Hardiness
Cold: USDA zones 3 to 7
Heat: AHS zones not available
Introducer Intrinsic Perennial Gardens
Source Klehm's Song Sparrow Farm and Nursery
800-553-3715
www.songsparrow.com
What's new? Fragrant flowers in the sun

'Mean Mr. Mustard' daylily
Hemerocallis hybrid

Almost everyone has a daylily or two. Here's a beautiful new rebloomer to add to your garden. The 5½-inch yellow and burgundy blooms start in late spring. Lucky for you, they keep coming through early summer. After a 2- to 3-week rest, 'Mean Mr. Mustard' starts blooming again.

Ever wonder how hybridizers come up with names for their plants? In this case, an old Beatles tune was the inspiration. When the introducer sat down and started trying to pull a name together, he put on his Abbey Road album. The song "Mean Mr. Mustard" came on, and he knew he had his name.

Type Perennial
Size 26 in. tall, 20 to 24 in. wide
Bloom Summer, rebloom in fall
Soil Well-drained
Light Full sun to part shade
Hardiness
 Cold: USDA zones 3 to 9
 Heat: AHS zones 9 to 1
Introducer Robert Blew
Source White Flower Farm
 800-503-9624
 www.whiteflowerfarm.com

What's new?
Big reblooming flowers

'Blackbird' spurge
Euphorbia 'Nothowlee'

There have been a number of new euphorbias introduced in the last few years, but this is one of the most striking. Chartreuse flowers on red stems with deep purple to black foliage — wow! The actual flowers are very small. It's the bracts, or brightly colored leaves around the flower, that are chartreuse.

To keep the foliage a deep, dark purple, make sure it gets plenty of sun. And fast-draining soil will ensure the crown doesn't rot. Once the flowers are spent, deadhead 'Blackbird' to keep the plant looking tidy.

As with all euphorbias, be careful when trimming 'Blackbird'. The milky sap can irritate your skin.

Type Perennial
Size 16 to 18 in. tall, 20 in. wide
Bloom Spring
Soil Sandy, well-drained
Light Full sun to part shade
Hardiness
 Cold: USDA zones 6 to 9
 Heat: AHS zones not available
Introducer Notcutts Nurseries, Ltd.
Source Plant Delights Nursery
 919-772-4794
 www.plantdelights.com

What's new?
Great color on one tough perennial

top perennials

'Toffee Chip' bugleweed
Ajuga reptans

You could say 'Toffee Chip' is a "chip" off the old block. A sport of the burgundy and green 'Chocolate Chip', this new variety has the same hardy constitution.

Along with blue flowers, 'Toffee Chip' leaves have a khaki brown center in spring that changes to the sage green you see above.

Once established, bugleweed spreads by stolons that root as they go, but it's not invasive like the species can be. I found out the hard way that 'Toffee Chip' needs good drainage to do well. The plant I grew in heavy clay soil disappeared. But others grown with good drainage did just fine.

Type Perennial
Size 2 in. tall, 12 in. wide
Bloom Spring
Soil Humus rich, well-drained
Light Full sun to part shade
Hardiness
   Cold: USDA zones 5 to 9
   Heat: AHS zones not available
Introducer
   Terra Nova Nurseries, Inc.
Source Great Garden Plants
   877-447-4769
   www.GreatGardenPlants.com

What's new?
   Beautiful new variegation

'Amethyst Falls' oregano
Origanum hybrid

You'll love 'Amethyst Falls'. This new hybrid is hardier, has bigger flowers, blooms longer and the foliage is more fragrant than other ornamental oreganos.

Go ahead and grow 'Amethyst Falls' in the ground — it overwinters outside as far north as zone 5 without a problem. It does best in fast-draining soil that's on the dry side so it's perfect for raised beds or a sunny southwest corner. For additional protection from wind and cold, leave the spent foliage in place through winter to insulate the crown. Remove the dead foliage in early spring to make room for new growth.

Type Perennial
Size 8 to 12 in. tall, 24 in. wide
Bloom Summer
Soil Well-drained
Light Full sun
Hardiness
   Cold: USDA zones 5 to 9
   Heat: AHS zones not available
Introducer
   Bluebird Nursery, Inc.
Source High Country Gardens
   800-925-9387
   www.highcountrygardens.com

What's new?
   Bigger flowers and more fragrant foliage

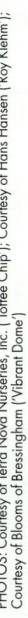

'Roy Klehm' hosta
Hosta hybrid

If you have shade, you'll want this hosta. It's just as easy to care for as others and mighty good-looking. What makes 'Roy Klehm' special? The green margin surrounding a yellow-gold interior is much larger than its parent plant 'Summer Serenade.' (This is another one of those sports.) It also has a more upright habit than other hostas, so you can underplant this new variety with other perennials. Like 'Summer Serenade', this new hybrid has big heart-shaped leaves that have good substance. That means they're thicker and less attractive to slugs. Thick leaves hold up better to wind and rain, too.

Type	Perennial
Size	18 in. tall, 36 in. wide
Bloom	White; midsummer
Soil	Moist, well-drained, organic
Light	Part shade to shade
Hardiness	Cold: USDA zones 3 to 9 Heat: AHS zones not available
Introducer	Shady Oaks Nursery, LLC
Source	Klehm's Song Sparrow Farm and Nursery 800-553-3715 www.songsparrow.com

What's new?
New variegation and a more upright habit than other hostas

'Vibrant Dome' aster
Aster novae-angliae

Nothing beats asters for fall color. This new hybrid supplies plenty. A sport of the old favorite 'Purple Dome', it has all the same terrific characteristics. It's tough, hardy, disease resistant and full of flowers even without pinching. But instead of purple flowers, this aster is covered in pink blooms through late fall.

'Vibrant Dome' has a compact habit that doesn't need staking to keep it from flopping. In fact, even the mildew-resistant foliage looks good. Short, lance-shaped leaves add a rough-looking texture that works well with other fall favorites like sedum or blue spirea.

Type	Perennial
Size	18 in. tall, 30 in. wide
Bloom	Late summer
Soil	Moist, well-drained
Light	Full sun
Hardiness	Cold: USDA zones 3 to 8 Heat: AHS zones 8 to 1
Introducer	Blooms® of Bressingham
Source	Local garden centers

What's new?
New flower color

top shrubs

Pinky Winky™ hydrangea
Hydrangea paniculata **'DVPpinky'**

There are a lot of hydrangeas around these days. But Pinky Winky is a stand out with 12- to 16-inch-long flower heads. In the photo you can see how the new flowers emerge white and change to pink. Since the flower heads keep growing, you get a colorful pink and white combination on each sturdy stem.

The only pruning you need to do is remove spent flowers in early spring. If the size is too much for you, cut Pinky Winky back to within a couple feet of the ground and it won't get as tall. Since this hydrangea blooms on new wood, it won't miss a beat.

Type Shrub
Size 6 to 8 ft. tall and wide
Bloom Midsummer to frost
Soil Well-drained
Light Full sun to part shade
Hardiness
  Cold: USDA zones 4 to 8
  Heat: AHS zones not available
Introducer
  Proven Winners® Color Choice®
Source Garden Crossings
  www.gardencrossings.com
What's new?
  Big colorful flowers

Dream Come True™ rose
Rosa **'WEKdocpot'**

The first bud on this rose was so pretty everyone here wanted one. As the flower opens, each petal is edged in pink, like the one above. Then the color changes to an orange-red blush. It's a grandiflora, so you'll have clusters of flowers in a multicolored show.

Besides the great flowers, Dream Come True has good disease resistance and a nice, upright habit. The size of a rose can vary depending on where it's growing. Our plant got 3 to 4 feet tall, which is common for areas where winters are below zero. The same rose in a milder climate can grow as tall as 6 feet!

Type Grandiflora rose
Size 3 to 4 to 6 ft. tall, 2 to 3 ft. wide
Bloom Spring to frost
Soil Well-drained
Light Full sun
Hardiness
  Cold: USDA zones 5 to 9
  Heat: AHS zones 9 to 1
Introducer
  Weeks Roses
Source Jackson and Perkins®
  800-872-7673
  www.jacksonandperkins.com
What's new?
  Big beautiful flowers

top tree

Royal Raindrops® crabapple
***Malus* 'JFS-KW5'**

This new tree is a four-season beauty. In spring, Royal Raindrops has pretty pink flowers like the tree in the large photo above. After the flowers fade, small red fruits start to form. (And the fruit stays on the tree instead of littering your drive.) In summer, deep-purple lobed leaves look almost like a Japanese maple. The leaves change to the red-orange in the inset in fall. Berries decorate the branches all winter long.

At 20 feet tall with an upright habit, Royal Raindrops can fit even in a small garden. With its great disease resistance, this beautiful tree will be around for years to come.

Type Tree
Size 20 ft. tall, 15 to 20 ft. wide (at 15 to 20 years)
Bloom Spring
Soil Well-drained
Light Full sun
Hardiness
  Cold: USDA zones 4 to 8
  Heat: AHS zones not available
Introducer J. Frank Schmidt & Son Co.
Source Forestfarm
  541-846-7269
  www.forestfarm.com

What's new?
Four-season interest and disease resistance

top bulb

'Tiny Bubbles' daffodil
***Narcissus* hybrid**

Wouldn't it be great to be greeted by these charming daffodils on a spring morning? Each stem sports several small 1-inch flowers. So no matter how many you plant, it looks like a multitude. Individual flowers open at different times but are quite long lasting and have a mild, sweet fragrance, too.

This new daffodil is small but just as resistant to deer, rodents and disease as its larger cousins. Plant 'Tiny Bubbles' in the fall, three times as deep as the height of the bulb. It spreads like bigger daffodils, too. So you'll have a big clump in no time.

Type Bulb
Size 12 in. tall
Bloom Midspring
Soil Well-drained
Light Full sun
Hardiness
  Cold: USDA zones 4 to 8
  Heat: AHS zones not available
Introducer Brent and Becky's Bulbs
Source Brent and Becky's Bulbs
  877-661-2852
  www.brentandbeckys bulbs.com

What's new?
A small fragrant daffodil with lots of flowers

Fragrant Flowers

More than any other, the sense of smell has the power to evoke memories. Maybe that's why we favor some plants — their scents revive memories of people or times we love to recall.

Not everyone enjoys the same kinds of scents. Some people like strong perfumes that permeate the area, like those of lilacs or lily-of-the-valley. Other people lean more toward lighter scents — the sweeter, the better. The scents of wisteria and Peruvian daffodil have this type of fragrance. Fortunately for all of us, there are plants with lots of different perfumes, so choose the ones that appeal to *your* nose.

But what if you like many kinds of fragrances? How do you keep them from clashing with each other? Think "pockets." Place the plants with the strongest scents in different areas of the garden. That way, they won't overlap and you'll be delighted with different perfumes as you move along a path or from the path to a seating area. I show my favorite spots in the illustration below.

Lightly scented plants can be grouped more closely. If possible, buy new fragrant plants in flower and try them out near other fragrant bloomers to see if they blend well. You can also plant lighter scents in raised beds or containers, closer to nose level.

Space the fragrances out over time by planning for different bloom periods. This is a good idea in any garden to ensure fragrance all season, but it's especially helpful in a small garden, where you really need to make the most of your space.

On the next pages, I've shared 10 of my favorite fragrant annuals, perennials, bulbs, shrubs and vines. Using these and your own favorites, you can delight your nose — as well as your eyes — from spring right up until winter! □

— *Deborah Gruca*

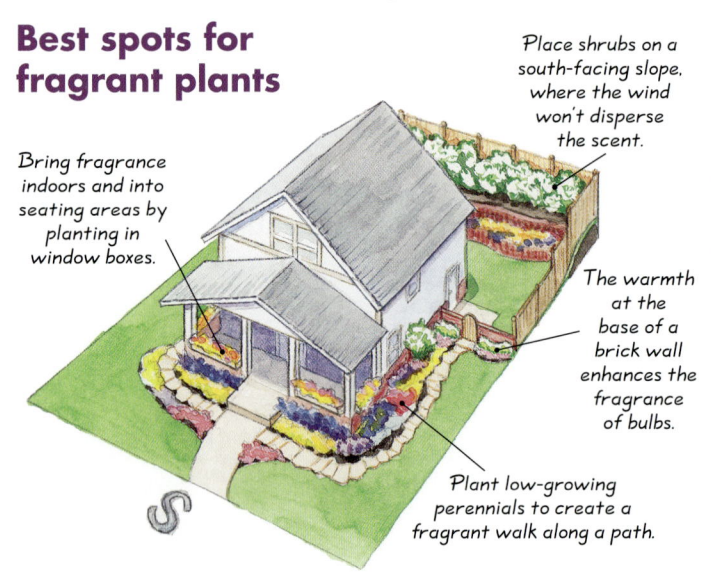

Best spots for fragrant plants

Bring fragrance indoors and into seating areas by planting in window boxes.

Place shrubs on a south-facing slope, where the wind won't disperse the scent.

The warmth at the base of a brick wall enhances the fragrance of bulbs.

Plant low-growing perennials to create a fragrant walk along a path.

top fragrant annuals

Stock
Matthiola incana

In summer, bright-colored, flower-packed spikes of stock rise a foot or more above the handsome gray-green foliage. Those lush flowers in the photo above are beautiful, but this annual also offers a rich, spicy scent that's a joy to have around.

Stock grows best in cool conditions in spring or fall in a sunny, well-drained spot. It'll even tolerate some shade, though you may get fewer blooms. Pinch back the growing tips before it buds out and you'll get a fuller plant.

To take full advantage of that lovely fragrance, plant young plants in a window box, where the perfume can waft in on the breeze.

Type Treat as an annual
Size 12 to 32 in. tall, 12 to 16 in. wide
Bloom White, pink, red, lavender or purple in late spring to early summer
Light Full sun to part shade
Hardiness
　Cold: USDA 10 to 11
　Heat: AHS 11 to 1
Fragrance Clovelike; most intense in the evening

Heliotrope
Heliotropium arborescens

Heliotrope is an unbeatable container plant. Not only is it one of the few purple annuals (that's 'Marine' with the deep violet-blue clusters in the photo), but it also has fascinating, wrinkled leaves. And if you like butterflies, growing heliotrope is a great way to entice them.

The plant can be a little tricky to grow. Keep the soil evenly moist and don't let it dry out completely or the lower leaves will drop. When the flowers start to turn brown, lightly brush them with your hand to remove the faded blooms. When the whole cluster fades, pinch it back to a set of leaves to encourage more beautiful blooms.

Type Treat as an annual
Size 18 in. tall, 12 to 18 in. wide
Bloom Clusters of purple or white flowers in summer
Light Full sun
Hardiness
　Cold: USDA 10 to 11
　Heat: AHS 11 to 1
Fragrance Vanilla; best on warm evenings

www.GardenGateMagazine.com　*the* YEAR IN GARDENING

top fragrant perennials

Lily-of-the-valley
Convallaria majalis

Smaller plants, like lily-of-the-valley, can get overlooked in the garden. With tidy, elegant dark-green leaves, it easily spreads into a lush mass even in deep shade, but it doesn't exactly jump out at you. That is, until late spring, when it blooms and exudes a strong, rich fragrance. Suddenly, you notice the delicate white bell-shaped flowers. Cut a few stems and enjoy the perfume indoors. The flowers last for a week in a vase.

Lily-of-the-valley is a spreader and can get invasive after four or five years. In summer or fall, dig up the rhizomes and move them to another spot or give them to gardening friends.

Type Perennial
Size 8 in. tall, 2 to 3 in. wide
Bloom White or pink in late spring
Light Part shade
Hardiness
  Cold: USDA 2 to 7
  Heat: AHS 7 to 1
Fragrance
  Heavy and sweet; most intense on calm evenings

Pinks
***Dianthus* hybrids**

A wide range of color choices and a heady, clovelike scent make this flower a great companion when you're out in the garden. Grow it in the very well-drained soil of a rock garden or along a stone or brick path. The sun's warmth on the hard surfaces brings out the plant's fragrance.

As a group, pinks are pretty fragrant, but 'Firewitch', above, is a standout even in this bunch. Attractive, gray-blue foliage sets off the fringed blooms from late spring into early summer. Sometimes, a few flowers will appear again in summer if the weather doesn't get too hot, especially if you keep deadheading the faded blooms.

Type Perennial
Size 10 to 12 in. tall, 12 in. wide
Bloom White, pink, red or purple in late spring to summer
Light Full sun
Hardiness
  Cold: USDA 3 to 9
  Heat: AHS 9 to 1
Fragrance
  Clove; strongest in warm sun

78 *the* YEAR IN GARDENING www.GardenGateMagazine.com

top fragrant bulbs

Hyacinth
Hyacinthus orientalis

Colorful, fragrant hyacinths have been grown for hundreds of years. Luckily for us today, the new varieties are just as fragrant as the older ones.

For the prettiest display, plant bulbs in bunches of at least three to five, about 6 to 8 inches deep and 6 inches apart. In zones 7 and colder, plant in fall, in zones 8 and warmer, in late winter.

Add compost to moist, well-drained soil to ensure the biggest and most colorful blooms. But even in the best conditions, hyacinth bulbs last just a couple years, so plant new ones each year. Use different varieties to extend the bloom from early to late spring.

Type Bulb
Size 8 to 12 in. tall, 3 to 5 in. wide
Bloom Blue, purple, yellow, pink and white in spring
Light Full sun to part shade
Hardiness
   Cold: USDA 4 to 8
   Heat: AHS 9 to 1
Fragrance Heady, floral scent; strongest on warm, damp days

Peruvian daffodil
Hymenocallis xfestalis

Even if they had no fragrance, the intriguing spiderlike white flowers are reason enough to grow this plant. Two to five blooms atop tall, sturdy stems last well in a vase, if you can bear to cut them.

This fast-growing summer bulb grows and blooms in less than a month once the weather warms. Plant bulbs two to three weeks apart in late spring to keep the flowers coming. In moist or even boggy soil, the bulbs quickly multiply, the new ones reaching blooming size in a year or two. Lift the bulbs in the fall before the first frost and store them in a cool, dry area until nighttime temperatures stay above 60 degrees.

Type Bulb
Size 32 in. tall, 12 in. wide
Bloom White flowers in summer
Light Full sun to part shade
Hardiness
   Cold: USDA 8 to 10
   Heat: AHS 11 to 3
Fragrance Lightly sweet; best in the evening

top fragrant shrubs

French lilac
Syringa vulgaris

Of all the fragrant flowering shrubs, lilacs are some of the best loved. And French lilacs are the most fragrant group in the lilac family. Their scent can't help but trigger warm childhood memories.

Lilacs need at least six hours of sun each day to produce the most blooms. In spring, loads of large, red-purple blooms form on the long stems of 'Monge', shown above.

Powdery mildew is often a problem with lilacs, but newer cultivars are much more resistant than some of the older ones. But even if they do get powdery mildew, the unsightly fungus won't harm the plants or reduce the bloom.

Type Shrub
Size 10 to 12 ft. tall, 8 to 10 ft. wide
Bloom Red, purple, blue, pink or white flowers in late spring
Light Full sun
Hardiness
Cold: USDA 2 to 8
Heat: AHS 8 to 1
Fragrance Sweet; very strong when wet with rain

Mockorange
***Philadelphus* spp.**

If you have room for just one shrub in your garden, mockorange would be a great choice. You'd be hard-pressed to find a less-fussy plant. It grows in all types of soil, from sandy to heavy clay, as long as it has a little moisture.

Reaching to just 10 feet tall, this shrub is covered with flowers with the fragrance of orange blossoms in early to midsummer. If it starts to look a little leggy after several years, prune back a third of the older stems down to the ground. Do this after the blooming is finished to encourage it to put out new growth, which will form next year's flowers. Be patient with a new plant — it takes several years for it to begin to bloom.

Type Shrub
Size 4 to 10 ft. tall, 8 ft. wide
Bloom White in summer
Light Full sun to part shade
Hardiness
Cold: USDA 5 to 8
Heat: AHS 8 to 1
Fragrance Orange blossom; best on warm days

top fragrant vines

Japanese wisteria
Wisteria floribunda

The dramatic, hanging flower clusters of this climber may make you think of the Deep South, but think again. Japanese wisteria is cold-hardy to zone 5. You'll need to wait several years for a young plant to begin blooming. But once it does, it sometimes flowers even before the leaves have fully emerged from the twining stems. The vanilla-scented flowers open gradually, starting at the bases and working out to the tips. Often, the flowers are followed by 6-inch-long beanlike green pods.

This is a hefty vine, so give it a sturdy support. And cut new shoots back by half in July to get the most flowers and to keep the plant under control.

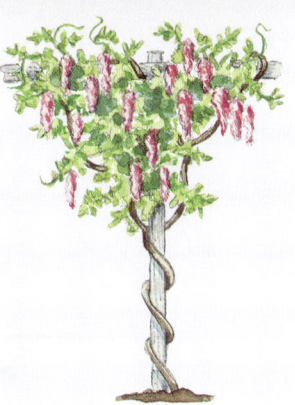

Type Vine
Size 30 ft. tall
Bloom Purple, pink or white in late spring
Light Full sun to part shade
Hardiness
   Cold: USDA 5 to 9
   Heat: AHS 9 to 1
Fragrance
   Vanilla; best on warm evenings

Passion flower
Passiflora caerulea

If you like unusual flowers, take a look at passion flower. "Exotic" is a good word to describe its 4-inch-diameter blooms. White, pink or red petals, ringed with a blue corona, last for just a day or so. But each plant has enough flowers to go from summer to frost. The blooms are slow to open on dark, cloudy days, yet stay open all night long.

Where it's hardy, this fast-growing vine can reach 40 feet or more. In areas where it's not hardy, passion flower is a great container plant. Twining tendrils hold it to the nearest plant or support.

It prefers sandy or gravelly soils and too much moisture can cause the crown to rot.

Type Vine
Size 40 ft. tall
Bloom White, pink or red with purple in summer to fall
Light Full sun to part shade
Hardiness
   Cold: USDA 6 to 9
   Heat: AHS 9 to 1
Fragrance
   Delicate; best on calm, sunny days

LOCATION: The Ewing and Muriel Kauffman Memorial Garden of Kansas City (wisteria)

www.GardenGateMagazine.com   *the* YEAR IN GARDENING   81

Readers' Favorite
Flowering Shrubs

Shrubs add structure to a landscape, no matter what the season. In fact, they're often referred to as the backbone of a garden. I especially like flowering shrubs because they add so much color. But these woody plants are also workhorses, adding height to block unwanted views or stiff winds. Some have interesting branching habits or unique foliage shapes to add texture to the garden. And colorful foliage is nice, especially where you want a focal point.

We asked readers to share the name of their favorite flowering shrub. As you might guess, the answers were as diverse and varied as any group of gardeners can be. Most of these shrubs will be familiar to you. But what's better than revisiting an old friend? As we started sorting the list, these seven tried-and-true flowering shrubs quickly rose to the top.

In some cases, readers shared specific species or cultivars — hydrangeas are a good example. Hydrangeas as a group got lots of votes, so we selected the number one cultivar, 'Annabelle', to profile. In other cases, like forsythia, they just told us they liked the whole family, not a specific one. So, starting with spring bloomers and ending in fall, let's take a look at what you, our readers, chose as your favorite flowering shrubs. ▫

— *Jim Childs*

Forsythia
Forsythia* ×*intermedia

What better way to welcome spring than with a burst of bright sunshine? Just look at the rays of gold on the 'Lynwood' forsythia in the photo above. It's an older cultivar that's still popular because the flowers completely line the upright branches.

Even though the plant is hardy into zone 4, the buds can be killed by late freezes. If you live where the buds *blast*, or don't open, try one of the newer cultivars, such as 'Meadowlark', with buds that are hardy down to -30 degrees Fahrenheit.

Forsythia is quite shade tolerant; however, you'll find it tends to grow more loose and open there. And the flowers are not as lush as they are in full sun.

Size   8 to 10 ft. tall, 8 to 12 ft. wide
Bloom   Early spring
Soil   Adaptable to almost any soil
Light   Sun to part shade
When to prune   Immediately after flowering
Hardiness   Cold: USDA zones 4 to 8
Heat: AHS zones 8 to 1

More than a one-hit wonder
Forsythia has healthy, clean foliage all summer and some varieties turn purple in fall

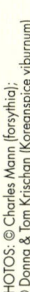

Rhododendron
Rhododendron **species and hybrids**

There are so many gorgeous rhododendrons to choose from, but 'Nova Zembla', above, is definitely a favorite. A Catawba hybrid with evergreen foliage, it's one of the hardiest of the large leaf types. And those vivid flowers almost completely cover the shrub and last for several weeks each spring.

All rhododendrons need an acid pH soil with excellent drainage. Wet soil will quickly kill the plant. When you plant, set the crown 2 to 6 inches higher than the surrounding area. Add a 4- to 6-inch-thick layer of shredded leaves or pine bark mulch to keep the roots cool and moist.

Size 5 to 7 ft. tall and wide or more with age
Bloom Spring
Soil Well-drained, acid
Light Sun to part shade
When to prune After blooms fade, pinch out spent flowers and prune to shape the plant at the same time
Hardiness Cold: USDA zones 5 to 9
Heat: AHS zones 9 to 1

More than a one-hit wonder Large evergreen leaves and fat flower buds look good all winter

Koreanspice viburnum
Viburnum carlesii

There are more viburnums than you can shake a stick at! But Koreanspice, in the photo above, headed the list of favorites. I think its spicy carnation scent is what makes it so popular.

Up close the scent can be a bit strong. But when it's wafting through the cool spring air, the fragrance will certainly draw your attention. Use it near an entrance or a window you open frequently.

Satiny gray-green pest-resistant foliage makes this shrub perfect in a starring role or great as a companion in a foundation planting. Yet its rather loose branching habit makes it casual enough to mix into the background of a colorful perennial border.

Size 4 to 6 ft. tall and wide
Bloom Spring
Soil Well-drained, slightly acid
Light Sun to part shade
When to prune Immediately after flowering
Hardiness Cold: USDA zones 4 to 8
Heat: AHS zones 8 to 1

More than a one-hit wonder Clean foliage that sometimes takes on burgundy tints for fall

top flowering shrubs *continued*

Korean lilac
***Syringa meyeri* 'Palibin'**

Maybe it's the sweet-scented hybrids you think of when someone says lilac. But when it comes to good-looking workhorses, spicy-scented Korean lilac, in the photo above, is near the head of the list. This species is smaller than many lilacs, and its leaves are smaller, too. Like all lilacs, it's the blooms you're after and this one is almost completely covered in late spring.

Have you ever spotted a white substance on the leaves of your French hybrid lilacs? Powdery mildew can be a serious problem. Korean lilac, sometimes referred to as dwarf Korean, is extremely resistant to this unsightly fungus.

Size   4 to 5 ft. tall, 5 to 7 ft. wide
Bloom   Late spring
Soil   Well-drained, but adapts to most soils
Light   Sun
When to prune   Immediately after flowering
Hardiness   Cold: USDA zones 3 to 7   Heat: AHS zones 7 to 1
More than a one-hit wonder   Clean, healthy foliage all season and occasionally a pale burgundy and yellow fall color

Weigela
Weigela florida

When weigela is in full flower, it can be a showstopper. The branches are lined with funnel-shaped flowers in shades of red, pink or white. And even without deadheading, you'll often get another smaller burst of flowers to enjoy later in the season.

There are newer cultivars with colored foliage, especially in shades of burgundy. Look for Wine and Roses® or Midnight Wine®. And the variegated leaves of 'Variegata' in the photo are almost more striking than the flowers.

To me, the hardest thing about planting a weigela is asking for it at the garden center. You'll hear all kinds of pronunciations, but it's correctly spoken wy-JEE-lah.

Size   4 to 6 ft. tall, 3 to 10 ft. wide
Bloom   Early summer
Soil   Well-drained
Light   Full sun
When to prune   After flowering
Hardiness   Cold: USDA zones 4 to 8   Heat: AHS zones 8 to 1
More than a one-hit wonder   Often blooms sporadically during summer and well into fall

Hydrangea
Hydrangea arborescens 'Annabelle'

Every year it seems there are more new hydrangeas to choose from. But white-flowered 'Annabelle', above, is still a top pick when it comes to easy-to-grow favorites. Unlike most of the mophead or lacecap varieties, this hydrangea doesn't need a specific pH to adjust its color or bloom beautifully.

Some hydrangeas need to be pruned right after they bloom. But if you're pruning-challenged, 'Annabelle' is easy to work with. Just cut all of the stems back to 10 to 12 inches tall in late winter.

And if you want more hydrangeas, most all of them can be divided just like perennials. Dig and split them in early spring.

Size 3 to 5 ft. tall, 4 to 6 ft. wide
Bloom Summer
Soil Moist, well-drained
Light Full sun to part shade
When to prune Late winter
Hardiness
 Cold: USDA zones 3 to 9
 Heat: AHS zones 9 to 1

More than a one-hit wonder
Blooms dry on the plant to add garden interest well into winter

Rose-of-Sharon
Hibiscus syriacus

There are so many flowering shrubs in spring and summer that it's nice to have one blooming at the end of the season.

If you live in zone 5, you may discover this late-bloomer dies back to the ground, or snow line, after a severe winter. But as long as the roots survive, in just one season it'll still grow 4 to 6 feet tall and bloom!

You'll find flowers in shades of pink, lavender and white, often with a darker color in the throat like 'Woodbridge' in the photo above. And there are single as well as double flower forms.

Rose-of-Sharon will bloom for several weeks, even months, until cold weather finally stops it.

Size 3 to 12 ft. tall, 6 to 10 ft. wide
Bloom Late summer into fall
Soil Moist, well-drained
Light Full sun to part shade
When to prune Early spring
Hardiness
 Cold: USDA zones 5 to 9
 Heat: AHS zones 9 to 1

More than a one-hit wonder
Very fast growth if you need a quick screen; no major pests to damage the foliage

Drought-Tolerant Perennials

Leaves to look for

You'll often see these types of leaves when you're at the garden center. These traits help the plant retain as much water as possible in drought, so if you see them it usually means a plant is drought-tolerant.

- Waxy
- Fuzzy
- Gray-colored
- Thick, fleshy
- Tiny

Quick: What's the simplest way to save money, water and time in the garden? Easy! Grow drought-tolerant plants. They're especially good in low-water areas, but are also great if you just don't want to spend your summer dragging a hose around.

No matter where you live, you're bound to get some hot, dry periods during the summer. You know, those times when you use your hose or watering can so much that you don't even bother putting it away. And you hope that a long, withering dry spell doesn't happen while you're out of town! But if an irrigation system or a plant-sitter's not in the budget, what can you do?

There are tons of plants that, once they're established, don't require lots of water. The 10 plants I'll talk about here like a range of light conditions and hardiness zones, but each can stand up to hot, dry weather without breaking a sweat. (Don't be afraid to grow ones not hardy in your zone as annuals or in containers.)

Most of these plants have colorful flowers and a few have beautiful foliage, but all have features that allow them to survive, and even thrive, in drought. They may have very deep roots to reach moisture or fleshy ones that store water. Or they may have leaves with the special features listed in "Leaves to look for" at left.

I'll share some terrific traits of each of these plants along with tips to help them look and grow their best. In addition, I've included 10 drought-tolerant companions that make great growing mates.

Even the most drought-tolerant plant still needs water while it's young. A moisture-conserving layer of organic mulch is also a good idea for any of these plants. But once established, they're easy to grow and enjoy, even when rain is hard to come by. ◻

— *Deborah Gruca*

Jerusalem sage
***Phlomis* spp.**

The woolly leaves of this plant tell you right away that it can handle dry-soil situations. It also tolerates heat, clay or heavy soil and light shade. Best of all, it sends deer packing. (I guess they don't care for hairy leaves!)

I say it tolerates light shade, but it blooms best in full sun. The unusual fuzzy blooms are held in tight whorls around the upright gray-green stems. You can easily dry the flowers and use them in long-lasting bouquets.

If you deadhead the faded flowers, you may be rewarded with a sporadic repeat bloom in fall. But even if the plant doesn't flower again, the soft, fuzzy foliage looks handsome in its own right.

Size 4 to 6 ft. tall by 2 to 3 ft. wide
Bloom Pink, lavender, yellow or white flowers in summer
Soil Lean, very well-drained soil
Light Full sun to light shade
Pests No insect pests
Hardiness
Cold: USDA 7 to 11
Heat: AHS 12 to 1

Works well with
Purple coneflower *Echinacea purpurea*

Rock rose
***Cistus* spp.**

Of the 20 or so species of rock rose, most come from the rocky soils of the Mediterranean, so you'd expect them to like dry conditions. But with this plant growing in the gravelly soil and full sun that it prefers, you might be surprised to see the loads of crepe-paperlike blooms it produces. Each flower lasts just one day, but so many buds cover the plant that it can be in bloom for three weeks in summer. Flowers of different rock roses range from 2 to 4 inches across; many have a small dark blotch on each petal.

Plant rock rose in late spring to summer, instead of in fall. To create sharp drainage, add a handful of grit to the planting hole.

Size 2 to 6 ft. tall and wide
Bloom White to dark pink flowers in summer
Soil Gravelly, sharply drained soil
Light Full sun
Pests No serious pests
Hardiness
Cold: USDA 8 to 10
Heat: AHS 10 to 1

Works well with
Catmint *Nepeta xfaasenii*

top drought-tolerant perennials *continued*

Plumbago
Ceratostigma plumbaginoides

While it's small in stature, plumbago has as much to offer as any plant twice its size. This vigorous perennial can cover a lot of ground in the right conditions, including down the side of a dry rock wall.

Brilliant blue flowers are a welcome color in the late-summer garden. Along with these, plumbago offers sprawling, slender red stems and tidy bright-green foliage. An added bonus is the unusual fall combination of the still-blooming blue flowers with leaves red-tinged by cooler weather.

Dry conditions help keep this rambunctious spreader in check, where its rambling might be a bit too much.

Size 12 in. tall by 18 in. wide
Bloom Clusters of bright blue flowers in late summer
Soil Well-drained soil
Light Full sun to part shade
Pests No serious pests
Hardiness
Cold: USDA 5 to 9
Heat: AHS 9 to 1

Works well with
Daylily
Hemerocallis hybrids

Yucca
***Yucca filamentosa* 'Bright Edge'**

Huge spikes of blooms, long, swordlike leaves — everything about yucca is dramatic. And the roots of this sturdy plant are very deep and extensive. They help it survive in extremely hot, dry conditions. The stiff, 2½-foot-long leaves are evergreen, even in colder zones, and look great sticking out of the snow.

It takes lots of energy to produce such large clusters of flowers on 6-foot stalks. So most yuccas only bloom once every three to five years. If you'd like flowers more often than that, plant a blooming yucca each year for three years in a row. That way at least one should bloom every year.

Size 30 in. tall (6 ft. in flower) by 60 in. wide
Bloom White flowers in summer
Soil Well-drained soil
Light Full sun
Pests No serious pests
Hardiness
Cold: USDA 4 to 11
Heat: AHS 11 to 1

Works well with
Cinquefoil
Potentilla fruticosa

Alpine sea holly
Eryngium alpinum

With its almost alien look, sea holly is one of those plants that people either love or hate. The spiny flowers and foliage make it a bold accent in the garden. Cut the stems near the basal foliage before the flowers are fully open and use them to add interest to dried arrangements, as well.

Though this prickly plant is easy to grow and tolerant of many soils and conditions, there's one hitch: it doesn't live long. Sea holly usually grows for only three to four years. But, luckily, it self-seeds around the garden, so you'll find it sprouting in lots of unexpected places. Simply dig and replant the seedlings in spring.

Size   36 in. tall by 18 in. wide
Bloom   Silver-blue or white flowers from summer to fall
Soil   Well-drained soil
Light   Full sun
Pests   No serious pests
Hardiness
   Cold: USDA 5 to 9
   Heat: AHS 9 to 1

Works well with
   Yarrow
   Achillea millefolium

Spike speedwell
Veronica spicata

This rugged little plant makes an attractive, carefree addition to your drought-tolerant garden. Known for blue spikes that bloom most all season, newer cultivars sport flowers in colors from light blue to rosy red. Whatever the color, add the spikes to jazz up a boring border. The blooms may fade quicker during extremely long dry spells, so deadhead to keep the plant blooming and looking tidy.

Some varieties, such as 'Royal Candles', above, have a dense, compact form. If you grow the taller species, place it in lean soil to encourage an upright habit. Otherwise, stake the plant or give it supportive neighbors.

Size   12 to 24 in. tall by 18 in. wide
Bloom   Blue, pink or red flowers in summer
Soil   Well-drained soil
Light   Full sun to part shade
Pests   No serious pests
Hardiness
   Cold: USDA 3 to 8
   Heat: AHS 8 to 1

Works well with
   Lavender cotton
   Santolina chamaecyparissus

top drought-tolerant perennials *continued*

Autumn sage
Salvia greggii

You're lucky if you garden in warmer zones because that's where autumn sage thrives. Bright-colored tubular flowers cover this shrubby perennial most of the season, even in the most excruciating heat. And if that's not enough, the blooms are hummingbird magnets, too.

It's also simple to make more plants. Take 6-inch stem cuttings in spring and plant them in moist potting mix. Once they root, plant them out in the garden later the same year.

A mature plant gets leggy in part shade. Don't be afraid to cut it back severely (even mowing it!) after flowering is finished to encourage lush, compact new growth.

Size 12 to 20 in. tall and wide
Bloom Red, purple, pink or orange flowers in late summer to fall
Soil Well-drained soil
Light Full sun
Pests No serious pests
Hardiness
  Cold: USDA 7 to 9
  Heat: AHS 12 to 1

Works well with
  Black-eyed Susan
  Rudbeckia fulgida

Cushion spurge
Euphorbia polychroma

With its attractive mounding habit, cushion spurge grabs your eye, especially in spring when it's covered with bright-gold bracts. But it's also showy in fall, as it takes on a red cast.

Grow it in full sun for the best color, except in hotter areas, where it needs a little afternoon shade. Cushion spurge's roots don't like to be moved. But the plant reseeds and the small plants are easy to move or give to gardening friends. Sometimes plants will flop open in late summer. To prevent this, cut the plant back to 4 or 5 inches high after blooming. Be sure to wear gloves when you do this, as many people are allergic to the white sap.

Size 16 in. tall by 24 in. wide
Bloom Bright yellow bracts in late spring to summer
Soil Well-drained soil
Light Full sun to light shade
Pests No serious pests
Hardiness
  Cold: USDA 4 to 8
  Heat: AHS 8 to 1

Works well with
  Lavender *Lavandula* spp.

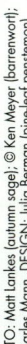

Barrenwort
Epimedium spp.

Barrenwort is not only drought-tolerant, but it also grows in a very challenging place: dry shade.

The foliage of many barrenworts shows a rosy glow in early spring, as well as a bronze tint in fall. In some areas (USDA zones 7 and warmer) the foliage is evergreen. But barrenwort also sports dainty flowers that vary greatly in shape and color depending on the cultivar.

Though it prefers a moist, humus-rich soil, the moisture-holding rhizome allows barrenwort to tolerate dry conditions with ease. Cut back the faded foliage in early spring before the new growth begins and apply a slow-release 10-10-10 fertilizer to give it a boost.

Size 6 in. to 20 in. tall, unlimited spread
Bloom White, cream, yellow, pink or red spring flowers
Soil Moist, well-drained soil, but adapts to dry conditions
Light Shade to part shade
Pests No serious pests
Hardiness
Cold: USDA 4 to 9
Heat: AHS 9 to 3

Works well with
False Solomon's seal
Maianthemum racemosum

Pine-leaf penstemon
Penstemon pinifolius

Named for its needle-like foliage, this durable perennial resembles a small evergreen shrub when it's not blooming.

But the plant's best feature is brightly colored, tubular flowers that can appear for as long as six to eight weeks in summer. The blooms attract hummingbirds along with human admirers.

Native to the desert Southwest, pine-leaf penstemon grows best in sharp-draining soil and with good air circulation, but is also adaptable to other areas. To keep yours happy and blooming, mix plenty of grit into the soil, plant the crown high and top it off with an inch or two of gravel mulch.

Size 16 in. tall by 10 in. wide
Bloom Red or orange flowers in summer
Soil Gritty, sharply drained soil
Light Full sun to part shade
Pests No serious pests
Hardiness
Cold: USDA 4 to 10
Heat: AHS 10 to 1

Works well with
Blanket flower
Gaillardia xgrandiflora

Back-of-the-Border Perennials

Are you vertically challenged? Not by your size, but by the plants you grow in your garden? Do you avoid tall perennials because you think they're gangly or will look out of place? No need to worry anymore! We've rounded up nine of our favorite stately flowers. And each one would be a grand addition to your garden.

Sure, tall plants are great for blocking a view. But their height also creates a visual bridge between the levels of a garden. Tall plants smoothly take your eyes from the lawn, often the lowest point, to the trees and buildings, the tallest points.

Just what qualifies as a back-of-the-border plant? That depends on the depth of your border. Here I'm showing you nine plants between 3 and 9 feet tall. As a rule of thumb, your tallest plant should be about two-thirds as tall as your border is deep. I'll show you how that works in the plan on page 97. However, if you like one of these plants but it's taller than you really need, go for it. Plant just one as a specimen among some shrubs. Or add it to your perennial border in a spot where you want to draw attention — a tall plant can make a striking focal point.

But first, meet these nine great tall plants and find out the best tips for growing them. I've even included information on whether or not you need to stake them to keep them standing straight and tall. □

— *Jim Childs*

Yellow meadow rue
Thalictrum flavum glaucum

Tall doesn't have to mean overwhelming. Yellow meadow rue has a delicate, wispy appearance. As the flowers fade, cut them off. This perennial won't reflower with deadheading, but the foliage stays healthy and clean, so it'll be a great backdrop.

The stems can be a bit floppy, so it's a good idea to plant it near shrubs, or between other tall plants for support. Or stake it early with a three-ring tomato cage that has several strings woven across each of the circles. The ferny foliage will cover the "corset" so it won't show, even after you remove the spent flowers.

Type Perennial
Size 3 to 5 ft. tall, 2 ft. wide
Bloom Early to midsummer
Soil Well-drained
Light Part shade
Stake? Tomato cage or grow-through grids
Hardiness
 Cold: USDA 5 to 8
 Heat: AHS 8 to 1
Mail-order source
 Big Dipper Farm
 www.bigdipperfarm.com
 360-886-8133

Queen-of-the-prairie
Filipendula rubra 'Venusta'

It's the cotton-candy pink flowers that make this a star performer. Give it a spot that's moist, even boggy, and it'll do fine. If the soil's too dry, the flowers will be small and the foliage will scorch.

After the flowers finish, cut them off, down to the first set of large leaves. Let the rest of the foliage stay standing, both to feed the plant and add visual interest to your border.

Given time, this perennial can spread and form a large colony. If you don't have room, there's no need to dig and divide the entire clump. Just dig along the edges and remove new sprouts.

Type Perennial
Size 4 to 8 ft. tall, 2 to 4 ft. wide
Bloom Midsummer
Soil Moist, well-drained to boggy conditions
Light Full sun
Stake? Rarely needed
Hardiness
 Cold: USDA 3 to 9
 Heat: AHS 9 to 1
Mail-order source
 Forest Farm
 www.forestfarm.com
 541-846-7269

Delphinium
Delphinium elatum and hybrids

Every garden needs at least a few tall spires; they add great visual interest. To grow spectacular delphiniums, like the Pacific hybrids above, start with new divisions every spring

Work compost into the soil as you plant. Then feed with an 18-18-18 fertilizer when the stems are 18 inches tall and again about two weeks later.

As the stems stretch, attach them to stakes with strips of fabric. Tie once when the stem is about 12 inches tall. When flower buds form, tie the stem to the stake just below that point. After the flowers finish, cut the stem down to the ground. You may get a second, shorter, batch of flowers in late summer.

Type Perennial
Size 4 to 6 ft. tall, 2 to 3 ft. wide
Bloom Early to midsummer
Soil Fertile, well-drained
Light Full sun
Stake? Tie flower stems to tall stakes with strips of fabric
Hardiness
 Cold: USDA 3 to 7
 Heat: AHS 7 to 1
Mail-order source
 Bluestone Perennials
 www.bluestoneperennials.com
 800-852-5243

top back-of-the-border perennials *continued*

Russian hollyhock
Alcea rugosa

Unlike most hollyhocks, this yellow one rarely has a problem with rust. And it tends to be perennial rather than biennial like many hollyhocks

Once most of the flowers have faded, cut the spires down to the low rosette of foliage. That way your plant won't waste energy producing seeds, and is more likely to survive the winter. It does come true from seed, so leave a few stems standing if you want to grow new plants. You can harvest the seeds when the pods turn brown, but I think it's easier to leave them and watch for seedlings coming up in early spring. Move them while they're small, before their taproots grow too deep.

Type Perennial
Size 5 to 9 ft. tall, 1 to 2 ft. wide
Bloom Midsummer
Soil Moist, well-drained
Light Full sun
Stake? Rarely needed
Hardiness
   Cold: USDA 3 to 8
   Heat: AHS 8 to 1
Mail-order source
   Select Seeds
   www.selectseeds.com
   800-684-0395

Bee balm
Monarda hybrids

Grow masses of bee balm and you'll not only get bees stopping by for a meal, but hummingbirds and butterflies, too.

'Jacob Cline', in the photo, is one of the tallest hybrids. It's quite resistant to powdery mildew, a gray fungus that grows on plants. It can be a problem so give all bee balms a spot where they get good air circulation. I also like to give them a "skirt" of a shorter perennial to hide the bare knees.

Bee balm can be a fast spreader. Every two to four years, lift the clump and divide it. If you occasionally spot a few wayward sprouts, give them a quick tug — they're shallow-rooted and easy to pull.

Type Perennial
Size 3 to 4 ft. tall, 2 ft. wide
Bloom Mid- to late summer
Soil Moist, well-drained
Light Full sun to light shade
Stake? Grow-through grids or tomato cages
Hardiness
   Cold: USDA 4 to 8
   Heat: AHS 8 to 1
Mail-order source
   Fieldstone Gardens, Inc.
   www.fieldstonegardens.com
   207-923-3836

Korean angelica
Angelica gigas

If you're looking for a conversation starter, this is it. It's not only tall, but the striking red-black flower buds and stems, set against the bright green leaves, are sure to attract lots of attention.

Korean angelica is a biennial, so once it sets seeds, its life is over. You can try to fool it into another year by cutting the stems down before the seeds form, but it's not always successful. Let a couple of the flower heads ripen. Then next spring, keep your eyes peeled for the seedlings. Their leaves are not as deeply cut as the mature plant.

It's a good idea to wear gloves when working with angelica. All parts of it can cause a skin rash.

Type Biennial, short-lived perennial; self sows
Size 3 to 6 ft. tall, 3 to 4 ft. wide
Bloom Mid- to late summer
Soil Rich, moist, well-drained
Light Full sun to part shade
Stake? Rarely needed
Hardiness
 Cold: USDA 4 to 9
 Heat: AHS 9 to 1
Mail-order source
 Annie's Annuals and Perennials
 www.anniesannuals.com
 888-266-4370

Crocosmia
Crocosmia hybrid

Hot colors are … well, they're hot. While there are other tall cultivars, 'Lucifer' is the best hot red. But don't buy just one or two corms — buy at least 10 and plant them in a tight clump no more than 4 inches apart. Go easy with fertilizer — too much and you'll get more leaves than flowers.

In USDA zone 5, it's a good idea to spread 4 or 5 inches of winter mulch over the clump for protection. But if you live further north you can still grow crocosmia. Purchase the corms in early spring and plant them as annuals. Just plan for them to grow only half as tall as the crocosmias in other zones that have been established for a couple of years.

Type Perennial
Size 3 to 4 ft. tall, 1 to 2 ft. wide
Bloom Mid- to late summer
Soil Moist, well-drained
Light Full sun
Stake? Rarely needed
Hardiness
 Cold: USDA 5 to 9
 Heat: AHS 12 to 1
Mail-order source
 Joy Creek Nursery
 www.joycreek.com
 503-543-7474

top back-of-the-border perennials *continued*

Culver's root
Veronicastrum virginicum

Butterflies find these fuzzy flowers a good source of nectar. Plus Culver's root is an excellent cut flower. And since it blooms just as fall gets started, the soft color, like 'Fascination' in the photo, is a nice contrast to autumn's other red and gold flowers.

Give Culver's root full sun and moist soil and it'll stand fine without staking. However, if you plant it in shade, you'll need to give it support.

Culver's root will eventually spread to form colonies that can be 4 feet or more in diameter. But if you divide clumps every few years, in either spring or late fall, it's easy to keep the width to about 18 inches.

Type Perennial
Size 4 to 6 ft. tall, 2 to 4 ft. wide
Bloom Late summer
Soil Moist, well-drained
Light Full sun
Stake? Rarely needed
Hardiness
  Cold: USDA 3 to 8
  Heat: AHS 8 to 1
Mail-order source
  Digging Dog Nursery
  www.diggingdog.com
  707-937-1130

Perennial sunflower
Helianthus hybrid

Rather than the strong golden yellows of other perennial sunflowers, 'Lemon Queen' above is a softer shade that looks great with fall asters. Pair it with pastel blues and pinks for an interesting late-season color scheme.

All perennial sunflowers are easy to grow. Keep them moist as they get established, but after that they're quite drought-tolerant. Plant them in full sun, or, like many other tall perennials, you may need to do some staking. And don't overfertilize early in the season, or you'll get lush foliage, weak stems and few flowers. To get sturdy plants, wait until they reach their full height before applying fertilizer.

Type Perennial
Size 6 to 7 ft. tall, 3 ft. wide
Bloom Late summer
Soil Moist, well-drained
Light Full sun
Stake? Tomato cages or grow-through grids
Hardiness
  Cold: USDA 4 to 9
  Heat: AHS 9 to 1
Mail-order source
  Busse Gardens
  www.bussegardens.com
  800-544-3192

96 *the* YEAR IN GARDENING www.GardenGateMagazine.com

GARAGE DRESS-UP

This garden is designed to hide that long, often blank, wall of a garage. We've selected a mix of perennials that will brighten this dull wall for most of the growing season.

The tallest plants should be about two-thirds as tall as the depth of the border? These hollyhocks are roughly 7 ft. tall. At its widest point, the bed is 10 ft. That works. When you design your border, you also want the plant heights to taper down to the level of your lawn or sidewalk to make a smooth transition.

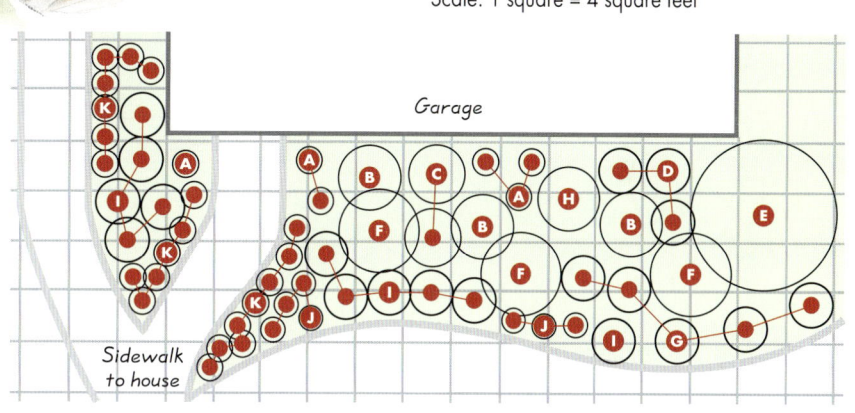

Scale: 1 square = 4 square feet

Code	Plant Name	No. to Plant	Blooms	Type	Cold/Heat Zones	Height/Width	Special Features
A	Russian hollyhock *Alcea rugosa*	6	Yellow; midsummer	Perennial	3-8/8-1	5-9 ft./ 1-2 ft.	Reseeds easily; young seedlings survive transplanting better than mature plants
B	Bog sage *Salvia uliginosa*	3	Blue; late summer	Perennial	6-10/10-1	4-6 ft./ 3-4 ft.	Reseeds; prefers moist soil; tends to flop, so plant next to other perennials for support
C	Queen-of-the-prairie *Filipendula rubra 'Venusta'*	2	Pink; summer	Perennial	3-9/9-1	4-8 ft./ 2-4 ft.	Spreads to form a colony; prefers moist soil; rarely needs staking
D	Meadow rue *Thalictrum 'Black Stockings'*	3	Lavender; summer	Perennial	5-8/8-1	4-6 ft./ 2 ft.	Lacy green foliage and black stems; often late to start new growth in spring; stays in a neat clump
E	Variegated giant reed grass *Arundo donax 'Variegata'*	1	Red-brown; late fall	Perennial	6-10/10-1	12 ft./ 6 ft.	Looks similar to giant corn; needs moist soil; leaves are striped with wide bands of green and white
F	Hibiscus *Hibiscus 'Blue River II'*	3	White; midsummer	Perennial	5-9/9-1	4-5 ft./ 2-3 ft.	Large, tropical-looking flowers; prefers moist soil; keep an eye out for Japanese beetles on late blossoms
G	Daylily *Hemerocallis 'Spanish Glow'*	5	Peach; midsummer	Perennial	3-9/9-1	26 in./ 24 in.	Rebloomer; remove spent flowers to keep the plant tidy; 5-in.-diameter flowers; semi-evergreen foliage
H	Goat's beard *Aruncus dioicus*	1	Creamy white; spring	Perennial	4-8/8-1	4-6 ft./ 2-4 ft.	Prefers moist soil; trim off spent flowers as they turn brown; no serious disease or insect problems
I	Big betony *Stachys macrantha 'Superba'*	11	Purple-violet; midsummer	Perennial	4-8/8-1	2 ft./ 2 ft.	Dense mounds of crinkled green foliage; lipped flowers arranged in spikes; easy to multiply by division
J	Coral bells *Heuchera* Dolce® Mocha Mint®	7	Coral-pink; midsummer	Perennial	4-9/9-1	8-16 in./ 10-14 in.	Dark foliage laced with lots of silver; remove spent flowers to keep the plant tidy and show off the leaves
K	Lilyturf *Liriope muscari 'Big Blue'*	21	Lavender-pink; late summer	Perennial	5-10/10-1	1-2 ft./ 1-2 ft.	Clumps expand but are not invasive; mow off old leaves in early spring to keep the plants looking good

Classic Lilies

Flat
Trumpet
Bowl
Recurved

Lily terms

Lily flowers range widely in shape. Here are some of the shapes, along with the terms you'll see in catalog descriptions.

Mail-order sources

Brent and Becky's Bulbs
www.brentandbeckysbulbs.com
804-693-3966. *Catalog free*

The Lily Garden
www.thelilygarden.com
360-253-6273. *Catalog free*

Van Engelen Inc.
www.vanengelen.com
860-567-8734. *Catalog free*

Nothing heralds the arrival of summer quite like a brightly colored mass of fragrant lilies. The gorgeous blooms compel you to drink in their beauty, as well as their wonderful perfume.

Lilies start blooming after the last tulips finish in late spring, and depending on the hybrid, continue until early fall. The drawings at left show you some of the different flower shapes available. And any of them may be upward-, outward- or downward-facing.

There are lots of different types or "divisions" of lilies available, but I'll be talking about four of the most popular ones here — Asiatics, trumpets and Aurelians, Orienpets and Orientals. I've picked 10 of my favorite hybrids: the prettiest, most durable and easiest to grow. (You can find them at the sources at left.) Many have been popular for decades and the North American Lily Society has placed some of them in their Lily Hall of Fame. But a few are newer hybrids that are just as outstanding.

GROW GREAT LILIES In humus-rich, moist but well-drained soils, lilies are easy to grow. For the healthiest plants and most flowers, plant the bulbs 6 to 8 inches deep in a spot where they'll get at least six hours of sun a day. You can plant bulbs in fall or early spring, but because of their tall, slim stems, lilies look best in groups of at least three to five, spaced 12 to 18 inches apart. Don't crowd the plants, though; they're prone to botrytis fungus in wet areas. Otherwise, mulch the soil to keep the roots moist and cool. In windy spots, you might need to stake your taller lilies.

As far as feeding, topdressing around the plants with compost or applying a single dose of fertilizer is about all your lily needs. Use a balanced, slow-release fertilizer, such as 10-10-10, in early spring.

Deadhead faded flowers so the plant will direct its energy to the bulb. After flowering is finished, don't cut back the ripening leaves and stems until they've turned completely yellow, so they can feed the bulbs as long as possible.

I'll share the lilies in the order they usually bloom. If you plan it right, you can plant a few and enjoy the color and perfume from the end of spring straight through to the beginning of fall. □

— *Deborah Gruca*

'Red Velvet'

True to its name, 'Red Velvet' produces lots of downward-facing flowers that look like they're made of the richest deep-red velvet. Displayed at the top of 3- to 4-foot-tall stems, blooms are shaped like large flat bowls, with petals recurved a little at the tips. You'll get the most flowers when you grow 'Red Velvet' in full sun, but this plant is tolerant of a little afternoon shade, as well.

'Red Velvet' blooms the first season after you plant it, with the number of flowers on the plant increasing with each passing year. As with other Asiatics, it's very cold-tolerant, carefree and easy to grow, even when grown in poor soil and full hot sun.

Type Asiatic
Height 3 to 4 ft.
Bloom Early to midsummer
Fragrance None
Hardiness
　　Cold: USDA 3 to 7
　　Heat: AHS 7 to 1

Early bloomer

Though these deep-hued blooms offer no scent, they are some of the first lily flowers to open in early summer — a real treat for gardeners and any nearby hummingbirds. The sturdy blooms are very fade-resistant and long-lasting.

'Tiger Babies'

You'll need to get very close to the 5-inch soft peach-pink flowers of this lily to enjoy their light perfume. The downward-facing, early summer flowers have a dark-peach throat with chocolate brown spots sprinkled generously over the petals.

'Tiger Babies' is valuable in the perennial border, as it brings its color to the garden early. It blooms at the same time as salvia, peonies and roses.

Gently arching 3- to 4-foot-tall stems carry dozens of flowers that shine in your garden as well as in a vase. Add it to colorful bouquets — the pastel flowers blend seamlessly with other blooms that have either brighter or darker colors.

Type Asiatic
Height 3 to 4 ft.
Bloom Early to midsummer
Fragrance Light
Hardiness
　　Cold: USDA 3 to 8
　　Heat: AHS 8 to 1

Good for northern gardens

With its well-earned reputation for being easy to grow, and because it's so cold-hardy, 'Tiger Babies' is a favorite of northern gardeners. This hardy hybrid is grown as far north as central Alaska without winter protection. But at the coldest end of its range, it may not bloom until later in summer.

top classic lilies *continued*

'White Henryi'

This classic lily hybrid sports large, fragrant white flowers with the deep-orange "sunburst" pattern in the center that is typical of trumpet hybrids. The petals have a light speckling of red spots.

Vigorous and disease-resistant, 'White Henryi' is very easy to grow — it's perfect for the beginning gardener. That same rugged constitution is the reason not only for its own popularity (it's a member of the Lily Hall of Fame), but why it's also been used in developing lots of other hybrids.

Starting in midsummer, 'White Henryi' can bloom for a good four weeks. And within just a couple of years, this lily can reach 7 feet or taller.

Type Trumpet
Height 4 to 7 ft.
Bloom Mid- to late summer
Fragrance Strong
Hardiness
    Cold: USDA 4 to 8
    Heat: AHS 8 to 1

Perfect partners

Phlox *Phlox paniculata* 'Robert Poore'
Shasta daisy *Leucanthemum xsuperbum* 'Becky'

The daisy-shaped flowers of 'Becky' echo the white 'White Henryi' flowers, while the large purple-pink flower clusters of 'Robert Poore' provide both a color and shape contrast.

'Black Beauty'

The very first Orienpet hybrid, 'Black Beauty' was introduced in 1957. It produces cascades of fragrant black-red flowers starting in August in most gardens. The petals, edged with a thin margin of white, are *recurved*, or tightly curved back, revealing a dramatic throat of green and white.

Loved by so many gardeners, 'Black Beauty' was the first lily inducted into the North American Lily Society's Hall of Fame and continues to be widely grown.

This rugged perennial favorite is very long-lived and multiplies readily by offsets, resulting in a large clump in just a few years. Plants do best in full sun, but tolerate a little shade in areas with very hot summers.

Type Orienpet
Height 3 to 5 ft.
Bloom Mid- to late summer
Fragrance Sweet
Hardiness
    Cold: USDA 3 to 8
    Heat: AHS 8 to 1

Long-bloomer

Because the sturdy 3- to 5-ft.-tall stems hold 20 to an amazing 50 buds each, 'Black Beauty' produces a very long succession of blooms. The total bloom period for one plant can last eight weeks or even longer into late summer!

'Silk Road'

Wide candelabras of huge 8-inch 'Silk Road' flowers are carried on sturdy stems that can reach to 6 feet the first year. In a few years' time the plant can easily top 8 feet or better. White flowers have dramatic crimson-pink throats that draw you near enough to enjoy the intense fragrance. The scent is a wonderful addition to the summer garden, but you may want to limit yourself to just a few cut stems for indoors, so the fragrance doesn't get overwhelming.

You may see this sold under the name 'Northern Carillon'. But whatever the name, it's been so popular in the dozen years it's been available, it's already made the Lily Hall of Fame.

Type Orienpet
Height 4 to 8 ft.
Bloom Mid- to late summer
Fragrance Spicy
Hardiness
  Cold: USDA 3 to 9
  Heat: AHS 9 to 1

A little support

'Silk Road' tolerates a little shade, especially in areas of hot summers, but you may need to grow it against a wall or fence to give it a little support. For a beautiful combination, grow it next to a trellis or arbor with a 'Jackmanii' clematis twined on it. Loosely tie the lily stems to the structure.

'Scheherazade'

There are plenty of reasons this classic Orienpet has been a favorite lily for 14 years. For one thing there are the breathtaking, 8-inch-diameter flowers with recurved deep-red petals. Edges of gold change to white at the tips. (Cooler weather or growing it in more shade brings out more of the gold color, while full sun makes the edges whiter.)

In addition, there's the sweet, spicy fragrance that permeates the garden. But also, after just a few years, the plants can reach a towering 8 feet tall. Imagine a mass of these flowers, with their dramatic good looks, perfuming the air and looming over your head — just the thing for adding some vertical impact to your border!

Type Orienpet
Height 8 ft.
Bloom Mid- to late summer
Fragrance Spicy
Hardiness
  Cold: USDA 3 to 8
  Heat: AHS 8 to 1

Easy to grow

On top of all of its other good qualities, 'Scheherazade' is simply a rugged, nearly indestructible plant, and one of the more cold-hardy lilies — in USDA zones 3 to 8. With no serious pests or diseases to speak of, this vigorous hybrid will be a favorite in your garden for years to come.

top classic lilies *continued*

'Orania'

Trumpet-shaped, 8-inch-diameter flowers of 'Orania' are a delicious pale tawny-melon color — rare in the world of lilies. Apricot midveins highlight the petals surrounding a splashy green starburst, with the undersides of the petals wearing a pale burgundy blush.

This hybrid tolerates a wide range of light conditions, though full sun will reward you with the most flowers. The amount of sunlight the plant gets, along with the daytime temperatures, affects the delicate color of the petals. They tend to be lighter (as the one in the photo above) in hotter areas or when situated in full sun, with a deeper apricot color in cooler areas or when grown in part shade.

Type Orienpet
Height 3 to 4 ft.
Bloom Mid- to late summer
Fragrance Mild, fruity
Hardiness
　Cold: USDA 5 to 9
　Heat: AHS 9 to 1

Great for cutting

'Orania' has a slightly fruity fragrance, perfect for cutting and bringing indoors, where the perfume of other lilies may be a bit too strong. When you refresh the water in the vase daily, 'Orania' cut flowers last longer than the average lily — an amazing two weeks!

'Satisfaction'

Compared to the other lilies shown here, 'Satisfaction' is a relative newcomer on the lily scene — but certainly no less outstanding.

'Satisfaction' has enormous 8- to 9-inch-diameter flowers in an unusual and intense deep red-pink. The outfacing blooms have throats splashed with an eye-grabbing yellow and are as durable and vigorous as you'd expect of an Orienpet lily. This intense color makes it stand out, even in a bed filled with other lilies. And as you draw near, you're enticed by an intoxicating perfume that makes it a joy to grow in your garden. In fact, if the opinion of some seasoned lily veterans counts, this hybrid may just be the next big favorite in the lily world.

Type Orienpet
Height 3 to 4 ft.
Bloom Mid- to late summer
Fragrance Strong
Hardiness
　Cold: USDA 4 to 9
　Heat: AHS 9 to 1

Perfect partners

Rose *Rosa* 'Sunshine Vigorosa'
Baby's breath *Gypsophila paniculata* 'Bristol Fairy'

The soft yellow of this carpet rose brings out the yellow lily centers. All the while, mounds of tiny white baby's breath blooms create an airy background.

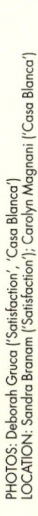

'Casa Blanca'

With richly perfumed, 10-inch pure white flowers, 'Casa Blanca' has been a perennial favorite lily for more than three decades. Its place in the Lily Hall of Fame is proof of that.

Type Oriental
Height 4 ft.
Bloom Late summer
Fragrance Very strong
Hardiness
  Cold: USDA 5 to 9
  Heat: AHS 9 to 1

The enormous blooms have a flocked surface, giving them a lovely textured look. To harvest them for use indoors, cut the stems just as the first buds open. But don't take more of the stem than you have to — it's needed to feed the bulb for the next year's blooms. On any lily, once the flowers have opened, hold the bloom upside down and carefully snip out the pollen-bearing anthers to avoid pollen stains on your clothes or furniture. Cut flowers last in the vase for five to nine days.

Lovely in low light

The enormous blooms of 'Casa Blanca' have ruffled edges and deeply contrasting anthers. As a result, the flowers show up well and entice lots of night pollinators in moon gardens. Happily, the end of the day is also when the perfume is at its peak.

'Star Gazer'

'Star Gazer' was one of the first modern oriental hybrids. With its large, durable flowers, it's still one of the most popular lilies, both for growing in flower gardens and for use in the cut flower industry. Most florist shops carry the cut stems in their stores almost year round.

Type Oriental
Height 3 to 4 ft.
Bloom Late summer
Fragrance Light
Hardiness
  Cold: USDA 4 to 8
  Heat: AHS 8 to 1

The large, upfacing white-edged crimson-red flowers are carried at the tops of 3- to 4-foot stems. This compact size means 'Star Gazer' needs no staking and is a perfect choice near the middle or front of garden beds and in containers. Place the containers in full sun to part shade, and move them to wherever you need a dash of bright color in the garden.

Perfect in pots

Dwarf fountain grass *Pennisetum alopecuroides* 'Hameln'
Sedum *Sedum* 'Vera Jameson'

Tuck plants into the pot with three to five bulbs to shade them and keep them cool, and don't let the mix dry out. Top with compost or shredded leaves to hold in the moisture.

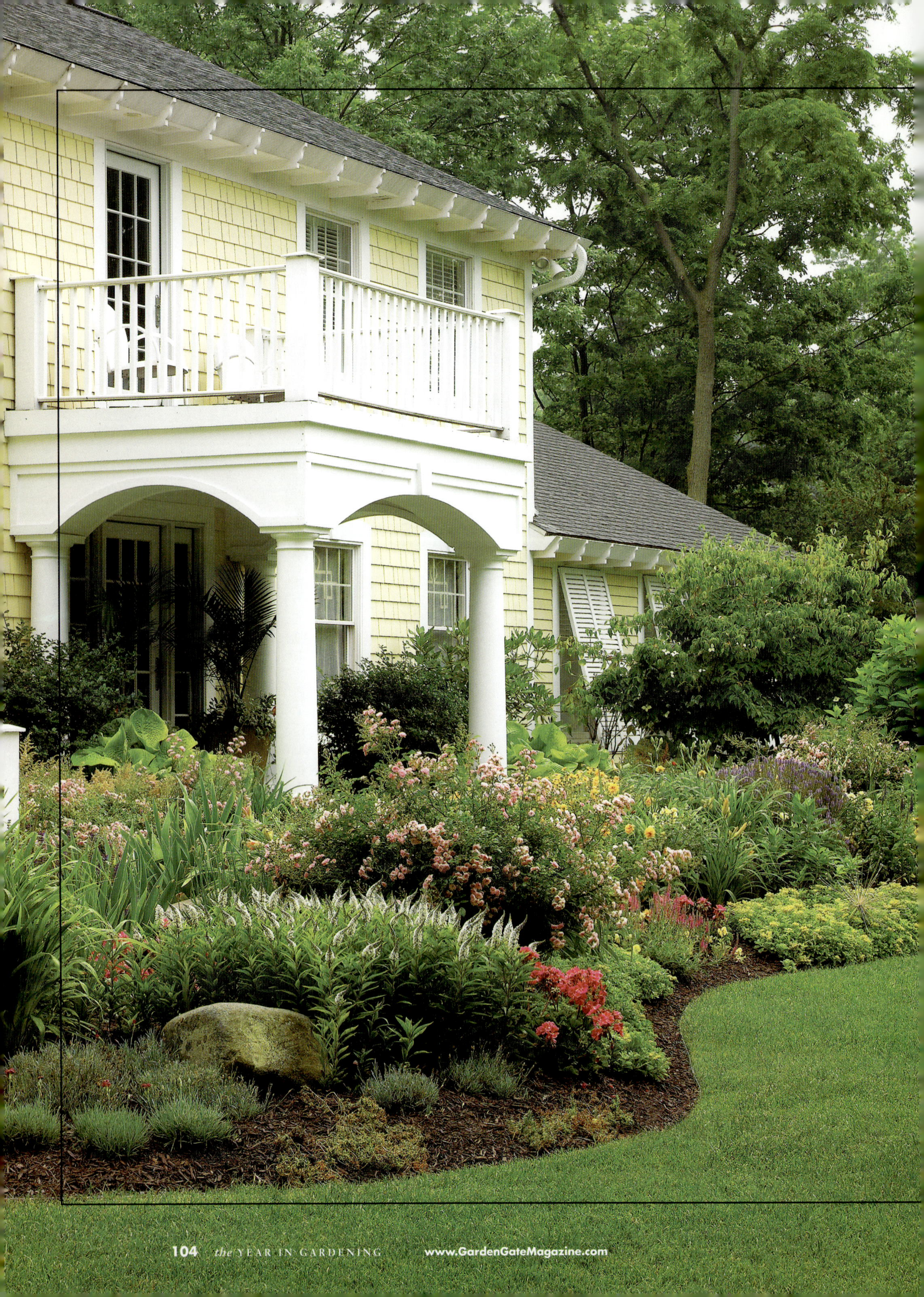

before & after

transform *your* garden, we show you how

THERE'S NO MAGIC INVOLVED IN A BEAUTIFUL GARDEN. The truth is, it's know-how and hard work. Here's how seven gardeners took everyday challenges and turned them into dream gardens. Their solutions range from quick fixes to major projects, but you're sure to get tips you can use from every one.

Starting from Scratch	**106**
From 'Oh, Dear' to 'Oh, Boy!'	**110**
Shade Garden Makeover	**114**
Midsummer Makeover	**118**
7 Tips for a Wonderful Water Garden	**120**
Sunny Side of the Street	**124**
Keep the Color Coming!	**128**

BEFORE & AFTER | BACK YARD

Starting From Scratch

A big expanse of lawn can be intimidating to even experienced gardeners. Take a tip from the pros and make a plan first, before you start digging. That's how Carolyn Magnani got started transforming her Iowa yard in the "before" photo below. She took a garden design class, made a plan and has used it as a guide over the years to create the beautiful garden you see at right.

WHAT YOU HAVE Start by taking stock of what's already there. Measure along the property line to see how long and wide the yard is, then transfer the measurements to some graph paper. Add in the house, trees and other permanent features. Be sure you indicate the windows on the house so you can plan a nice view from inside, too. Carolyn's favorite easy chair in the family room has a great view of the garden around the arbor. Or, make washing the dishes more enjoyable by planning a colorful flower bed that you can see from the kitchen window.

Next, take note of how much sun and shade there is. It also helps to get your soil tested to see if it's acid or alkaline. You can get a kit from garden centers or send a sample to your local extension agency.

WHAT YOU WANT Once you know what you have, you can daydream about your ideal garden. Maybe your list would include plenty of room for plants, space for the grandkids to play and some privacy. Plan for big things like a path or garden shed now. In this garden the arbor was the first addition. It's a lot easier to install hardscaping early on so you don't have to work around plants later.

PULLING IT ALL TOGETHER Now's your chance to get creative. Take a look at your map of the yard, garden conditions and wish list. Experiment with different bed shapes, using both straight and curved lines. The undulating edge of this border creates a casual feel with plenty of room for plants. On the other hand, a garden with a lot of straight lines and symmetrical plantings usually seems more formal. If you find it hard to get started, follow the example to the left. Make some copies of a photo of your yard so you can sketch ideas right on the print.

Another way to kick-start your design is to get something out there that you can build around. This arbor and the arborvitaes on either side are the biggest things in the border, so they serve as a focal point. For extra emphasis, the two beds sweep in and end at the edge of the arbor, highlighting it a bit more. On a more practical note, this structure and the trees are on the south so they protect the garden from wind and sun. Evergreens planted on the north can help block cold winter winds.

Remember, you don't have to install everything in one year. This garden has been a work in progress for 18 years, with new beds and even a pond being added as time and budget allowed.

Now that you know about garden planning, the next step is choosing plants. Let's take a look at the plants in this garden on the following pages.

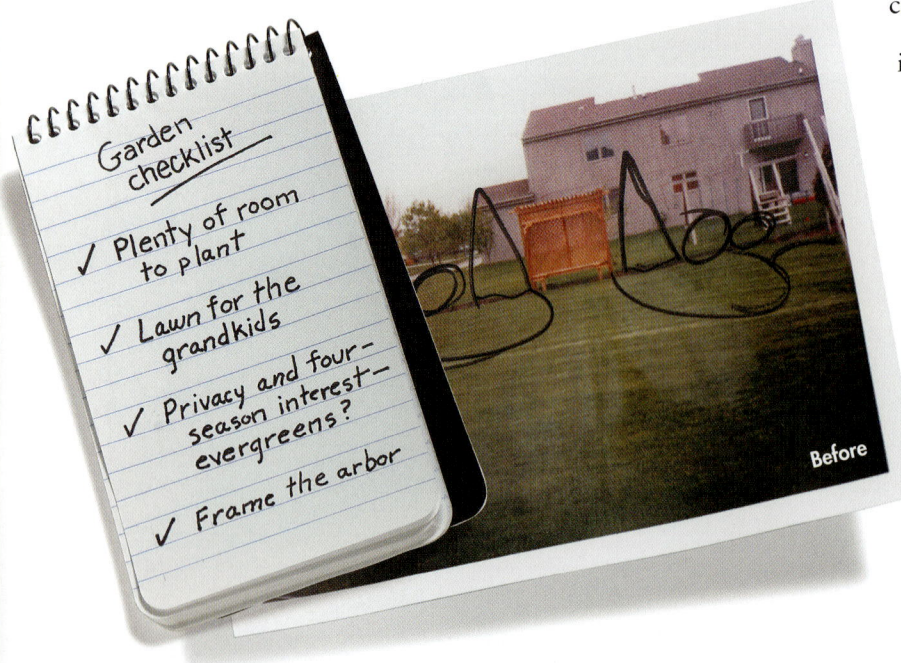

PHOTOS: Carolyn Magnani (before); John Holtorf (lead)

Garden checklist
- ✓ Plenty of room to plant
- ✓ Lawn for the grandkids
- ✓ Privacy and four-season interest—evergreens?
- ✓ Frame the arbor

Before

106 *the* YEAR IN GARDENING   www.GardenGateMagazine.com

Turn the page to learn how to grow this garden.

COLOR-FILLED BORDER

No matter what your garden plan looks like, you can use the hardy, easy-care plants from this garden to fill it up. This is a large garden so there isn't room to show everything, but this area of colorful flowers and foliage is a good representation of the whole thing. The small photo shows the same area you saw on the previous page from a different angle. That's the plan you'll see on the next page. If you have a large yard to fill, repeat the planting plan a few times to fill the space.

NO FENCE NEEDED Like a lot of suburban areas, this yard backs up to several other unfenced yards. How do you give yourself some privacy without seeming unneighborly? Those hefty arborvitaes are as good at screening the view as any privacy fence but make a prettier backdrop for the planting in front. And the shorter plants like the lilies and daylilies in front of the arborvitaes bridge the space to the lawn. In the illustration below you'll find more tips for creating privacy in any garden.

COLOR ALL SEASON Carefully staggering bloom times keeps the garden looking good even with only one or two types of plant. There are a lot of lilies and daylilies here, but some bloom early in the season and others show off later. That way,

(1) The sweeping line of this bed curves out and back to the arbor. A deeply curved edge like this, seen from an angle, can stir curiosity since you can't see what's around the corner.

there's plenty of color most of the summer and into fall. Some of these daylilies even rebloom.

This garden peaks in summer with phlox, daylilies, balloon flowers and lilies. But that doesn't mean the garden isn't beautiful the rest of the season, too. Colorful foliage from a full moon maple and the 'Tiger Eyes' sumac on the right side of the photo dress up the border in between stages of blooms. From a distance, the false sunflower is a splash of gold flowers in the center right of the photo. But up close, the leaves are variegated with stripes of white, so it's colorful even when it's not blooming. If you keep deadheading this beauty, you'll have a non-stop show from early summer until fall.

Foliage isn't the only way to brighten the pause between blooms. Tuck some containers filled with annuals into the beds near perennials that are done blooming. With regular water and fertilizer, annuals will keep the color coming all season. Did you notice that pink flowering "shrub" in the middle of the photo? It's actually a strawberry pot filled with begonias. Once the small plants filled out, they covered the container, making it look like one large plant.

As you can see, any garden can look as good as this one. All it takes is a little planning! □

— *Sherri Ribbey*

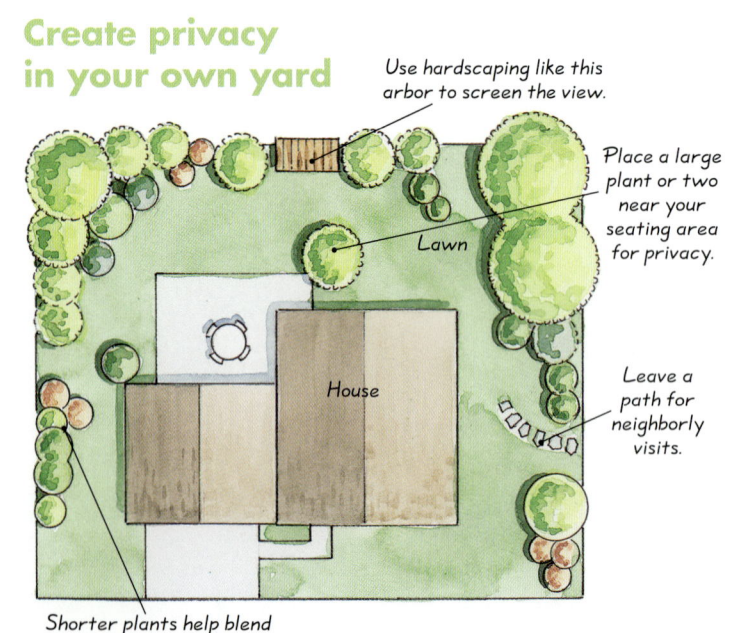

Create privacy in your own yard

Use hardscaping like this arbor to screen the view.

Place a large plant or two near your seating area for privacy.

Leave a path for neighborly visits.

Shorter plants help blend trees into the landscape.

A clematis on the arbor adds height and color.

Scale: 1 square = 1 square foot

Remove the spent stalks of reblooming daylilies to keep them flowering.

QUICK TIP

If you have a big yard to fill, flip the garden plan over to repeat the same planting on the right.

SUMMER COLOR

Code	Plant Name	No. to Plant	Cold/Heat Zones	Height/Width	Special features
A	**Balloon flower** *Platycodon grandiflorus* 'Sentimental Blue'	4	3-8/8-1	6-12 in./12-15 in.	Dwarf cultivar; balloonlike buds open into 3-in. single flowers; midsummer
B	**Daylily** *Hemerocallis* 'Razzamatazz'	2	3-9/9-1	20 in./18-24 in.	Medium-purple flowers with a yellow throat and ruffled edge; early to midsummer; reblooms
C	**Daylily** *Hemerocallis* 'So Lovely'	1	3-9/9-1	30 in./24-36 in.	Large pale-yellow blooms; mid- to late summer; very fragrant
D	**Daylily** *Hemerocallis* 'Shari Harrison'	1	3-9/9-1	24 in./18-24 in.	Lavender flowers with yellow eye-zone; early summer; reblooms
E	**Full moon maple** *Acer japonicum* 'Aconitifolium'	1	5-7/7-1	8-19 ft./8-10 ft.	Serrated green leaves turn orange-red in fall; slow growing; multi-stemmed; good variety for containers
F	**Daylily** *Hemerocallis* 'Wilson Spider'	1	3-9/9-1	28 in./18-24 in.	Purple-pink petals with a yellow throat; midsummer
G	**Daylily** *Hemerocallis* 'Strutter's Ball'	2	3-9/9-1	28 in./18-24 in.	Deep-purple petals with lemon-green throat; midsummer
H	**Phlox** *Phlox xarendsii* 'Miss Mary'	2	3-9/9-1	15-22 in./24 in.	Cherry-red flowers; midsummer; mildew-resistant
I	**Oriental lily** *Lilium* 'Sorbonne'	1	4-8/8-1	48 in./10-12 in.	Rose-pink petals edged in white; mid- to late summer; fragrant
J	**Asiatic lily** *Lilium* 'Iowa Rose'	2	4-8/8-1	3-4 ft./1 ft.	Pale-pink flowers with recurved petals; early summer
K	**Phlox** *Phlox paniculata* 'Blue Paradise'	1	4-8/8-1	40 in./18-24 in.	Blue-violet flowers with white eye; midsummer; mildew-resistant
L	**False sunflower** *Heliopsis helianthoides* 'Helhan' (Loraine Sunshine)	1	4-9/9-1	30 in./24-30 in.	Yellow daisylike flowers; mid- to late summer; green veins on white leaves; deer-resistant
M	**Asiatic lily** *Lilium* 'Ruby Tuesday'	2	4-8/8-1	36 in./10-12 in.	Ruby-red blooms with a hint of white in the center; early summer
N	**Daylily** *Hemerocallis* 'Imperial Edge'	1	3-9/9-1	22 in./18-24 in.	Peachy-pink flowers with lighter eye-zone; early summer; reblooms
O	**Asiatic lily** *Lilium* 'Nove Cento'	1	4-8/8-1	24-32 in./10-12 in.	Clear-yellow flowers; early summer
P	**Orienpet lily** *Lilium* 'Catherine the Great'	1	3-8/8-1	48-60 in./10-12 in.	Yellow-gold flowers; midsummer
Q	**Clematis** *Clematis* 'Hagley Hybrid'	1	4-9/9-1	8 ft./2-3 ft.	Shell-pink flowers with dark anthers; mid- to late summer; reblooms
R	**Chinese lily** *Lilium henryi*	1	5-8/8-1	48-72 in./12 in.	Tawny-orange recurved petals; mid- to late summer
S	**Penstemon** *Penstemon digitalis* 'Husker Red'	1	3-8/8-1	24-36 in./12-24 in.	Maroon leaves with white-blushed pink flowers; early summer

BEFORE & AFTER | BACK YARD

From 'Oh Dear' to 'Oh, Boy'

Botanical Names

Beardtongue
  Penstemon strictus
Ice plant
  Aptenia cordifolia
Salvia *Salvia* spp.
Yucca *Yucca* spp.

A run-down house and a neglected back yard were just the thing for an energetic gardener and do-it-yourselfer like Dan Johnson. He transformed his Colorado back yard in the small "before" photo into the beautiful garden in the photo at right. How? By employing lots of color, tucking in small planting areas and taking advantage of microclimates.

First thing on the agenda was getting rid of the 10-foot-by-70-foot concrete driveway to make room for the garden. A contractor demolished the drive and hauled away some of the debris. Dan used the rest in the garden. Part of the concrete became the foundation for the more than 150 feet of path that winds through the yard. The rest ended up as backfill behind some of the boulders and combined with soil to improve drainage here and there.

COLOR AND STONE You probably noticed that the house color is similar to the warm tones of the flagstone path. Shades of this color weave through the garden, creating a common thread. Tucked here and there, colorful flowers, such as the pink ice plant along the path or the violet beardtongue in the foreground, keep things lively.

Choosing a type of stone found in your area can save you money on shipping charges. This native red flagstone has a rich color, and the smooth surface is easy to walk on. In different parts of the country or for a different color scheme, slate could be a good choice, too. It has the same look but comes in shades of gray. Or save a little money and install a gravel path.

Whatever material you choose, remember the layout of the path affects the look and feel of the garden, too. It's easy to see in the illustration below how the path branches and winds through the yard in a relaxed and casual style. A straight path or two made of brick and a few right-angled turns would provide a more formal feel.

SMALLER IS BETTER This branching path also divides the yard into smaller planting areas. These small spaces are easy to fill, especially if you're prone to those onesy-twosy purchases from the garden center. It's also easier to see if plant combinations are working — there's not as much space or as many plants to worry about. So if the grass grows too tall and floppy or the flowers are the wrong shade of pink, move them somewhere else or give them to a friend. You can even get a whole new look with just a few plants.

GET THE LAY OF THE LAND This is a zone 5 garden. Some of these cactus, salvia and yucca up near the house and between the two doors are usually only hardy in warmer zones. Why do they keep coming back year after year? Well, it all has to do with microclimates. Sun, wind, soil and the topography of your garden, neighborhood and even region all play a part in forming microclimates. You can take advantage of those spaces in your yard that get hotter, colder, wetter or drier than the rest of the garden to grow plants that like those conditions.

In this garden, the cactus are able to survive because they're planted near the house, which provides protection from the wind and cold in winter. Plus the soil has been modified to create the excellent drainage these plants demand.

Want to see some other great plant combinations? Just turn the page.

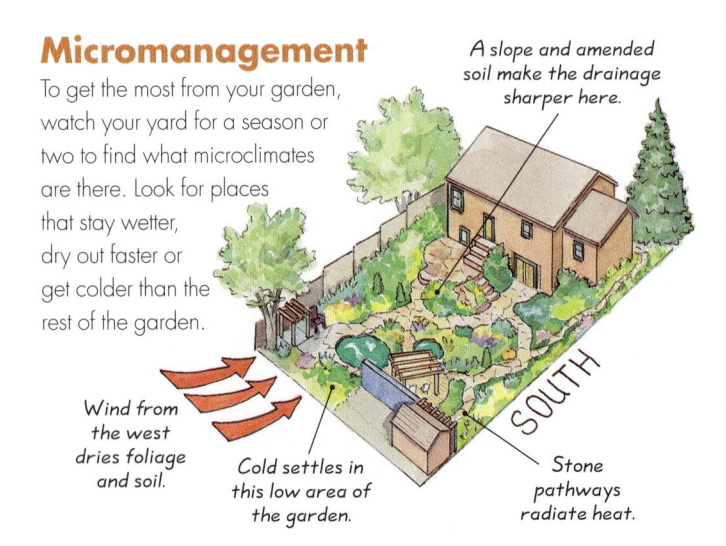

WEB extra

Find out how to create your own microclimate with this downloadable *article*.

Micromanagement

To get the most from your garden, watch your yard for a season or two to find what microclimates are there. Look for places that stay wetter, dry out faster or get colder than the rest of the garden.

A slope and amended soil make the drainage sharper here.

Wind from the west dries foliage and soil.

Cold settles in this low area of the garden.

Stone pathways radiate heat.

Turn the page to find some great plant combos.

3 HEAT-DEFYING **PLANT COMBOS**

In this Colorado garden, the rain can be sporadic. It faces west so it gets the hot afternoon sun, and drying winds can cause soil and plant foliage to really suffer. For a garden that looks good without endless watering or a major soil overhaul, Dan chose plants that don't mind these conditions.

Even drought-tolerant plants need some water. Regular watering the first year they're planted helps establish a good root system. After that, they'll be able to withstand longer periods without water. Of course, a 2- to 4-inch layer of mulch helps cut down on watering, too. For plants like those in photos 1 and 3, ordinary bark mulch is fine. Even better, use compost. It helps preserve moisture, adds lots of organic matter and has a finer texture than bark.

But bark mulch isn't the best choice for dry-loving plants like those in photo 2. It actually holds too much moisture, which can sometimes cause crown rot. In this case, rock mulch is the way to go. True, the small pea-gravel-sized mulch that's used here radiates heat. But these plants can take it — in fact, they like it that way.

Everybody has difficult situations in their gardens. What you need are solutions. Here are some combos you may find helpful. They're tough, hardy and grow almost anywhere. □

— *Sherri Ribbey*

1 EASY-CARE PLANTS around this deck allow you to relax and enjoy the view. They love the soil found here. A mix of sand, clay and loam covers the yard, but generous applications of compost over the years have improved its texture and nutrients.

Cold air settles in this low area of the garden. But these plants won't suffer because it's also the first place hit by the rising sun, so it warms up quickly.

You can deadhead the coneflowers to get more blooms. But if you let a few flowers go to seed in late summer you'll get a different kind of show. Goldfinches and other birds love coneflower seeds. Sit quietly on the deck and you can watch them swoop in and perch on a stem to grab a quick snack.

Fountain grass foliage and dried allium flowers persist into winter, adding another season of interest to this garden. Don't be surprised if kiss-me-over-the-garden-gate shows up where you didn't plant it. It reseeds in places where it's happy.

- **A Coneflower** *Echinacea purpurea* 'Magnus'
- **B Kiss-me-over-the-garden-gate** *Persicaria orientalis*
- **C Fountain grass** *Pennisetum orientale* 'Karley Rose'
- **D Allium** *Allium hollandicum* 'Purple Sensation'

2 THESE PLANTS ARE MADE TO BEAT THE HEAT. The sunny south-facing slope they sit on — and heat reflected from the nearby path — keep this combo high and dry. This is a spot where concrete debris was mixed with the soil to create the sharper drainage these plants thrive on.

That soaptree yucca is usually only hardy in zone 6 but the extra heat and drainage keep it coming back each year. If you think sage flowers are boring, think again. This species has big rose-colored bracts in summer and butterflies love it. But keep it dry or you won't have it long. Starting out as red-tinted buds, sulfer flowers open yellow and then dry to orange and red. Beardtongue is perfect for this lean soil — it doesn't like a lot of fertilizer. To keep blooms full and numerous, use a slow release 14-14-14 formula, such as Osmocote®, once in spring.

A Soaptree yucca *Yucca elata*
B Sulfur flower *Eriogonum umbellatum*
C Beardtongue *Penstemon strictus*
D Mountain desert sage *Salvia pachyphylla*

3 KEEP YOUR PATHWAY LOOKING GOOD with colorful flowers. Repeating the bright-orange California poppies draws your eye along the path. The different flower form of the iris adds interest to the planting while the deep red chair acts as an anchor *and* gives you a place to sit down for a while.

Besides being colorful, these plants are tough. They're growing in full sun with additional heat reflected off the stone path. Wind further dries out the soil and foliage, making this a difficult place for plants. With all that, this is still a low-maintenance planting. Removing spent blossoms is about all that needs to be done in spring. In late fall a layer of mulch keeps soil temperature even through winter. But during the summer, these plants are on their own, and you can see the results.

A California poppy *Eschscholzia californica*
B Allium *Allium hollandicum* 'Purple Sensation'
C Bearded iris *Iris* hybrid

BEFORE & AFTER | BACK YARD

Shade Garden Makeover

Bonnie Moore likes being on her local garden tour. She also likes her two big golden retrievers. But dogs are hard on grass, and she was tired of replacing damaged areas of the lawn every year before the tour. Her solution for her Michigan garden: Get rid of the lawn and plant a shade garden with mulch paths for dogs and visitors. Sound like a good idea? Keep reading to learn how to replace your lawn with a lush planting like this.

NO MORE LAWN Removing a big area of grass is a lot of work, no matter how you do it. But isn't more space to garden worth it? The lawn in the before photo was removed the old-fashioned way, with a spade. If you're pressed for time, rent a sod cutter. It's like using a tiller, and will make the job go faster.

Once you're done and there's a big pile of sod in the yard, what can you do with it? You can add it to your compost pile, or if the grass is in good shape, use it to patch damaged areas elsewhere in the yard. Or build a berm by turning the newly cut sod over and piling it up. Cover it all with a mixture of soil and compost for a raised planting area.

When the grass is gone, you have a blank slate for planting. To get started, add a few inches of compost on top of the soil. Don't till, though, or you might damage tree roots.

GOT SHADE? Any garden looks best if you choose plants that like your conditions. In this shady yard, you need to figure out exactly how much shade you have before you start to plant.

You see shade terms in catalogs and magazines all the time. What does it all mean? I've defined some basic terms that cover most situations:

- **Light** — 2 to 4 hours of shade per day
- **Filtered** — Sunlight peeks through tree branches all day
- **Part** — 4 to 5 hours of shade per day
- **Full** — Shade lasts all day

Botanical Names

Brunnera *Brunnera macrophylla*
Holly *Ilex xmeserveae*
Hosta *Hosta* hybrid
Japanese painted fern *Athyrium niponicum pictum*
Rose *Rosa* spp.

This garden has 4 to 5 hours of shade each day. The deepest is in the back near the fence. Hollies work well here — they can take the lack of sun and drier conditions from root competition. As you move away from the fence, the pink roses in the foreground have plenty of sun.

To find out what type of shade you have, watch your garden for a year and keep a shade journal. It can be hard to wait but the amount of shade can change throughout the season. If you watch your garden and keep track of where the shade falls and for how long, you won't have to move plants later.

ADD SOME PIZZAZZ How do you make your shade garden look great? Think color *and* texture. Then you'll have a garden that inspires visitors to take notes.

Shade plants often have pastel flowers. They may not be showy, bright colors, but the pale blossoms are easy to see in a shady spot. And remember that foliage can be just as colorful as flowers and lasts longer, too. Just think of all the shades of green you've seen at the garden center. Variegated foliage with white or silver reflects light and keeps the garden from feeling closed in.

Color isn't the only "tool" you have when it comes to designing your shade garden. Combining a variety of leaf shapes makes the garden interesting to look at. Take a look at the contrasting shapes of feathery Japanese painted fern, elongated hosta and heart-shaped brunnera in the center of the photo.

Turn the page for tips to help you grow great-looking shade plants like these.

Turn the page to learn how to grow this garden.

GROW BEAUTIFUL SHADE PLANTS

Botanical Names

Barberry *Berberis* hybrid
Hosta *Hosta* hybrid
River birch *Betula nigra*
White pine *Pinus strobus*

Every garden has its challenges. With shade, it's low light, root competition from trees and lack of air circulation. But you can still have a beautiful garden. Check out the plan at right, as well as these tips on how to grow plants that thrive in the shade.

LIGHTEN UP When it comes right down to it, some shade spots are easier to work with than others. The more light that's available, the more plant choices you have. Trees like the river birch in this garden have fine twigs and small leaves. The branches are high, so plenty of sun reaches the ground. With light to part shade like this, it's possible to grow even sun-loving plants like the barberries in this garden. Plants may be a little taller and leggier, the foliage color may be different and blooming plants have fewer flowers in part shade. But these versatile plants still look good. Even shade plants like hostas react to different light levels. Blue hostas are bluer in full shade and some variegated varieties can have very different shades of green depending on how much sun they get.

MOISTURE MATTERS There's no getting around the fact that the plants in the photo on p. 115 need regular moisture to grow large and full. With shallow-rooted trees like white pines nearby, this is a challenge. Mulch and a soaker hose make this job a lot easier.

Every year this garden gets a new layer of finely chopped bark mulch. It conserves moisture and adds texture and nutrients to the soil as it decomposes. Plus, the smaller pieces are less noticeable than big chunks of bark and give the open areas a woodland feel. If you're concerned about using mulch in your shade garden because of slugs, check out "Slugs no more" at lower left to see how Bonnie got rid of hers.

To make watering easier, snake a soaker hose around the plants and under the mulch. This gets water near the roots where it's needed. Add a timer and you won't even have to remember to turn it off and on.

KEEP IT MOVING Branches, fences and other structures that make shade also block air movement, which makes it easier for fungal diseases to thrive. To keep plants healthy, avoid overcrowding. It's tempting to place those small sprouts close together but remember how big they will eventually get and plant them that distance apart. During the growing season, don't fertilize too much. Nitrogen promotes a lot of lush growth that's susceptible to disease. A good fall cleanup gets rid of debris where spores overwinter.

Big trees are beautiful by themselves, but a great-looking garden on the ground below makes the yard look like something special. You'll never miss that piece of lawn! ☐

— *Sherri Ribbey*

WEB extra

Welcome toads to your garden — build a toad house with our *instructions!*

SLUGS NO MORE

Slugs feel right at home in the cool, moist soil and leaf litter of a shade garden. While iron phosphate baits are a safe solution, Bonnie found that installing a pond took care of the problem. Frogs and toads showed up and the slugs disappeared. Even without a pond, you might be able to attract toads to your garden because they can tolerate drier environments. Did you know a single toad can eat up to 100 insects a day? Welcome these amphibians to your garden with a toad house like the one made from a broken pot in the photo above. To find out more about these fascinating creatures and how to make a toad house, check out our Web extra.

QUICK TIP

Water early in the morning to help prevent the spread of fungal disease. That way, moisture evaporates and doesn't sit overnight.

Scale: 1 square = 4 square feet

THE GARDEN'S PALETTE

Code	Plant Name	No. to Plant	Cold/Heat Zones	Height/Width	Special features
A	Hosta *Hosta* 'Frances Williams'	4	3-8/8-1	32 in./50 in.	Broad, leathery leaves are slug resistant
B	Holly Berri-Magic® China holly combination *Ilex xmeserveae* 'Mesdob' and 'Mesog'	3	4-9/9-1	10 ft./8-10 ft.	This holly is sold with a male and female plant in the same pot to ensure bright red winter berries
C	Hosta *Hosta sieboldiana elegans*	3	3-8/8-1	24 in./48 in.	Corrugated leaf texture shows up more as plant matures
D	Hosta *Hosta* 'So Sweet'	3	3-8/8-1	16 in./28 in.	Yellow edge fades to white later in the season
E	Brunnera *Brunnera macrophylla* 'Jack Frost'	3	3-8/9-1	12-15 in./12-15 in.	Tolerates heat better than other varieties
F	Hosta *Hosta* 'Ground Master'	2	3-8/8-1	10 in./16 in.	Low-growing hosta; makes an excellent ground cover or edging
G	Japanese painted fern *Athyrium niponicum pictum*	9	5-8/8-2	12-18 in./24 in.	Silver-gray leaves really show up in shade; good ground cover
H	Mugo pine *Pinus mugo* 'Mops'	1	2-7/7-1	36-48 in./30-36 in.	Dwarf cultivar; grows slowly so it takes years to reach full size
I	Hosta *Hosta* 'Wide Brim'	2	3-8/8-1	16 in./24-36 in.	Broad, mounding habit; heavily puckered leaves
J	Hosta *Hosta* 'Krossa Regal'	2	3-8/8-1	30 in/36-72 in.	More upright than other hostas; flower stalks grow up to 5 ft. tall
K	Rhododendron *Rhododendron* 'Roseum Elegans'	1	4-8/8-1	6-8 ft./6-8 ft.	Hardy evergreen variety; plant in protected site, away from wind
L	Barberry *Berberis thunbergii atropurpurea* 'Atropurpurea Nana' (Crimson Pygmy)	3	4-8/8-3	24 in./36 in.	Red foliage in spring and summer changes to orange in fall
M	Hosta *Hosta* 'Tot Tot'	1	3-8/8-1	6 in./18 in.	Miniature hosta; dark green leaves; does well in rock gardens
N	Hosta *Hosta* 'Ginko Craig'	5	3-8/8-1	10-12 in./18 in.	Dense, low-growing mounds; good ground cover or edging
O	Astilbe *Astilbe* 'Sprite'	5	4-9/8-1	12-15 in./10-12 in.	Dwarf variety; pale pink flowers in spring; slow growing
P	Swamp milkweed *Asclepias incarnata*	1	3-9/9-1	5-6 ft./2-3 ft.	Tolerates a wide range of soils; deep taproot is best left undisturbed
Q	Hardy geranium *Geranium* 'Johnson's Blue'	4	4-8/8-1	15-18 in./18-24 in.	Large flowers; shear plant back after flowering for rebloom
R	Rose *Rosa* 'F. J. Grootendorst'	1	4-9/9-2	4-6 ft./3-4 ft.	Rugosa hybrid; tolerates part shade; pink flowers; repeat bloomer

BEFORE & AFTER | BACK YARD

Midsummer Makeover

By midsummer, your garden's usually looking pretty good. The perennials you planted are growing and your annuals are starting to bloom like mad. Yes, everything is doing well — except for that one little bed. Hmm…now what?

Just because the calendar says it's the middle of summer, don't think it's too late to rejuvenate an existing bed that's become sparse-looking. Here are a few things you can do to perk up a lackluster perennial border.

1 SIZE IT UP First, take a close look at what you can salvage in the bed. There's not much going on in the before photo, except for a young Japanese aster starting to bloom. A tiny blanket flower, phlox and some other skimpy plants struggle there also. We decided to keep the aster in place and tuck the other plants into gaps in some other beds.

2 GO "SALE-ING" Take advantage of late-season plant sales at garden centers and pick up perennials for a lot less than you'd pay in the middle of May. Buy a few annuals, like the red begonias we found, to help fill in around the perennials while they're small. Or scratch in the seeds of fast-growing annuals like zinnias, celosia or cosmos. These seeds actually need the heat of summer to sprout. Next year, the perennials will be much bigger and you won't need as many annuals to fill in the bed.

3 DIG IN Summer heat and drought can be tough on young plants. Mix moisture crystals into the soil of your planting holes to keep the new starts moist while they're getting established. Give them a shot of fertilizer and top the soil with 2 to 3 inches of mulch to help hold moisture and cut down on your watering chores. Along with plants, crystals and mulch are often on sale by midsummer.

4 SPOT SOME POTS Many container plants are at their peak in midsummer. Place a few colorful pots among the plants to quickly fill in thin areas. A pot of coleus adds texture and color to this bed. Other plants that look great in late-summer containers are dahlias, sedums and asters.

5 ADD A PERSONAL TOUCH Finally, don't forget to include some hardscaping or a piece of garden art to personalize your garden. We placed the whimsical rusty cat at the left side of this bed. Whether bold or subtle, art should accent your plants, but not topple over onto them. It should be sturdy enough to withstand summer wind and rain without falling over, but easy to move to other parts of the garden wherever you want a fun finishing touch. □

— Deborah Gruca

Transform a sad bed into a colorful sunny one. See our Web extra for our makeover plan and plant list.

Botanical Names

Aster *Aster* spp.
Blanket flower *Gaillardia* xgrandiflora
Celosia *Celosia* spp.
Coleus *Solenostemon* hybrids
Cosmos *Cosmos* spp.
Dahlia *Dahlia* spp.
Japanese aster *Kalimeris pinnatifida*
Phlox *Phlox* spp.
Sedum *Sedum* spp.
Zinnia *Zinnia* spp.

WEB **extra**
Plant our summer spruce-up *plan!*

www.GardenGateMagazine.com the YEAR IN GARDENING 119

BEFORE & AFTER | BACK YARD

7 Tips For a Wonderful Water Garden

Water gardens add a new dimension to any garden, but this one is more dramatic than most. It's not often you can actually walk on a pond without getting wet!

As a garden designer, Darcy Daniels loves experimenting in her Oregon yard. She's always appreciated the sound and reflection of light and shadow on the water's surface, so she decided to add a pond to the area you see in the "before" photo above. (By the way, to see more of Darcy's garden, visit www.bloomtowngardendesign.com.) Thinking of adding a pond to your own garden or wondering how you can spruce up the one you have? Check out these seven tips to make your pond as beautiful as the one in the large "after" photo at right.

1 SHADE IS OK When you think of water gardens, you often think of plants like water lilies. But most aquatic plants need at least four hours of direct sun each day to bloom. If you don't have that much sun, look for shade-loving perennials to plant *around* the pond instead. Hosta, bergenia, perennial geranium and astilbe all look great near a pond and don't need a lot of light. Another shade bonus? Less algae grows in the water in shade.

2 TREE TROUBLE While shade is nice, deciduous trees directly over a pond can be a real pain. Falling leaves cause water quality problems if they aren't removed promptly. They sink to the bottom and decompose, robbing the water of valuable oxygen. Be sure to keep a skimmer handy so you can get rid of leaves daily, if needed.

3 POND PLACEMENT While it's tempting to put a pond in the middle of an empty space, it can look artificial there. Find a place in your yard where water seems appropriate. After all, you don't usually see ponds on a hillside. Instead, tuck it in near the garden's edge so it's a part of the whole yard. Placed near a border filled with perennials and shrubs, this pond has a seamless fit and looks fantastic.

4 MAXIMIZE ENJOYMENT If you're going to go to all the work of installing a pond, you want to get the most out of it. So make sure it's placed where you'll see it often. This one is near the deck and the path so there's plenty of opportunity to enjoy the view.

5 GO NATURAL Help your pond fit into its surroundings by giving it a natural look. How? Plant right up to the edge. Here, the feathery Scotch moss softens the hard edge of the stone around the pond. With the 'Tricolor' hebe nearby, there's no shortage of interesting foliage! If you'd like to see what else is planted here, look over the plant list in "Fine-looking foliage" at right.

6 HOW LOW TO GO Generally it's a good idea to keep the height of the plants nearest the pond's edge down low. That way you have a good view of the pond no matter where you are. And if you're walking nearby, you want to be able to see where you're going. But as you can tell by this photo, it's still a good idea to work a few taller plants in to add variety and keep it interesting.

7 TWO FOR ONE Speaking of walking near the pond, this water feature cuts through a natural traffic pattern. But that's no reason not to put it there. Redirecting the path around the pond would have looked awkward. So why not incorporate the path into the pond? You can get closer to the water this way and these "floating" steppers are pretty dramatic, too.

Think these steppers look complicated to build yourself? They're not. Turn the page to find out how to make them for your own pond.

Botanical Names

Astilbe
  Astilbe hybrid
Bergenia
  Bergenia cordifolia
Hebe
  Hebe speciosa 'Tricolor'
Hosta *Hosta* hybrid
Perennial geranium
  Geranium hybrid
Scotch moss
  Sagina subulata glabrata 'Aurea'
Water lily
  Nymphaea hybrid

FINE-LOOKING FOLIAGE

A **Chameleon plant** *Houttuynia cordata* 'Chameleon'; 10 to 18 in. tall and 12 to 24 in. wide; cold-hardy in USDA zones 4 to 10; heat-tolerant in AHS zones 12 to 1

B **Japanese sweet flag** *Acorus gramineus* 'Ogon'; 6 to 12 in. tall and wide; cold-hardy in USDA zones 5 to 11; heat-tolerant in AHS zones 12 to 1

C **Hebe** *Hebe speciosa* 'Tricolor'; 4 ft. tall and wide; cold-hardy in USDA zones 10 to 11; heat-tolerant in AHS zones 12 to 1

D **Scotch heather** *Calluna vulgaris* 'Dark Beauty'; 8 to 10 in. tall and 12 to 18 in. wide; cold-hardy in USDA zones 5 to 7; heat-tolerant in AHS zones 7 to 1

E **Scotch moss** *Sagina subulata glabrata* 'Aurea'; 2 in. tall and 8 in. wide; cold-hardy in USDA zones 4 to 7; heat-tolerant in AHS zones 7 to 1

Turn the page to make your own "floating" steppers.

MAKE "FLOATING" STEPPERS

This unique stepping stone path *looks* difficult to make but is actually pretty simple. I'll give you all the details you need to build it. Take a good look at the photo of the pond during construction and the illustration at right to see how it all goes together. With modifications, you can build a pedestal (or two) that fits the size and shape of your own pond or stream. There's a list of what you'll need from the hardware and pond supply store in the "Materials & tools" list below. These supplies will help you build one stepper in a 24-inch-deep pond. You'll notice in the "after" photo that it looks like there are three "floating" steppers. But the two outer ones actually sit on solid ground. The water there is only a few inches deep.

To make the steppers comfortable to walk on, place them so the distance to the center of each stone is about the same as your natural stride. To find your stride, walk a few feet in sand or with wet shoes on a sidewalk. Then measure several of the steps from left heel to right heel, average them, and you have your stride measurement.

FROM THE BOTTOM UP Once you've dug the pond but before you put in the liner, make sure the ground is level where the pedestal base will go. Check it with a carpenter's level and use sand to fill in, if necessary. Measure the width and depth of your pond to determine how much pond underlayment and liner you'll need. (Be sure to include a little extra!)

Next, lay down the underlayment along the bottom of the pond. This feltlike fabric doesn't stretch and protects the pond liner from punctures. Cover the underlayment with pond liner. You can see the layers clearly in the illustration at right. Make sure to get pond liner, not roofing rubber. They look similar but the rubber used for pond liners is safe for plants and fish.

MAKE A BASE Bring the liner over the pond edge and secure it with stones. Now you're ready to pour the concrete base for the pedestal. To make a form, cut four 16-inch lengths of 2x4 and nail them together at the corners. Set the frame on the liner. Mix up the concrete and fill the form halfway. Add a piece of hardware cloth for strength and finish filling the form with concrete. Level off the top and let the base dry according to directions on the bag. This can take one to several days, depending on the weather.

STACK 'EM UP Once the concrete is dry, remove the form and spread mortar on top of the base. Set the first two concrete blocks on the mortar and check them with a carpenter's level. Turn the next set of blocks 90 degrees and stack them on the bottom set without mortar. Their weight will hold them in place. Add another layer of mortar on the top two blocks, and cap them with your stepping stone.

Apply liquid pond liner (available at the pond supply stores) to the pedestal and base. Bare concrete makes water too alkaline for fish and plants. Plus, liquid liner is black, so it's harder to see under water, adding to the illusion of "floating" steppers.

MORTAR MATTERS In Oregon, Darcy doesn't have to worry much about freezing temperatures. But if you live where your pond will freeze in the winter, pressure from ice can damage the mortar so that it needs to be replaced every three to five years. There are a couple of things you can do to prolong the life of the mortar. Both will help keep ice from forming directly beneath the stepper and weakening the mortared joint.

First, make sure the pedestal is at least 12 inches tall from the concrete base to the mortared joint just below the stepping stone. (Don't get carried away, though — a pedestal that's too tall is more likely to tip.) Second, in late fall, before a hard freeze, drain some of the water from the pond to keep the water line below the upper mortared joint.

When all the work is done on your stepping stone pedestal and pond, you can fill it with water and enjoy the benefits of a water garden from every point of view. □

— Sherri Ribbey

PHOTO: Darcy Daniels (pond under construction)
DESIGN: Darcy Daniels, Bloomtown Garden Design

MATERIALS & TOOLS

Here's what you need to make one floating stepper. Modify sizes and amounts for larger or smaller ponds.

Underlayment and 45-ml. pond liner (measure to fit your pond)
- 4   8x8x16 in. concrete blocks for each stepper
- 1   8-ft.-long 2x4
- 1   18-in.-square stone stepper at least 3 to 4 in. thick
- 1   bag of concrete mix
- 1   bag of mortar mix
- ¼-in. hardware cloth
- Liquid pond liner
- Nails

Shovel, carpenter's level, ruler, hammer, trowel for mortar, tub and hoe for mixing concrete, gloves

A fountain made from a broken stone adds the element of sound.

This stone is sitting on solid ground.

Choose stone that's native to your area for a natural look.

Pond under construction

"FLOATING" STEPPING STONES

Not every stepper needs a pedestal. This one is sitting on a "shelf" near the edge.

Stepper

Mortar

Paint the blocks with liquid liner to prevent water quality problems.

Keep water level below the upper mortared joint in winter to prolong the life of your stepper.

Existing soil

Mortar

Concrete base reinforced with hardware cloth

Concrete blocks

Pond depth — 24 inches

45-ml. pond liner

Underlayment

Sand

BEFORE & AFTER | FRONT YARD

Sunny Side of the Street

When Anne Warburton first moved into her southern California home, there was just the island bed and foundation planting you see in the before photo. It didn't take her long to determine that things would have to change — there wasn't nearly enough room to garden! By adding a big, beautiful border out by the street in the after photo, she had plenty of space for plants and a garden that showed off her house at the same time.

FRONT YARD FIRSTS The first thing to consider with a front yard garden is the size of the beds in proportion to the house. Generally, the bigger the home, the bigger the border needs to be to balance it out. This home is just one story but it's quite long and has a fairly narrow front yard. The foundation planting can't be enlarged because of the sidewalk that runs along the front. That leaves the rest of the yard — but where? Out by the street, of course. Without a public sidewalk and parking strip, there's no barrier between traffic and the house. This big border is a great way to frame the house and provide a bit of a buffer from the traffic going by.

STYLE MATTERS When you have a garden in front, its style should complement the look of the house. After all, the house is a backdrop for the garden and you want the whole yard to have a cohesive feel.

A wide border full of low-growing plants reflects the silhouette of this house. Short plants make it easier to see the house from the street and visitors can easily find the front door. From inside, you can enjoy the view of the garden and see what's going on in the neighborhood at the same time. And the border is wide enough to easily incorporate the old island bed into it, instead of having to re-sod that area. In fact, absorbing the island into the border created a nice curve that sweeps up the sidewalk to the front door.

Don't avoid height completely, though. Ornaments, such as the obelisk, arbor and bee skep, help bridge the gap visually between the ground and the house. These taller structures aren't too bulky, so they don't overwhelm the rest of the garden or block the view from the window. If you have a two-story house, you may need more trees, shrubs or tall perennials to balance out the additional height of the house.

The edging of small stones next to the street is a nice finishing touch and echoes the larger stones in the border. Anne finds them whenever she digs a planting hole and adds them to the edge. If you'd like the same look but don't have rocky soil, a few bags of river rock should do the trick.

PAVEMENT PLANTS Gardening next to pavement can be a challenge, whether it's a street, driveway or sidewalk. Paved areas radiate extra heat, which dries out both plants and soil. Plus, pedestrians or their pets can cause damage. These are tough spots, but you can still garden there. Choose drought-tolerant and hardy plants for your region. (Check out our Top Picks story on p. 86 for plants that thrive on less water.) Save more sensitive plants for the side of the garden closer to the house and the garden hose.

Once you have a plan, it's time to think about plants. On the next page you'll find out how to grow these plants even in tough growing conditions.

PHOTO: Courtesy of Anne Warburton (before)

Add height to the garden with structures, such as this obelisk.

Unwanted pebbles from the soil make an easy-care edging. Brush any stray rocks back in line with a broom.

Turn the page to learn how to grow this garden.

CURB-WORTHY PLANTS

When you think of sunny southern California, which is USDA zone 9, you'd assume it would have perfect conditions for gardening, right? Well, sort of. Actually, wind, heat and hardpan soil sometimes make gardening there difficult. But hard work, some low-growing plants and a good layer of mulch can take care of these difficulties. Check out "Three garden challenges" below to find out how to deal with these situations.

Want a colorful and welcoming border like the one on p. 125? Take a look at the plan below. And if you live where temperatures fall below zero, I've listed some cold-hardy alternatives below right.

Every area has its challenges but with a little hard work and know-how, you can turn any front yard into a garden that welcomes visitors and provides you with a great view at the same time. □

— Sherri Ribbey

Three garden challenges

WIND Hot, dry winds can devastate any garden. Try growing dwarf varieties and low-growing plants that won't get blown over by the wind.

New transplants can dry out quickly, too. Give them shelter with some row cover or snow fencing to block the wind until they get established.

HEAT Keep soil cool with organic matter and mulch.

Compost is an easy way to add organic matter. The rough texture creates spaces that allow oxygen to circulate, keeping soil cooler. It also prevents a heat-reflecting hard crust from forming.

A 3- to 4-in. layer of organic mulch also cools soil temperature and helps retain moisture.

HARDPAN Have you ever run into a hard, almost impenetrable layer of soil while digging in your garden? You've found hardpan, soil so dense it's impervious to roots and water. Break through thin layers with a garden fork. If that's not possible, work compost and top soil into the layer above the hardpan. Then grow shallow-rooted plants like the ones found in the plan.

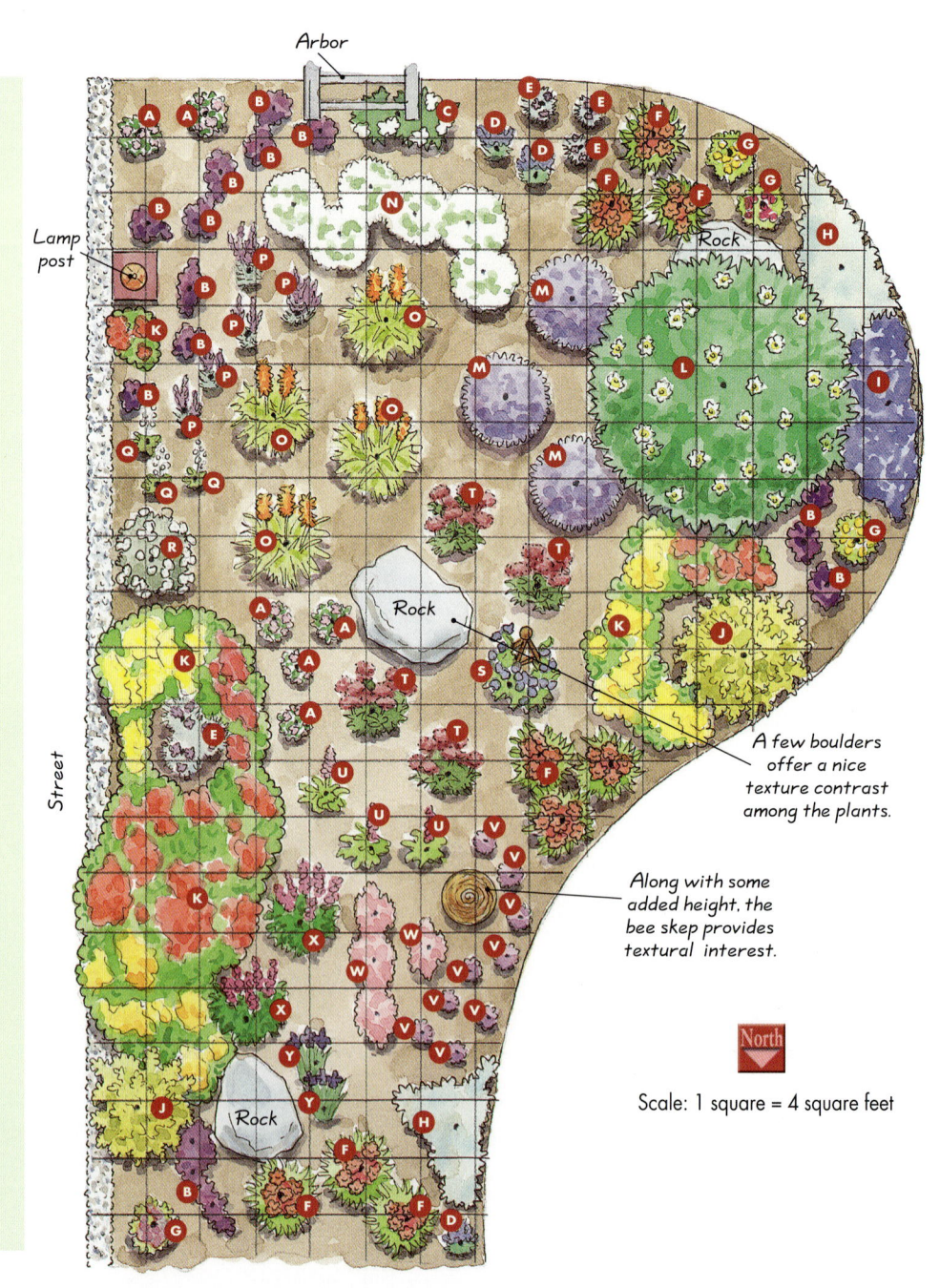

A few boulders offer a nice texture contrast among the plants.

Along with some added height, the bee skep provides textural interest.

Scale: 1 square = 4 square feet

HEAT-LOVING FRONT ENTRY GARDEN

Code	Plant Name	No. to Plant	Blooms	Type	Cold/Heat Zones	Height/Width
A	Pacific chrysanthemum *Ajania pacifica* 'Pink Ice'	6	Pink; fall	Perennial	5-9/9-1	1-2 ft./1-3 ft.
B	Verbena *Verbena* 'Balazplum' (Aztec™ Plum Magic)	15	Violet; summer	Annual	annual/12-1	8-10 in./12-18 in.
C	Climbing rose *Rosa* 'Climbing Iceberg'	1	White; spring to summer	Shrub	5-9/9-1	8-10 ft./6 ft.
D	*Beardtongue *Penstemon heterophyllus*	3	Violet; early summer	Perennial	7-10/12-1	20 in./18 in.
E	*Society garlic *Tulbaghia violacea* 'Silver Lace'	6	Violet; summer	Perennial	7-10/12-7	24 in./15 in.
F	Daylily *Hemerocallis* 'Persian Market'	9	Salmon; early summer	Perennial	3-9/9-1	27 in./18-24 in.
G	*Persian buttercup *Ranunculus asiaticus* Tecolote hybrids	4	Mix; spring	Tuber	8-10/12-1	12-30 in./24 in
H	Lamb's ear *Stachys byzantina*	2	Violet	Perennial	4-8/8-1	15 in./spreading
I	*Dampiera *Dampiera diversifolia*	1	Violet; summer	Tender perennial	10-12/12-1	6 in./spreading
J	Licorice plant *Helichrysum petiolare* 'Limelight'	2	N/A	Tender perennial	9-11/12-1	12-18 in./spreading
K	Nasturtium *Tropaeolum majus* Whirlybird mix	1 pkg.	Mix; summer	Annual	annual/12-1	14-16 in./24 in.
L	*Magnolia *Magnolia grandiflora* 'Little Gem'	1	White; summer	Tree	7-9/9-3	15-25 ft./10-15 ft.
M	Lavender *Lavandula angustifolia* 'Hidcote'	3	Violet; summer	Perennial	5-9/12-7	18 in./24 in.
N	Feverfew *Tanacetum parthenium*	6	White; summer	Perennial	5-10/7-3	2-3 ft./2-3 ft.
O	Red-hot poker *Kniphofia* 'Bee's Sunset'	4	Red to orange; summer	Perennial	5-9/9-1	4 ft./3 ft.
P	Toadflax *Linaria purpurea*	5	Violet; summer	Perennial	5-9/9-1	18-36 in./6-12 in.
Q	*Saxifrage *Saxifraga umbrosa*	3	White; summer	Perennial	5-8/12-1	12 in./12 in.
R	*Silver bush morning glory *Convolvulus cneorum*	1	White; spring to fall	Shrub	8-10/12-8	2-3 ft./2-3 ft.
S	Morning glory *Ipomoea indica*	1	Blue; summer	Annual vine	annual/12-1	15-30 ft.
T	Joe-Pye weed *Eupatorium dubium* 'Little Joe'	4	Mauve; summer to fall	Perennial	4-8/10-3	3-4 ft./2-3 ft.
U	Foxglove *Digitalis purpurea* Excelsior Group	3	Mix; summer	Biennial	4-8/8-1	3-5 ft./1-2 ft.
V	Pincushion flower *Scabiosa* 'Butterfly Blue'	9	Violet; summer to fall	Perennial	5-9/8-1	12-15 in./12-15 in.
W	Rose yarrow *Achillea millefolium rosea*	4	Soft pink; summer	Perennial	3-9/9-1	24 in./24 in.
X	*Salvia *Salvia chiapensis*	2	Pink; summer	Tender perennial	8-10/11-8	18-24 in./24-36 in.
Y	Siberian iris *Iris sibirica* 'Caesar's Brother'	2	Deep violet; spring	Perennial	4-9/9-1	40 in./18-24 in.

* Cold-hardy replacement listed below

COLD-HARDY ALTERNATIVES

CHOICES ARE GOOD Not everyone can grow all of the plants in the original garden. Below, I've included cold-hardy alternatives that look similar to the original plant. And even though the saxifrage is technically cold-hardy to USDA zone 5, it may not make it through severe, open winters.

There are a lot of magnolia cultivars out there. But 'Butterflies' blooms a little later than other species, so it's not as likely to lose its flower buds to a late frost. Don't worry about the rest of the plants on the list. They're tough enough to make it through cold winters without any pampering.

Code	Plant Name	No. to Plant	Blooms	Type	Cold/Heat Zones	Height/Width
D	Rough blazing star *Liatris aspera*	3	Violet; summer	Perennial	3-8/9-1	24-36 in./12-15 in.
E	Blue fescue *Festuca glauca* 'Elijah Blue'	6	Tan; summer	Perennial	4-8/8-1	10-12 in./6-10 in.
G	Pink *Dianthus* 'Helen'	8	Salmon; spring	Perennial	5-8/9-1	6-12 in./6-12 in.
I	Bugleweed *Ajuga reptans* 'Valfredda' (Chocolate Chip)	6	Blue; spring	Perennial	4-9/9-1	2-3 in./spreading
L	Magnolia *Magnolia* 'Butterflies'	1	Yellow; spring	Tree	5-9/9-1	15-20 ft./10-15 ft.
Q	German statice *Goniolimon tataricum*	3	White; summer	Perennial	3-9/12-1	12-18 in./12 in.
R	Globe thistle *Echinops sphaerocephalus* 'Arctic Glow'	1	White; summer	Perennial	3-9/9-1	30-36 in./6-18 in.
X	Salvia *Salvia nemorosa* 'Sensation Rose'	4	Pink; early summer	Perennial	4-9/9-4	12 in./12 in.

BEFORE & AFTER | FRONT YARD

Keep the Color Coming!

You know how those small home-improvement jobs can turn into big projects. Joyce Baumgardener set out to update her kitchen, but before it was finished, the outside of her Michigan home, in the "before" photo, got spiffed up, too. And that meant some new plantings were definitely in order.

UPDATED STYLE Traditional architecture like this is the perfect backdrop for a cottage garden. A formal planting would look at home, too. But this gardener wanted lots of flowers and a more casual, cottage-garden design. Choosing a garden style to match your home helps the house and landscape look unified.

Just because you want the kind of garden that's been popular for generations doesn't mean you have to choose the same plants Grandma would have. The garden here has the feel of a classic cottage garden, but with a modern twist: There are plenty of flowers along with that cottage-garden sense of exuberant growth. But this garden is tidier than traditional cottage gardens and doesn't have as many different plants.

COLOR, COLOR, COLOR You can't miss the color in this beautiful flower-filled border. But how do you get lots of color and still have a garden that looks pulled together? Choose a palette of colors and stick to it. Take a look at the large "after" photo and you'll see a lot of purple, pink and yellow flowers. Color is often a matter of personal preference, so you won't find anything blooming in red-orange, peach or orange in this garden. But if you think this color palette is limiting, think again. Look at all the different shades of pink and yellow — it's still a very bright, colorful effect.

Since an entry garden is the first thing visitors see as they approach the house, you want it looking great all the time. A garden with a color scheme that complements the house helps both look good. Here, bright yellow coreopsis and yellow stonecrop flowers along the garden's edge echo shades of the house color, while pale pink and purple provide added interest. If the house were deep rust-red with white trim, more pink and even a few orange flowers would be in order to reflect the color of the house.

Reblooming plants, such as the rose, daylily and coreopsis here, do an excellent job at providing color all season. But once-blooming varieties, such as allium, hydrangea, astilbe and butterfly bush, are still well worth growing. Did you know that you can keep those flowers showy, even when they're spent? Get some floral spray paint at your local hobby store. When the flowers fade, spray paint the seedheads. The "blooms" look so nice that sometimes even the butterflies are fooled!

INSTANT GRATIFICATION Joyce admits that she's not a patient person — she wants everything gorgeous right now. So how do you hurry a garden? Many easy-to-find perennials are popular for a reason. They may not be glamorous and exotic, but they're hardy, tolerate a variety of growing conditions and bloom all season. With just minimal care, plants such as coreopsis, daylily, stonecrop and pinks will reward you by looking like a million bucks, even the first season. And when you're shopping for perennials, buy the largest plants you can afford. You'll get a bigger bang for your buck right away.

Even with these hard-working plants, it takes some planning to have something blooming all the time. I'll tell you more about the layering technique that keeps this garden going strong on the next page.

(1) Shapely curves tie the house and garden together. The curved garden beds echo the arches over the front door.

Botanical Names

Allium
Allium spp.
Astilbe
Astilbe spp.
Butterfly bush
Buddleja spp.
Coreopsis
Coreopsis spp.
Hydrangea
Hydrangea spp.
Rose
Rosa spp.
Yellow stonecrop
Sedum kamtschaticum

Before

Turn the page for more colorful flowers

www.GardenGateMagazine.com the YEAR IN GARDENING 129

LAYER THE COLOR

Botanical Names

Baby's breath
 Gypsophila paniculata
Crocus *Crocus* spp.
Gaura *Gaura lindheimeri*
Geranium
 Pelargonium hybrids
Tulip *Tulipa* spp.

Joyce has a garden that's always filled with color, from the front of the border to the tallest plant in the center. This technique of layering, planning beds so plants bloom from smallest to the tallest, is just good garden design.

LAYERS OF FLOWERS In many cases, tall perennials bloom later because it takes them longer to grow to maturity. Use this natural progression to your advantage by arranging plants that bloom at the front, middle and back of the border. Take a close look at the plan at right and you'll notice large groups of flowering plants at each level, or layer. They aren't placed in stairstep fashion but in staggered groupings to repeat color and texture throughout the garden.

In this garden, crocus and early tulips start things off in spring at the front of the border. When they fade, pinks and iris draw your eye further up. Later, the coreopsis and soon-to-bloom daylilies in photo 2 brighten up the center of the garden like icing on a cake. Reblooming varieties at each level keep the color going from spring to fall. And annuals tucked in here and there provide season-long color. Find out about another great role for annuals in the garden in "Repeat yourself" below.

THE BIGGER THE BETTER A large two-story house like this needs a big garden in front to balance it out. There are many theories on how large to make a garden bed in relation to the house but there isn't one simple answer. Here, the entry walk and beds near the house are wider now than they were originally, which really helps. Added depth in front is just one way you can integrate house and landscape. There are other ways to balance out a large house, too; it isn't just about the size of the bed. A planting full of wispy or fine-textured plants, such as gaura or baby's breath, just wouldn't have the visual "weight" to pull this off. The large, dense planting that you see here really anchors the house to the landscape. Taller plants, such as the rose and hydrangea, or drifts of smaller plants, such as the stonecrop, are easier to see from a distance. That way, this colorful bed has a big impact all season long, even from across the street. ◻

— *Sherri Ribbey*

(2) Repeat colors to create harmony. The yellow coreopsis and white gooseneck loosestrife help draw the house and garden together.

Repeat yourself

A big garden has a lot of opportunities but it presents challenges, too. For example, how do you keep it all looking coordinated? Staying with a color scheme through the whole yard, whether it's plants or hardscaping, really helps. In this garden, the house trim, fencing and furniture are all painted white. When it comes to plants, bright pink geraniums do the job. These two showy containers flank the gate. Throughout the garden you'll see other containers and bedded-out geraniums, all of the same variety. So whether you're walking to the front door or strolling across the back patio, you'll see the familiar pink and white.

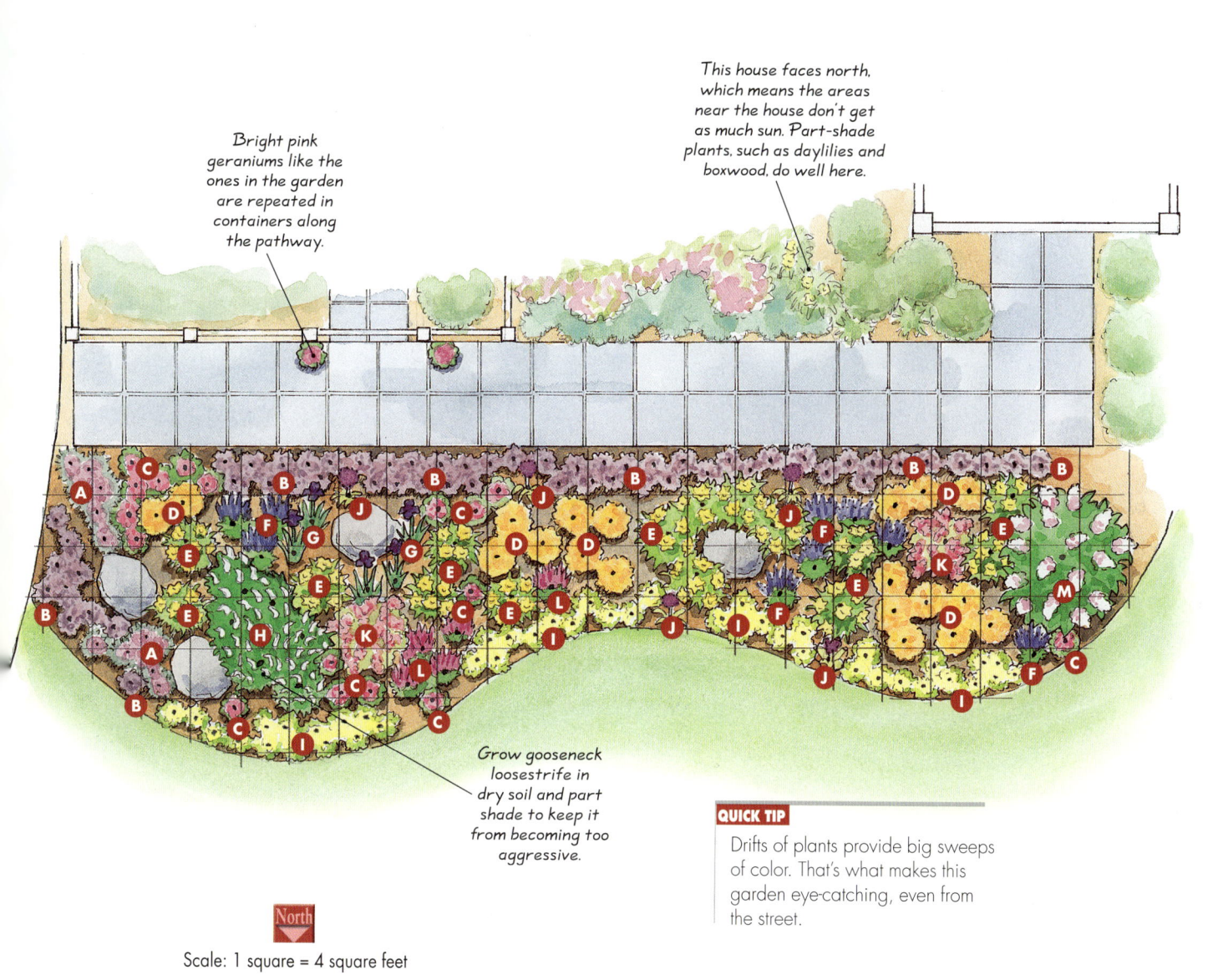

Bright pink geraniums like the ones in the garden are repeated in containers along the pathway.

This house faces north, which means the areas near the house don't get as much sun. Part-shade plants, such as daylilies and boxwood, do well here.

Grow gooseneck loosestrife in dry soil and part shade to keep it from becoming too aggressive.

QUICK TIP
Drifts of plants provide big sweeps of color. That's what makes this garden eye-catching, even from the street.

North

Scale: 1 square = 4 square feet

THE GARDEN'S PALETTE

Code	Plant Name	No. to Plant	Blooms	Type	Cold/Heat Zones	Height/Width
A	**Pinks** *Dianthus* 'Horatio'	13	Maroon and white; spring	Perennial	4-8/9-1	6-12 in./12-24 in.
B	**Red stonecrop** *Sedum spurium* 'Voodoo'	57	Rose red; summer	Perennial	3-8/9-1	2-6 in./12-18 in.
C	**Geranium** *Pelargonium* 'Strawberry Sizzle'	17	Bright pink; spring to fall	Annual	Annual/12-1	12-14 in./12-14 in.
D	**Coreopsis** *Coreopsis grandiflora* 'Sunray'	19	Yellow with maroon eye; spring to fall	Perennial	4-9/9-1	18-24 in./12-18 in.
E	**Daylily** *Hemerocallis* 'Buttered Popcorn'	15	Yellow; late spring to fall	Perennial	3-9/9-1	32 in./18-24 in.
F	**Salvia** *Salvia xsylvestris* May Night ('Mainacht')	9	Violet; spring	Perennial	4-8/9-4	18-24 in./12-18 in.
G	**Iris** *Iris* 'Badlands'	5	Deep violet; spring	Perennial	4-9/9-1	38 in./8-10 in.
H	**Gooseneck loosestrife** *Lysimachia clethroides*	6	White; late spring	Perennial	3-8/8-1	2-3 ft./2-4 ft.
I	**Yellow stonecrop** *Sedum kamtschaticum*	44	Yellow; summer	Perennial	3-9/9-1	4-6 in./6-15 in.
J	**Star of Persia** *Allium schubertii*	5	Rose; late spring	Perennial	5-8/8-4	12-24 in./15 in.
K	**Rose** *Rosa* 'The Fairy'	2	Double pink; spring to fall	Perennial	5-9/9-1	3 ft./3 ft.
L	**Speedwell** *Veronica spicata* Red Fox ('Rotfuchs')	5	Pink; spring to fall	Perennial	3-8/8-1	12-18 in./12-18 in.
M	**Hydrangea** *Hydrangea paniculata* Pink Diamond ('Interhydia')	1	Pink; summer	Shrub	3-8/8-1	6 ft./6 ft.

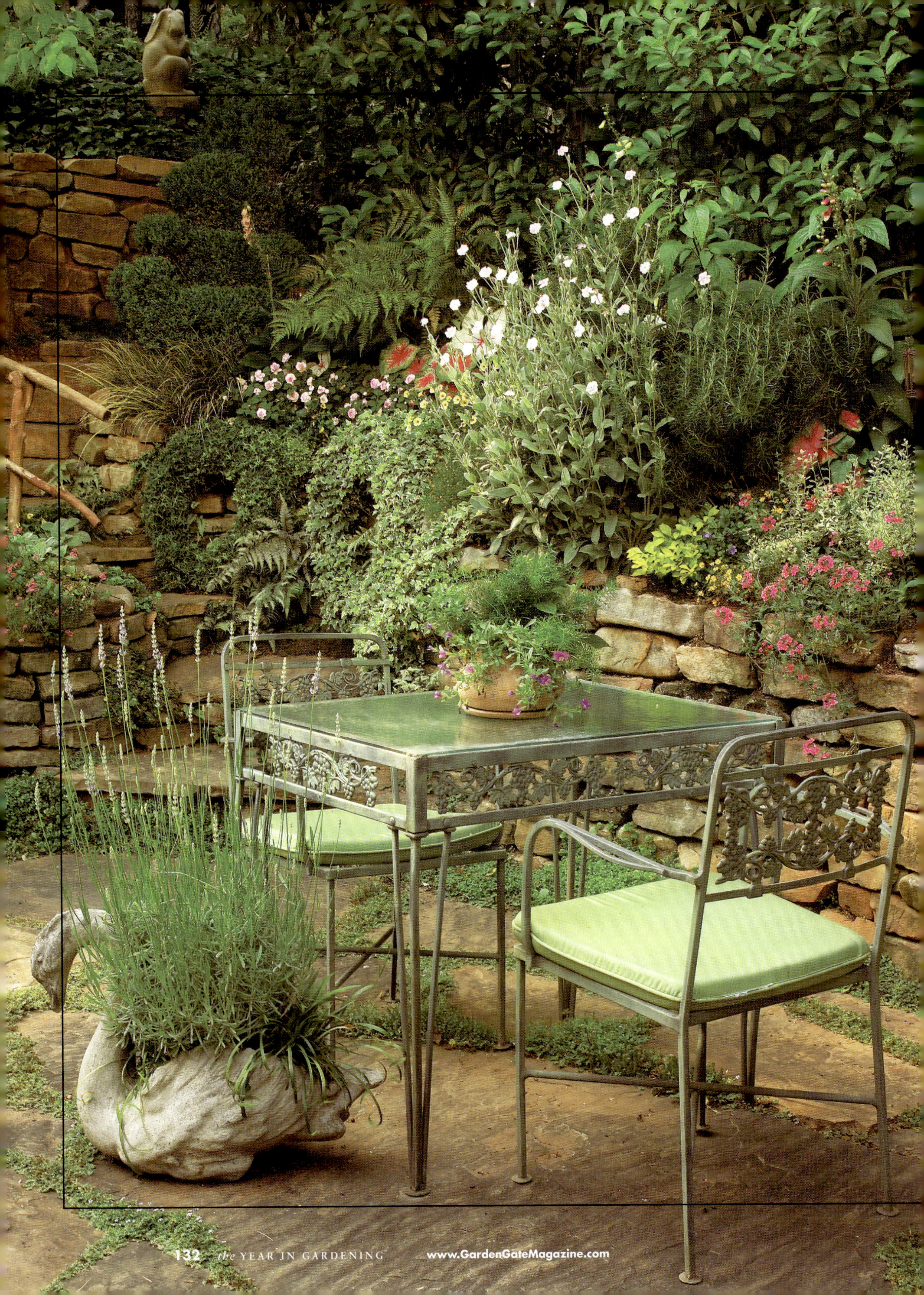

garden design
great *ideas* you can use!

CREATE A GORGEOUS GARDEN...LET US HELP! We'll give you solid design ideas for creating a beautiful yard, whether you want to transform your patio into a private getaway, dress up a small entry or tackle your entire back yard. Plus we'll show you how to combine plants like a pro, share tips for for making the color last and offer time- and money-saving ideas we can all use.

Restful Retreat	134	Vegetable Medley	176
Quick & Easy Shade Border	140	Combine Bulbs and Perennials Like a Pro	180
Small and Sensational	142	Fall Splendor	182
Best of Both Worlds	148	Bring on the Blue	186
Inviting Spaces	154	Color That Won't Quit	190
Small-Space Secrets	158	Nine Tips for Season-Long Color	196
Design on a Budget	160	Winter Wonders	198
Think Big	164	Did You Know	200
Create Great Island Beds	170		

DESIGN | ALL AROUND THE YARD

Carve out a getaway, even in a small space.

Restful Retreat

Have you ever walked into a garden and immediately felt like you'd left the world behind? This is that kind of garden. Even though it's situated on a small lot, you completely forget about the real world. Dense plantings do a great job of screening the view and sound.

See the bench in this garden? Go ahead, take a seat. Tom Vetter is the owner of this Oregon garden, and I'm sure he won't mind. It's nice, isn't it? Look at all the relaxing textures of green and gold foliage. There aren't many flowers, but that lets you take your time to examine and appreciate the ones that are there, like the spiky purple monkshood and the mound of bright pink geranium. No need to hurry when there are just a few perfectly grown prime specimens among the lush foliage. If you want to learn how you can create your own garden like this one, turn the page and we'll get started on a tour.

Botanical Names

Geranium
Geranium spp.
Monkshood
Aconitum spp.

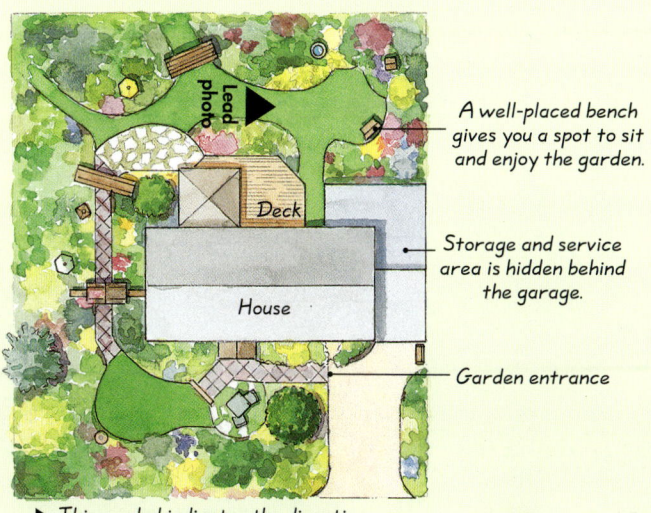

A well-placed bench gives you a spot to sit and enjoy the garden.

Storage and service area is hidden behind the garage.

Garden entrance

▶ This symbol indicates the direction the photo was taken in the garden.

DESIGN PERFECTION

Botanical Names

Hakonechloa
Hakonechloa macra
Honeysuckle
Lonicera spp.
Hosta
Hosta hybrid
Ligularia
Ligularia spp.
New Zealand flax
Phormium hybrid

Let's begin our tour in front. The first thing you'll notice is that this garden is packed with plants. However, it's not haphazard, looking like you hit a great plant sale and bought the last one of everything. It's a carefully crafted mix of conifers, deciduous trees and shrubs, as well as lots of perennials and a few annuals. But let's not get ahead of ourselves. I'll talk more about combining plants later. For now, let's learn more about design tips.

MAKE A FOCAL POINT As you walk up the driveway and step onto the sidewalk, you'll spot the small seating area in photo 2. It's right outside the front door. It might seem odd to have a table and chairs in the front garden, but it breaks up the masses of plants. And since the front yard is very sheltered, why not sit there and enjoy the space? Dense plantings like these create lots of private areas so you can use your entire yard without being on public view. You don't have to be relegated to just the back. In fact, did you notice how well the driveway and parking area have been screened off from this area? Look closely in photo 2 and you can just see the top of a car behind the shrubs.

(2) Create privacy, even in your front yard, with dense plantings to screen the street and driveway. A small tree near this table and chairs makes a natural canopy to complete the feeling of enclosure.

The table and chairs also create a wonderful focal point, no matter what season it is. If you don't want a seating area, try a sculpture or even a large container with or without plants. But in this front garden, a small seating area seems to say, "Come on in and visit awhile."

Notice how some of the plants spill out of the beds and creep under the table? If you want to add a similar casual look to your flagstone patio, tuck a few plants between the stones. And to blend furniture or other structures into their surroundings better, paint them a dark shadowy color like this and they won't distract from your plantings.

STICK TO A COLOR SCHEME As you look around, you'll notice the plantings in the front garden focus on shades of gold and yellow. Why? They add a warm, inviting feel as you enter the garden. But the scheme isn't too strict — there are a few small spots of other colors, such as the burgundy New Zealand flax in the terra-cotta container.

Photo 3 shows a small portion of the border in the back yard. Even here there are bright spots of gold. However, there are more plants with burgundy

(3) Who needs lots of flowers? Bold color and texture contrasts keep this garden interesting.

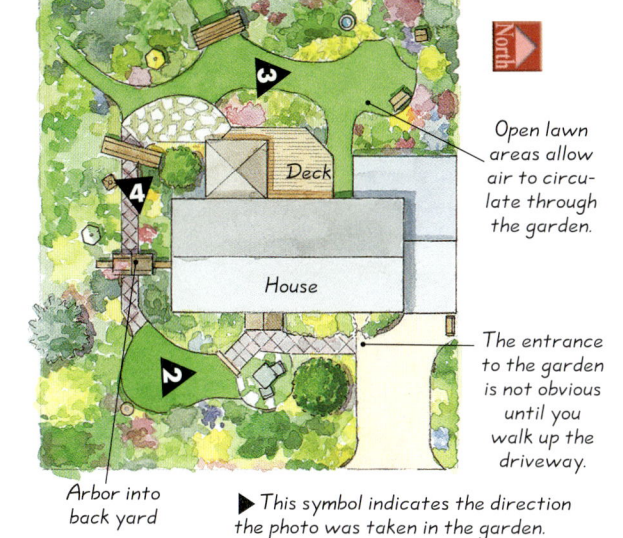

Open lawn areas allow air to circulate through the garden.

The entrance to the garden is not obvious until you walk up the driveway.

Arbor into back yard

▶ This symbol indicates the direction the photo was taken in the garden.

foliage in this part of the garden. Colorful foliage, such as golden hakonechloa grass and variegated hosta, take the place of flowers. That means there's very little deadheading for you to do. And you don't have to worry about the sequence of flowers: The foliage is there, and stays the same most of the growing season.

But every garden needs flowers. You can have both if you plant flowering shrubs and perennials that have flowers and great foliage. Just check out the ligularia in the center of the photo, behind the birdbath. It has bold foliage with a hint of burgundy *and* tall spikes of golden yellow flowers.

BACK YARD IDEAS Lots of gardens make a transition from front to back with nothing more exciting than a patch of lawn. Not this garden. It's a much more interesting journey along a patterned brick path that goes through not just one, but two dramatic arbors. You see one of them in photo 4. Arbors are like doorways in a garden. Granted, they're usually open doors, but an arbor lets you change the feel of the separate areas, just like rooms inside your house.

As long as it slows, or even stops, your eye as you travel forward, any arbor helps create a transition. It doesn't need to be custom made, or even fancy, but it should be in scale with the surroundings. A small, delicate-looking arbor in a large garden just doesn't look right. And one from massive timbers would look out of place in a small formal garden. But you can help any arbor fit in your garden better by placing it in a bed of shrubs or large perennials. And arbors are meant to hold vines like this fragrant honeysuckle, which helps them blend into their surroundings even better.

Speaking of plants, there are some unique specimens in this garden. Occasionally these plants can be temperamental, or need a bit of extra protection from hot sun or strong rain. Here, a patio umbrella sometimes comes to the rescue. Learn more about using this plant-saving, as well as ornamental, tip in "Protect delicates," below.

Plants really are what you notice first. And, they're planted in well-thought-out combinations, too. On the next pages I'll highlight some of the companions, and share tips about how to create beautiful combos in your own garden.

(4) Dramatic transitions, like this arbor, make you feel you're entering into a completely different garden.

Protect delicates

Transplanting on a hot day? Trying to preserve the rich colors of a flower a bit longer? Attempting to prevent scorched foliage during a hot spell? Any size umbrella can come in handy to shade a fragile plant or two. Stick the shaft into the soil or secure it in an umbrella stand. Just be careful that it doesn't blow over in windy weather and do more damage than good.

COMBINATIONS THAT SHOW OFF

Designing a garden is similar to cooking, except it's creating a visual recipe. While taste is not important in a garden design, color and texture are. You still start with a main ingredient, in this case a plant, and gradually add in more flavors. Just like cooking, a bit of guidance always helps create a great end result.

Looking at the finished product — in this case a beautiful garden like the one you've just seen — can seem overwhelming, or at best confusing. Where and how do you start? Let's take a look at some practical tips you'll need to know to make your own great combinations. Then we'll examine three from this garden. With each combo you'll find a list of plants, as well as a few design pointers on why it works.

First you'll want to find the right plant for the light conditions you have. There's no point putting sun plants in shade. They'll be floppy and probably won't bloom well. And the reverse means plants will scorch, or even dry up and die. Same with soil — a moisture-loving plant in sandy soil means you'll be watering all the time. Better to find something that tolerates dry conditions.

Almost every garden has several microclimates within it. These are areas that have different growing conditions from the rest of your garden. Think of that low spot where the first light frost knocks out the annuals long before the same plants wither in containers up on your deck. Both areas are microclimates you can use to your gardening advantage. As you learn where they are (and they can change as the garden matures) take advantage of them to grow special plants. Or try things there that may have a reputation for being temperamental in your zone.

Gardens are meant to be enjoyed. Tips like these will help you create a beautiful oasis where you can sit back and relax. I bet you'll feel as if you've stepped into a photo in a magazine! ◻

— *Jim Childs*

Golden touch

Bright greens and shades of gold that catch and reflect sunlight are especially effective in a shaded spot. This combo works because there are several shades of green and gold mixed together. And one or two variegated plants in a combination like this are often enough. Too many variegated leaves can make the combo look busy and cluttered.

A **Ostrich fern** *Matteuccia struthiopteris*
  4 to 5 ft. tall and 2 to 3 ft. wide; cold-hardy in USDA zones 2 to 8; heat-tolerant in AHS zones 8 to 1

B **Dogwood** *Cornus alba* Ivory Halo™ ('Bailhalo')
  4 to 6 ft. tall and wide; cold-hardy in USDA zones 3 to 7; heat-tolerant in AHS zones 7 to 1

C **Hosta** *Hosta* 'Wide Brim'
  18 to 22 in. tall and 30 to 36 in. wide; cold-hardy in USDA zones 3 to 9; heat-tolerant in AHS zones 9 to 1

D **Sword fern** *Nephrolepis cordifolia*
  24 to 32 in. tall and 3 to 5 ft. wide; cold-hardy in USDA zones 9 to 11; heat-tolerant in AHS zones 12 to 1

E **Spotted deadnettle** *Lamium maculatum* 'Aureum'
  8 in. tall and spreading; cold-hardy in USDA zones 4 to 8; heat-tolerant in AHS zones 8 to 1

Dramatic texture

Color is good, but it's the bold texture contrast that really makes this combination work. Large ligularia leaves set against the tiny leaves of a honeysuckle energize this group. But color plays a role, too. Small bright-green barrenwort, pale honeysuckle and white-edged dogwood leaves visually jump forward. The dark ligularia recedes into the background, adding depth to this combination. That's a good design technique to give an illusion of more size in a tight space.

A Dogwood *Cornus alba* Ivory Halo™ ('Bailhalo')
4 to 6 ft. tall and wide; cold-hardy in USDA zones 3 to 7; heat-tolerant in AHS zones 7 to 1

B Ligularia *Ligularia dentata* 'Othello'
3 ft. tall and wide; cold-hardy in USDA zones 4 to 8; heat-tolerant in AHS zones 8 to 1

C Barrenwort *Epimedium xversicolor* 'Sulphureum'
12 in. tall and spreading; cold-hardy in USDA zones 5 to 9; heat-tolerant in AHS zones 9 to 1

D Boxleaf honeysuckle *Lonicera nitida*
8 ft. tall and 6 ft. wide; cold-hardy in USDA zones 7 to 9; heat-tolerant in AHS zones 9 to 1

Bountiful burgundy

Combinations of deep tones, like these rich burgundies, can look dark and dreary. But toss in a touch of light green or gold and they will brighten up just fine. Add a few bold, contrasting shapes, such as the spiky New Zealand flax and large-leafed catalpa, and this combination is anything but depressing.

A Barberry *Berberis thunbergii atropurpurea*
3 to 4 ft. tall and wide; cold-hardy in USDA zones 5 to 8; heat-tolerant in AHS zones 8 to 1

B New Zealand flax *Phormium tenax*
1 to 6 ft. tall and 1 to 3 ft. wide; cold-hardy in USDA zones 7 to 11; heat-tolerant in AHS zones 11 to 1

C Catalpa *Catalpa bignonioides* 'Aureum'
30 ft. tall and wide; cold-hardy in USDA zones 5 to 9; heat-tolerant in AHS zones 9 to 1

D Northern sea oats *Chasmanthium latifolium*
2 to 5 ft. tall and 1 to 3 ft. wide; cold-hardy in USDA zones 3 to 8; heat-tolerant in AHS zones 8 to 1

E Mourning widow geranium *Geranium phaeum*
24 to 30 in. tall and 24 to 28 in. wide; cold-hardy in USDA zones 4 to 7; heat-tolerant in AHS zones 7 to 1

F Lady's mantle *Alchemilla mollis*
18 to 24 in. tall and 24 to 30 in. wide; cold-hardy in USDA zones 4 to 7; heat-tolerant in AHS zones 7 to 1

DESIGN | ALL AROUND THE YARD

6 tips every shade gardener can use

Quick & Easy Shade Border

Loads of bright-colored flowering annuals and perennials. That's what you can grow in a full-sun garden. But what if your garden is part or even full shade? Well, believe it or not, a shade garden can be just as beautiful as a sunny one and often needs much less care!

With lower sunlight for photosynthesis, plants grow slower in shade than in sun. And that can mean you don't have as much work to do. First of all, they need less fertilizer and water, and you won't have to deadhead or divide plants as often. Weed seeds aren't as likely to sprout in shade, so there are fewer weeds to deal with, as well.

Sheltered from harsh sun, part-shade flowers last longer without fading, and foliage isn't as likely to scorch, either. Even dealing with pests is less time-consuming in a shady situation. With the exception of slugs and snails, there are fewer plant-hungry insects in shady areas.

With all the work and time you'll save in your garden, you'll be able to appreciate the best thing about shade: It's perfect for a relaxing seating area. So pull up a chair, put your feet up and take a break. Then check out my six tips below for making shade gardening even easier. □

— *Deborah Gruca*

Botanical Names

Bird's nest spruce
  Picea abies 'Nidiformis'
Hosta *Hosta* spp.
Periwinkle *Vinca minor*
Sedum *Sedum* spp.
Yellow corydalis
  Corydalis lutea

WEB extra
Read our *tips* for a quick and easy berm.

1 TO GARDEN IN TOUGH AREAS where tree roots compete for moisture, plant in containers. Sink plastic pots in the ground between the roots or use tall pots set on the ground (or on a wall, as here) to add height.

2 BUILD TERRACED, RAISED OR BERMED BEDS to make plants more visible and to make weeding a breeze. Make sure the area of the bed covers no more than a third of the tree's roots so you don't harm the tree. Find out an easy way to make a bermed bed in our Web extra.

3 GROW DROUGHT-TOLERANT GROUND COVERS, such as this yellow corydalis, in areas where rain is blocked. Save money and buy corydalis as small plants — they reseed and spread quickly. Periwinkle and some sedums also work well in dry shade.

4 PLANT VARIEGATED HOSTAS and other variegated or light-colored foliage plants to brighten shade. Unlike flowers that bloom and then fade, they'll be colorful all season. Instead of a scatter-shot placement, create "rivers" of color flowing through your bed to carry your eye along.

5 FOR A FAST FILL-IN, buy larger anchor plants, such as this bird's nest spruce. Place them closer together than normal, since they'll grow slower in shade.

6 IN FALL, TUCK IN SPRING BULBS or perennials to extend the season. The bulbs will provide early season color, and early plants will put on the most growth before trees leaf out in spring. By the time the bulb foliage fades, the other plants will be tall enough to hide it.

GOT SHADE?

There are different degrees of shade. And sometimes it's hard to tell if your particular spot is dappled, part or full shade. To find out exactly how much light your garden gets, place a sunlight calculator in the bed on a sunny day. The SunCalc® Sunlight Calculator measures the amount of light falling on the area over a 12-hour period and helps you choose plants that'll thrive there. When I tried this in my garden, I found you need to set the calculator straight up and down in a pot so it's above the surrounding plants to get an accurate reading. It's available at www.GardenGateStore.com or www.leevalley.com for $29.95 to $32.95.

DESIGN | ALL AROUND THE YARD

Small and Sensational

Any size spot can be the right size for a gorgeous garden!

Botanical Names

Impatiens
Impatiens walleriana
Lavender
Lavandula spp.
Rose campion
Lychnis coronaria
Verbena
Verbena spp.

Waste not, want not. How many of us grew up hearing that phrase? It fits many situations, including garden design. If you don't waste any space, you can have everything you want or need — even in the smallest area. Chris and Bob Semisch's Georgia garden is a good example.

In the illustration below you'll find a layout of their property. It's roughly 80 by 120 feet. But if you walk into this garden you probably wouldn't notice the small size. Why? Well, one reason is that the space has been divided into rooms. For example, the front garden is one room. Walk along the right side of the house and you're in a "hallway" that leads to the back. Walk up the steps and around the corner and you'll find the flagstone patio you see in this photo. It's bordered on one side by stone walls that terrace a steep hill. Not only does the hillside give the area a sheltered feeling, but it also provides several levels for planting. The lower beds are all filled with flowers like these pale-pink rose campion, medium-pink impatiens and hot-pink verbena. Elevated planting beds bring the flowers up close to you. That means you can enjoy them, and do your planting and weeding, without stooping or bending.

TIE IT ALL TOGETHER When you turn the page, you're going to discover that all of the rooms don't look alike. Like the interior of your home, they don't need to. But using coordinating colors is one way to tie the rooms together. So are repeated elements, such as the stone used for steps, walls and the terrace you see here. Matching something this simple links the rooms together beautifully.

The charming bistro table and chairs are perfectly in scale with this small area. So is the graceful lavender-filled swan planter. This is a great spot for quiet meals for two. And though the table's small, it's roomy enough for two dinner plates.

As you look at the plan, you'll spot several areas to sit and enjoy this garden. On the next pages I'll show you those areas, as well as more design tips you can use in your own garden, no matter what the size or shape. And later, I'll share some of Chris and Bob's tips for clever cover-ups. After all, in a small area you don't want to have to be stuck looking at your air conditioning unit. But first, let's take a closer look at more of this garden.

This patio area is protected from wind and neighboring views by the steep hillside.

A small water feature near the deck covers noise from nearby neighbors.

This narrow area could be wasted space, but here it's a beautiful entrance to the back garden.

▶ *This symbol indicates the direction the photo was taken in the garden.*

www.GardenGateMagazine.com *the* YEAR IN GARDENING 143

DESIGN DETAILS

This is a well-thought-out garden with lots of interesting details. For example, in the illustration at right, to the right of the house is a wide room, or hall. The gravel path through the middle of this hall widens just past the center. That little bit of extra width slows down your eye as it moves along the path and it helps disguise how long and narrow it really is. And the steps at the end curve to the left so you can't see what's around the corner, adding mystery to the space.

Photo 1 below shows you the other side of the house where there's a path made of large flagstone steppers. They're big enough to walk on comfortably without really having to look down or step off into mud or gravel. Even in a narrow spot like this, setting the stones in a gently curving pattern makes you slow down and enjoy the stroll. And like the gravel path on the other side of the house, the curve also helps keep the area from looking longer than it really is.

DIVIDE AND DEFINE Notice the airy iron gate in this photo? Look again. There's another one in the distance. They help divide and define this corridor as a room. As you enter through one, you spot the one in the distance and it visually pulls you forward to enter the next room.

The open design of these gates lets you easily see through and doesn't distract from the plants. They're used more like sculptures and help add height to a narrow garden. Vines on both walls do the same thing. If there were a small tree or medium-sized shrub, it would take up valuable walking space, block the view and look much too confining here. You could even end up creating a tunnel effect with too much dense height in a narrow area like this. Vines, whether they're on a trellis or attached directly to the wall, don't take up much room. They're perfect choices in this space.

Once you're in the back yard, there's a lovely deck with comfortable furniture next to the flagstone patio. Photo 2 shows this area from the top of the hill. What you can't see is how you could sit here even on a rainy day. There's a large sheet of

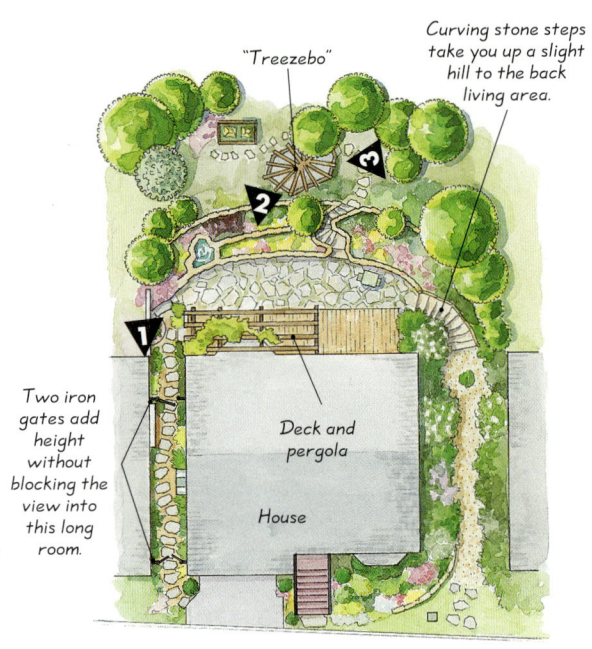

▶ *This symbol indicates the direction the photo was taken in the garden.*

"Treezebo"

Curving stone steps take you up a slight hill to the back living area.

Two iron gates add height without blocking the view into this long room.

Deck and pergola

House

(1) *A curving path is more interesting than a straight one.* Plus, this space is only about 8 ft. wide, so the bend in the path adds an illusion of width. And the tall gates add height so the area doesn't feel like a tunnel.

144 the YEAR IN GARDENING   www.GardenGateMagazine.com

clear Plexiglas® on the pergola. It was set in place before the vines grew. Now the foliage disguises the Plexiglas so you may not notice the protection unless it's raining.

GET READY FOR SOME EXERCISE Climb the stone steps up the terraced hillside to a rustic gazebo. Chris and Bob call it a "treezebo" because some of the posts are live trees while others are cut logs. It's another of those relaxing rooms with comfortable furnishings where you can sit after your steep climb. And there are lights, both electric and candles, so you can stay up there late into the evening. And as you noticed in photo 2, the gazebo gives visitors a great viewing spot where they can look down on the patio.

As a child, did you ever look at a drawing where there were things hidden in the picture? Well, this garden has utilities that are well hidden. On the next pages I'll give you some clues so you can disguise your own "uglies."

(2) Height adds to a feeling of distance. Whether you're looking down at this deck or up toward the structure in the photo below, the distance between them seems greater than it really is because of the steep hillside.

(3) Create a restful destination. This seating area gives you the perfect place to relax after you climb the hillside. And the look is different from the rest of the yard so you feel you're in another garden.

www.GardenGateMagazine.com

HIDING IN PLAIN SIGHT?

Botanical Names

Boston ivy
Parthenocissus tricuspidata
Creeping fig
Ficus pumila
English ivy
Hedera helix

No matter where you garden, I bet there's something you wish wasn't visible to your visitors. Everyone has similar problems. Too much concrete, or hardscaping, in a small spot looks out of proportion. Big central air conditioning units and heat pumps just don't fit the look of my garden, how about yours? And don't get me started on those green telephone junction boxes. Does anyone really think that shade of green will disguise them? This Georgia garden had all of those things to contend with and more. Here are some solutions you can use to "hide the uglies."

SOFTEN HARSH HARDSCAPING Steps are often a necessity to get guests to the front door. This house has a large, and very high, set of them next to the street. Brick is fairly easy on the eyes, but by covering the front of each step with creeping fig, a clinging vine that is hardy in USDA zones 7 to 11, this staircase almost disappears. Any small-leafed vine that attaches to a solid surface with rootlets, such as English or Boston ivy, can be substituted. All of these vines need to be clipped frequently to keep them close to the surface and off the top of the step. After all, you don't want guests tripping over aggressive vines. Don't have time for that kind of maintenance? Try painting the front of wood or concrete steps the same color as your house to make them blend in a bit better.

USEFUL UTILITIES One way to disguise a big outdoor heat pump or air conditioning unit is with a lattice screen — it's quick and easy. But let's face it; you still know what's behind that big screen. Can you spot the AC in photo 5? I didn't at first. Look closely at the potting bench. There are two big

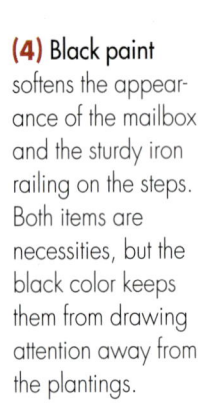

(4) Black paint softens the appearance of the mailbox and the sturdy iron railing on the steps. Both items are necessities, but the black color keeps them from drawing attention away from the plantings.

146   the YEAR IN GARDENING   www.GardenGateMagazine.com

utility units under each end. The front and sides are louvered so plenty of air can circulate. And the top is slatted over the units so air moves easily. You probably won't do heavy potting on this bench, because you don't want soil falling into the fans. However, the center area is solid so you can do some light potting when the need arises.

TAKE A MESSAGE Telephone junction boxes are relatively recent inventions. They mean you don't have to worry about, or look at, overhead wires. But they do seem to pop up in the most visible locations. There's one in this front yard. The disguise? The wooden "sleeve" you see in photo 6, with a faux birdhouse on top. Why a fake birdhouse? You don't want a family of birds moving in and being disturbed should the phone company need to do repairs. But before you build one, check with your phone or utility company. It may have restrictions about what you can and can't do to disguise the box. Look for the contact information on the front of the metal box.

The next time you wish you had more space to plant, or you're stuck looking at an "ugly" that ruins your view, don't fret. These tips are sure to stimulate your own creativity, no matter what size garden you have. ◻

— *Jim Childs*

(5) Add to the disguise by placing decorative items on top of the bench. Friends will focus on them rather than the units underneath.

(6) Hide a phone junction box with a custom-made wooden "sleeve." You can't attach it to the box, so make sure it's heavy enough to stay put in a strong wind, but light enough to lift off easily for repairs.

DESIGN | ALL AROUND THE YARD

Welcome the neighborhood or take a break from the hustle and bustle.

Best of Both Worlds

It used to be that people spent leisure time in their front yard, not the back. A back yard was to hide the garbage cans, hang the laundry, grow a vegetable garden and shake the rugs on Saturday morning. Somewhere along the line, we all started living in the back yard and the front yard became a place just for show. But Tom Palamuso and Carol Siracuse have capitalized on both areas. They often retreat to the private space you see in photo 1. This is in their back yard, away from public view. It's a quiet, secluded place where they can relax.

But they also enjoy the front garden in photo 2. With its bright colors and inviting porch, this is a perfect spot for chatting with neighbors or making new friends. Unfortunately, as building styles changed, front porches were left off houses. But older neighborhoods, like this one in Buffalo, New York, still have them. And now, many new homes in all areas of the country are being built with front porches. They're a place where folks can share their garden with all who pass by. At the same time, the owners can keep up with what's going on in the neighborhood.

DESIGN SEPARATE AREAS Having two distinct gardens like these can be a great advantage, especially if you like variety. The planting areas could be tied together by hardscaping, plant material or design elements, such as color. Or they can be completely different. You'll discover that the two areas in this garden are separated by a long, narrow house. Since there's a great deal of distance between the two garden spots, there was no reason to tie them together visually.

So, when it comes to design, the front and back areas have almost nothing in common. That's exactly what the owners wanted. This garden, just like many people, has a public persona and a private one. To attract attention, the front area is colorful and open with an inviting feeling of energy. But the private back garden is designed with less color and more calming, restful texture.

On the next pages, you'll discover tips to help you create your own colorful and interesting public garden. And later I'll share ideas on what you'll need to create a private retreat. Now, imagine you're walking down the sidewalk and you spot this front garden. Let's stop by and take a look.

(1) Peaceful and quiet are the goals in this secluded and private back yard.

(2) Bright colors draw attention and bring energy to this front garden. With careful plant selection, it's easy to have something in bloom most of the year.

www.GardenGateMagazine.com the YEAR IN GARDENING 149

DESIGNING THE FRONT GARDEN

Botanical Names

Agave *Agave* spp.
Crabapple
  Malus hybrid
Juniper
  Juniperus spp.

Front gardens should be inviting. That doesn't mean you have to encourage every passerby to come up onto your porch. But it should make people want to slow down and enjoy the scene. So, how do you do that? Here are some tips.

GROW CONVERSATION STARTERS It's a fact, people are curious. And when it comes to gardeners, if they see a plant they don't know, they want to learn all about it. Or, if they recognize a common plant, perhaps a rose, they want tips on how you feed yours or how you keep it so healthy.

Many of the plants in this garden are easy to identify. But notice the agaves in the containers at the first landing of the steps in photo 3? Being in a USDA zone 6 garden, they're pretty uncommon — perfect conversation starters. And since they're in containers, they can be moved or swapped with another plant to keep the garden looking fresh and different as the seasons change.

LEAVE A LITTLE LAWN To achieve all of that color, the first impulse for many of us may be to take out the entire lawn. But by leaving the bit of grass you see in the illustration, even though it's on a slope, folks have a place to step off the hard, sometimes hot, sidewalk while they chat. And the block of green gives a frame to the colorful garden. However, since the lawn area is small and very visible, it needs to be meticulously maintained. Lots of weeds or a patch of mud would stand out like a sore thumb.

TAKE TIME TO SIT A SPELL What's better than a spot in the front yard where you can watch the world go by? Notice the porch swing to the left of the front door in photo 3? Across from it, just out of sight, are a couple of small chairs. If you want to invite someone to come up for a chat, you don't have to worry about whether the inside of the house is picked up or not. And with a porch, you're protected if a rainstorm suddenly starts to pour.

Front garden

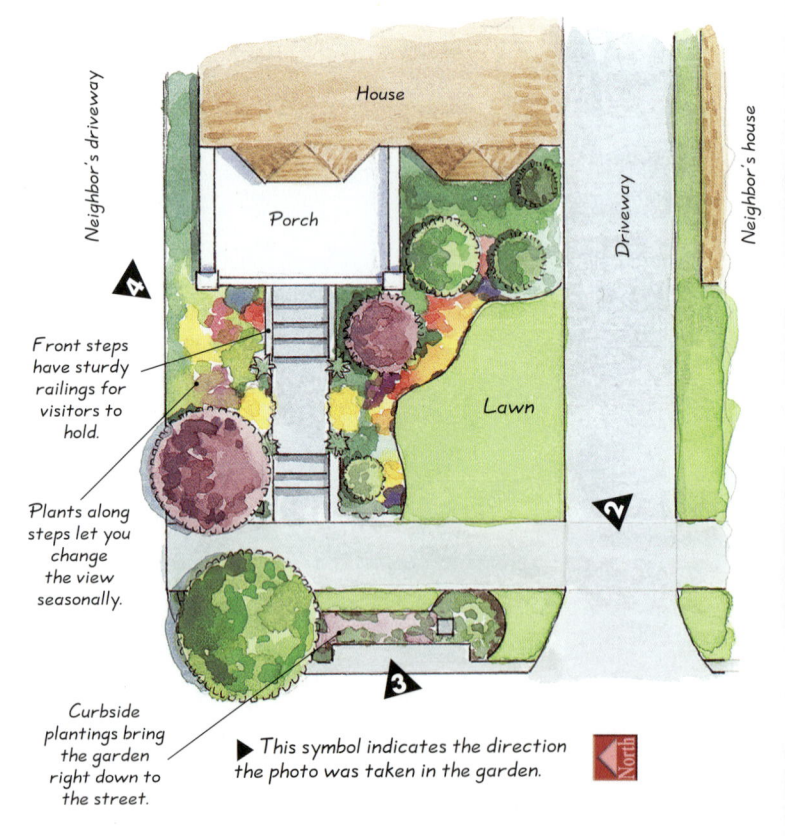

- Front steps have sturdy railings for visitors to hold.
- Plants along steps let you change the view seasonally.
- Curbside plantings bring the garden right down to the street.

▶ This symbol indicates the direction the photo was taken in the garden.

(3) Blend a high porch into the landscape by tapering plantings from the top of the railing down to the street.

150   *the* YEAR IN GARDENING   www.GardenGateMagazine.com

(4) To get the longest period of color, combine blooming plants with others that have interesting foliage.

TRY THIS BRIGHT IDEA You want people to see the garden, so vibrant, energizing colors, such as the ones above, are a great idea. To learn more about the perennials and annuals growing in this front yard garden, check out the information in "Keep it colorful" to the right. But be sure to add some height with a few shrubs or a tree. Dwarf or compact varieties are a perfect fit in a small garden. And don't forget evergreens for winter interest. The narrow, upright blue-tinted juniper on the left won't take up much space or block the view from the porch.

Now that you've enjoyed visiting the front garden, you've become a new friend. So, do you want to see the back garden? Turn the page and come on back. You'll learn about ideas you can use as you design your own hideaway.

Keep it colorful Front gardens are meant to be noticed. That usually calls for lots of color. This garden is on the north side of the front steps and under a small flowering crabapple. Color could be a challenge in this kind of shade. Rather than planting the bed with all hostas, three provide a framework for lots of other plants. Colorful foliage is one of the best ways to keep the color from lagging. And annuals can't be beat for both colorful foliage and flowers. Tuck in a tropical or two when it's in flower and you'll not only have more color, but you get a great conversation starter, too.

A **Hosta** *Hosta* hybrids
   Cold: USDA zones 3 to 9 • Heat: AHS zones 9 to 1
B **Coleus** *Solenostemon scutellarioides*
   Tender perennial • Heat: AHS zones 12 to 1
C **Clivia** *Clivia miniata*
   Tender perennial • Heat: AHS zones 12 to 1
D **Deadnettle** *Lamium galeobdolon* 'Hermann's Pride'
   Cold: USDA zones 4 to 8 • Heat: AHS zones 8 to 1
E **Creeping Jenny** *Lysimachia nummularia* 'Aurea'
   Cold: USDA zones 4 to 8 • Heat: AHS zones 8 to 1
F **Torenia** *Torenia fournieri*
   Annual • Heat: AHS zones 12 to 1
G **Daylily** *Hemerocallis* 'Happy Returns'
   Cold: USDA zones 3 to 10 • Heat: AHS zones 10 to 1

DESIGNING A PRIVATE RETREAT

Botanical Names

Calibrachoa
  Calibrachoa hybrid
Wisteria
  Wisteria spp.

When you feel like visiting with neighbors, a garden in the front yard is a perfect place to do it. But everybody needs a private space where they can relax and let their hair down. When Tom started designing the back garden, the only thing there, besides a driveway and garage, was the raised brick area you see under the pergola in photo 5. There were no plantings, paths or pergola.

DIVIDE AND CONQUER Splitting the back garden into rooms gives a feeling that it is a larger space than it really is. These rooms are not defined by walls, but are loosely divided by structures and plantings. The original square of bricks became the outdoor dining room. It's large enough for a table and four chairs. In a pinch, a couple more chairs can be added. Look at the illustration below and you'll see that it's very close to the back door. That makes it handy when you're carrying dishes and food to the table.

(5) Solid surfaces make footing secure and keep muddy holes from forming in a hard-use area like this path.

Back garden

A potting bench is hidden from the rest of the garden but easy to access.

This water garden has a small, shady seating area to relax and enjoy the sound.

Water feature

This low wall hides the driveway from the garden.

The "dining room" is covered by a pergola for shade and to screen the view from neighbors' windows.

Bluestone path

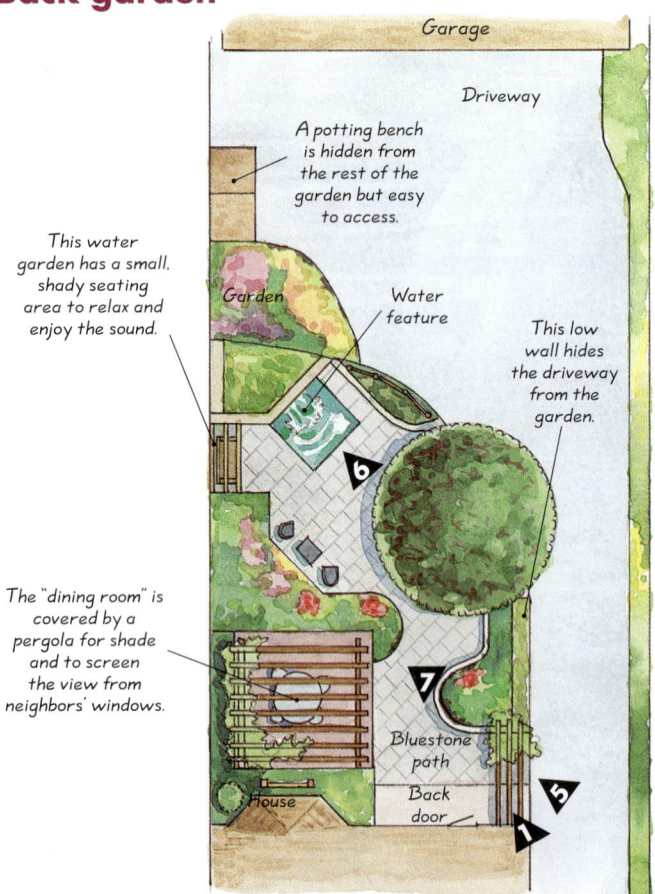

▶ *This symbol indicates the direction the photo was taken in the garden.*

ADD A CEILING This wisteria-covered pergola gives a more intimate, secluded feeling to the dining area. Just remember to prune the fast-growing vines to keep them under control.

Need extra lighting? Hang an electric light or even a rustic chandelier of candles from the pergola. Plus, it's a great spot to hang baskets of annuals, like these calibrachoas. You can change them occasionally to keep the "room" looking fresh. Or you can swap them out for different seasonal colors.

CREATE A DESTINATION The waterfall and small pond in photo 6 are at the opposite end of the garden from the back door and main garden entrance. You can hear the water as you step into the garden, but you can't see where the sound is coming from. That adds a bit of mystery, encouraging you to enter the garden and explore.

Once you find the water garden, you'll discover it's another room. The simple, unobtrusive design is ideal in this urban garden. It's small enough that it doesn't pull your attention away from other design features, such as the plants or hardscaping. If this was a rushing stream or a grand, large pond, it would overpower the garden. Not only would it be out of scale visually, but the sound of the water splashing might be so loud that holding a conversation would be difficult. And the best thing about a small water garden? It's easy to maintain so you have more time to relax and enjoy it.

152 *the* YEAR IN GARDENING www.GardenGateMagazine.com

SET THE MOOD Whether you're indoors or out in your garden, different color schemes really do help set distinctly different moods. In photo 7, you'll notice that, in contrast to the colorful front area, most of the back garden is in shades of green. It capitalizes on calming texture rather than energizing color. However, flashes of bright red direct your attention to things you need to find. Notice the red flowers by the back door? Now check out the other photos on these pages. See how red draws you to the dining table and emphasizes a curve in the path? There's even a splash of it near the water feature. Without small dashes of color, an all-green garden may be bland. But repeating one color helps blend the scene together better.

If you want to participate in your neighborhood, and get to know your neighbors better, plant a front garden everyone can enjoy. But keep a private place in back just for you and a few of your best friends. ☐

— *Jim Childs*

(6) Simple plantings show off the small waterfall, pool and even the fish without hiding them.

(7) Vary the height of plants to add interest in any size garden. Here, it also helps create curiosity about what may be around the corner or behind it.

www.GardenGateMagazine.com *the* YEAR IN GARDENING **153**

DESIGN | SMALL GARDENS

How to create perfect patios and decks

Inviting Spaces

Outdoor living — it's the best way to spend your leisure time during those warm summer months. We've come a long way from the cold steel chairs of the 1950s or the webbed folding lawn chairs of the 1960s. Now there are almost as many decorating options for your patio or deck as there are for the inside of your home. Just look at the colorful fabrics and comfortable furniture on this welcoming patio.

I'm going to assume you already have a deck or patio, so I won't focus on how to build one. Instead I'll share tips about things you can do with an existing area to make it more appealing. For example, have you ever visited a patio or deck, maybe even your own, that just doesn't have a comfortable feeling? Maybe it's too large and open and you feel like you're floating in a sea of bricks or decking. Or maybe you have to navigate around a clutter of furniture and accessories to get across the area. Most of us have had these experiences, but you'll be glad to know they can be corrected.

I'll start with tips for a large space at right. On the following pages you'll find ideas to use in smaller areas. But no matter how big your patio or deck is, these tips are sure to make your outdoor living area a spot where you and your guests will want to relax and sit a spell.

Turn the page to learn design tips for smaller decks and patios.

UMBRELLAS DO MORE THAN KEEP YOU DRY! A large patio is great for entertaining a large group. But when there are just a few folks, it can seem out of scale. The first thing to consider is a "roof" overhead. An umbrella is perfect for creating a smaller space inside a larger one, kind of like spreading an area rug in your living room. Plus, an umbrella like this one gives you the options you won't get with a pergola. You can switch from sun to shade at a moment's notice. Umbrellas can even be moved around to wherever you need shade. One is fine in a small space, but don't be afraid to use more if you have a large area to shade. This umbrella post goes through a flower-filled pot. The drainage hole has been drilled large enough for the post to go through into the weighted base.

SHED A LITTLE LIGHT I don't know about you, but I often don't sit on my patio until evening. I want a bit of light, but nothing too bright. You couldn't read by these outdoor lanterns, but they do give a relaxing warm glow to the area. They're also portable so they can be moved around as needed. Don't want the hassle of running electricity to your patio? Solar lights are much brighter and longer lasting than they used to be. Or if you're into a romantic feel on your deck, candles and oil lamps are the low-tech way to go.

MAKE IT AS COMFORTABLE AS YOUR LIVING ROOM Nothing's worse than trying to relax on hard, uncomfortable furniture. With today's weather-proof materials, finishes and fabrics, you have a wealth of options to choose from. I like cushions I can leave out in the weather if I feel like it. And I think the garden always looks inviting with the cushions in place when friends drop by. If rain is predicted, tip the cushions on edge before they get wet so they'll drain and dry faster.

RELAX IN A FIELD OF FLOWERS I know it's hard, if you're a dedicated gardener, to actually sit and enjoy your garden. I always see flowers that need deadheading or weeds to pull when I'm trying to relax. Place plants near your seating area that don't need constant staking or dividing, like these feverfew. Yes, you'll still have to pull a few weeds — unless you put down mulch! Afraid of or allergic to bees? Plant more foliage plants around the seating area and keep flowers in the distance.

MORE DESIGN TIPS

Maybe your patio is so small you just can't figure out what to do with it. The patio you see below takes up almost the entire back yard. Yet it still leaves room to garden and doesn't feel like a big slab of concrete. And the seating area in the photo to the right is one "room" on a long deck that's less than 10 feet wide. To keep the deck from feeling like a narrow passageway, the length has been divided into rooms. Furniture groupings define the sections. For example, you can see a small dining area with a table and chairs in the background.

No matter how you use your outdoor living area, or its size or shape, there are lots more ways to add a few special or personal touches. You'll find more tips with the photos on these pages.

Two deck and patio design features that are popular right now are firepits and small water fountains. In "Fire and water" I'll share information on ways to use both of them. But be careful. Soon all your friends will be dropping in to enjoy your newly decorated patio. Better keep lots of refreshments on hand!

— *Jim Childs*

PROVIDE PERMANENT SHADE
A pergola is a great way to shade a large area where you relax. Plus, it can add lots of style to any garden setting. These classic pillars supporting the canopy give an elegant feel to this small patio. So do the detailed ends of the beams on the top. If you like to display baskets filled with colorful annuals, pergolas provide lots of spots where you can hang them.

SURROUND YOURSELF A patio or deck is made much more inviting with a bit of enclosure. Like the walls in your home, a fence gives you privacy. And hiding the fence, as well as the house wall to the left, with lots of leafy shrubs or vines, helps soften the look. While a fence alone is fine, covering it with foliage also helps muffle unwanted noise.

FLOOR IT! Stone, like this bluestone, or brick is nice. But if you already have concrete, it can be stained or stamped for a similar look. Check home improvement stores for do-it-yourself concrete stains. Stamping a pattern into the surface will probably need to be handled by a pro. Consult your local yellow pages for a concrete contractor.

IMPROVE CIRCULATION No matter where you put your patio or deck, make sure air can circulate through the area. This deck is raised above the ground for a good view, and it catches cooling breezes on summer evenings. Even if you build fences or plant hedges for sight and sound control, make sure you don't cut off all of the breeze. Leave some space between the top of the fence and the pergola so air filters underneath your "roof" if you build one.

REDUCE A BIG AREA On a large deck, you can design or organize a small, separate conversation area. Two comfortable chairs, an umbrella overhead and a railing at your back make this spot feel more intimate. The railing gives a sense of security to this grouping. Imagine it out in the center of the deck — someone could sneak up behind you as you tell secrets. You feel more secure when the space is limited, or defined. Plus placing the seating area next to the railing allows for a comfortable traffic flow. You won't have to worry about people walking between you and your guest as you chat.

FIRE AND WATER

EXTEND THE SEASON Firepits can be as simple as a shallow depression dug in the dirt and surrounded by rocks. Or they can be more elaborate like the one below, which is made with mortared stone. Some firepits are portable and can be moved if you want. You'll find styles that burn gas or wood. For safety reasons, firepits are best on patios away from the house or other structures. And depending on the design of the firepit, you may not want to use it on a flammable wooden deck. My community ordinances don't allow wood-burning firepits, so check your local codes before building or purchasing a firepit so you can use it as you planned.

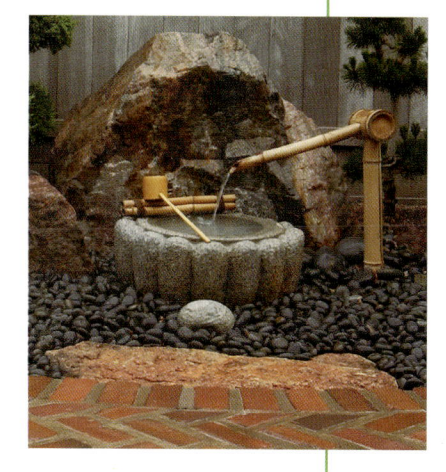

TRANQUIL SOUNDS What could be more relaxing than the sound of moving water? A small fountain is one of the easiest and most relaxing things you can add to your outdoor living space. Place one with a bubbler or a bamboo spout, like this one, near your seating area. The gentle sound is relaxing as it helps block out the neighbors' blaring TV. Why keep it small? You can bring it up close to the seating area so you can enjoy the sound best. And while you'll get more sound with a big waterfall and pond, the amount of work you'll have to do goes up dramatically. After all, this is about relaxing.

DESIGN | SMALL GARDENS

Small-Space Secrets
5 tips to make your tiny garden terrific

Take a look at this gorgeous, colorful garden. Pretty, isn't it? What you can't see are the winged visitors or the soft fragrance. Would you guess that a bed like this takes a lot of attention and time? Well, guess again! Actually, a small bed like this is easy to create and take care of, even if you can't spend lots of time on it. And besides saving you time and work, small beds have several other advantages.

First of all, they're less expensive to put in because you need fewer plants. The majority of the plants in this bed are perennials, so they'll come back each year. All you need to do is add a few annuals here and there.

Second, if you design the bed as an island or peninsula like this one, it's easy to reach and to admire from all sides. That means it looks as good from the house as it does from the yard or the sidewalk out front.

Finally, if you're new to gardening, you can create a small bed without getting in over your head. Once they're established, these plants need very little work to keep them looking nice. And if you feel like you want a bigger bed, you can always expand it later on. So whether you're an old hand at gardening or are just dipping your toe in for the first time, try planting a small bed. (You'll find this plan and plant list in our Web extra.) I'll share easy tips below to help you make it look great. For just a little time and effort, you'll get a large helping of enjoyment! □

— *Deborah Gruca*

Botanical Names

Bee balm
 Monarda didyma
Fountain grass
 Pennisetum alopecuroides
Garden phlox *Phlox paniculata*
Perennial sunflower
 Helianthus angustifolia
Purple coneflower
 Echinacea purpurea
Salvia *Salvia farinacea*
Snapdragon
 Antirrhinum majus
Zinna *Zinnia hybrid*

Do repeat splashes of color throughout the bed to help keep your eye moving.

Don't ring the island with the same plant or color — your eye goes to the edge and stays there.

Do include fine-leafed plants along with bold foliage for accents. Smaller leaves help the bed appear bigger.

Don't use lots of plants with bold foliage. It makes the bed look smaller.

1 HANDLE HEIGHTS Place the tallest plants in the center of the bed so you can't see the entire bed from one spot. Each "level" of plants should be 30 to 50 percent taller than the one in front of it.

2 PUT PLANTS IN THEIR PLACE Pick compact plants that won't take over the whole bed or need staking. Some good dwarf perennials are 'Kim's Knee High' purple coneflower, 'Little Bunny' fountain grass and 'Low Down' perennial sunflower. When you space these plants close together, they'll shade out most weeds and you won't have to mulch the bed.

If you do include a spreader, such as the red bee balm here, plant it in a plastic nursery pot sunk in the ground. Cut off the bottom of the pot first and drop it in the hole so the rim sticks up an inch or two above the soil. This will prevent the plant from spreading.

3 MIX IT UP To increase the visual interest of the bed, mix bright and pastel-colored flowers, such as the intense red bee balm and the soft pink garden phlox.

4 REACH OUT Make the bed no more than twice the length of your arm. You can care for it without ever having to step into it, so you won't compact the soil.

5 KEEP A TIDY EDGE Leave some space near the front edge of the border to plant short, upright annuals, such as these snapdragons, salvias and zinnias — plants that sprawl make it harder to mow and to maintain a tidy edge. And annuals let you change the look easily from year to year.

WEB extra
Want to grow this bed? Check out our *plan and plant list!*

DESIGN | SMALL GARDENS

Design on a Budget

Easy, inexpensive *and* you can do it yourself

Botanical Names

Barberry
Berberis thunbergii atropurpurea
Rose *Rosa* 'William Baffin'
Thyme *Thymus pseudolanuginosis*

Not everyone has a big budget to spend on their garden. So that means we need to use creativity to get the garden we want. Magda Martinez has done just that in her Colorado garden. There's not much in this 30-by-50-foot yard that's expensive to build, hard to find or that you can't do yourself, no matter what your budget is. Let's take a look at how Magda uses these items, along with some easy-to-grow plants, to make her garden beautiful.

Choose hardscaping materials in similar colors to tie the entire garden together.

Premade fence panels can be moved if you change your layout later.

▶ *This symbol indicates the direction the photo was taken in the garden.*

ESTABLISH THE PALETTE Starting with a well-defined color scheme makes it less likely you'll make impulse purchases that will be hard to fit in later. Limiting the colors also helps keep the garden from looking jumbled. That's why most everything here is in shades of red and pink — it unifies the look. From the bright red roses to the dark red leaves of the barberries and even the orange-red of the stepping stones and concrete edging, it all ties up into a neat garden design package.

PLANTING ON A BUDGET Just because you're working with a budget doesn't mean you have to put up with skimpy plantings. No matter what size your garden is, choose several large plants to give it some bulk and presence. Or choose one or two plants that have a long season of interest, like the repeat-flowering 'William Baffin' rose over the gate.

Next, fill in around those specimens. On a really tight budget? Use annuals you can start from seed. Or shop late-summer sales for perennials and shrubs. Great gardens don't have to be designed using the newest or rarest plant cultivars. Like those barberries, the plant choices in much of this garden are all fairly common. Many of them could even be shared, or friendship, plants from friends and neighbors.

DO-IT-YOURSELF HARDSCAPING These concrete steppers are a perfect solution for a do-it-yourself application. They're found at lots of retail stores, plus they're inexpensive and a snap to install. To add a finished appearance, a dense ground cover of woolly thyme has been planted between the steppers. No jumbled or impulse-buy look here!

Iron fencing gives any garden a classic feel. It looks as if it was custom made, but it, too, is an easy-to-install DIY project. Ready-made panels are available at home improvement stores and even some garden centers. Many styles have stakes that you simply drive into the ground before you attach the panels. And if you change your design, it's easy to remove the panels, pull up the stakes and rearrange them.

Those are just a few of the design tips this garden has to share. On the next pages, you'll learn more budget-minded ideas you can use in your own garden.

HOMEOWNER TIP
Make color work for you. Limiting the color choices can make any garden look organized. Coordinate flower and foliage colors with the hardscaping, like these easy-to-install steppers, to get a finished, unified feel.

MORE DO-IT-YOURSELF DESIGN

HOMEOWNER TIP
Sections of low fencing along a narrow path serve a dual purpose. They keep visitors from stepping off the sidewalk. And they keep sprawling plants that might trip people, like this bleeding heart, off the sidewalk.

(2) Hanging baskets filled with colorful annuals are a great way to keep narrow garden areas colorful. Hang them from brackets or shepherd hooks.

Botanical Names

Calibrachoa
  Calibrachoa hybrid
Honeysuckle
  Lonicera sempervirens
Hyacinth bean
  Lablab purpureus
Morning glory
  Ipomoea purpurea
Sweet autumn clematis
  Clematis terniflora

Walk through the gate you saw on the last page and photo 2 is what you'll find. No matter what size budget you're working with, narrow garden spaces like this can be difficult to design. It's impossible to plant against the wall to soften the hard angles or keep it from looking large and looming.

BROADEN YOUR WALKWAY This concrete sidewalk's in good shape, so removing it really wasn't an option. Besides, it would be expensive. Instead, several containers with lots of green plants really improve the appearance. But because they take up sidewalk space, you'd have to step onto the grass to get around them. Rather than pour more concrete (that wouldn't match anyway), you can see the solution in the photo — a row of alternating bricks and steppers. It's an easy do-it-yourself weekend project. And since they're the same color as the ones in front, the bricks carry the color scheme into the back garden.

WATCH YOUR TUNNEL VISION In the illustration on the next page, notice how narrow the planting bed is to the right of the walk? With a fence on one side and the house on the other, this area felt like a tunnel. To get the most out of the space, and to make it feel more like a garden, vines cover the stark board fence. And several inexpensive hanging baskets filled with red calibrachoas add long-lasting color. Planting a few choice shrubs, perennials and ground covers at the ends and the base of the fence create an illusion that this area is wider, or deeper, than it really is.

PLAN A CONTAINER COLLECTION
Go around the corner you see in the distance of photo 2 and you're in photo 3. On the left is a planting bed. It has some permanent plants, but you'll notice flower-filled containers, too.

Buying lots of matching pots all at once could get expensive. If you're like most of us, you pick up a new container or two every year or so. (I often wait for fall clearance sales.)

Keep your color scheme in mind as you buy, and it becomes easier to create groupings that look well-planned. These pots all have similar warm colors to help tie them together. Flower and foliage colors planted in them also add to the unified look. And all of the colors coordinate with the rest of the garden. Containers like these also let you move plants around now and then for a fresh look.

WIDEN THE VIEW A fence gives almost any garden a more intimate, sheltered feeling. It also gives you control of the entire space so you don't have to worry about trying to tie your garden into its surroundings. However, that fence can also make the area feel confined. In this small

162 *the* YEAR IN GARDENING   www.GardenGateMagazine.com

(3) Need room for pets? The gate in the distance leads to a dog run. And to the right is a rabbit hutch, painted to become a garden focal point.

▶ This symbol indicates the direction the photo was taken in the garden.

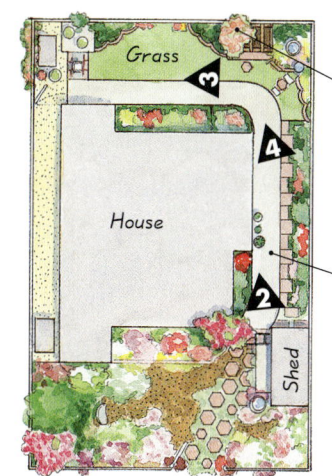

As you enter the gate near the shed, this bench and arbor create a great focal point.

This garden's small, but covering the fences with plants blurs the boundaries and helps give an illusion of more size.

HOMEOWNER TIP
Need more height to screen a view? Use 8-ft.-long premade lattice panels cut into two-foot wide strips. Fasten them to the top of the fence with wood screws. Now you also have a great place to grow colorful vines.

garden, all of the hard lines become much more noticeable, too. Fasten a trellis to the fence and cover it with vines. Since no one will see it, a plain, inexpensive one is fine. That's a fast-growing honeysuckle in the background of photo 3. Or you could grow sweet autumn clematis to soften the hard top edge. You can start with a small plant, even a cutting shared from a friend, and in a year or two you'll have a lush, leafy cover. Faster yet? Annuals, such as morning glories or hyacinth beans, are very economical and can be started from seed.

PLANT WITH EXUBERANCE There's no room in this small garden for the drifts or sweeps of plants we often recommend. And if you're a plant collector who picks up a wide variety of plants at seasonal closeout sales, it's probably not important to you. Instead, you'll end up with lots of individuals, like this garden has. Coordinating colors and textures will help avoid a cluttered look.

INSTALL SUPERB STRUCTURES
Nothing makes a garden look more put together than well-built structures. But if you've ever priced having an arbor or other small structure custom-made, you probably didn't add it to your landscape. And if you're not up to building your own, what can you do? You can pick up lots of different styles of ready-made garden structures at lots of stores.

Unfortunately many of these ready-made structures don't tie into their settings. The arbor and bench in photo 4 are stock items. Placing them into the border, surrounded by plants and against the fence, helps. So does including some of the bricks and steppers used in other parts of the garden. Plus, staining the two pieces to match gives this grouping a custom look.

With some easy planning, you can have the garden of your dreams, and some cash left over for what every gardener wants — more plants! ☐

— *Jim Childs*

(4) Avoid mudholes by installing inexpensive steppers or bricks in grassy areas where you frequently walk.

DESIGN | BACK YARD

Put these great design ideas to work in any size garden!

Think Big

You've found your dream home — and with it comes a big area for a garden. Do you simply plant it all to lawn and invest in a big riding mower? Not if you enjoy having a flower-filled garden. But a plot this size requires some special design ideas. Otherwise, you'll end up spending all of your spare time taking care of your garden, not enjoying it.

WHERE DO YOU START? When Bob and Becky Shaw bought this property in Iowa, it was a blank canvas. The first order of business was to gather design ideas. They had some specific "wants" in mind, one of which was privacy on this corner lot. A water feature to cover neighborhood noise was another must-have. And since they occasionally host large events in their garden, they wanted sturdy paths and other hard surfaces. That way they and their guests could enjoy the garden without getting muddy.

You can see just a portion of their efforts in this photo. Beautiful, isn't it? This yard takes up just over an acre, so the landscape ideas had to be big, too. On the next pages you'll learn some of the design techniques that fit the scale of the space and make sure the garden is beautiful no matter what the season. Yet it's easy to maintain, in some cases even more so than the average small garden. And finally, there are some tips on choosing and designing hardscaping so it visually fits into its surroundings. So put on your walking shoes and let's go!

FOCUS ON PLANTINGS

I bet you've thought, "If only I had a bigger garden, I could grow more plants!" But then you think how a larger garden usually translates to more work. To save time and energy, start by adapting these simple design techniques:

PLANT IN MASS If you want a big impact, add big groupings of the same plant into your design. In photo 2 there are lots of perennial sages, shrub roses and daylilies growing in large masses. Visit this garden earlier in the season and you'll find sweeps of spring bulbs in the same beds. Bold groupings of plants that are still just foliage will bloom later. Generous plantings are in scale with the size of this garden. Too many clusters of plants, or individuals, look wimpy in a large space.

Big groupings of the same plant don't just look pretty, they also simplify care. How does that work? Well, when it comes time for maintenance, such as watering, fertilizing, pest control, deadheading and winter protection, you can take care of large areas all at once. There's no need to remember individual requirements for lots of different plants. When the sages in photo 2 are finished, you can cut all of them to the ground at one time. In a traditional border with smaller groupings of perennials, simply remembering when to do what to which plants can be a chore.

REPEAT A FEW GROUPINGS Even with masses of plants, you still need to tie the garden together visually. You can see the purple spikes of perennial sage in almost every photo on theses pages. Repeated groups help unify any garden, big or small.

Not everything *has* to be repeated. But if it has a bright color or interesting texture, unless you want it to be a focal point that draws attention, try to repeat it at least three times. The bigger the garden, the more you may want to repeat an element to keep the look unified.

KEEP THE COLOR COMING Away from the house, green trees and shrubs provide privacy and low maintenance. Color is focused near the patio where you spend the most time and you'll enjoy flowers the most. Unfortunately, there are very few plants that will stay in flower for the entire growing season. No matter what size garden you have, you'll want to choose an assortment of plants that bloom at different times.

The shrub roses in photo 2 are a great choice because they bloom for almost of the entire summer, even without deadheading. Rebloomers, such as the purple sages, are another option. They'll give you one big burst of

Botanical Names

Daylily
Hemerocallis hybrid
Rose *Rosa* hybrid
Russian sage
Perovskia atriplicifolia
Sage
Salvia xsylvestris
Zinnia
Zinnia elegans

(2) Maintenance is easy if you repeat the same plants. You won't need to memorize lots of different care schedules, such as deadheading or fertilizing.

A mix of trees and shrubs is more interesting than a hedge of a single type of plant.

▶ *This symbol indicates the direction the photo was taken in the garden.*

166 the YEAR IN GARDENING www.GardenGateMagazine.com

(3) Extend the season with colorful annuals, such as these red 'Cherry Profusion' zinnias. They bloom continuously from midsummer until a hard freeze knocks them out.

color early in the season and then you cut them back. Later they reward you with more flowers.

Annuals, like the 'Profusion Cherry' zinnias in photo 3, are indispensable for long-lasting color. Many will bloom much of the summer. Late into fall, as the grasses reach their peak, most annuals will still look terrific. You don't need huge beds of them, but you can't beat a few annuals for lots of fast, long-lasting color.

Yes, you will have to plant annuals every year. But planting in big sweeps of the same plant is easier than ones and twos. Plus, it's often more economical. You can direct sow seeds, such as these zinnias. Or you can buy full flats of seedlings and get a better price than if you pick up just a few small four- or six-packs.

And did you notice? The plants in this garden are not fancy or hard-to-find items, yet with careful design, they make a big impact. Photo 4 has repeated groupings of purple sages and silvery-gray Russian sage, which hasn't started to bloom yet. A repeat flowering daylily stays in bloom from spring through late summer. And a few grasses near the back will carry the garden even after frost.

Plants are all well and good. But great gardens also have great hardscaping. As we continue touring, you'll find tips on structures, water features and paths for gardens of any size.

(4) Keep the color coming by combining perennials that bloom at different times. After the purple sage finishes, the gray spikes of Russian sage will open to soft blue-purple.

HARDSCAPING HOW-TO

Botanical Names

Juniper
Juniperus spp.
Sedum
Sedum spp.
Thyme
Thymus spp.

When I think of great gardens I've visited, the first thing that comes to mind is usually the plants. But close on their heels is the hardscaping — almost anything in the garden that isn't plants. Here it includes the stream with its ponds and waterfalls, as well as paths, several stone walls, a wooden deck, stone terrace and spectacular pavilion.

MAKE ROOM There's nothing worse than having lots of elbow room out in the garden and then being squeezed into a small gazebo or pergola. The pavilion in photo 5 can hold a small party. It's perfectly in scale with the surrounding space. If it were smaller, or built with small timbers or delicate-looking materials, it just wouldn't look right.

A solid roof on the pavilion is also a great idea in this big garden. It shades you and your guests, as well as helping keep you dry during rainy weather.

(5) Large structures need large plantings around them. Without them, this pavilion would appear bigger than it is, and out of scale in this back yard.

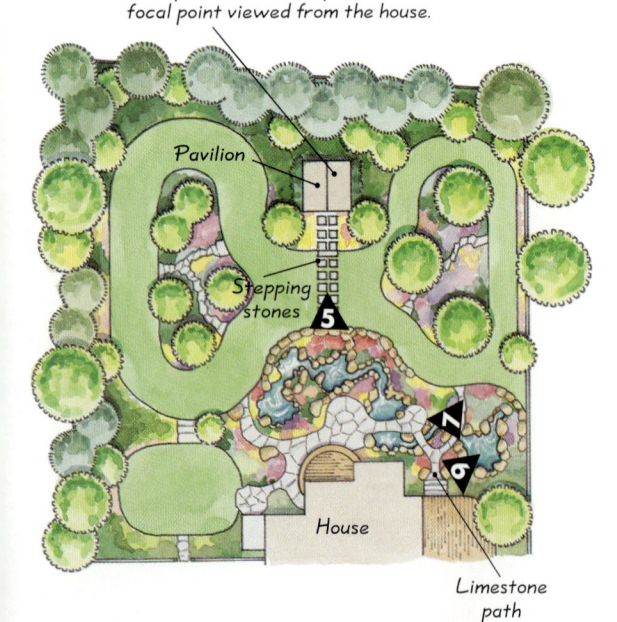

The pavilion makes a permanent focal point viewed from the house.

Pavilion
Stepping stones
House
Limestone path

▶ This symbol indicates the direction the photo was taken in the garden.

Did you happen to notice the arched opening over the entrance? It's more than just a decorative architectural feature. It's designed to let breezes carry the hot air out of the roof area so the pavilion stays cooler on those hot summer days. You could even put in a ceiling fan to keep the air moving when there isn't a breeze.

Small, geometrically placed stepping stones to the pavilion have a clean, crisp look compared to the rest of the garden. Not only do they keep your feet dry when the grass is wet, but they lead your eye from the house and patio directly to the pavilion.

WATER, WATER EVERYWHERE Between the pavilion and the house, is a large, recirculating water feature. Bob wanted a waterfall that reminded him of a mountain stream — one you could hear, but not always see from all areas of the garden. Since there's a slight slope to this area, the stream has several waterfalls built in. Each fall is made by water spilling over a large flat stone. The one in photo 6 shows how the stone sticks out a bit, leaving a hollow spot underneath called an "echo chamber." This open space takes the sound of the falling water as it hits the pool, amplifies it and directs it outward. That means you'll get more sound from even a small water feature.

Plantings, like these tough junipers, weave around the stones that edge the stream, helping disguise the fact that this water feature is manmade. Scattering lots of random-sized boulders along the edge of the stream also helps create a natural look. You can even sprinkle a few more away from the edge to make it appear as if the stones have just tumbled down a hillside.

168 *the* YEAR IN GARDENING   www.GardenGateMagazine.com

(6) Intensify the sound of falling water by making an echo chamber. The hollow space under the stone amplifies the sound as the water hits the pool.

BUILD STURDY PATHS Have you ever noticed how new guests to your home may take a tour of the entire house, but they always congregate in the kitchen? Well, in a garden, visitors tend to look over the whole area when they first arrive and then head back to the terrace or deck. To accommodate all that foot traffic, the area around the wooden deck has stone paths. Even after a rain, you won't have to worry about guests tracking mud into your house from this garden!

Many of the stone slabs used to build the paths are massive. One even makes a bridge over the stream in photo 7. But as with the pavilion, these big slabs look just right in the large space. Try to imagine the paths made from bricks. They'd look much too small and busy, wouldn't they? Plus, the large stone slabs are quicker to install. Granted, this is not a do-it-yourself kind of job — it takes some heavy equipment and strong workers to move these massive pieces.

Plants help disguise the hard edges of the paths. Plant them tight to the edge so they spill out onto the path. Sedums, creeping thymes and many other plants can even take a bit of foot traffic. They'll bounce right back if they occasionally get stepped on.

So as you can see, a big garden doesn't have to mean big work. However, I won't lie; it does take *some* work — all gardens do. But with careful planning, you'll still have lots of time left over to sit back and relax. □

— *Jim Childs*

(7) Make wide paths so you not only have a place to stroll, but gathering places throughout the garden, too.

DESIGN | BACK YARD

Smart design ideas every gardener can use
Create Great Island Beds

A big sweep of lawn is nice — it gives you a spot to stand and admire a garden. Or if you're into croquet, it's a great place to play. But if you love flowers, you want as much garden space as possible. So when the borders around their lawn were filled, Chris and Don Hoerner in Washington decided to take out some of the lawn and add island beds. However, island beds are more than just a place to catch the overflow of plants.

BREAK UP THE SPACE There really aren't any hard and fast rules about where you can put islands. They're great for breaking up a large expanse of lawn. Visually these separate gardens make a large space seem smaller and more intimate. However, if you need space for children, or yourself, to play, you still want to keep some open lawn. Leave generous amounts of lawn around each bed, kind of like a picture frame. Make these grassy areas at least 4 feet wide so two people can walk comfortably side-by-side around your island.

DETERMINE THE SHAPE AND SIZE The casual shapes of the beds in the photo match the gentle curves of the borders. In a garden with more formal lines, an island or two with straight edges would probably look best.

Also, keep the size of each bed in mind. You just want an island, not an entire continent! How can you determine a size to start with? Here's a tip: Take your hoe, stand and reach as far as you can with it. Measure that distance and then double it. That's a size that will let you work in the bed without stepping into it. If you don't mind crawling into the bed, go ahead and make it a bit wider.

After you mark the edges but before you remove the sod, walk around the island to see how you like it. Or you can even check it out from a second story window. And if you're adding a decorative ornament, set it in place to see how it'll look.

On the next pages, I'll share more tips on installing an island bed, or even several, in your lawn. And later, I have design tips on adding ornaments, like the steel augers you see here, into any garden, whether you have an island bed or not.

(1) Gentle curves make for easy mowing. After you lay out a garden hose to mark the edges of your island bed, get out the lawn mower and without starting it, run it around. You can adjust the hose to easier curves before you cut the edge and remove the sod.

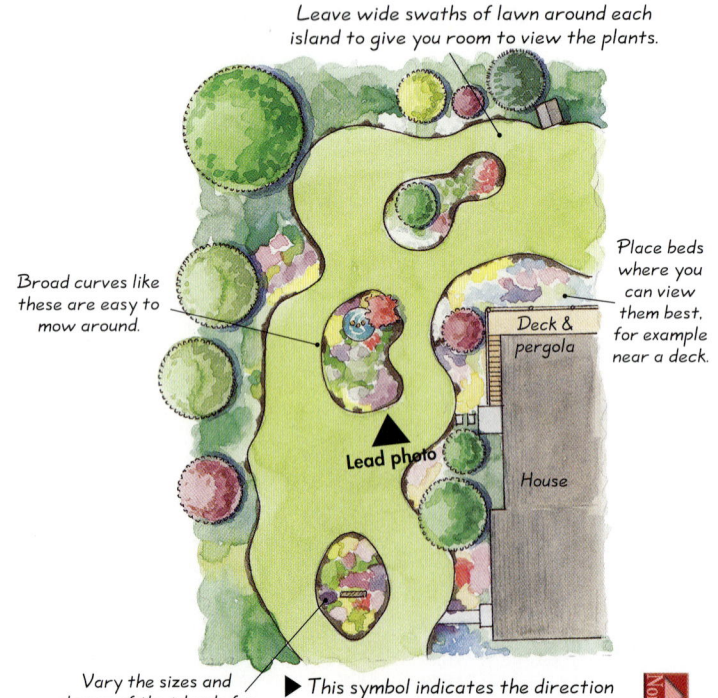

Leave wide swaths of lawn around each island to give you room to view the plants.

Broad curves like these are easy to mow around.

Place beds where you can view them best, for example near a deck.

Deck & pergola

Lead photo

House

Vary the sizes and shapes of the islands for more interest.

▶ *This symbol indicates the direction the photo was taken in the garden.*

North

170 the YEAR IN GARDENING www.GardenGateMagazine.com

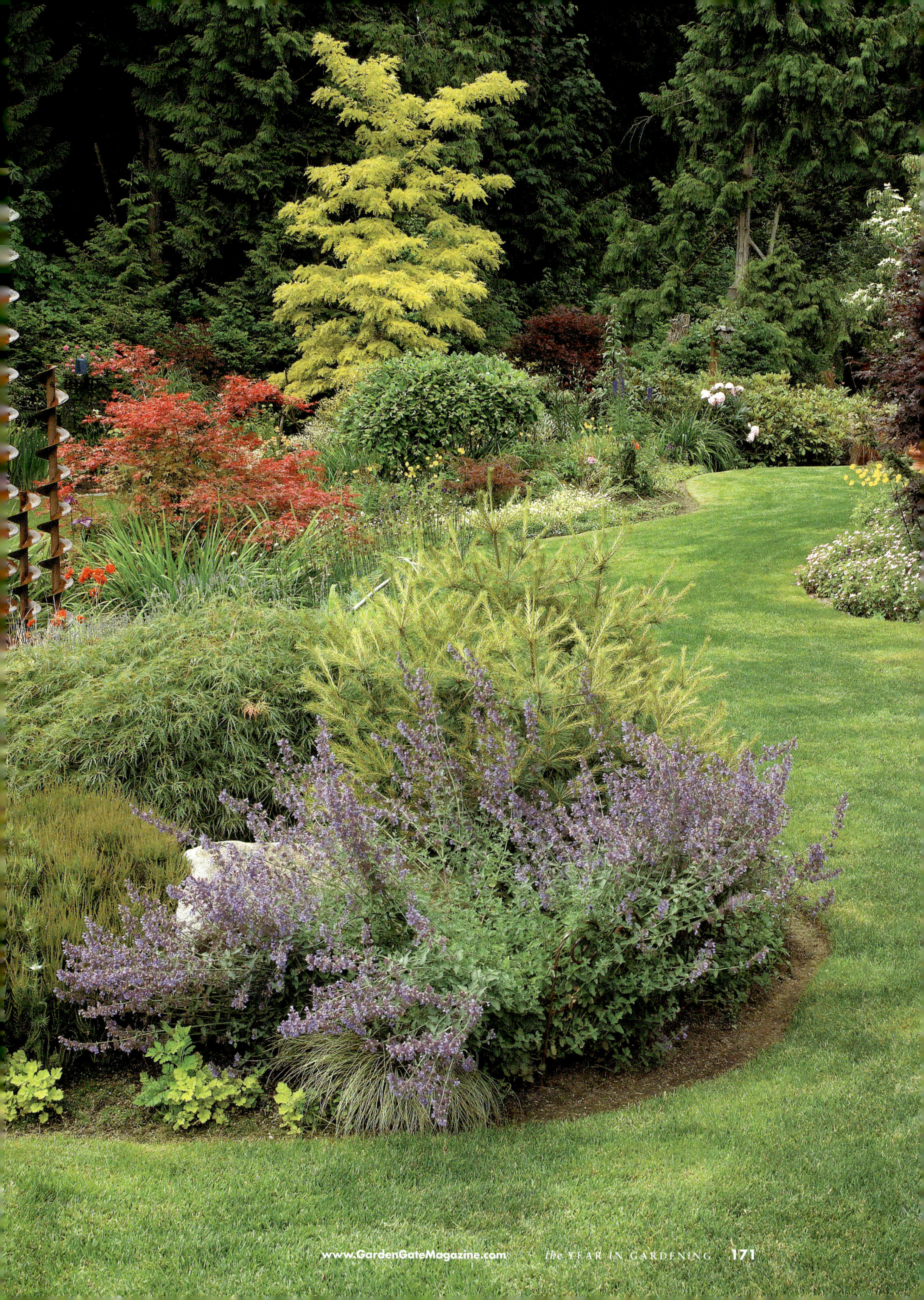

BUILDING YOUR OWN ISLANDS

Botanical Names

False cypress
Chamaecyparis spp.
Hosta
Hosta hybrids
Lily
Lilium hybrids
Lupine
Lupinus hybrids
Penstemon
Penstemon spp.

Island beds are great places to showcase plants, and I think much more interesting than just lawn. Let's take a look at some of the ways you can build, and personalize, your own island bed.

ADD SOME HEIGHT IF YOU LIKE Island beds can be flat, on the same grade as the surrounding lawn. Or, like the bed in photo 2, they can be bermed, or built up slightly. A berm like this shows off plants best because it brings them up closer to your view. And island beds with height are a great way to highlight a piece of sculpture, like this crackled glass panel. Extra height gives the ornament more importance and makes it a strong focal point for the surrounding garden.

Raising the level of the bed slightly, and carefully placing it in the best spot, can screen a view, such as a busy street. And a berm makes the topography of your garden much more interesting than if it was flat. But don't worry, you don't need a bulldozer to build a berm.

After you determine the location, size and shape, remove a 2- or 3-foot-wide strip of sod from around the inside edge of the bed. Pile this excess sod, upside down, in the center of the area and simply bring in some good soil to pile on top. Smooth the soil out a bit, tapering it down to the edges and surrounding lawn, and you have an island bed. Leave a shallow trench at the edge so soil won't run down the hill and into your lawn. And last but not least, be sure to make the berm a foot or two higher than the height you'll want when it's finished — soil settles and you'll lose some of the height.

As you build the bed, you also have a great opportunity to amend your soil. If you've always wanted to grow acid-loving evergreens, or other plants that need a specific soil, amend now. Simply mix the amendments into the soil as you build the berm. Every few years you'll probably need to add more of these amendments to your soil.

PLANT CREATIVELY Do you have room in your garden for more than one island bed? If so, tie several together visually by growing similar plants or using similar colors and textures in each. You can even coordinate them with the surrounding borders. Or if they are a distance apart, each one can have a completely different theme or color scheme. For example in photo 2, there are lots of colorful perennials, like penstemons and lupines. Combine them with a few gold false cypress for some winter interest and you're set. But in photo 3, the bed in the background is planted with more shrubs, and much more subtle colors.

Are you a plant collector? Island beds let you keep your collections separate if you choose. Make one in a shady spot for hostas and another in the sun for lilies. Beds can even peak at different times so one bed is drawing your attention while the other is not at its best. Separate beds are a great way for couples to garden together. They let each person exercise his or her individual tastes.

(2) Plan ahead. These gold false cypress are still young. But leave room for them to grow and you won't need to adjust the size of the island later.

(3) Well-defined edges and wide paths of grass help these beds stand out as individuals. Imagine what this scene would look like if it were all lawn with only the border in the distance. It would look much larger, and not as friendly.

Freestanding beds like these let you view plants from all sides. None of that putting the tallest plants in back and shorter ones in front. Here you'll want the tallest near the center, with the rest tapering down to the edges. But notice in photo 3 that the left side of the bed has a tall shrub near the edge? It prevents you from seeing the entire bed from any one angle, keeps things from being too predictable and creates a bit of mystery about what might be behind it.

These individual beds can be anything you want them to be — they're sort of a freestyle form of gardening. Like many aspects of designing and planting a landscape, island beds are a great way to personalize your garden. Another way is with ornaments. On the next pages, I'll share some tips from several gardens on different ways to use ornaments. I'll show you easy design techniques to display them as focal points or accessories. □

— *Jim Childs*

A bermed island blocks the view from the house into the neighbors' yard.

A large shrub obscures part of the island, adding the element of mystery about what might be on the other side.

▶ This symbol indicates the direction the photo was taken in the garden.

Shades of red and purple visually tie these islands together.

Crackled glass panel ornament placed as a focal point.

www.GardenGateMagazine.com · *the* YEAR IN GARDENING · 173

GARDEN DECORATION

You don't *have* to have sculptures or ornaments in your garden — it may not be your style. But like finding the right tie to go with a new sport coat, ornaments add something special. And they can take an average landscape to a new level. The Hoerner garden you've just seen has ornaments, like the augers to the right, as focal points in its island beds. But take a look at the rest of these photos from other gardeners to see more ways to add an ornament or two to your beds.

Too many of us find it hard to limit our "collections." We find things we like, or friends give us gifts, and we keep adding them to our gardens. Soon we have a cluttered hodge-podge that looks more like a garage sale than a landscape. When it comes to ornaments, the truth is, less is more. On these pages I'll show you two great ways to show off garden ornaments.

Focal points

DRAW YOUR ATTENTION Place an ornament where you can't miss it because of its size, shape, color or movement, and you have a focal point. These ornaments are often specimens, like the large concrete leaf in photo 4. It makes a statement and draws your eye to it, so one is usually enough in a small garden. The garden we've been looking at on the previous pages has three islands and several garden rooms that create distinctly different views. So it makes sense to have one in each. How do you know if you can use several focal points? When you stand in the most-used viewing spot, such as the patio or an entrance gate, it's best if you can't see more than one large ornament. That's true with the cluster of metal augers in photo 5. Although there are several other ornaments in the garden, they're placed so you can only see one from this vantage point.

Curving paths are a great place to use ornaments. Place one as a focal point in the distance, at a bend in a path, where you can't see around the corner. Your eye will be drawn to it as you stroll along. Once you get close to the first focal point, or turn the corner, another one placed in the distance pulls you toward that spot. Since you only see one at a time, this is a good way to place several striking ornaments in one garden.

CONSIDER THE SCALE Choosing an ornament that's in scale with the surroundings is hard to explain because there are so many different kinds of ornaments. But you wouldn't set a tiny figure in the middle of a sweeping expanse of lawn — you wouldn't notice it. And you wouldn't put a life-sized figure of a giraffe in a tiny courtyard or it would overwhelm the surrounding garden.

Accessories

TUCK IN SURPRISES Just the opposite of focal points, ornaments that are smaller in size or are neutral or subtle colors *accessorize* your garden. They're often tucked into their surroundings, partially hidden by foliage, to add a bit of surprise to the garden. You can place several of

(5) One at a time, please. One large ornament in an area is enough. Since these augers are the same material and grouped close together, they're seen as one unit.

(4) Frame your focal point. Contrasting the foliage around an ornament draws even more attention to it.

these pieces throughout your garden. While you may be able to see more than one from where you stand, don't overdo it. After all, you want your plants to have some room and still be the most interesting part of the garden.

Ornaments that accessorize work best if they have a style or theme in common. For example, all your ornaments might be made from rusted metal. Or perhaps you have a fondness for rabbits. The person who owns the garden in photo 6 does. That's why she tucked several rabbit statues among her plantings. Just be careful not to mix too many different styles and colors together — it could get confusing.

MOVE THINGS AROUND One of the best things about accessory pieces is that they can be moved easily. The dragonfly in photo 7 looks right at home resting on the red stone. Later you could swap it for a small turtle figure. Either piece would get a bit of added importance sitting on the red rock. Or move the dragonfly to a different place altogether. Visitors might have fun looking for its hiding spot each time they stop by.

If you have lots of ornaments, store a few of your pieces for a year or two and replace them occasionally with something completely different. It's a great way to keep your garden looking fresh.

(6) Go for the unexpected. Tuck accessories among foliage for a whimsical surprise.

(7) Not the main event. Why would you want to take attention away from this showy flower garden? The dragonfly patiently rests on the rock at the garden's peak. Then when the flowers are between blooms, it catches your eye.

www.GardenGateMagazine.com · the YEAR IN GARDENING · 175

DESIGN | GREAT COMBOS

Ripe tomatoes

Summer squash

Feast your eyes on these 5 great design ideas!

Vegetable Medley

I've never had enough room to grow a separate vegetable garden. But I always thought well-grown veggies were pretty, so I finally decided they could have a place in my perennial border. After all, many vegetables and flowers need the same things for success — sun, water and good soil. And as long as you keep the foliage texture, color and size of each plant in mind, there's not a lot of difference in designing with these two groups.

Let me show you a few ways vegetables can hold their own in any flower bed. I'll share design ideas, as well as some "growing concerns," to keep your garden producing and looking good. Whether you start from seed or buy young plants at the greenhouse, you'll find that you can get double-duty out of your beds and borders. And you won't have to sacrifice a thing when it comes to good looks. □

— *Jim Childs*

Grow up and out with vines

Want lots of produce? Grow vine crops, such as squash or cucumbers. If you've ever grown a zucchini or other summer squash, such as the yellow one in the upper right inset, you know you'll have enough for friends. But while a tomato or two and a few lettuces might look good, they won't give you enough produce to put up for the winter or share.

BE BOLD! Look at all those lush squash vines in the center of the back border. Their foliage makes a bold statement. Just be sure to give them some room to spread. Or look for bush varieties that stay in a clump. Pair low plants with vertical ones, such as the sunflowers along the wall. Notice the grasses to the right and the spiky gladiolus in front? They're good texture contrasts to all of these large leaves

A large area planted with spring bulbs makes a great spot for sprawling vines. You only need to water at the base of the vegetable, so the surrounding area stays dry — just what those tulip and daffodil bulbs require during summer dormancy.

OH, GROW UP Tomatoes that sprawl or grow tall in cages might seem difficult to work into an ornamental garden. But plant them on interesting wood obelisks to add height to a border or bed. Later, when the structure is covered with vines, just imagine how easy to pick, pretty to look at, and tasty the red fruit you see at far left will be.

MORE TO SAVOR...

Tuck them in Cottage gardens are usually loose and casual in design, perfect for tucking in a few veggies here and there. You can even add a few herbs. Now your cottage garden becomes a colorful kitchen garden. Just look at what a great combination these plants make.

ENJOY THE HARVEST Most vegetables won't look good all season, so you'll need to plan ahead to remove or cover plants that are past their prime. Cabbages are typically one-time producers — plant spreading or sprawling flowers nearby. This vivid pink petunia will cover the bare spot when the cabbage is gone. Or sprinkle seeds of late-season crops, such as lettuce, spinach, turnips or radishes, to keep the garden looking fresh.

WATCH FOR PESTS Some veggies are pest magnets. For example, cabbage loopers love these cabbages and purple kale. Sure, you'll enjoy watching small white or pale yellow butterflies flitting about your garden. But later, voracious little green worms quickly turn leaves into something resembling Swiss cheese. You can enjoy the lacy look if you like. Or an application of *Bacillus thuringiensis* (Bt) will keep your crop looking good. And it won't hurt you or any of your flowers.

FILL EVERY NOOK In any garden, narrow leaves are a good texture contrast with coarse foliage. Tuck a few onions into almost any sunny garden for some interesting foliage combinations. And the white flowers in summer aren't bad, either. Another nice thing about designing with onions? You can pull a few as you need them and you won't notice a big empty spot in the flower bed.

GARDEN DESIGN: Karen Guzak and Warner Blake/AngelArmsWorks

Forget the flowers Often the foliage and fruit of a vegetable plant is attractive enough that you don't even need flowers around it. The shiny dark purple fruit, large foliage and architectural form of the eggplant in this photo definitely hold your attention just as well as any flower would.

All of these purple shades coordinate well with the ground cover of dark ajuga and the purple fountain grass behind. Protect vegetables with mulch. These pine needles not only keep the plants evenly moist, but also keep the fruit looking good until you harvest it, free of splashing soil during heavy rains.

Block a view Are you stuck with a narrow spot between a sidewalk and the garage wall? A trellis is a great way to beautify that situation. But trelliswork doesn't have to be against a wall. It can also be set free-standing to block a view where you don't have room for a tall shrub. That's how this sturdy trellis is used. Sure, you could cover it with a clematis or other flowering vine, but why not cover it with climbing, or pole, beans? They're very fast growers, easy to start from seed and dense enough to block an unwanted view. Best of all, they do all of those things, *and* you also get to feast on fresh veggies.

DOUBLE CROP Pole beans are a warm weather crop. That means if you only grow them on the trellis, it could be bare until midsummer. To remedy this, start out in early spring with a cool season crop of climbing peas. After harvest, as the temperature rises, the vines dry up and you can plant the bean seeds.

Check out the inset — did you know beans don't have to be green? Look for purple 'Blauhilde' pole beans to add color to your trellis. Bean vines often have "bare knees" — their lower leaves sometimes drop off. Solve the problem by planting tall, colorful perennials, such as these coneflowers, in front as a cover-up.

PHOTO: Greg Ryan/Sally Beyer

SHORT ON SPACE?

Plant veggies in a container. In this window box, after the lettuce is finished, these compact tomatoes will fill the box with red fruit — that is, until you eat them. The red celosia and tufts of bloodgrass make a colorful background that will coordinate well with the red tomatoes when they ripen.

Any container needs constant watering. But if veggies dry out, they won't produce well. And in a container you'll need to supply extra nutrients. Since the tomatoes are the focus of this combo, and the pickiest eaters, choose a fertilizer specifically for them, such as Miracle Gro® for tomatoes. Flowering plants will tolerate it just fine.

DESIGN | GREAT COMBOS

Combine Bulbs and Perennials Like a Pro

with Jo Ellen Meyers Sharp

Botanical Names

Bearded iris
Iris hybrid
Daffodil
Narcissus hybrid
Pinks *Dianthus* spp.
Sedum *Sedum* spp.

PHOTOS: Courtesy of Jo Ellen Meyers Sharp (portrait); Courtesy of the Netherlands Flower Bulb Information Center (hyacinth, Spanish bluebell); © Joseph G. Strauch Jr. (trout lily)

Every spring I marvel at gardens filled with spring bulbs. But then I begin wondering, "What does this garden look like in summer?" Bulbs have pretty specific growing requirements, especially while they're dormant. Is there any way to mix bulbs and other plants together in borders so both are happy? Jo Ellen Meyers Sharp, editor of *Indiana Living Green*, has planted bulbs with her perennials for years and has some useful tips to share.

CHOOSE YOUR FRIENDS WISELY
The companions you choose will have to grow in the same kinds of conditions the bulbs need. Most bulbs like it dry in summer. That's why dry-loving companions are often ideal. Many annuals tend to be water hogs, needing constant moisture to keep them looking good so they're not the best choice if you want your bulbs to last more than one season. And if you have heavy soil that stays moist, you'll need to choose both bulbs and companions that can tolerate it.

The illustrations below show you tips for choosing good companions. Then on the next page you'll find charts with three distinct growing conditions — dry sun, moist soil and shade. With each section I've included some well-known bulbs, as well as a few perennial companions that like those situations.

MAKE THE NEIGHBORS WORK
You know how you always hear that you shouldn't cut off bulb foliage before it's fully ripened? That's hard to do when you have a big clump of ugly falling-down yellow leaves in the middle of a bed. The planting below helps you do the right thing. Perennials with dense foliage, such as these tall sedums, grow up and over the withering leaves, allowing them to gather sunlight and store energy for as long as they need.

EXTEND THE ENJOYMENT You don't want the neighboring plants to be too tall when the spring bulbs are in bloom. In the small combo below you see how the neighbors are short, and not flowering, while the bulbs are at their peak. The daffodils are the center of attention and you can easily see them.

WHICH CAME FIRST? It's often best to plant the perennial garden first and the bulbs second. That way you can leave at least 6 to 12 inches of open space between the perennials and the bulbs. The spacing gives the perennial room to expand without interfering with the bulbs. And it makes it easy to feed each plant with exactly what it needs, when it needs it.

Not only does choosing the right plant companions make gardening chores easier, it makes your garden beautiful, too. Pair your spring bulbs and perennials carefully and everyone will be happy. □

— *Jim Childs*

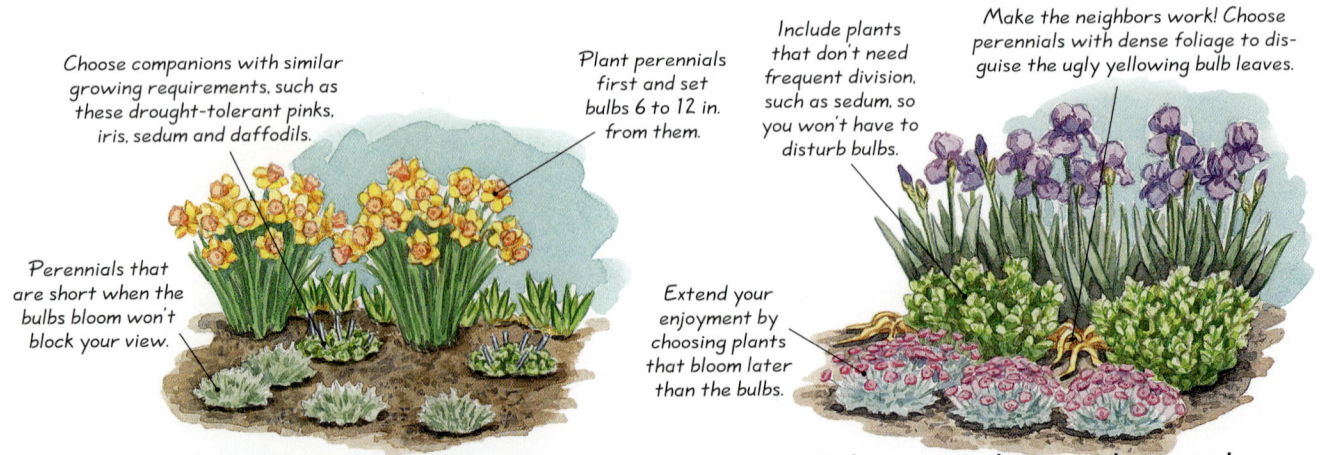

Choose companions with similar growing requirements, such as these drought-tolerant pinks, iris, sedum and daffodils.

Perennials that are short when the bulbs bloom won't block your view.

Plant perennials first and set bulbs 6 to 12 in. from them.

Include plants that don't need frequent division, such as sedum, so you won't have to disturb bulbs.

Make the neighbors work! Choose perennials with dense foliage to disguise the ugly yellowing bulb leaves.

Extend your enjoyment by choosing plants that bloom later than the bulbs.

Spring, when the bulbs are in bloom

Early summer, as the perennials start to take over

GOOD NEIGHBORS

Bulbs | Perennials

Got hot, dry sun? These plants will grow great

Daffodil *Narcissus* spp. and hybrids
5 to 20 in. tall and 5 in. wide; most are long-lived — avoid growing near perennials that need to be dug and divided frequently; cold-hardy in USDA zones 3 to 9; heat-tolerant in AHS zones 9 to 1

Hyacinth *Hyacinthus orientalis* (photo at right)
8 to 12 in. tall and 3 in. wide; bulbs usually not long-lived, so can be planted with perennials that may need frequent division; cold-hardy in USDA zones 4 to 8; heat-tolerant in AHS zones 9 to 1

Tulip *Tulipa* spp. and hybrids
4 to 24 in. tall and 3 to 5 in. wide; species tulips are often longer lasting than some hybrids, so choose companions to fit the variety; cold-hardy in USDA zones 3 to 8; heat-tolerant in AHS zones 8 to 1

Bearded iris *Iris* hybrid
8 to 40 in. tall and 18 in. wide; shallow-rooted rhizomes; almost unlimited color choices; foliage helps disguise ripening bulb foliage; divide frequently; cold-hardy in USDA zones 4 to 9; heat-tolerant in AHS zones 9 to 1

Lamb's ear *Stachys byzantina* (photo at right)
18 in. tall and wide; bushy growth great for covering ripening bulb foliage; cold-hardy in USDA zones 5 to 9; heat-tolerant in AHS zones 9 to 1

Common yarrow *Achillea millefolium*
12 to 36 in. tall and spreading; needs frequent division to keep it in check; grow it near bulbs that don't mind being disturbed frequently; cold-hardy in USDA zones 4 to 9; heat-tolerant in AHS zones 8 to 1

Great companions for moist soil

Fritillaria *Fritillaria meleagris*
6 to 12 in. tall and 3 in. wide; very tolerant of moist soil; purple or white flowers; often reseeds, forming colonies or drifts; cold-hardy in USDA zones 3 to 8; heat-tolerant in AHS zones 8 to 1

Quamash *Camassia leichtlinii*
3 to 4 ft. tall and 12 to 15 in. wide; flowers can be blue or white; likes acid soil; sun to part shade; cold-hardy in USDA zones 4 to 10; heat-tolerant in AHS zones 10 to 1

Spanish bluebell *Hyacinthoides hispanica* (photo at right)
16 in. tall and 12 in. wide; pale blue, pink or white blooms; prefers dappled shade; naturalizes easily; cold-hardy in USDA zones 4 to 9; heat-tolerant in AHS zones 9 to 1

Astilbe *Astilbe* spp.
6 to 36 in. tall and 8 to 36 in. wide; good foliage for covering ripening bulb leaves; cold-hardy in USDA zones 3 to 9; heat-tolerant in AHS zones 9 to 1

Cardinal flower *Lobelia cardinalis*
36 in. tall and 12 in. wide; late to start growing, so won't overshadow spring bulbs; cold-hardy in USDA zones 2 to 8; heat-tolerant in AHS zones 8 to 1

Goatsbeard *Aruncus* spp.
10 in. to 5 ft. tall and 15 in. to 4 ft. wide; clumps rarely need dividing; cold-hardy in USDA zones 3 to 9; heat-tolerant in AHS zones 9 to 1

Ligularia *Ligularia* spp. (photo at right)
3 to 6 ft. tall and 2 to 3 ft. wide; large leaves of one plant can cover lots of bulb foliage; cold-hardy in USDA zones 4 to 9; heat-tolerant in AHS zones 8 to 1

Good neighbors that like shade

Trout lily *Erythronium americanum* (photo at right)
6 to 9 in. tall and 3 in. wide; multiplies and naturalizes well; tolerates dry soil but best in moist, well-drained; cold-hardy in USDA zones 3 to 8; heat-tolerant in AHS zones 8 to 1

Windflower *Anemone blanda*
6 in. tall and wide; tolerates both sun and shade; needs to be kept dry while dormant; cold-hardy in USDA zones 4 to 8; heat-tolerant in AHS zones 8 to 1

Wood hyacinth *Hyacinthoides non-scripta*
8 to 16 in. tall and 3 in. wide; moist soil; naturalizes easily; pendulous blue flowers; cold-hardy in USDA zones 4 to 10; heat-tolerant in AHS zones 10 to 1

Celandine poppy *Stylophorum diphyllum*
12 in. tall and 12 in. wide; easy to divide and move; also reseeds, but is not invasive; cold-hardy in USDA zones 5 to 8; heat-tolerant in AHS zones 8 to 1

Ostrich fern *Matteuccia struthiopteris*
5 ft. tall and 3 ft. wide; spreading fern great for hiding bulb foliage; cold-hardy in USDA zones 2 to 8; heat-tolerant in AHS zones 8 to 1

Solomon's seal *Polygonatum* spp.
8 to 36 in. tall and 12 to 24 in. wide; clumps will eventually form large colonies, but rarely need to be lifted and divided; cold-hardy in USDA zones 4 to 9; heat-tolerant in AHS zones 9 to 1

WEB extra
Want more perennials that make terrific bulb companions? Check out our *list*.

Lamb's ear won't need any extra watering during the summer. And with dry summers, a hyacinth bulb will live longer.

Ligularia and Spanish bluebell both like moist soil. Plus, the large ligularia leaves will disguise the ripening bluebell foliage.

Trout lilies like the shade found at the base of a tree trunk. In too sun, the leaves will burn.

DESIGN | GREAT COMBOS

5 colorful and easy-to grow combos
Fall Splendor

There's something about the autumn garden. Maybe it's that slanting, golden sunlight that makes colors glow with a richness they don't have in spring or summer. Or maybe it's because gardeners know that time is short and we have to soak up as much garden atmosphere as we can to get us through the winter. Whatever it is, fall is a great time for gardeners — and for plants.

I don't know about you, but I often feel revived and ready to get out in the garden again once the heat of summer is finally over. But instead of just spending time pulling weeds, deadheading and getting your beds ready for winter, why not make plans for a beautiful garden. One (or all!) of these late-season combinations will brighten your garden and give you great enjoyment as you go about your autumn chores.

Let's start with two autumn classics, chrysanthemums and goldenrod. Then turn the page for three more great fall looks using some well-known combinations and a few out-of-the-ordinary pairings.

1 UNCOMMON MUMS Chrysanthemums, or mums, are often the first plants you think of when you notice a nip in the air. But they don't have to be those tight mounds you see every fall being sold in full bloom. Take a look at the old cultivar 'Sheffield' in this photo. It's a looser, more casual style that doesn't need pinching. Plus it's more cold-hardy than the mums you pick up in bloom. Plant it in spring. It'll start blooming in late September and continue well after a frost. And the fall foliage color of shining sumac brings out the autumn fire in this combo.

A Chrysanthemum *Chrysanthemum* 'Sheffield'
24 to 36 in. tall and 18 to 24 in. wide; cold-hardy in USDA zones 5 to 9; heat-tolerant in AHS zones 9 to 1

B Shining sumac *Rhus copallina latifolia* Prairie Flame™
15 ft. tall and wide; cold-hardy in USDA zones 4 to 9; heat-tolerant in AHS zones 9 to 1

2 GREAT FOR SMALL SPACES Breeders are growing more and more dwarf varieties of perennials for today's smaller gardens. For example, 'Laurin' goldenrod grows less than 18 in. tall. Its late blooms are perfect companions to the foliage of an almost black bugleweed and the short pale green leaves of a miniature iris. The color and foliage texture contrast is what makes this combo effective. Plus there's something in this mix that will hold your interest from spring, when the bugleweed and iris bloom, until late fall when the goldenrod finally fades. And the evergreen boxwood foliage carries this combo through the cold days of winter, until the flowers start again.

A **Miniature bearded iris** *Iris* hybrid
6 to 10 in. tall and 12 in. wide; cold-hardy in USDA zones 3 to 10; heat-tolerant in AHS zones 10 to 1

B **Bugleweed** *Ajuga reptans* 'Binblasca' (Black Scallop)
4 to 6 in. tall and 10 in. wide; cold-hardy in USDA zones 4 to 11; heat-tolerant in AHS zones 11 to 1

C **Goldenrod** *Solidago* 'Laurin'
12 to 18 in. tall and 18 in. wide; cold-hardy in USDA zones 5 to 9; heat-tolerant in AHS zones 9 to 1

D **Boxwood** *Buxus* 'Green Velvet'
2 to 4 ft. tall and wide; cold-hardy in USDA zones 5 to 8; heat-tolerant in AHS zones 8 to 1

WEB extra
See a *slide show* of even more great fall combos.

MORE FALL COMBOS!

What does it take to make a gorgeous combination? Well, the first thing is that all the plants have to show interesting color or texture at the same time.

Autumn combos can be created from all kinds of plants. You don't have to rely on that old burning bush in the corner of your yard to carry the whole season. Capitalize on other woody plants like sumac or maple to add color very late into the season, even after frost. Go ahead and grow annuals, such as the orange zinnias at right or chartreuse sweet potato vine below. Annuals often reach their peak of color and look great for several weeks before a hard freeze knocks them out. And last but not least, there are many hardy perennials, like the asters in photo 5, that start blooming in late summer, and continue even after a frost.

Whatever you plant for fall, it may last for weeks if the weather is mild. Or, just like spring pairings, a frost may change them overnight. The nice thing about fall combos? That frost could turn the foliage, or even the flowers, a different and sometimes surprising color you never expected. ☐

— *Jim Childs*

3 PREPARE FOR THE SEASON Burgundy and chartreuse — classic autumn colors. But this foliage-based combo has those shades much of the summer, too. When fall approaches, the colors become richer, more vibrant hues in the golden light of the season. And with cooler temperatures, the leaves of some plants, such as the sumac, take on a coppery cast that intensifies before they finally drop off for winter. You'll want to cut off or pull out the frozen sweet potato vines, but don't cut back the sedum just yet. Wait until spring so you can enjoy the dark bronze flower heads all winter.

A Smokebush *Cotinus coggygria* 'Velvet Cloak'
6 to 12 ft. tall and 3 to 12 ft. wide; cold-hardy in USDA zones 5 to 9; heat-tolerant in AHS zones 9 to 1

B Sumac *Rhus typhina* 'Bailtiger' (Tiger Eyes®)
3 to 6 ft. tall and wide; cold-hardy in USDA zones 4 to 8; heat-tolerant in AHS zones 8 to 1

C Sedum *Sedum telephium* 'Purple Emperor'
16 in. tall and 18 in. wide; cold-hardy in USDA zones 3 to 9; heat-tolerant in AHS zones 9 to 1

D Sweet potato *Ipomoea batatas* 'Margarita'
6 to 12 in. tall and 6 ft. wide; cold-hardy in USDA zones 9 to 11; heat-tolerant in AHS zones 12 to 1

4 A BLAST OF ANNUALS As summer winds down, annuals know their days are numbered. Their goal is to set as many seeds as possible before they die. Before they can produce seeds, they have to make flowers. To keep those flowers coming until frost, keep deadheading spent blooms. That'll prevent seeds from forming too early and stopping the show. The purple heart and salvia in the background are terrific texture and color contrasts to the vivid orange zinnia and red geranium. While some of these plants are hardy if you live in very warm zones, all of them can be treated as annuals, no matter where you live.

- **A Purple heart** *Tradescantia pallida*
  6 to 10 in. tall and 12 to 18 in. wide; cold-hardy in USDA zones 10 to 11; heat-tolerant in AHS zones 12 to 1
- **B Salvia** *Salvia farinacea* 'Victoria'
  18 to 24 in. tall and 12 in. wide; cold-hardy in USDA zones 5 to 9; heat-tolerant in AHS zones 9 to 1
- **C Geranium** *Pelargonium* hybrid
  1 to 3 ft. tall and wide; cold-hardy in USDA zones 10 to 11; heat-tolerant in AHS zones 12 to 1
- **D Zinnia** *Zinnia elegans* 'Profusion Orange'
  12 in. tall and 15 in. wide; annual; heat-tolerant in AHS zones 12 to 1

5 AMAZING ASTERS If it's not mums, it's often asters that brighten the autumn garden. Usually in shades of pink, white or blue, they bring with them a pastel color scheme. Soft pink 'Harrington's Pink' and lavender-blue 'Jindai' look great with grasses. Compared to many asters, both are quite tall. That puts the flowers at about the same level as the fuzzy seedheads of this Korean feather reed grass. If the spiky New Zealand flax is not hardy in your zone, grow it in a large nursery pot you can sink into the ground. Before freezing temperatures damage the leaves, it's easy to dig up the pot and move the plant indoors for the winter.

- **A Korean feather reed grass**
  Calamagrostis brachytricha
  3 to 4 ft. tall and 2 to 3 ft. wide; cold-hardy in USDA zones 4 to 9; heat-tolerant in AHS zones 9 to 1
- **B Aster** *Aster novae-angliae* 'Harrington's Pink'
  4 to 6 ft. tall and 2 to 3 ft. wide; cold-hardy in USDA zones 3 to 8; heat-tolerant in AHS zones 8 to 1
- **C Tatarian aster** *Aster tataricus* 'Jindai'
  3 to 4 ft. tall and 2 to 3 ft. wide; cold-hardy in USDA zones 4 to 8; heat-tolerant in AHS zones 8 to 1
- **D New Zealand flax** *Phormium tenax purpureum*
  1 to 6 ft. tall and 1 to 3 ft. wide; cold-hardy in USDA zones 9 to 11; heat-tolerant in AHS zones 12 to 1

DESIGN | COLOR PALETTE

Cool down the summer heat

Bring on the Blue

For gardeners, blue is a coveted color. In part, that's because it's so hard to find truly blue flowers. But it's more than that. Surveys show that, by a large margin, people choose blue as their favorite over all the other colors in the rainbow. This cool hue is perceived as stable and reliable, peaceful and soothing, thoughtful and meditative. And isn't that just what you want in your garden? But blue can be exciting, as well. We'll show you four ways to use blue in your own garden to make it a beautiful place you can enjoy, whatever your mood.

COOL BLUE Like your favorite pair of jeans, blue combines easily with most colors. Even though it's hard to find truly blue flowers like the speedwell and grape hyacinth in photo 1, it's well worth the effort. What a refreshing sight to see these similar shades of blue blooming in a spring garden! A few other pastel-colored flowers like pink hyacinths and yellow daffodils will give you a spring combo to brighten your garden after a long, cold winter.

Blue flowers are pretty but they eventually fade. To have color all season, add blue foliage plants like hostas or blue fescue.

REV UP YOUR BLUES If you want a garden with lots of pizazz, try the combination in photo 2. Adding orange or yellow to blue really spices things up. But even when you're combining colors, you still want a pulled-together look. That's where blue comes in. Just as repeating a plant throughout a border provides unity, repeating a color does the same thing. Take a look around this garden. The blue wall and container stand out. Look further and you'll see blue foliage, decorative chunks of blue-green glass — even the path gravel is blue-gray.

Feeling a little cramped in your garden? Add blue. Whether it's flowers, foliage or hardscape, this cool color provides depth in a garden. Why? Because cool colors recede visually. Place your blue at the back of the garden and it will make the space seem bigger. Or repeat clumps of blue throughout a mixed border to add a sense of depth to the planting.

Find out more about using blue in the garden on the next pages. You'll also find some color "recipes" in "New looks for blue," too.

Botanical Names

Blue fescue
 Festuca glauca
Daffodil
 Narcissus hybrid
False indigo
 Baptisia australis
Forget-me-not
 Myosotis sylvatica
Hosta
 Hosta hybrid
Hyacinth
 Hyacinthus orientalis
Morning glory
 Ipomoea hybrid
Plumbago
 Ceratostigma plumbaginoides
Siberian bugloss
 Brunnera macrophylla

1 GROW TRUE BLUE FLOWERS Flowers that are truly blue are hard to find. Most of the time what's called "blue" in catalogs and on plant tags is really a blue-violet. But the flower color of the two plants in this photo is no trick — they really are blue. For more blue flowers every season, look for Siberian bugloss, forget-me-not, false indigo, morning glory and plumbago.

A Grape hyacinth *Muscari armeniacum* 'Valerie Finnis'
B Speedwell *Veronica umbrosa* 'Georgia Blue'

2 MIX HOT AND COLD The cool blue wall behind the water feature creates the illusion of space, making the garden seem bigger than it actually is. Using orange, which contrasts strongly with blue, makes this one hot combo. Besides grabbing your attention, those bright-orange red hot pokers in the foreground help the blue look more intense. And in turn, blue acts as a foil, brightening the orange. Keep it simple with strong contrasts; if you have a lot of different colors, the effect won't be as striking.

A New Zealand flax *Phormium* 'Jack Spratt'
B Hen and chicks *Sempervivum* hybrid
C Blue fescue *Festuca glauca* 'Elijah Blue'
D Red hot poker *Kniphofia* 'Orange Crush'

MOODY BLUES

How do you feel about blue? Is it peaceful and soothing, calm and thoughtful or bright and cheerful? Blue can be all these things, depending on how you use it. Color is more than just the physical reaction of light reflecting off surfaces. Different shades of blue can actually create different moods.

CHANGING SHADES Soft blue-grays, like the hosta in photo 3, are a good choice for toning down warm, intense colors that could otherwise overwhelm a garden. The chartreuse hosta below is great for reflecting what little light does penetrate the shade, but a whole bed of chartreuse might look too harsh. This quiet blue adds depth and calms the planting.

Now take a look at the bright blue bench in photo 4; it's quite a contrast to the soft blue of photo 3, isn't it? More intense shades of blue have a more upbeat feel. Even though this blue is bright, the space is still relaxing and peaceful because there's plenty of green to give your eye a resting place. And nearby plants have flower colors with some blue in them, providing a cohesive look to the garden.

So the next time you're wondering what can tone down a wild-looking bunch of colors, add some depth or create a place to relax, plant some blue-flowered favorites or paint a lawn chair a nice shade of blue. Then sit back and relax.

—*Sherri Ribbey*

3 DON'T FORGET FOLIAGE

Foliage may not be as bright as flowers but it's just as beautiful. And leaves come in blue, too! The blue-gray of 'Halcyon' hosta is muted, so it goes well with almost any color. Here, the soft shade is perfect for toning down the chartreuse hosta and light-green baneberry. For a completely different effect, pair the blue-gray hosta with burgundy coral bells. Now it's the blue-gray that's the star of the show.

A Hosta *Hosta* 'Halcyon'
B Hosta *Hosta* 'August Moon'
C White baneberry
 Actaea pachypoda

4 MIX AND MATCH Want color but think blue and orange might be too jarring for your garden? Try purples and reds with blue instead. The colors here work because they're similar — they all have some blue in them. It's almost as if a painter added a little more red to each plant's flowers, starting with the blue hydrangea, then moving on to the blue-violet clematis and lastly to the red bee balm. The important thing here is that this red has blue undertones. A red that has more orange in it would create too much contrast for this cool combo.

A Hydrangea *Hydrangea macrophylla* 'Nikko Blue'
B Clematis *Clematis* 'Niobe'
C Bee balm *Monarda* 'Jacob Cline'

NEW LOOKS FOR BLUE

Cobalt blue has been all the rage in garden containers and ornaments for several years. But you've probably noticed some other shades of blue showing up in garden centers, too. Here are two blue "recipes" to use in your own garden. The two containers are a similar shade of green-blue — but these looks are totally different! And don't feel confined to the items that are shown in the photos. Use flowers, foliage, ornaments, cushions or anything else with these "new blues."

BRIGHT AND CHEERY Take a soft shade of blue like the teal container at left, add some bright colors and you have a combination that's perfect for entertaining or grabbing attention. With a cool background like this, the orange, yellow and red really stand out. And if you're worried about trying this kind of eye-popping color combination on a large scale, give it a try with a small planter and table setting like the one at left. If you like it, move on to a bigger container or an in-ground planting that can give your home landscape real curb appeal.

SOFT AND SUBTLE Why not use blue to remind you of a day at the beach? To create a laid-back mood, use colors that are all nearly the same intensity. That way, no one color grabs all the attention and the whole planting looks good. Stick with plants that have warm foliage colors in brown, soft green and burgundy. This turquoise container, paired with sandy browns and a tropical palm, can take you on a vacation, even if it's only in your imagination.

www.GardenGateMagazine.com   *the* YEAR IN GARDENING   **189**

DESIGN | COLOR PALETTE

Color That Won't Quit! 6 tips to make it easy

Botanical Names

Azalea
   Rhododendron spp.
Boxwood
   Buxus spp.
False cypress
   Chamaecyparis spp.
Geranium
   Pelargonium hybrids
Japanese maple
   Acer palmatum
Juniper *Juniperus* spp.
Rose *Rosa* spp.
Sedum *Sedum* spp.
Yarrow *Achillea* spp.

Everyone has opinions about color. Things like favorite color or which ones look best together can be different from person to person. However, no matter what you think about these things, most everyone likes color — and lots of it — especially in their gardens!

But how do you know what plants to grow to get the most possible color all of the time? Well, surprisingly, it doesn't really take that many plants to create a garden with long-lasting color. It just takes a little planning. I'll talk more about that later. First, I'll share six tips on different ways to achieve three-season color success.

(1) Color for every season Choose plants to highlight each season, such as the soft pink flowers of azaleas in spring. Annual geraniums and evergreen boxwoods offer color summer through fall.

1 USE PLANTS WITH MORE THAN ONE SEASON OF INTEREST Most plants have one or two times of the year when they're at their peak. Usually it's when they flower — that bed in photo 1 wouldn't be nearly so striking without the pink azalea blooms in spring. But there are often "secondary" features that can make a plant look great at other times of year as well, such as this azalea's evergreen leaves. Many plants display brightly colored berries later in the season or reveal interesting and colorful winter bark once the leaves fall. Include plants that offer some of these things to help your bed look good from early spring to winter.

2 ADD ANNUALS FOR ALL-SEASON COLOR Now that you have each season covered, add some annuals that will provide flower power from early summer all the way to a killing frost. Plant them right in the garden or grow them in a pot, like the geraniums in photo 1. That'll give you the option of moving the color right where you need it. You can span a lull in the blooming of other plants, for example, or add a contrasting or complementary color to the other flowers in the bed.

3 PICK LONG-BLOOMING PLANTS Not into annuals? The red roses and yellow yarrow in photo 2 both flower for much of the summer and will return each year. And, in addition, many perennials, such as this yarrow, can be coaxed to bloom even longer with a simple tip: In early summer, before it flowers, cut back a portion of the clump by half. The unpruned part will bloom at its normal time. But the stems that were cut will bloom a bit later, extending the period later into the summer.

4 PERGOLAS, PEDESTALS AND POTS Don't think that plants are the only way to get color into your garden; hardscaping can also help. Technically, anything that's not a plant is hardscaping, including everything from buildings to benches to porch banisters. The owner of the garden in photo 2 used the beautiful chartreuse pot in the inset to inject color into this bed. It adds color even without any plants

(2) Run-on color To get long-running color easily, think hardscaping, such as the white pergola and chartreuse container here. They shine no matter the date or the weather. Long-bloomers, like these red-pink roses and yellow yarrows, are also must-haves.

in it! Paint choice plays a large role, too — imagine how different the scene would look if the gazebo was black or bright blue.

5 RAISING ANCHORS Remember that green is a color, too! Every garden needs good-looking anchor plants for constant color. A 'Compressa' juniper in the middle of photo 3 creates a year-round green exclamation point in this hillside bed. The blue-green foliage of the false cypress adds more all-year color.

6 FAB FOLIAGE Incorporate lots of colored foliage plants, like the red Japanese maple and the repeated bloodgrass in photo 3, into your bed — it's an easy way to get many hues of long-lasting color without flowers. And if you use plants with leaves that turn a different color in fall, like low-growing sedums, you'll get even more bang for your buck!

On the next pages, I'll share two different plans, one for full sun and one for part shade. Each garden uses the tips I share here, and has just six plants that provide the bulk of the color from spring through fall. Turn the page to start your colorful stroll through the seasons.

(3) Who needs flowers? Junipers, acting as anchor plants, and grasses with bright leaves provide a palette of colors without a single bloom. Fall foliage adds yet another dimension to the garden when cool weather hits.

3 SEASONS IN THE SUN

A good foundation planting should showcase your house and look beautiful all year long. And if it provides lots of color in every season, so much the better!

The paint and trim colors of the house provide a neutral background for all the plants in this small bed. All through the year, the burgundy-leafed smokebush anchors this garden. Spring bulbs add a little early season color with summer annuals following close behind them. By midsummer, the smokebush and the Virginia sweetspire add their flower power. Reblooming daylilies repeat their bright-pink flowers until fall, when sedum's dramatic blooms take over the show. Meanwhile, the foliage of lamb's ear and feather reed grass contribute long-lasting and interesting texture.

Turn the page for a colorful plan that grows well in part-shade situations.

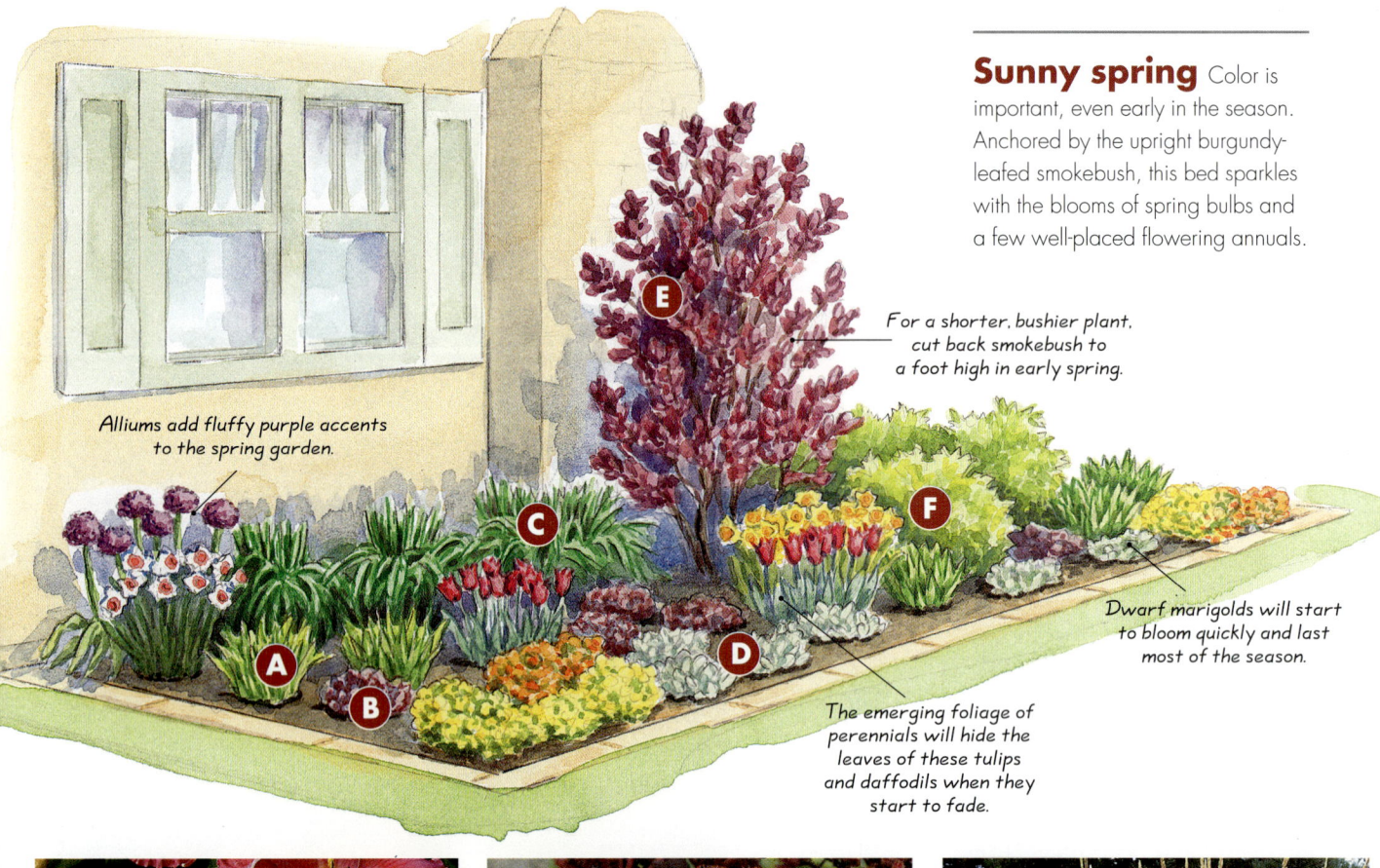

Sunny spring Color is important, even early in the season. Anchored by the upright burgundy-leafed smokebush, this bed sparkles with the blooms of spring bulbs and a few well-placed flowering annuals.

For a shorter, bushier plant, cut back smokebush to a foot high in early spring.

Alliums add fluffy purple accents to the spring garden.

Dwarf marigolds will start to bloom quickly and last most of the season.

The emerging foliage of perennials will hide the leaves of these tulips and daffodils when they start to fade.

A — **Daylily** *Hemerocallis* 'Romantic Returns' Pink flowers from early summer to midfall; 24 in. tall and 30 in. wide; cold-hardy in USDA zones 3 to 10; heat-tolerant in AHS zones 10 to 1

B — **Sedum** *Sedum telephium* 'Lynda Windsor' Burgundy foliage spring to fall; red flowers late summer to fall; leave dried flower heads for winter interest; 18 in. tall and wide; cold-hardy in USDA zones 3 to 10; heat-tolerant in AHS zones 10 to 1

C — **Feather reed grass** *Calamagrostis* ×*acutiflora* 'Karl Foerster' Pink-tan flowers summer to fall; 4 to 5 ft. tall and 18 to 30 in. wide; cold-hardy in USDA zones 5 to 9; heat-tolerant in AHS zones 9 to 1

Summer show

By summer, the smokebush and the sweetspire are bursting with blooms. And the reblooming daylily starts its bright-pink flower show. The lamb's ear and feather reed grass have also reached their full size by midsummer.

Pick off the damaged leaves of lamb's ear to keep it looking tidy.

Keep deadheading the daylily and it'll bloom until early fall.

Fall into foliage

After the daylilies stop blooming in early fall, the sedum flowers shine, changing slowly from red to red-brown. Autumn colors the leaves of the shrubs and burnishes the grass to a tawny tan.

Smokebush's purple leaves turn bright red in fall.

For a different look, replace summer annuals with cool-weather ones in fall.

Leave the sedum flowers on the plant to provide winter interest.

Lamb's ear *Stachys byzantina* 'Big Ears' Rarely flowers; clean fuzzy foliage; 6 to 18 in. tall and 12 to 18 in. wide; cold-hardy in USDA zones 4 to 9; heat-tolerant in AHS zones 10 to 1

Smokebush *Cotinus coggygria* 'Velvet Cloak' Red flowers in summer; burgundy foliage spring to fall, bright red in fall; 10 ft. tall and wide; cold-hardy in USDA zones 4 to 8; heat-tolerant in AHS zones 8 to 1

Virginia sweetspire *Itea virginica* 'Henry's Garnet' White flowers in summer; red fall leaves; 3 to 4 ft. tall and 4 to 5 ft. wide; cold-hardy in USDA zones 5 to 9; heat-tolerant in AHS zones 9 to 1

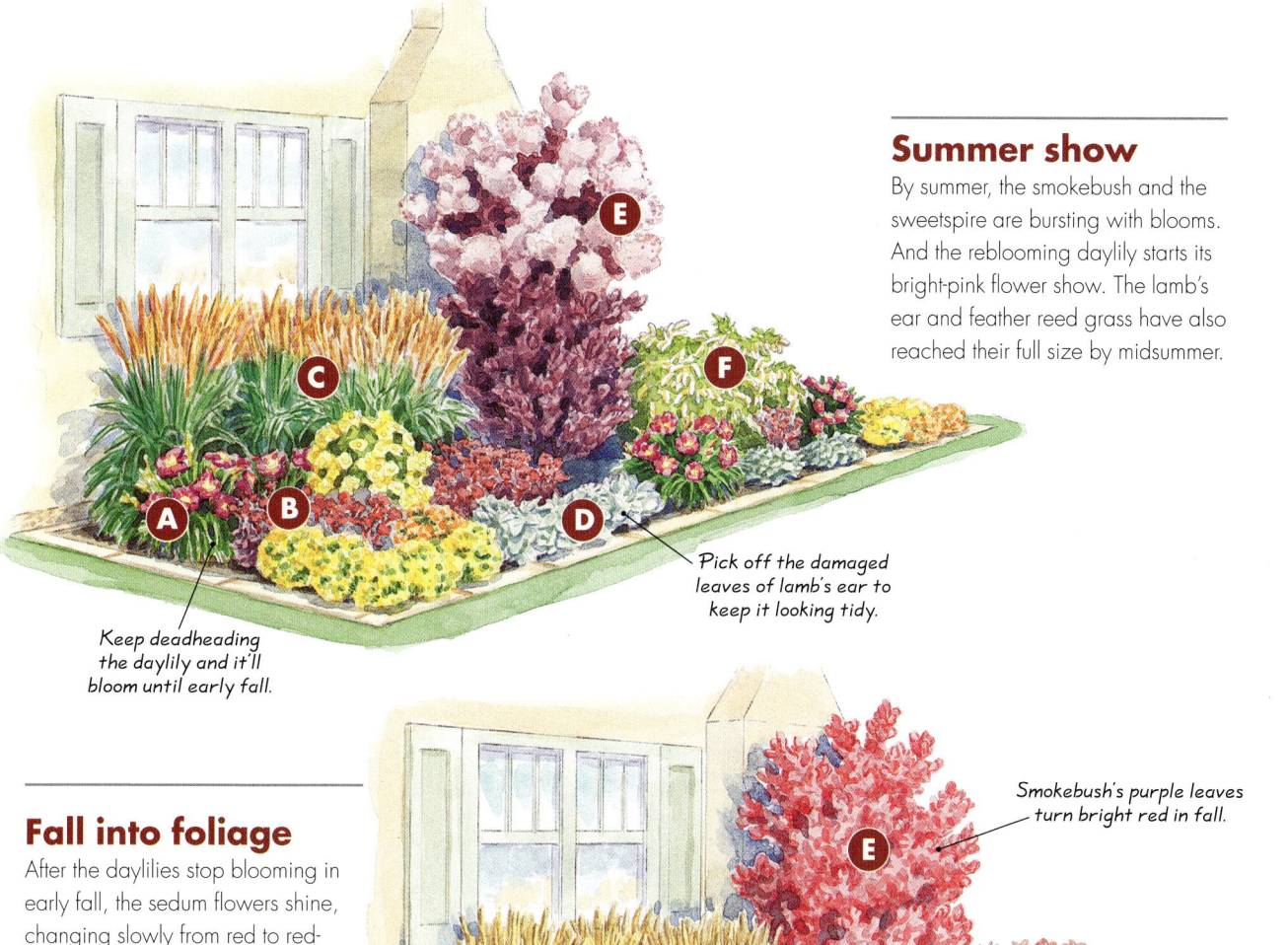

www.GardenGateMagazine.com   *the* YEAR IN GARDENING   **193**

3 SEASONS IN THE SHADE

Believe it or not, you *can* have lots of color in a part-shade garden. This shady corner bed that receives only morning light is proof of that.

Pansies and other cool-weather-loving annuals in containers provide color in early spring, as other plants emerge. Later, the foundation plants of the bed, two types of flowering shrubs, take the stage. White oakleaf hydrangea flowers and the rose-red spikes of summersweet embellish the border in summer. Also in midsummer, long-lasting flowers of astilbe and coral bells add their shades of pink and white, while the silvery leaves of the brunnera brighten this shady retreat.

As late summer turns into fall, the eye-catching blooms of the hydrangea turn a lovely papery brown. And the foliage of all the shrubs turns colors for real fall impact. □

— *Deborah Gruca*

Great spring look

Spring color is provided by the foliage of emerging brunnera and coral bells, along with cool-weather annuals in containers set in the bed. Paint or choose colorful pedestals for even more pizzazz through the seasons.

Tiny blue brunnera flowers are easy to enjoy at the front of the border.

Brunnera *Brunnera macrophylla* 'Jack Frost'
Blue spring flowers; silver variegated leaves all season; 12 to 18 in. tall and wide; cold-hardy in USDA zones 3 to 8; heat-tolerant in AHS zones 8 to 1

Coral bells *Heuchera* 'Montrose Ruby'
Early summer white flowers; burgundy and silver foliage all season; 12 to 18 in. tall and wide; cold-hardy in USDA zones 4 to 9; heat-tolerant in AHS zones 9 to 1

Columbine meadow rue *Thalictrum aquilegiifolium* Lavender-pink flowers in late spring to early summer; 24 to 30 in. tall and wide; cold-hardy in USDA zones 5 to 8; heat-tolerant in AHS zones 8 to 1

In the summer Midseason is the highlight of this shady corner. Flowers of oakleaf hydrangeas, astilbe and summersweet adorn the bed with pink and white.

As temps warm, switch out cool-weather pansies with long-blooming impatiens or begonias.

The tiny white flowers of coral bells are a treat for passing hummingbirds.

Autumn splendor Cool fall temperatures spark the foliage of the summersweet to turn a warm yellow while the leaves of the hydrangeas become a mix of reds, oranges and rich browns.

Papery brown hydrangea blooms add movement to the scene with the slightest breeze.

PHOTO: © Joan de Grey [B]; © Joseph G. Strauch, Jr. [E]; © Jerry Pavia [F]

D
Oakleaf hydrangea *Hydrangea quercifolia* 'Snow Queen' White summer flowers; multicolored fall foliage; peeling bark adds winter interest; 4 to 6 ft. tall and 6 ft. wide; cold-hardy in USDA zones 5 to 9; heat-tolerant in AHS zones 9 to 1

E
Summersweet *Clethra alnifolia* 'Ruby Spice' Pink summer flowers; yellow fall foliage; 6 to 8 ft. tall and 4 to 6 ft. wide; cold-hardy in USDA zones 4 to 8; heat-tolerant in AHS zones 8 to 1

F
Astilbe *Astilbe* Ostrich Plume ('Straussenfeder') Pink summer flowers; 2 to 3 ft. tall and 2 ft. wide; cold-hardy in USDA zones 4 to 8; heat-tolerant in AHS zones 8 to 1

www.GardenGateMagazine.com   *the* YEAR IN GARDENING   **195**

DESIGN | COLOR PALETTE

Nine Tips for Season-Long Color

with Kerry Mendez

Botanical Names

Astilbe
Astilbe spp.
Bee balm
Monarda spp.
Black-eyed Susan
Rudbeckia spp.
Bleeding heart
Dicentra hybrid
Coral bells
Heuchera hybrid
Coreopsis
Coreopsis verticillata
Daylily
Hemerocallis hybrid
Delphinium
Delphinium hybrid
Geranium
Geranium hybrid
Heliopsis
Heliopsis helianthoides
Phlox
Phlox paniculata
Sedum
Sedum spp.
Snakeroot
Actaea simplex

When you ask most gardeners what they want from their perennial garden, they'll say, "Color." And they want it to keep coming all season. It's easy in those grand English borders we all enjoy looking at. There are lots of plants that bloom at different times to get constant color. But it takes time to plant, feed, weed, stake, prune, deadhead, dig and divide all of those perennials. In today's smaller gardens, what can you do when you want lots of color from the space you have time to care for?

I talked with garden designer Kerry Mendez, owner of Perennially Yours in Ballston Spa, New York. She shared design secrets as well as care tips. After all, if the plants aren't healthy and well-maintained, they won't perform to their full potential. First, let's take a look at the design ideas.

Design strategy

PLAN FOR SEASONAL BALANCE Spring arrives and many of us head to the garden center. There we buy only the perennials that are in flower. Soon our gardens bloom heavily in spring, with almost nothing from midsummer into fall. Notice how this bed in Kerry's garden has plants in flower and others that are still to bloom? To make sure you have later color, read labels on the plants that aren't flowering yet. Try to limit yourself so no more than one-third of your spring purchases are in bloom when you take them home. Or better yet, drop by the garden center every two weeks to see what's in flower and buy a few things.

PLANT POWERHOUSE PERENNIALS Look for flowering perennials that go on and on, just like that Energizer Bunny®. 'Rozanne' geranium, 'Moonbeam' coreopsis and 'King of Hearts' bleeding heart bloom for months with little or no deadheading. And don't forget about reblooming perennials, like the daylilies in this photo.

PLAY UP THE FOLIAGE Use foliage to round out your color scheme. The burgundy coral bells in the photo looks good on its own, and it ties to the pink tones of the astilbes in the distance. But how do you know how many colorful or interesting foliage plants to use in your beds? Well, there are no hard-and-fast rules, but one plant with great foliage to every two or three blooming plants is a good place to start. And if you choose plants that have colorful foliage *and* flowers, like variegated 'Lorraine Sunshine' heliopsis and burgundy 'Hillside Black Beauty' snakeroot, they'll do double duty.

Now let's take a look at Kerry's care and culture techniques for keeping that color coming as long as possible.

Maintenance matters

PICK THE BEST POSITION Often, poorly performing plants are in the wrong light. Too much sun burns foliage and flowers. But a lack of light makes sun-lovers grow floppy. Keep a record of sun patterns and read plant labels to help you plan. And never be afraid to move plants around to find the best spot.

PREPARE THE SOIL Soil isn't the fun, or sexy, part of gardening but it's the most important thing to get healthy plants. And healthy plants produce the best flowers and foliage. Most perennials need a humus-enriched soil, so work in lots of compost. Learn the requirements of your plants to see what they like best.

PHOTO: Courtesy of Kerry Mendez (portrait)

196 the YEAR IN GARDENING   www.GardenGateMagazine.com

Choose perennials that flower at different times so there is always something in bloom.

Colorful foliage, like this coral bells, will last much longer than most flowers, so give it a prominent spot in the border.

PROPER HYDRATION Watering isn't glamorous either, but plants won't flower if they aren't hydrated. An inch of rain, or supplemental watering, per week is a good rule of thumb. Some perennials, such as astilbes, need more while sedums require less. You'll save time, and water, if you group plants that have similar needs.

PLENTY OF FOOD Heavy feeders, such as the astilbes and delphiniums in this photo, bloom best with extra nutrients. If you have a busy schedule, a timed-release fertilizer, such as Osmocote®, is easy. One application in spring feeds up to four months.

PROPAGATE FOR PRODUCTION When an old perennial clump begins to decline, so does its flowering. It's time to dig, divide and replant. Young divisions have more aggressive root systems to take up moisture and gather nutrients. Healthy, robust roots will reward you with more, and larger, flowers on sturdy stems. Your beds and borders will always be in top form.

PERENNIAL PINCHING You probably know how deadheading spent flowers can prolong blooming. But in early to mid-summer, before they bloom, prune back a few garden phlox, bee balm, coreopsis, heliopsis and black-eyed Susans. Just cut off the front part of a clump. Or, prune back an entire plant or two here and there in your border. As you see in the illustration below, unpruned stems will bloom at their regular time, while the stems that were trimmed back will bloom a few weeks later. What could be easier to get more long-lasting color in your perennial garden? □

— *Jim Childs*

Prune back the front of the clump so it will bloom later.

DESIGN | THE GARDEN IN WINTER

Don't deadhead these flowers — you'll miss out on their final act!

Winter Wonders

If you've ever seen a seedhead swaying in the breeze on a snow-covered winter day, you know how welcome the subtle color and texture are. Maybe a hungry bird flew in looking for a quick snack. Who says the winter garden is boring?

Seedheads are a lot like flowers — they come in all kinds of sizes, shapes, and colors. You'll find everything from the large, smooth pods of false indigo to fine, wispy switchgrass. Colors are usually subtle, from pale, almost white, to dark brown and black. But set them against dark evergreens or give them an icing of snow, and they take on a magical quality.

DESIGNING WITH SEEDHEADS
There's no need to design your entire garden around seedheads — they're more of a charming byproduct from not deadheading. But there are some easy ways to get a big impact from them.

Just as you design your flower borders, you'll get the best show by leaving large clumps or masses of seedheads. And mix up the head shapes, too. Grow spike forms, such as goldenrod, near rounded

Grasses have stiff stems that will hold the seedheads up even with snow.

Don't cut off these heads!

Plant Name	Cold/Heat Zones	Height/ Width	Comments
Amsonia *Amsonia hubrichtii* and *A. tabernaemontana*	3-9/9-1	2-3 ft./3 ft.	Seedheads are clusters of narrow, pointed pods; blue star-shaped flowers in late spring; foliage turns yellow in fall; full sun to part shade
Astilbe *Astilbe* spp.	4-9/9-1	8-48 in./ 15-36 in.	Pointed or arching panicles containing seeds stand long after the flowers fade; many cultivars and colors; needs moist soil and shade
Blackberry lily *Belamcanda chinensis*	5-10/10-1	2-3 ft./2 ft.	Orange flowers dotted with red change into shiny blackberrylike heads; needs well-drained soil and full sun
Butterfly weed *Asclepias tuberosa*	4-9/9-1	18-36 in./ 24 in.	Narrow, pointed pods open to release silky seeds; orange flowers in summer; needs dry, infertile soil or the roots will rot; full sun
Chinese lantern *Physalis alkekengi*	3-9/9-1	18-24 in./ 18-24 in.	Orange bladders, or lanterns, contain seeds of this sometimes invasive plant; white flowers are not showy; prone to flea beetle; full sun
Clematis *Clematis* spp.	3-8/8-1	3-25 ft./ 3-10 ft.	Perennial vines or low, shrubby plants; twisting, fuzzy seedheads; don't deadhead late flowers and prune in spring; full to part sun
False indigo *Baptisia australis*	3-9/9-1	3-4 ft./3-4 ft.	2- to 3-in.-long pods change from green to black; blue flowers in mid- to late spring; slow to establish but long-lived; full sun
Goldenrod *Solidago* spp. and hybrids	2-8/8-1	1-6 ft./1-3 ft.	Fuzzy, flat-topped or pointed seedheads; yellow to gold flowers in late summer; some spread fast; full sun
Japanese anemone *Anemone xhybrida*	4-8/8-1	2-4 ft./2-4 ft.	Fuzzy seedheads on tall stems; late-summer flowers are white or pink; most spread by underground runners; full sun to part shade
Jerusalem sage *Phlomis russeliana*	4-8/8-1	3 ft./3 ft.	Seedheads clustered along square stems change from green to brown; yellow flowers in midsummer; dry soil in full sun

198 the YEAR IN GARDENING www.GardenGateMagazine.com

heads, such as purple coneflower, like the one in the photo at left.

I like seedheads near paths where I walk in the winter. That way I can enjoy them up close. But if you're trapped indoors, you'll want to have larger seedheads, such as false indigo, out in your borders so you can see them from the window.

Most seedheads last well into winter, almost until spring. That is, many of them will until they're eaten by birds or animals. Leave some seedheads standing near bird feeders so your feathered friends are sure to find them.

A WORD OF CAUTION Some plants may be aggressive seeders, even to the point of becoming pests. If your garden is small, or you don't want to deal with lots of spring seedlings, here's what to do: Deadhead at least some of the spent blooms, leaving just a few for winter interest.

Below you'll find a list of some of my favorite plants with seedheads. You may have some of them in your garden already. In that case all you need to do is stop plucking off the spent flowers.

That way you'll get to enjoy the flowers *and* the interesting seedheads. Plus, you saved time because you didn't have to deadhead in the summer heat. What a great way to garden!

— *Jim Childs*

Plant Name	Cold/Heat Zones	Height/Width	Comments
Lily *Lilium* hybrids	4-9/9-1	2-6 ft./1 ft.	After the flowers fade, swollen green pods take their place; later they turn papery brown; huge variety of cultivars; full sun
Moneyplant *Lunaria annua*	4-9/9-1	24-36 in./18-24 in.	Biennial; panicles of flat silvery discs by late summer; pink or purple flowers in late spring; may be invasive in some gardens; full sun
Poppy *Papaver orientale*	3-7/7-1	2-4 ft./3-4 ft.	Stiff stems hold turbanlike seedheads even after the spring foliage disappears; large flowers in late spring; well-drained soil, full sun
Purple coneflower *Echinacea purpurea*	3-8/8-1	2-3 ft./2 ft.	Dense cones on sturdy stems stand well all winter if not eaten; wide variety of flower colors in late summer; reseeds; full sun
Russian sage *Perovskia atriplicifolia*	5-9/9-1	3-4 ft./3-4 ft.	Purple bracts remain long after the flowers fade, giving the illusion the plant is still in flower; silvery stems and seedheads; full sun
Sea holly *Eryngium amethystinum*	3-8/8-1	18-28 in./18-28 in.	Large thistlelike bracts surround clusters of seeds; often retains a blue tint late into fall; silvery blue blooms; dry soil, full sun
Siberian iris *Iris sibirica*	3-8/8-1	24-48 in./18-24 in.	2- to 3-in. seed pods turn brown and stand long after the foliage withers; late spring flowers; fertile, moist soil and full to part sun
Switchgrass *Panicum virgatum*	5-9/9-1	4-6 ft./2-3 ft.	Wispy red-purple heads turn pale brown; heads sway easily in the wind; forms medium-sized clumps; full sun
Tall sedum *Sedum* hybrids	3-10/9-1	18-24 in./18-24 in.	Flat clusters of pink flowers eventually turn brown; sturdy, stiff stems hold up with heavy snow; full to part sun
Yarrow *Achillea filipendulina*	3-8/8-1	36-60 in./18-24 in.	Large flat heads on tall stems change from golden yellow to brown; often fall under the weight of wet snow; full sun

Flat-topped heads, like this tall sedum, look more interesting with a frosting of snow.

did you know...

Holiday topiary
Sue Bresnahan, Minnesota
Don't throw away those lighted wire holiday forms when the lights stop working. Move them to the garden! Sue had two reindeer ornaments with worn-out lights. Instead of throwing them away, she removed the lights. Then she painted the deer green with an outdoor spray paint, such as Rustoleum®. In spring, with the deer relocated to the garden, Sue planted one clematis near each frame. The vines twined up and through each form.

You could even plant around an ornament that still has working lights for a good-looking evening garden accent.

Easy overflow
Tatiana Lary, Maryland
Tatiana's draining sump pump was a problem — water was pooling in the neighbor's lawn. So she installed a small preformed pond with a spillway (a lip where water is directed over the pond edge) at the mouth of the sump pump pipe. From the spillway, Tatiana laid river rock to form a natural-looking streambed that flowed down the slight incline in her yard. At the bottom, she added a slightly larger preformed pond to help hold the extra water.

Occasionally, a heavy downpour causes some overflow, but much less than before. Her family has enjoyed the ponds so much that they added some plants, a bridge and a small fountain, too. What was a source of trouble has become the most beautiful spot in the yard.

Bottles up!
Mary Ann Riggs, Wisconsin
Garden ornaments can be so expensive that Mary Ann decided to make her own. She slips green and blue glass bottles on copper pipe cut to various lengths. The pipe diameter will depend on the size of the bottle mouth. Odd-numbered groupings usually look best, and pushing one or two pipes in the ground at an angle adds a little flair, too.

product pick

Ultimate Lounger

Wouldn't you like to be as comfortable in the chair on your deck as you are in the one in the family room? You can be with the Ultimate Lounger. It's the most comfortable lounge chair we've tried. This mesh fabric is good-looking yet durable, and it's attached to the frame with heavy elastic cords. The steel frame is sturdy and powder-coated to protect it from the elements, and wooden arm rests give it a stylish look.

Bottom line Once you sit down, don't be surprised if you fall asleep in this comfy chair.
Source Gardener's Supply at 888-833-1412 or www.gardeners.com
Price $159

product pick

Citronella incense coils

Mosquitoes bugging you? Try these citronella incense coils. Most insect repellents don't double as garden art. But these coils are so colorful and festive, someone might mistake them for just that.

Made of compressed wood and citronella oil, they burn slowly just like incense. One 11½-inch coil lasts about 20 hours, releasing the familiar lemon-like fragrance as it burns. Keep it out of the rain, though. When ours was left out in a downpour, it lost its shape and sagged. After drying, it still worked, but it didn't look as nice.

Bottom line An attractive way to keep mosquitoes away.
Source Gardener's Supply at 888-833-1412 or www.gardeners.com
Price $12.95 for a set of three in blue, green and orange

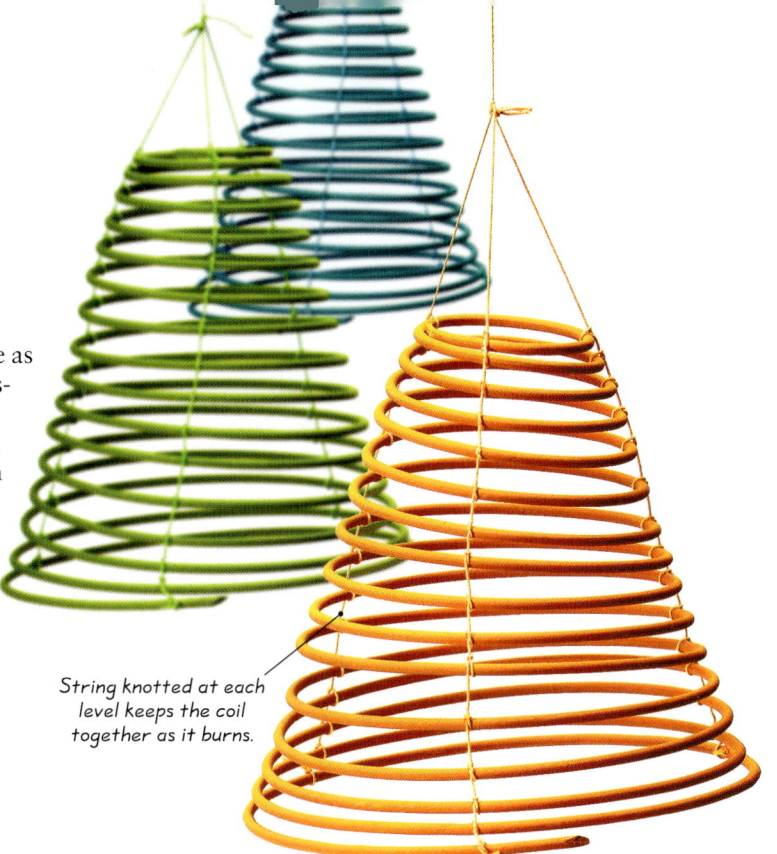

String knotted at each level keeps the coil together as it burns.

in the news

Forest-friendly garden furniture
The National Wildlife Federation has set up a Web site to help conscientious folks find garden furniture they can relax on without worrying about rainforest loss. Go to www.nwf.org/forests/gardenfurniture.cfm to download information on Forest Stewardship Council (FSC) certified garden furniture products from companies like Crate & Barrel and Lowe's. Haven't heard of the FSC? It's an organization that promotes responsible forestry management worldwide. So when you see the FSC-certified logo, you'll know it identifies products that contain wood from well-managed forests, certified in accordance with the rules of the Forest Stewardship Council.

Plants add $$ to your home
A study from the University of Michigan and the Horticultural Research Institute found that good landscaping adds 5 to 11 percent to the value of your home. Location is still the most important determiner of price, but adding plants will nudge the price a little higher. Even if you're not moving right now, adding a shade tree or some shrubs helps cut down on energy costs, as well as adding to your property value as they mature. So no matter when you sell, investing in your landscape makes good "cents."

product pick

Down to Earth with Helen Dillon

Down to Earth with Helen Dillon is just that — a down-to-earth and humorous look at gardening. Helen walks you through some basics of garden design that everyone will find useful. Then she moves on to such diverse topics as compost, weeding, Mediterranean style, burglar-proof plants and red borders. This is definitely a British book and some of the plants she mentions will do much better in Ireland, where the author lives, than in North America. But the experiences and garden ideas she talks about are universal and you'll come away having learned, and laughed, a lot.

Bottom line Not many books can talk about garden design and give you a good laugh at the same time.
Source Local and online bookstores or www.GardenGateStore.com
Price $29.95; hardcover; 208 pages

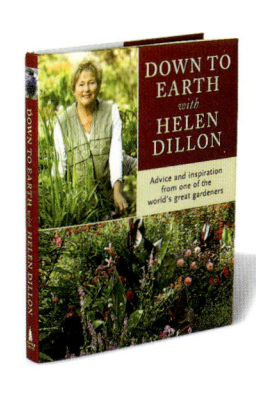

did you know... (CONTINUED)

Baffle the squirrels

After losing pounds of birdseed to the squirrels in her New Jersey neighborhood, Clancey Mitchell was frustrated. But her husband, John, found an HVAC reducer from a local hardware store worked wonders. An HVAC reducer is a piece of metal that connects two ducts of different sizes. To attach the reducer, John removed the bird feeder from its 4-inch wooden post. The mouth of the reducer was wider than the post, so he wedged a shim in on each side of the post. A couple of screws held it all in place. John and Clancey haven't had any squirrels poaching the birdseed in months!

Shims fill the gap between the reducer and the post

This reducer has an 8-in. mouth that tapers to 6 in.

in the news

Hi-tech bird-watching

If you like to watch birds, now you can go online and keep track of what you've seen. eBird is an online database sponsored by the Cornell Lab of Ornithology and the National Audubon Society. You fill in the data about what birds you've seen where. Then everyone, including bird-watchers across the country as well as scientists, can see what birds are in your state. Canada and Mexico are included, too. So take a walk, visit a local birding site or just sit back and watch your feeder. Then go to www.ebird.com, log in and share the birds you saw with everyone.

product pick

No/No Bird Feeder

This is a great feeder for attracting sunflower lovers, such as cardinals, woodpeckers and chickadees. It's made of recycled metal that lasts for years and won't be shredded by aggressive squirrels looking for a snack. The collapsible wire mesh makes this feeder easy to store and doesn't harbor avian diseases that could harm your wild friends. No cleaning is required, but it's dishwasher safe, just in case.

No/No Feeders attract both perching and clinging birds and can feed up to 15 at a time. The cardinal feeder in the photo holds up to 2½ pounds of seed. Other styles and colors are available.

Bottom line The only problem you'll have with these feeders is keeping track of all the birds that visit.
Source Sweet Corn Products at www.no-nobirdfeeder.com or call 877-628-6115. Or visit www.GardenGateStore.com.
Price $33.95.

202 the YEAR IN GARDENING   www.GardenGateMagazine.com

product pick

Hot Meats bird seed

Fill up your bird feeder instead of the neighborhood squirrels! Hot Meats™ sunflower seed is coated with safflower oil and habanero chili pepper. Squirrels will leave the seed for the birds, who can't taste the pepper. Like feeding suet-loving birds, such as woodpeckers and nuthatches? Get the Hot Meats suet cake, too.

Bottom line A great way to feed birds instead of squirrels.
Source Birdwatcher's Supply Company at 888-552-4737 or www.birdwatchersupply.com. Find a local retailer online at www.coleswildbird.com
Price $15.39 for a 5-lb. bag; $1.89 for a suet cake

Hot Meats is the latest from the Cole's® line of gourmet bird foods.

Fill feeders faster
Steve Warren, Oregon

Steve likes to feed hummingbirds but filling those narrow feeders without spilling nectar can be a hassle. He found a solution that makes for neat filling and easy storage — a water bottle.

You can use any size, but be sure to get the type that has a pull-top cap. Just pour nectar into the empty water bottle, replace the top, then squeeze the nectar into the feeder. When you're done, close the pull-top cap and store the bottle in the refrigerator until your feeder needs refilling. When the bottle is empty, wash it in hot, soapy water and it's ready to be filled and used again.

Water the birds
Gerald Grover, OR

For birds, source of water is just as important as food during winter months. Gerald's found an easy way to get rid of ice that forms in the birdbath — a garbage bag. He takes a kitchen-sized plastic garbage bag, slips it over the dish and loosely ties the opening around the pedestal. If ice forms, he gently lifts one edge of the bag and the ice slips over the edge of the birdbath onto the ground. He then refills the bath with warm water and his feathered friends have a place to drink again.

This tip works well in areas like Oregon that only occasionally have freezing temperatures. For USDA zones 7 and colder, it's still best to use a birdbath heater to keep the water open for birds in winter.

product pick

The Wildlife Gardener's Guide

Gardens and wildlife just seem to go together. But it helps to have some advice on how to make your garden even more attractive to birds, butterflies, bees, bats and beneficial insects. This book from the Brooklyn Botanic Garden is packed with information, tips, regional plant lists and plans to encourage wildlife to visit your garden. You'll find 10 steps to a bird-friendly garden and five feeders every yard should have. Don't have much space? Plant a container sure to bring in the hummingbirds. Plus, check out a list of regional plants they love.

Bottom line It's a small book but has lots of great advice for attracting the kind of wildlife you want to see in your garden.
Source Local or online bookstores or www.GardenGateStore.com
Price $9.95; softcover; 119 pages

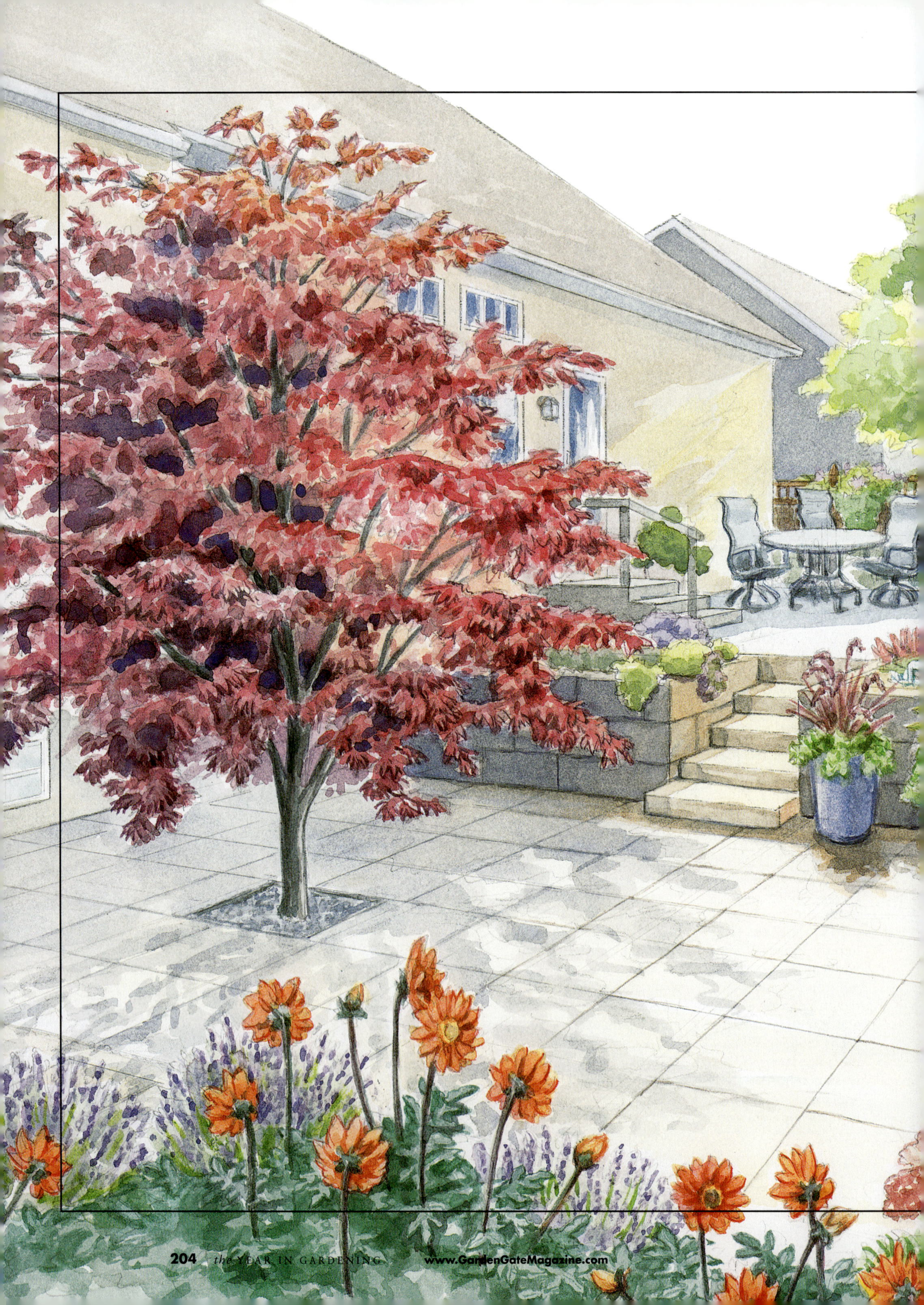

design challenge
and drawing board
plans to solve *your* most challenging garden situations

HOW'D YOU DO THAT? is what most folks want to know when they see a gorgeous garden. Let us give you the solutions for six common situations gardeners face. From tips you can apply to your yard to specific planting plans for great-looking beds, it's all here!

Show Me the Door	**206**
Windowbox Wonders	**208**
Take Back Your Bed!	**210**
Flower Garden Makeover	**212**
Peace and Quiet	**214**
Patio Perfection	**216**
Weedy to Wonderful	**218**
As Easy as You Please	**220**
Divide and Disguise	**222**
One Hot Planting	**224**
A Change of Scenery	**226**
Room to Grow	**228**
Building Blocks of Design	**231**

DESIGN CHALLENGE | FRONT YARD

Show Me the Door

Think about a child's drawing of a house. A front door, two windows and a tree off to one side. It's a look that feels friendly and safe to most people. But what do you do when your house is missing two of those three important elements? Deborah Mirando's New York house doesn't have a tree beside it…and it doesn't have a front door, either! It does have two windows, but they look a little off balance.

Instead of the narrow planting she has now, she'd like a tree for a little shade and a charming cottage-style garden with lots of flowers. And she wants to direct visitors to the door on the right side of the house. (Even if your front door is on the front of the house, you may want to play it up a bit. And these tips will work for that, too.)

Let's take a look at a few design ideas to give this little house a big garden look.

Create curb appeal

This may be a small house, but that doesn't mean the foundation planting needs to be small, too. In fact, a too-narrow foundation planting just looks wimpy. And don't limit yourself to low-growing plants, either. Choose some medium-sized shrubs and a small ornamental tree like the one that shades this southwest corner. Then make the bed wide enough to give them plenty of room. Sticking to a simple palette of pink, burgundy and chartreuse makes designing a great-looking planting easy.

PHOTO: Courtesy of Deborah Mirando

206 the YEAR IN GARDENING   www.GardenGateMagazine.com

Cover the pump

Every house has a little something that needs to be concealed. In this case, it's a sump pump drain right in the middle of the front foundation planting. The perennials and annuals in the current bed cover it up in summer, but it shows up again as soon as everything dies back. A couple of strategically placed shrubs will keep it covered all year. (Choose plants that won't mind a little extra water every now and then.)

Work with the windows

A bay window gives a great view from inside, but from the front, it doesn't seem to match the rest of the house. Minimize the different style by filling the space under the bay window with tall perennials or medium-sized shrubs.

WEB extra

See the complete *planting plan* for this garden.

Enter here

It's easy for guests to go to a door that's clearly visible, but here, the door is tucked around on the right side. This planting tapers from the high point of the tree on the left to the lowest plants right near the driveway, like an arrow pointing at the entry. And the colors get brighter as you move to the right, which also leads your eyes in the right direction. A small patio gives guests a place to stand and chat, and it also allows room for a couple of big containers — the last step in attracting your attention toward the door.

DRAWING BOARD | FRONT YARD

Windowbox Wonders

A lush windowbox is the perfect finishing touch for a cottage-style garden. Multiple windowboxes look best if you use the same plants in all of them.

When you were looking at the Design Challenge on p. 206, you probably noticed the windowboxes. This small house has two distinct styles of window, but matching windowboxes keep a theme going along the front of the house. These are both painted blue to match the shutters on the front of the house.

SUN-WARMED This topiary adds height and flair. It takes time to get ivy to cover a frame, so grow it in a separate, individual pot and slip the pot into the windowbox. (Or buy an established one and leave it in the original pot.) Keep it watered — ivy doesn't mind full sun, but it'll stay healthier with plenty of moisture. Magenta geraniums add summer-long color, and a trailing burgundy coleus underlines it all. (Many newer coleus, like this trailer, tolerate plenty of sun.) Last, 'Oriental Limelight' artemisia adds a splash of chartreuse. This plant spreads like crazy in the ground, but it's perfect in a windowbox, where it fills in quickly but can't get out of control. □

— Stephanie Polsley Bruner

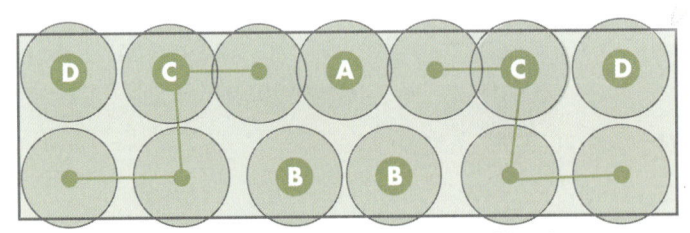

Windowbox is approximately 36 in. long and 10 in. deep.

A sunny window

Code	Plant Name	No. to Plant	Special Features
A	**Ivy** *Hedera helix*	1	Grow on wire topiary frame in individual container; prune as needed to maintain shape
B	**Coleus** *Solenostemon* 'Trailing Plum'	2	Very vigorous; pinch back to keep compact and direct growth downward
C	**Geranium** *Pelargonium* hybrid	8	Choose a magenta-flowered variety for maximum impact; nip back faded blooms to keep flowers coming
D	**Artemisia** *Artemisia vulgaris* 'Janlim' (Oriental Limelight)	2	Perennial spreader is too vigorous in the garden, but performs well in a windowbox

QUICK TIP

Ivy trained on a wire frame gives this planting height, but you could get the same effect with a small evergreen or a simple ornament or obelisk.

DESIGN CHALLENGE | DECKS AND PATIOS

Take Back Your Bed!

Have you ever had a flower bed turn out completely different from your original plan? If so, you're not alone. Eventually, most gardeners find themselves in the situation of having a flower bed that just doesn't work anymore. Pam Argubright of Illinois has that situation right now. When she planted the bed along her patio several years ago, she really liked it. Each plant had its own space and looked tidy. But now those little plants are all grown up and have taken over the bed. It's hard to tell where one plant ends and another begins. In addition to being a bit messy, this garden blends into the house because all of the colors and textures are so similar. What can we do to spice up this bland bed?

Instead of designing a whole new bed, we decided to work with some of the existing plants. (You could also use the plan to start a new garden from scratch.) Pam wants a garden that complements the rest of her yard and containers (which have bright colors). And she doesn't want to block the view from the patio.

Let's take a look at a few ideas for renovating a troubled patio bed.

Spice up the color

The "before" color combo — purple and tan — just didn't show up very well against the house. You could paint the house, but it's a lot easier to add a few colorful plants! Spice up the impact with some bright pinks, purples and yellows. Pairing two contrasting colors, like these purple and yellow shades, makes them both stand out better. Combine two similar colors, like red and pink, and they tend to blend together.

Turn up the texture

When you talk about texture, think about contrasts. The original bed included wispy, fine-textured plants that tangled together and got lost against the house. Dense shrubs make a great backdrop for fine-textured plants. Plus, they add long-lasting shape and structure that keep any garden looking good even when nothing's blooming. And coarse-textured perennials, with big leaves and flowers, offer a lot of contrast too, making the wispy plants stand out even more.

PHOTO: Courtesy of Pam Argubright

WEB extra
See the complete *planting plan* for this garden.

210 *the* YEAR IN GARDENING www.GardenGateMagazine.com

Bring some balance

A tree at the corner of a house or bed is a great anchor for a border. This magnolia was a bit overgrown, making the planting feel lopsided. But it's a beautiful tree, and it's easy to work with it, instead of removing it. Balance the visual weight of the tree with a mockorange near the patio area. This offsets the size of the magnolia and adds another focal point, as well as fragrant white spring flowers. Plus, the mockorange hides a big patch of blank wall. (You can also prune up the magnolia a little — read more about how to do this on p. 212.)

Vantage point

Some gardens can only be seen from one angle, but this one can be seen from both sides — the yard and the patio. We didn't want to block the view with large shrubs or ornamental grasses. Instead, a container on a pedestal echoes the pedestals in the patio wall. It'll add height, making the patio feel more enclosed and cozy, but you can still see around it. Plant the container with annuals for a different look each year.

DRAWING BOARD | DECKS AND PATIOS

Flower Garden Makeover

Maybe the plants got too big or you lost a tree that used to shade your garden. Or maybe a planting just didn't turn out the way you anticipated. There are lots of reasons to redo a flower bed. If you're reworking a bed, you have two options: Rip everything out and start over, or keep a few plants you like and replace the rest. We're renovating this bed, but you could also use this plan for a new bed.

WHERE DO YOU BEGIN? First, identify all the plants you have and decide which ones you want to keep. Use plant stakes to mark spring bulbs so you remember where they are later. Some perennials, like catmint, are easy to transplant and could be moved to another bed or given to a friend. It's best to move perennials in spring or early fall. When you're transplanting, figure out where you want to put the plants before you dig them — that way they won't dry out while you decide. Treat transplants like new additions and keep them watered during the first year.

PICK NEW COMPANIONS Other perennials, like the Russian sage here, are best either left alone or removed entirely. Russian sage has a taproot that makes it very difficult to transplant successfully. These are large, mature plants, so we left them in the new plan. However, we picked some new companions for them, including yellow false indigo and black-eyed Susans. False indigo's clean green foliage makes a great backdrop for wispy stems of Russian sage. And the round, golden-yellow flowers of black-eyed Susan are a great color contrast.

WORK WOODY PLANTS IN When it comes to trees and shrubs, it's usually hard to just dig them up and move them! But you can make a big difference with a little careful pruning. Thinning a few branches from the middle of the magnolia highlights the branching pattern and makes the tree look less "heavy."

And removing a few lower limbs creates enough space and light to plant perennials around the base. This is a great spot for catmint. It tends to spread vigorously, but it'll stay contained inside the edging.

Timing is everything when it comes to pruning woody plants. It's best to prune magnolias after they've finished blooming. As a general guide, plants that bloom on new wood, like spirea, should be pruned in early spring. Plants that bloom on old wood, like mockorange and lilac, should be pruned after they flower. ☐

— *Stephanie Polsley Bruner*

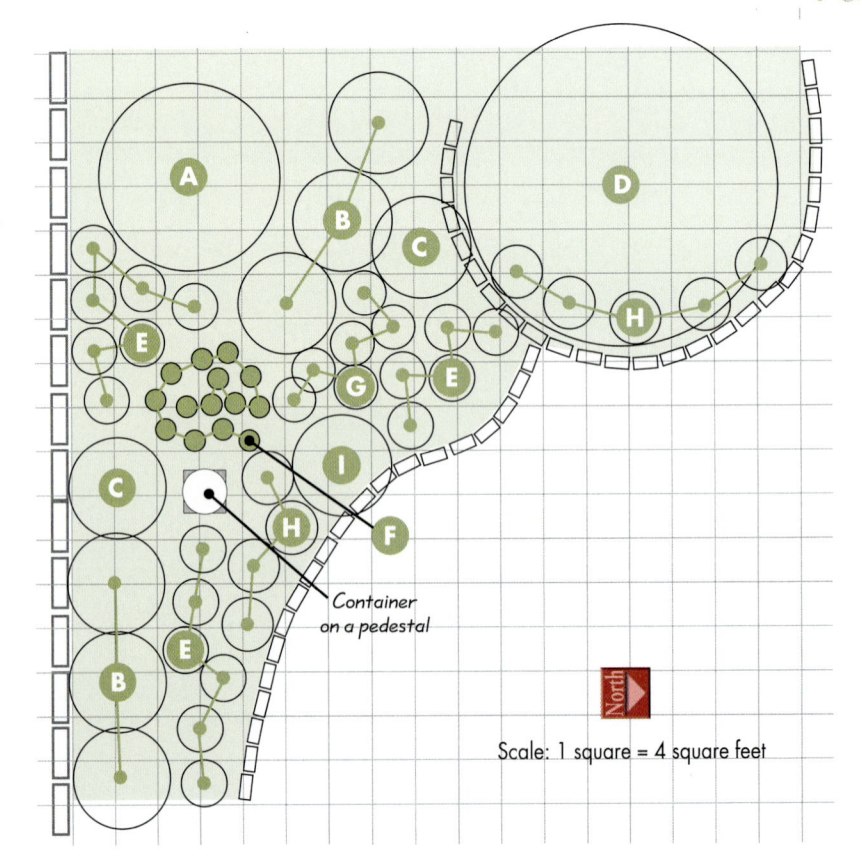

Container on a pedestal

Scale: 1 square = 4 square feet

QUICK TIP

Building a garden pedestal can be as simple as stacking up several layers of bricks or cinder blocks. This works best for short pedestals. For taller pedestals, you'll want to mortar the bricks together so your container doesn't tumble off.

THE GARDEN'S PALETTE

Code	Plant Name	No. to Plant	Blooms	Type	Cold/Heat Zones	Height/Width	Special Features
A	Mockorange *Philadelphus* 'Belle Etoile'	1	White; spring	Shrub	5-8/8-1	5-7 ft./ 4-6 ft.	Fragrant flowers; blooms on old wood; prune after flowering; can be cut back hard to rejuvenate
B	Yellow false indigo *Baptisia* 'Carolina Moonlight'	6	Yellow; spring	Perennial	4-9/9-1	3-4 ft./ 3-4 ft.	Attracts butterflies; clean green foliage; attractive seed pods in fall; rarely needs staking
C	Russian sage *Perovskia atriplicifolia*	2	Lavender; summer	Perennial	4-9/9-2	3-4 ft./ 3-4 ft.	Long bloom time; feathery gray-green foliage; drought-tolerant; rarely needs staking; pest-resistant
D	Star magnolia *Magnolia stellata*	1	White; spring	Tree	5-9/9-1	15-20 ft./ 10-15 ft.	Early spring flowers give way to clean green foliage in summer; best to prune after it flowers
E	Black-eyed Susan *Rudbeckia fulgida* Viette's Little Suzy ('Blovi')	18	Yellow; summer	Perennial	3-8/9-2	12-18 in./ 12-18 in.	Many blooms on compact plants; deadhead to encourage rebloom
F	Blazing star *Liatris spicata* 'Kobold'	14	Purple; summer	Perennial	4-9/9-1	24-30 in./ 6-12 in.	Attracts butterflies; long-lasting as cut flowers; green, grasslike foliage
G	Garden phlox *Phlox paniculata* Volcano® Red ('Barthirtysix')	6	Red; summer	Perennial	4-9/9-1	24-28 in./ 18-24 in.	Fragrant flowers; upright, disease-resistant cultivar
H	Catmint *Nepeta xfaassenii* 'Kit Cat'	9	Purple; summer	Perennial	3-8/9-1	12-18 in./ 12-24 in.	Attracts butterflies and hummingbirds; fragrant flowers; cut back to 6 in. if it gets leggy
I	Boxwood *Buxus* 'Green Velvet'	1	NA	Evergreen shrub	4-9/9-3	3-4 ft./ 3-4 ft.	Tolerates shearing; protect from harsh winter winds

DESIGN CHALLENGE | DECKS AND PATIOS

Peace and Quiet

You come home and you just want to relax on the patio. But it's tough to relax when you can see all the neighbors…and they can see you!

Teresa McCann loves her low-maintenance Kansas home, but she wants something more outdoors. The back yard is only about 30 feet deep and 60 feet wide. And the existing patio is 12 x 14 feet, just big enough for a table and chairs. Sitting down outside, you see similar back yards all the way down the street. She'd like more privacy and a bigger patio space, while still leaving room to plant. And she wants to cover a big, blank wall at the back of the house. Is all of this possible in a small space? Of course!

A fence and shrubs add privacy, with perennials and annuals for color. An existing maple tree will add much-needed shade in a few years. The little-used lawn is replaced by extra patio space.

Now when Teresa sits on her patio, she won't feel like she's sharing the space with all of her neighbors, all of the time!

PHOTO: Courtesy of Teresa McCann

Plant a tree

A large blank wall seems to loom over the patio. Normally, a trellis with a vine would solve the problem, but it won't work here because of the basement window. Instead, a Japanese maple (*Acer palmatum* 'Red Emperor') softens this wall without blocking the window. And there's a little surprise: A landscaping light, tucked into the border on the other side of the patio, casts the shadow of the tree's branches on the wall at night. A 24-in.-square planting opening in the patio leaves plenty of room for this small tree.

Gain some space

Who needs lawn? Well, maybe you do if you want space for kids and dogs to play, but sometimes a hard surface, especially in a small space, is more practical. Here, we extended the patio by adding another, lower level. Extra space for furniture, plus no more mowing! The original patio was poured concrete, and Teresa had used big limestone blocks to create a planting area. We used cut limestone squares to extend the hard surface. That way, there aren't too many different materials, which would look cluttered against the simple lines of the house.

Do fence me in

Many beautiful gardens don't begin with plants — they begin with a fence. A fence gives a garden a visual boundary as well as an actual one. In other words, your eye stops at the fence, instead of wandering off down the row of houses. And a fence is the fastest, easiest way to give yourself some privacy without taking up a lot of space. But be careful about the height and materials. You don't want your patio to feel like a stockade. Here, spaces between the slats allow a little air circulation, and the height of the fence is adjusted for the changing levels of the patio. You can still see over the top when you stand up, but when you're seated, you won't feel that you're on a stage.

Take it to a different level

It's easier to work *with* a slope than against it. Here, the yard slopes up toward the original patio. Creating the additional patio on a lower level adds visual interest. It's much simpler to dig out a little more soil to finish the lower level than it is to add more soil to bring the whole patio up to the original height. A few limestone steps make it easy to go from one "room" to the other, as well as create some raised planting areas to enjoy up close. The final touch: A bubbling fountain helps mask noise from nearby yards.

DRAWING BOARD | DECKS AND PATIOS

Patio Perfection

Who needs a lawn? In this small back yard, a patio surrounded by bright plantings is the easy way to go. No mowing, more privacy and a beautiful place to relax. There's still plenty of room for planting, and a limited plant palette keeps your garden colorful without being completely overwhelming.

KEEP IT SIMPLE Choosing two main colors, in this case purple and red, makes choosing plants and coordinating the garden easy. You can use different shades of these colors, from the pale lavender-pink of the lilacs to the darker purple of the salvia. Next, throw in some plants with bronze or burgundy foliage. They'll help tie the garden together and keep the brighter colors from looking too harsh.

YEAR-ROUND SURROUNDINGS When you're planting a small garden, it's natural to think of small plants. But even the tiniest gardens need some shrubs. Around this patio, they help provide some much-needed height and privacy. Evergreens add texture and color, even in the winter, and the flowering lilacs have wonderful spring fragrance.

Another great thing about shrubs is that they take up a lot of room! That may sound like a strange "benefit" when you don't have much planting space. But adding a few shrubs makes any garden more low-maintenance. They cover a lot of ground and choke out weeds. And they provide a permanent backdrop for perennials and annuals without needing a lot of special care themselves. If you're planting a garden in stages, put the shrubs (and trees) in first, so they'll have a chance to fill in before you surround them with smaller plants. Of course, if you're planting everything at once, be sure to leave enough room for those little shrubs to grow! □

— *Stephanie Polsley Bruner*

THE POWER OF PURPLE AND RED

Code	Plant Name	No. to Plant	Blooms	Type	Cold/Heat Zones	Height/Width	Special Features
A	Arborvitae *Thuja occidentalis* 'Smaragd' (Emerald)	3	NA	Evergreen shrub	2-7/7-1	12-14 ft./ 3-4 ft.	Stays upright and compact without pruning; spray with antidesiccant in winter in dry, windy locations
B	Yew *Taxus xmedia* 'Taunton'	3	NA	Evergreen shrub	4-8/8-1	3-4 ft./ 3-5 ft.	Prefers well-drained soil; tolerates some shade
C	Dwarf Korean lilac *Syringa meyeri* 'Palibin'	4	Lavender-pink; spring	Shrub	3-7/7-1	4-5 ft./ 5-7 ft.	Shiny foliage is disease resistant; very fragrant blooms; prune right after flowering to shape
D	Clematis *Clematis* 'Lady Betty Balfour'	1	Purple; early to midsummer	Vine	4-9/9-1	10-12 ft./ spreads	Cut back hard to first or second set of buds in early spring
E	Clematis *Clematis* 'Gravetye Beauty'	3	Red; summer	Vine	5-9/9-1	10-12 ft./ spreads	Unusual tulip-shaped flowers; cut back hard to first or second set of buds in early spring
F	Yarrow *Achillea millefolium* 'Paprika'	15	Rust-red; early to midsummer	Perennial	3-8/8-1	18-24 in./ 24 in.	Red flowers fade to pink and orange; cut back after flowering to encourage fall rebloom
G	Salvia *Salvia nemorosa* 'Caradonna'	11	Purple; early to midsummer	Perennial	4-8/8-1	20 in./ 12-18 in.	Striking dark-purple stems; cut back to encourage fresh new growth
H	Lavender *Lavandula angustifolia* 'Munstead'	9	Lavender; early to midsummer	Perennial	5-8/8-1	12-18 in./ 12-18 in.	Needs well-drained soil; prune back to 8 in. high in early spring to shape
I	Dahlia *Dahlia* 'Bishop of Llandaff'	8	Red-orange; midsummer to fall	Tender perennial	8-10/10-1	2-3 ft./ 1 ft.	Shiny bronze foliage looks great all summer; dig and store tubers indoors over winter

QUICK TIP

Spring bulbs will love the warm, well-drained soil in these beds. Tuck them in among the perennials and shrubs for spring color and fragrance. The emerging perennial foliage will hide the bulbs' leaves as they start to fade.

Scale: 1 square = 4 square feet

DESIGN CHALLENGE | BACK YARD

Weedy to Wonderful

There's starting from scratch and then there's *really* starting from scratch!

Faced with this weedy back yard, it'd be tempting just to go back in the house and shut the door. But Christine Broughton knew when she bought this home in Washington state that she wanted a garden. She'd like flowers and space for her dog to play, but she also wants easy care, as she's new to gardening.

Homeowners often assume that a formal look, with straight lines and brick paths, is high maintenance. But actually, it's not. Straight bed edges and a path that doubles as edging make mowing the lawn a snap. Wide paths clearly define the bed shapes so you don't have to do a lot of experimenting to get the right look. Last, but not least, a short list of easy plants is a must. Most of these plants just need a quick spring cleanup.

When you're planning your garden, think about how you'll see it. You enter this back yard through a gate that's to the left of the illustration. So the first thing you see is the little gazebo, a great focal point. And there's room on the patio surrounding it for some big containers that echo the colors of the plantings. While you're sitting in the gazebo, there's a gorgeous border to gaze at — check out the plan on p. 220.

Let's take a look at how we combined all these elements (and more) to create a garden that will give you time to relax. ◻

Get out of the sun

Every garden needs a place where you can sit out of the sun and rain. And this garden needs it worse than most, because this house doesn't have a door into the back yard. Curtains at the back of this gazebo add privacy and hide the chain-link gate on the property line. But the "floor" of the gazebo is the same level as the sidewalk and patio. So if you need to push a wheelbarrow through the gate, just roll up the curtains — you'll have plenty of space to maneuver. The wide sidewalk doubles as patio space, so there's lots of room to entertain.

Be doggone friendly

It's great to have a pooch for company as you garden, but you do need to make a few allowances as you plan. A big rectangle of lawn in the middle gives a dog plenty of room to run and play. And if you want to install an invisible fence to keep your furry friend out of the flowers, it's easier to do that with these straight lines than with curved beds. Just be sure there's access to shade if your dog is going to be outside a lot. Steer clear of poisonous plants in the areas where your dog can roam free.

PHOTOS: Courtesy of Christine Broughton

Hide the chain link

When you have a dog, a completely enclosed back yard is a bonus. Three sides of this yard have attractive, solid backdrops — the house, a garage and a privacy fence. But most gardeners would agree that chain-link fencing, which you can catch a glimpse of on the left in this photo, isn't their favorite material. On the other hand, it does a fine job of keeping the dog within bounds, and it's actually pretty easy to disguise. Dense, twiggy Van Houtte spireas are tall enough to hide the fence both summer and winter. (Evergreen shrubs would do the same.) And another handy tip: Paint chain-link fence black or dark green — it'll practically disappear.

Make it easy

Sidewalks that edge the beds make this yard easy to mow. And it's also easy to trim around the low, shallow pool with its wide brick edging — just don't blow the grass clippings into the water! Getting the sidewalks and patio in place might take some time and effort, but once they're installed, all you have to do is sweep. (And these red bricks really echo the trim on the house.) Think a brick sidewalk sounds too expensive or like too much work? Try stained, stamped concrete instead.

WEB extra

For the complete **garden plan**, see our Web extra.

DRAWING BOARD | BACK YARD

As Easy as You Please

Low-maintenance doesn't mean boring! These flowery borders are proof of that. But how do you get from a list of plants to a beautiful garden? Let's take a look.

GOOD ADVICE Any garden designer will tell you to plant in "drifts." If most of your plants are in groups, like the daylilies in this design, it makes your garden look lush, not spotty. That doesn't mean you shouldn't tuck in a single plant or two here and there for emphasis. But clump plants together in groups of four or five (or more!) for a polished look. You'll really notice their color and shape better that way, too.

These pale colors — whites, lavenders and yellows — are great for relaxing or entertaining in the evening. You'll be able to see and enjoy the plants as it begins to get dark.

KEEP IT GOING Don't forget about winter. Evergreens and ornamental grasses give you something to look at even when there's snow on the ground. And the "exclamation points" of the upright hollies help break up the expanse of privacy fence, while still leaving room for lots of other plants.

TIDY UP All these plants are easy-care. Just cut the perennials back in early spring, along with the grasses, the hydrangeas and the bluebeards. Hollies are slow-growing and need little, if any, pruning or shaping. There's enough room here for the spireas to spread out — you can enjoy their lovely vase shape without needing to cut them back at all. Last but not least, this crabapple holds onto its fruits right into winter, and they're usually eaten by birds. So it looks beautiful for a long time and it doesn't make a mess all over your path! □

— *Stephanie Polsley Bruner*

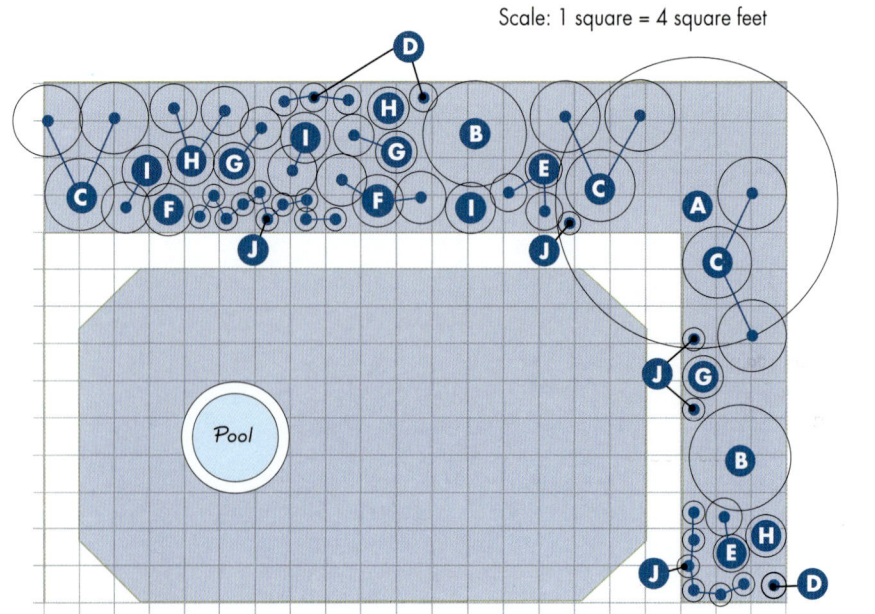

Scale: 1 square = 4 square feet

QUICK TIP
Want a little extra punch? These soft pastels are beautiful just as they are, but you could add more color by tucking a few spring bulbs and long-blooming annuals into the edges of this border.

EASY AND ELEGANT

Code	Plant Name	No. to Plant	Blooms	Type	Cold/Heat Zones	Height/Width	Special Features
A	**Crabapple** *Malus transitoria* 'Schmidtcutleaf' (Golden Raindrops®)	1	White; spring	Tree	4-8/8-1	20 ft./15 ft.	Unusual, fine-textured leaves turn yellow-orange in fall; heavy load of yellow fruit is very ornamental
B	**Van Houtte spirea** *Spiraea xvanhouttei*	2	White; late spring	Shrub	3-8/8-1	6 ft./6 ft.	Graceful, arching branches; fine-textured blue-green foliage stays clean all summer
C	**Smooth hydrangea** *Hydrangea arborescens* 'Annabelle'	9	White; early to midsummer	Shrub	3-9/9-1	3-4 ft./3-4 ft.	Huge white flower heads gradually fade to green, then tan, for interest into fall and winter; cut back hard in early spring for best shape
D	**Japanese holly** *Ilex crenata* 'Sky Pencil'	5	NA	Shrub	6-8/8-1	6-8 ft./12-18 in.	Glossy dark-green foliage year-round; maintains narrow shape without pruning; protect from drying winter winds
E	**Agastache** *Agastache* 'Blue Fortune'	5	Lavender-blue; midsummer to fall	Perennial	5-9/9-1	24-36 in./18-24 in.	Attracts butterflies; cut back 8 to 12 in. after the first flush of blooms to maintain nice plant shape
F	**Shasta daisy** *Leucanthemum xsuperbum* 'Becky'	4	White; midsummer to fall	Perennial	5-9/9-1	3-4 ft./2-3 ft.	Strong, upright stems don't need staking; deadhead to keep new flowers coming
G	**Garden phlox** *Phlox paniculata* 'David'	5	White; midsummer to fall	Perennial	3-8/8-1	2-4 ft./2-3 ft.	Fragrant blooms make good cut flowers; deadhead to prolong blooming; good resistance to powdery mildew
H	**Maiden grass** *Miscanthus sinensis* 'Morning Light'	5	Silvery plumes; late summer to fall	Perennial	5-9/8-1	4-5 ft./2-4 ft.	Variegated foliage stays upright; tiny reddish flowers fade to silvery plumes that hold on into winter
I	**Bluebeard** *Caryopteris xclandonensis* 'Longwood Blue'	5	Purple-blue; late summer to fall	Shrub	5-9/9-1	2-4 ft./2-4 ft.	Attracts butterflies; cut back hard in spring to remove winter damage and promote full growth
J	**Daylily** *Hemerocallis* 'Happy Returns'	19	Lemon yellow; early summer to fall	Perennial	3-9/9-1	15-20 in./15-20 in.	Reblooming daylily; cut spent flower stalks to the ground to tidy plants and encourage rebloom

DESIGN CHALLENGE | BACK YARD

Divide and Disguise

This yard is like an outfit that doesn't quite work. The fences don't match, and the yard is too long for comfort.

When you think of a fenced-in yard, you probably visualize one style of fence around the entire yard. But Wendy Hesselbein has *two* fences in her Massachusetts yard. One is a privacy fence that belongs to her neighbor, while the shorter split-rail fence is hers. Plus, there's a 5-foot gap between the fences that attracts a lot of unwelcome attention, both to the gap itself and to the mismatched fences.

And the fences aren't the only problem. At 90 feet by 40 feet, this yard is long and narrow. Although it's logical to soften the strong lines of the fences with plantings, the existing skinny beds don't work very well. They aren't wide enough for big plants that will cover the fence. In fact, the narrow bed lines just accentuate the length of the yard. Wendy has a collection of beautiful plants, but she's not sure how to arrange them into a cohesive plan.

A few simple design ideas come to the rescue. Strategically placed shrubs hide the gap in summer and winter, while colorful perennials soften the fences. Dramatic curved bed shapes create two separate spaces in this long, narrow yard, showing off different planting color themes.

Now, when the Hesselbeins want to enjoy their yard, they'll admire their lush garden instead of focusing on fences.

Use common themes

These beds sweep in toward the center, creating two distinct areas in this yard. In a space that's divided this way, you can use slightly different color themes in the separate spaces. If you like a lot of colors, this is a great way to organize them. But try to stick to a common color thread — too many areas with completely different color palettes would be confusing. Weave a few of the same elements through each space to create a sense of familiarity for garden visitors because they've seen that element before. Here, red flowers, similar textures and specific plants, such as tall sedum and coneflowers, tie the "rooms" together.

PHOTOS: Courtesy of Wendy Hesselbein

WEB extra

Want this garden? Check out the complete *plan*.

Hide the gaps

Think about seasonal issues when you're planning a cover-up planting. A deciduous shrub will cover this gap in summer, but a shrub with a striking shape may make it even more noticeable in the winter by drawing your eye to the trouble spot. However, this trio of evergreen arborvitae will make the gap disappear year-round. Plus, they'll form a great backdrop, either for these bright perennials, a garden ornament or a flowering deciduous shrub.

Cover up quickly

Whether you want to cover up a fence completely depends on the style and material of the fence. This fence, like most privacy fences, isn't very exciting. But it makes a great support for vines. Sweet autumn clematis is vigorous enough to scramble over almost anything, but you'll need to provide some strings or wires for it to get started up the fence. (Make sure that's OK with your neighbor first.) Vines grow quickly and can cover up an eyesore faster than shrubs. So planting a combination of vines and shrubs provides both an immediate and a long-term solution. Planting shrubs with winter interest, like holly and redtwig dogwood, makes the garden attractive during the drab winter months. Take a closer look at the plantings that cover this fence on p. 224.

Change the shape

In long, narrow spaces, it's tempting to use long, narrow planting beds, too. But repeating that shape in the flower bed actually makes the yard look longer. Instead, use a dramatic curving bed shape to bring the planting away from the fence several feet. The curved bed and a small island bed directly opposite effectively break this big yard into two smaller "rooms." These smaller areas feel more enclosed and comfortable, but you can still catch a glimpse of other exciting spaces to explore.

Botanical Names

Arborvitae
 Thuja occidentalis
Coneflower
 Echinacea hybrids
Holly *Ilex* spp.
Redtwig dogwood
 Cornus spp.
Sweet autumn clematis
 Clematis terniflora
Tall sedum
 Sedum hybrids

www.GardenGateMagazine.com   *the* YEAR IN GARDENING   223

DRAWING BOARD | BACK YARD

One Hot Planting

A privacy fence can be an asset in your garden, but it definitely needs to be dressed up with a lush planting. We've used evergreen shrubs and late-blooming vines along this fence as a backdrop for colorful perennials.

MASSES OF COLOR Choosing a color theme and sticking to it is an easy way to make any garden look unified. A theme can be as simple as a one-color garden or two contrasting shades. Or it can be a group of colors, like the reds and oranges here. This planting of yarrow, coneflower and butterfly weed blend into a very warm-hued garden. At the far end, a rusty-pink sedum signals a transition into another color "room," but without creating a jarring contrast.

WHERE TO FIND COLOR The obvious places to look for color in the garden are flowers and leaves. But don't forget about berries and twigs. Holly, for example, has tiny white spring flowers. But in fall, the plants are covered with bright-red berries. And those will last until spring, as long as the birds don't eat them! Some dogwood shrubs are grown for their yellow or red twigs — they'll show up against an evergreen background for winter interest, too.

Use different bloom times to give your garden a changing color theme. White, pink and yellow spring bulbs can give way to cream, red and orange summer perennials. Follow with red berries, red or yellow twigs and bronze or evergreen foliage for winter. ◻

— *Stephanie Polsley Bruner*

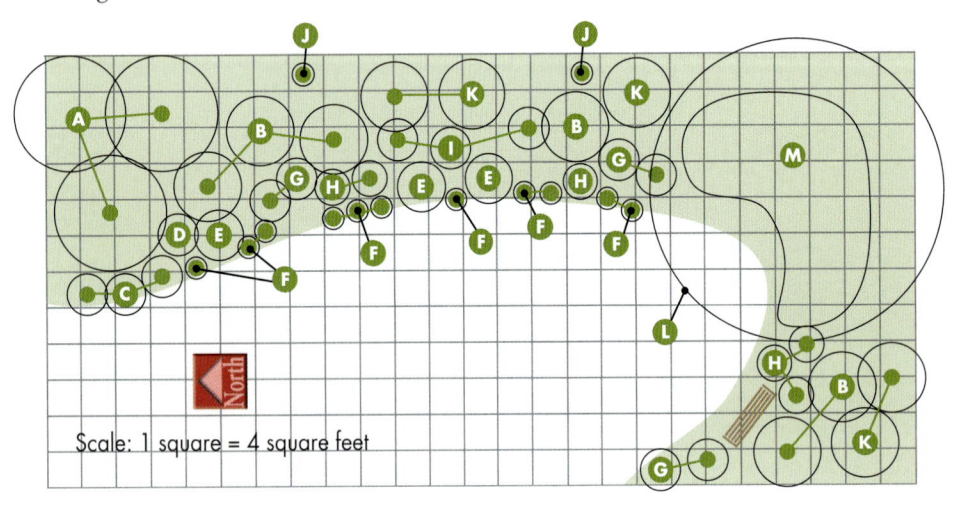

Scale: 1 square = 4 square feet

THE GARDEN'S PALETTE

Code	Plant Name	No. to Plant	Blooms	Type	Cold/Heat Zones	Height/ Width	Special Features
A	Arborvitae *Thuja occidentalis* 'Brandon'	3	NA	Evergreen shrub	3-8/8-1	12-15 ft./ 6-8 ft	Year-round interest; excellent choice for hedges or screens; needs little pruning
B	Red-osier dogwood *Cornus stolonifera* Arctic Fire™ ('Farrow')	6	White; late spring	Shrub	3-9/9-1	3-4 ft./ 3-4 ft.	Compact habit makes it great for smaller spaces; bright red-orange twigs provide winter interest
C	Tall sedum *Sedum* 'Autumn Fire'	3	Pink; summer to fall	Perennial	3-11/11-1	2-3 ft./ 2 ft.	Attracts butterflies; drought-tolerant; dried flower heads add winter interest
D	Coneflower *Echinacea purpurea* 'Green Eyes'	1	Dark magenta; summer	Perennial	4-9/9-1	25-30 in./ 24 in.	Flowers have green center when young; seedheads attract birds; can self-seed
E	Common yarrow *Achillea millefolium* 'Red Velvet'	3	Red; summer	Perennial	3-9/9-1	1 ft./3-5 ft.	Attracts butterflies; fast spreader; drought-tolerant; bloom stalks can be 3 ft. tall
F	Blue fescue *Festuca glauca* 'Elijah Blue'	11	Tan; summer	Perennial	4-11/11-1	8-12 in./ 8-12 in.	Evergreen, blue-gray grass; tight, mounded shape; cut back in spring to refresh
G	Coneflower *Echinacea* Sundown Big Sky™ ('Evan Saul')	6	Red-orange; summer	Perennial	4-9/9-1	32-40 in./ 20-30 in.	Fragrant blooms in waves through summer; deadhead to prolong blooming

Code	Plant Name	No. to Plant	Blooms	Type	Cold/Heat Zones	Height/ Width	Special Features
H	**Butterfly weed** *Asclepias tuberosa*	6	Orange; summer	Perennial	4-9/9-1	3 ft./2 ft.	Attracts butterflies; tolerates variety of soils; drought-tolerant
I	**Foxglove** *Digitalis purpurea* 'Camelot Cream'	3	Cream; early summer	Biennial	5-9/9-1	30-38 in./ 24-30 in.	Attracts butterflies; blooms heavily first year; biennial or short-lived perennial
J	**Sweet autumn clematis** *Clematis terniflora*	2	White; late summer to fall	Perennial vine	4-9/9-1	20 ft./ spreads	Sweet fragrance; heavy blooming; prune hard in early spring
K	**Holly** *Ilex* x*meserveae* Berri-Magic® Kids ('Blue Girl' & 'Blue Boy')	5	White; spring	Evergreen shrub	5-9/9-1	6-8 ft./ 3-6 ft.	Red berries in late fall and winter; needs male and female plants for berries (Berri-Magic Kids has both male and female plant in one container)
L	**Japanese maple** *Acer palmatum* 'Bloodgood'	1	Insignificant	Tree	5-8/8-1	15 ft./ 15 ft.	Delicate burgundy foliage; interesting branch structure provides winter interest; best in sheltered location
M	**Japanese spurge** *Pachysandra terminalis* 'Green Sheen'	40	Insignificant	Ground cover	4-8/8-1	6-10 in./ 24-36 in.	Glossy evergreen leaves; spreads slowly, so plant closely for a full look

www.GardenGateMagazine.com *the* YEAR IN GARDENING

DESIGN CHALLENGE | BACK YARD

A Change of Scenery

Don't look now

Why an island bed to hide an ugly view? Why not a border garden right along the edge of the yard? Well, it's a matter of perspective. Hold your hand a few inches from your face. Can't see much around your hand, can you? Now move it out to arm's length. You can see a lot more now. This island bed works the same way. It's a little closer to the house, so it's going to block more of the view than a planting farther away would.

Maybe you're one of those gardeners lucky enough to have a view of the mountains or a beautiful tree. But most of us aren't so fortunate. Usually there's something we'd like to hide, whether it's a busy street, garbage cans or, in Kathy Hoffmeister's Maryland garden, a weedy parking lot.

However, the right combination of plants can help you out of almost any situation. In this case, the solution is simple: Plant something big enough to block the view. Kathy wants plenty of color and a year-round screen. She also wants a planting that's wildlife-friendly — the tangle of trees is home to lots of birds and small animals. They're fun to watch, and Kathy doesn't want to spend all her time trying to keep them out of the garden.

Take a look at how this island screens an unsightly view. Then turn to p. 228. You'll find a timeline planting plan that'll keep this bed looking great until the trees reach their full size.

PHOTO: Courtesy of Kathy Hoffmeister

Make a big bed

Of course, when you're trying to screen a large area, the bed needs to include a couple of evergreen trees if it's going to work year-round. And that brings up the subject of scale. The bed needs to be big enough to contain the full-sized trees, and you'll need some other large plants nearby to bridge the height difference between the trees and the surroundings. A little "ruffle" of perennials won't look right, so we've included some crape myrtles and winterberries — plants that are halfway between the trees and the perennials in size.

Invite them in

You can view wildlife as pests, or you can decide to get along with them. In this garden, evergreens offer shelter for birds, and a mix of shrubs and perennials provides cover for small animals. A little pond is a bonus for wildlife, but be sure there's a gentle slope and a shallow end an inch or two deep. You don't want your furry friends to drown! (A couple big rocks will also give small animals a way to climb out if they slip into the water.) Skip the fish — some wildlife visitors, such as raccoons, will think you're providing snacks.

Catch your eye

Although the larger plants will end up doing most of the work in this bed, you still need some bright color. Color will help attract the birds and butterflies this gardener loves. And it'll also draw your eye down, so you'll be looking at the color, not at the background. In a few years, the trees will grow into a good screen and this won't matter as much. But while the bed is just getting started, some color is going to play a big role in improving the view.

www.GardenGateMagazine.com   *the* YEAR IN GARDENING   **227**

DRAWING BOARD | BACK YARD

Room to Grow

It's always a jolt. You imagine a beautiful garden, buy the plants and put them in the ground. Then you step back — and it doesn't look anything like what you'd expected. The problem is, you imagined the garden full-grown, but it's still just a baby.

So how do you deal with the time lapse between digging the planting holes and actually having a mature garden? There are a few things you can do to make the wait for this island bed a little easier.

INVEST WISELY Two Norway spruces will be the biggest plants in the final garden. You're usually better off planting smaller trees, because they get established and grow more quickly than larger trees do. But in this case, where the trees are to provide a screen, you might prefer to start off with the largest size your budget will allow. You may need to get a landscaper to plant them for you, because big trees are heavy and hard to manage. It's not cheap to plant trees that size, but they'll have much more immediate impact than smaller ones.

TAKE IT SLOW Think in stages. In the end, you want a big bed around some big trees, but those trees still aren't anything close to their full size. So you don't have to make the bed the final dimensions either. In fact, it's better if you don't. If you dig up the whole area now, you'll have to look at a lot of bare mulch for several years, or spend all spring tucking in hundreds of annuals to fill it up.

The first stage bed is highlighted in green at right. There's plenty of room for the trees to mature, but the bed around them is small.

However, the planting can still look good. You don't want to plant shrubs, because those are hard to transplant later, but what about perennials? In the illustration above, you'll see how we've filled out the bed with tall perennials, such as ornamental grasses and false sunflower, with annuals in front for color. This bed will look great for several years while the trees get going. What happens next? Turn the page to find out.

JUST GETTING STARTED

Code	Plant Name	No. to Plant	Blooms	Type	Cold/Heat Zones	Height/Width	Special Features
A	Norway spruce *Picea abies*	2	NA	Tree	3-7/7-1	40-60 ft./25 ft.	One of the fastest-growing spruces; branches become pendulous as the tree matures
B	False sunflower *Helianthus* 'Lemon Queen'	3	Pale-yellow; late summer	Perennial	4-9/9-1	6 ft./6 ft.	Covered with pale-yellow blooms in late summer to fall
C	Dwarf zebra grass *Miscanthus sinensis* 'Hinjo'	8	Silver-white; late summer	Perennial	5-9/9-1	4 ft./2 ft.	A compact zebra grass; silvery plumes rise above foliage in late summer
D	Black-eyed Susan *Rudbeckia fulgida sullivantii* 'Goldsturm'	5	Yellow; summer	Perennial	4-9/9-1	24-30 in./18-24 in.	A garden classic; golden-yellow flowers in midsummer
E	Purple coneflower *Echinacea purpurea* 'Vintage Wine'	7	Magenta; summer	Perennial	3-8/8-1	36-40 in./18-24 in.	Petals stand out instead of drooping as they do on most coneflowers; leave seedheads for goldfinches and other songbirds to eat

Scale: 1 square = 4 square feet

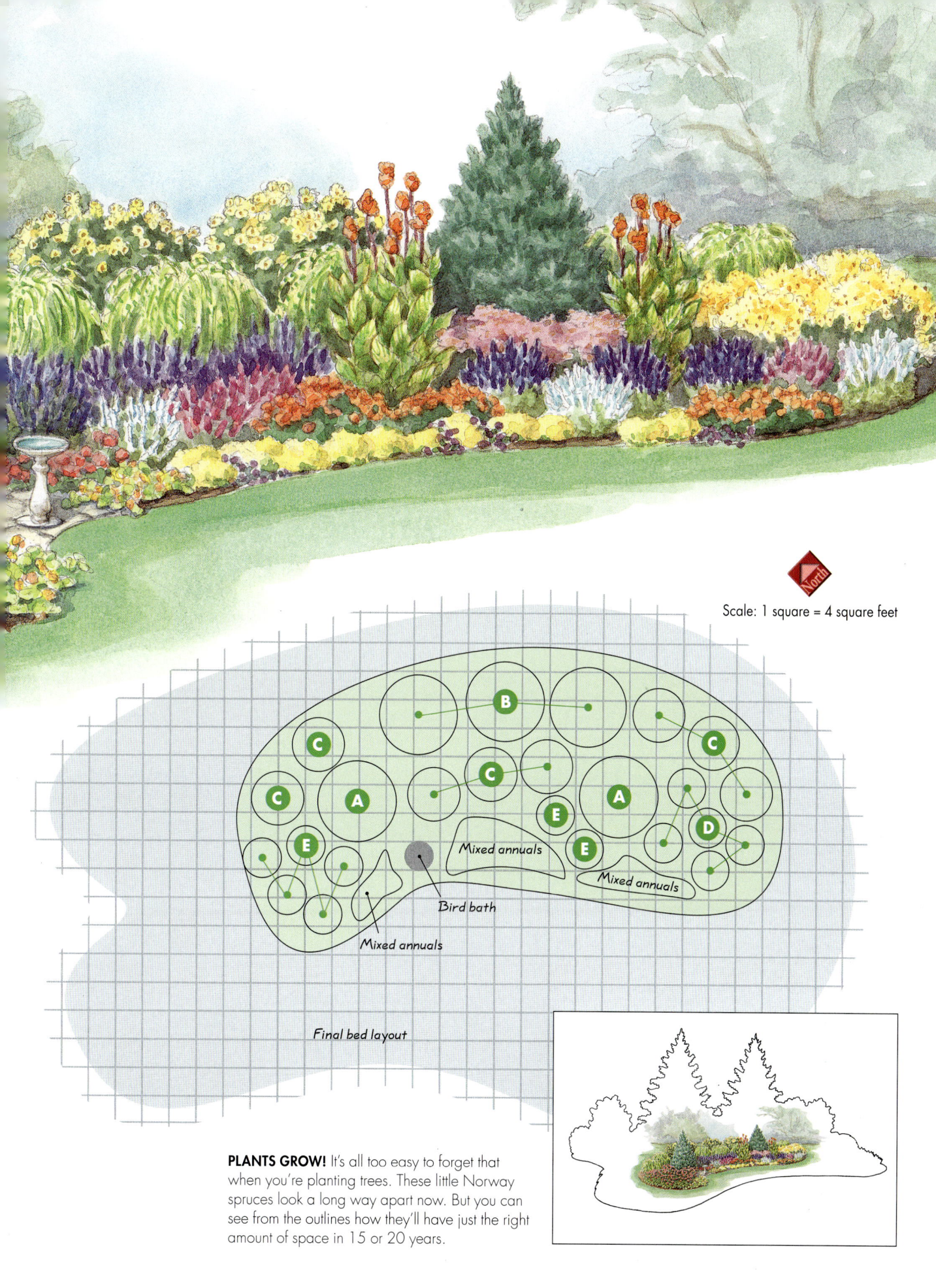

B
C
C
C
A
E
E
A
C
E
D
Mixed annuals
Bird bath
Mixed annuals
Mixed annuals

Final bed layout

PLANTS GROW! It's all too easy to forget that when you're planting trees. These little Norway spruces look a long way apart now. But you can see from the outlines how they'll have just the right amount of space in 15 or 20 years.

www.GardenGateMagazine.com   *the* YEAR IN GARDENING   229

DRAWING BOARD | BACKYARD CONTINUED

Fast forward five or ten years. Your trees aren't at full height yet, but they've grown several feet, and you're ready to make the bed bigger and add some shrubs. (Norway spruce can grow 1 to 2 feet per year, so your garden will get to this point sooner than you think.) You'll need to strip off more sod and make the bed its "finished" size.

Shrubs will add structure to the bed, and bridge the gap between the height of the trees and the much-smaller perennials. 'Osage' crape myrtle has showy pale-pink flowers and good fall leaf color, while winterberries add a bit of interest during the cold months. (Winterberries have male and female plants. The females bear the showy fruit, but you still need one male.) Be sure you leave room for the shrubs to reach their full width, too.

Those perennials you planted when you first put in the bed are about to come in handy. They've grown and some of them need to be divided, so you'll have plenty to fill in a bigger bed. Split them if they need it, and move them forward to fill in the area in front of the trees. We added another ornamental grass, and left space for the small pond you read about on p. 226, where you saw what the mature garden will look like.

Planning a garden in stages this way will keep it looking great from the first year you plant it. □
— *Stephanie Polsley Bruner*

Just getting started

Code	Plant Name	No. to Plant
A	Norway spruce	2
B	False sunflower	3
C	Dwarf zebra grass	10
D	Black-eyed Susan	6
E	Purple coneflower	11

These numbers are for the second phase of planting. See p. 228 for plant details on A-E.

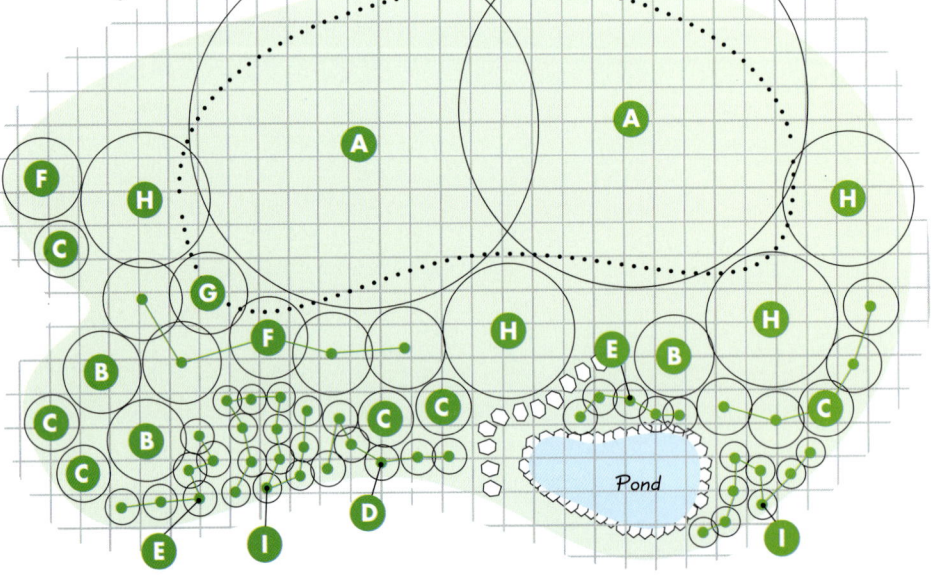

Scale: 1 square = 4 square feet

GOING STRONG

Code	Plant Name	No. to Plant	Blooms	Type	Cold/Heat Zones	Height/Width	Special Features
F	Winterberry *Ilex verticillata* 'Afterglow'	6	White, inconspicuous; spring	Shrub	4-8/8-1	6 ft./6 ft.	Glossy green foliage is deciduous; showy red winter berries; female
G	Winterberry *Ilex verticillata* 'Jim Dandy'	1	White, inconspicuous; spring	Shrub	4-8/8-1	6 ft./6 ft.	Male pollinator for 'Afterglow'
H	Crape myrtle *Lagerstroemia* 'Osage'	4	Pale-pink; mid- to late summer	Small tree	6-10/10-1	12-15 ft./10-12 ft.	Exfoliating bark; can have some winter damage in the coldest part of its hardiness range
I	Little bluestem *Schizachyrium scoparium* 'The Blues'	20	Purple-bronze; late summer	Perennial	3-9/9-1	18-36 in./18-24 in.	Blue-gray leaves change to red-orange in fall and winter; purple-bronze seed heads in August turn silver-white in fall

building blocks of design

« Most gardens incorporate several of these design building blocks. In the photo at left, the LINE of the path leads your eye to the FOCAL POINT of the arbor. Clumps of plants are REPEATED along the path. The petals of the poppy below have a silky TEXTURE and the purple and orange are a great color CONTRAST.

As you read *The Year in Gardening*, you'll notice design terms like "line," "shape," and so on. These are the building blocks of good design, whether you're planting a garden, painting a picture or decorating a room. Below, find out how to put these tools to work in your own garden.

COLOR Everyone has different taste in color. But keep in mind that warm colors (browns, oranges, reds and yellows) can feel either energetic or cozy, and warm-colored flowers or objects often seem closer. Cool colors (blues, greens, lavenders, purples) are serene and soothing, and they usually recede, making a cool-colored object seem farther away. There can be some overlap; for instance, a pink flower might be a warm pink with undertones of salmon and orange, or it might be a cool pink with a touch of lavender or blue.

CONTRAST Contrast happens when two dissimilar objects are compared. That's the textbook definition, but what does it really mean? Pair a fuzzy-leafed plant with a plant that has smooth, glossy leaves, or plant bright-red flowers next to bright-blue ones — that's contrast. A black iron bench blends in against a dark-green yew hedge, but a white bench stands out because of the color contrast. Use contrast to call attention to a special plant or ornament and to keep the garden exciting and interesting.

FOCAL POINT A focal point is where your eye goes first when you look at a scene, like a bold shape against a finer-textured background or a bright splash of color that draws your eye. If part of your garden looks bleak at a certain time of the year, place something bright in a different part of the garden. Your eyes will go to the bright spot without noticing the less-attractive area.

LINE A line can be straight, curving, vertical or horizontal. Edging, a sidewalk or a row of plants can create a line. Use lines to direct people's eyes to a certain view (for instance, position a statue at the end of a straight pathway; your eyes will follow the path directly to the statue). Lines also define shapes, as a well-defined edge (the line) shows off a bed shape.

REPETITION Repetition is exactly what it sounds like: A garden element that's repeated over and over. It might be clumps of one type of plant scattered through the garden, or it could be the same bricks used in a patio, in a path and as edging. Repetition makes your design look planned and deliberate, so all the small, separate areas are clearly part of one garden. (Think of it as having your shoes and your belt match — everything just looks more pulled together.)

SHAPE Flower shapes (like spikes or daisies) can create a mood or feeling in the garden. A planting with a lot of spiky, upright flowers has lots of energy, while round or daisy-shaped flowers look cheerful and serene. Bed shapes are important too. Simple geometric shapes like circles and rectangles look at home in a formal garden, while curving, irregularly shaped beds are more casual.

TEXTURE Texture is the surface quality of an object. A leaf might be furry or smooth. A pea gravel path has a finer texture than a flagstone path, while a tree with large, bold twigs has a coarser texture than a tree with fine, wispy twigs. If you want to show off a specimen tree or shrub, it's best to set it in front of a group of fine-textured plants, which blend together to create a backdrop that won't distract.

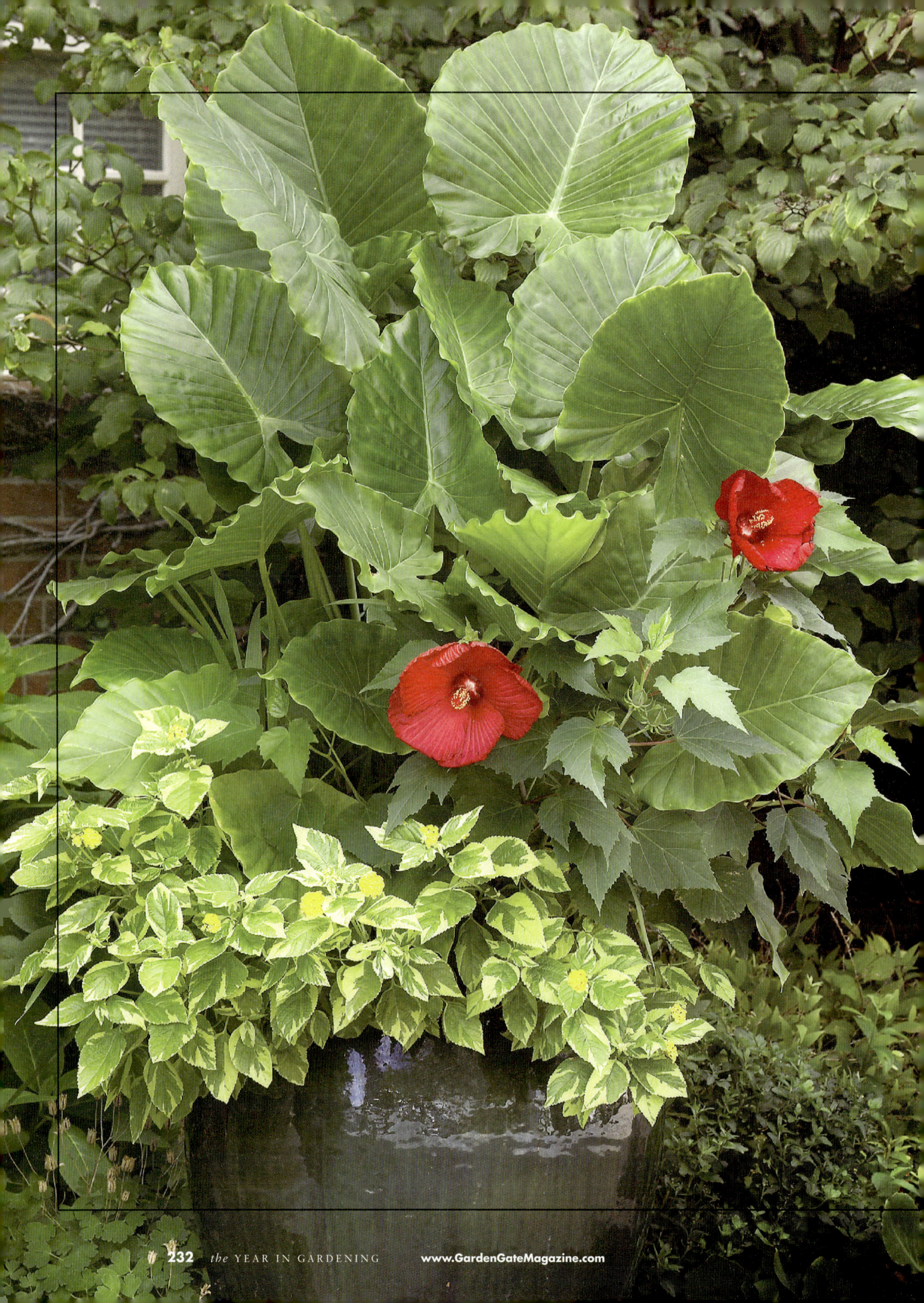

all about containers

grow the *best containers* on the block!

IF YOU WANT INSTANT IMPACT, growing container gardens is one of the best ways to get it. Want to punch up your entry this weekend? Plant a container! Tired of your deck's color scheme? Do a quick switch of your pots. Here you'll find dramatic container plans as well as some great advice on how to buy containers. Plus we'll show you the winners of the *Garden Gate* Reader Container Challenge. Now get growing!

Choosing Containers	234
Double Delight	236
Dark and Dramatic	238
Garden Gems	239
First-Class Containers	240
Tropical Flair	244
Bold Combinations	245
Watering	246
Gold Rush	248
Holiday Packages	249
Condense Your Garden	250
Did You Know	252

CONTAINERS | BASICS

Choosing Containers

DECISIONS, DECISIONS Walk into a nursery or landscape center, and you're faced with row after row of containers. Tall or short, heavy or feather-light, wide or skinny — there are so many options. How do you know which one to choose?

Much of it depends on your own personal sense of style and the colors you like. But it's also important to consider what the container is made of. After all, the material doesn't just affect how a container looks, but also how it performs. Did you know that metal containers can burn tender trailers? Or that composite containers can help even the largest plantings stay lightweight?

On these pages, you'll discover everything you need to make smart container choices, compiled in one easy-to-read chart. We'll walk you through what's included in each category (from the types of terra-cotta you might find to what hypertufa is actually made of), tell you the pros and cons of each option and give a few tips to ensure that your container looks great and works well, no matter what type you choose.

So this year, whether you're purchasing new containers or pulling old favorites out of the garage, you'll know how to make the container's material work to your advantage.

SHOPPING TIP

If you're unsure of whether or not a container will work in your yard, grab a digital camera. Take shots of the pots you like, then print out the photos and look at them in your yard. You can also take shots of plants you like, and use prints to piece together successful plant combinations.

	TERRA-COTTA	METAL
material	"Terra-cotta" is Italian for "baked earth," and that's just what this is — kiln-fired clay. It can range from the rich orange-brown color seen here, to a pale, creamy color. Find it either glazed or left bare. Containers made from Italian clay are considered the finest, and are the most expensive.	Metal containers can be made of cast iron, copper, stainless steel or zinc, for a range of weights and looks. They can be left as bare metal, or can be powder-coated with a range of colors, as the one above is.
upside	Unglazed terra-cotta is porous, so air can get in and water can evaporate out, keeping roots cool. It's a durable material (as long as it's cared for properly) and it can give either a casual look or a formal feel.	These pots are durable — they won't chip or crack. They can be modern and sleek, or stately and formal. And some gain a patina with use, which many believe increases their beauty.
downside	Dry terra-cotta wicks moisture away from soil, can't withstand freezing temperatures and cracks and chips easily.	Metal heats up quickly in the sun, drying soil and searing delicate plants. Cast-iron containers are very heavy and can be difficult to move. Some metal will rust. Thin containers may dent.
price	Can be less than $1 or more than $250. Size and shape of pot, and type of clay used are factors.	Can be less than $10 or more than $250. Cast iron and copper are generally more expensive than steel or zinc.
tips	To keep containers from sucking plants dry, get them wet before planting. Submerge small terra-cotta containers in a bucket of water until air bubbles stop rising. For larger containers, use a hose to soak them through.	If your copper container has lost its shine, it's time to polish. Many sources recommend using lemon, vinegar or salt. They're OK to use on some metals, but not copper. Acidic lemon juice and abrasive salt can damage copper's finish. Stick with commercial copper polish for a safe shine.

CONCRETE	**GLAZED**	**FAUX MATERIALS**	**WOOD**
Concrete (top) makes solid, sturdy containers. They can be left unfinished, for a rough, rustic appearance, or concrete can be stained for a little color. An alternative, hypertufa (bottom), is a lightweight cement mixture with properties similar to concrete.	These containers are made of clay that's been coated with a glaze and fired in a kiln. Glazed containers are available in almost any shape, size or combination of colors.	These containers are made of fiberglass, resin, plastic or a composite of materials. They're made to look like glazed, metal, terra-cotta or stone containers, and come in a wide range of colors, styles and sizes.	Wooden containers are available as planters, like the one above, windowboxes, whiskey barrels, and other styles. They can be unfinished, finished with clear oil, stained a rich color or painted.
Concrete containers are heavy, which means they won't tip over. Plus, they're durable, so they'll last for years and years. They're perfect for containing the strong root systems of trees and shrubs. Hypertufa is lighter in weight, easy to move and only slightly less durable.	Glazed containers offer the widest variety of color and style for a container garden, and they withstand cold temperatures better than unglazed clay containers (but they aren't completely frost-proof). With proper care, glazed containers can last for years.	Composite or fiberglass containers are extremely lightweight, durable, weather-resistant and affordable. They can be left outside during a freezing winter, look very realistic and can fit any style.	Wood planters and boxes can create versatile looks, especially when combined with trellises or benches. Choose to maintain their new-wood look, let them weather to deep gray or paint or stain them to fit your color scheme.
Concrete containers are heavy, which means they're difficult to move. Concrete and hypertufa are both porous, so they can wick water away from soil.	Glazed containers can chip and crack, and need to be pulled indoors or protected in freezing temperatures.	The major drawback to composite or fiberglass is that, while they look like other materials, they just aren't the real thing.	Unfinished, untreated wood will rot over time, and wooden containers can attract pests. Wood is usually used for large planters, rather than small pots.
High-quality concrete pots tend to be more expensive than other containers of similar size. Hypertufa is more affordable than concrete.	**Can be less than $10 or more than $250. Size, shape and type of glaze used determine price.**	**Faux containers tend to be less expensive than other containers of similar size. Expect to pay less than $100.**	**Can be less than $50 or more than $250. Size of container, type of wood and quality of construction determine price.**
To keep your concrete looking clean and new, paint the exterior with a coat of Thompson's Water Seal®. However, if you like the aged, mossy look that concrete gets, mix a cup of buttermilk with a handful of moss in a blender. Paint the mixture over your container to encourage moss growth.	If your glazed container is too large or too heavy to move indoors during freezing temperatures, you can still protect it from damage. Remove the plants and soil, and wrap the empty container, inside and out, with bubble wrap. Or tip the container on its side to keep moisture out.	Because these containers are so lightweight, they can be top-heavy when planted. To keep yours from tipping over in wind, put a brick or a few heavy stones in the bottom of the pot to weight it down. Just be careful not to cover the drainage hole, or your potting mix may get soggy.	Look for containers made from redwood, cypress, white oak, teak or cedar. These containers will be naturally rot-resistant, and will stand up to weather much better than containers made from other types of wood.

CONTAINERS | DESIGN IDEAS

Double Delight

Create combinations that go from inside to out and back again.

Looking for ways to save more of your time and your money? Get double duty out of your containers by creating ones you can use inside in the winter and move outside when summer arrives.

Most house plants are tender tropicals that can't survive temperatures lower than about 45 to 50 degrees. They generally don't need or like full sun conditions either, the trait that makes them great indoors. But many also thrive in sheltered spots outside. Just keep them out of harsh sun and damaging wind. A covered porch or deck is a perfect summer hangout. For no-hassle tips on bringing plants back indoors in fall, see our Web extra.

PICK THE PLANTS Instead of planting a single plant per pot, combine different kinds in each container. After all, you do that with your outdoor containers all the time. Keep your home's color scheme in mind when you pick plants and make sure they like similar light and moisture conditions. The plants in both the terracotta dish and the large pot at right need moderate to bright light. All of the plants in these two recipes grow well indoors in winter. And you can see how they really perk up and put on new growth when they're outside on the porch in summer.

WEB extra

Don't let tender plants go! Use our foolproof *tips* for bringing them indoors in fall.

1 LIGHT AND LEAFY

Lots of foliage contrast keeps this container interesting through the seasons. And the key to keeping it looking this good? Let the soil dry out between waterings. The most common cause of house plant problems is overwatering. That's why terracotta containers, which dry out faster than plastic, metal or glazed containers, work well for indoor plants.

Small, deep-brown aquarium rocks dress up the surface of the soil. I added some water to more of the gravel in the waterproof saucer to provide a little humidity and to give the pot a finishing touch.

Code	Plant Name	No. to Plant
A	Flamingo flower *Anthurium andraeanum*	1
B	Bromeliad *Neoregelia* spp.	1
C	Friendship plant *Pilea mollis* 'Moon Valley'	2
D	Nerve plant *Fittonia albivenis* 'Red Angel'	2
E	Variegated ivy *Hedera* spp.	4

INDOOR CARE Remember that no plant will do well in the most difficult areas in your home — places that are very dark or are exposed to drafts, either hot or cold. But even in the brightest spots in your home, your plants will grow more slowly indoors and will need much less water than they do outside in summer. Only water when the soil's surface is dry; use a waterproof saucer under the pot to protect your furniture. A dose of half-strength house plant food twice a month will keep plants looking their best. □

— *Deborah Gruca*

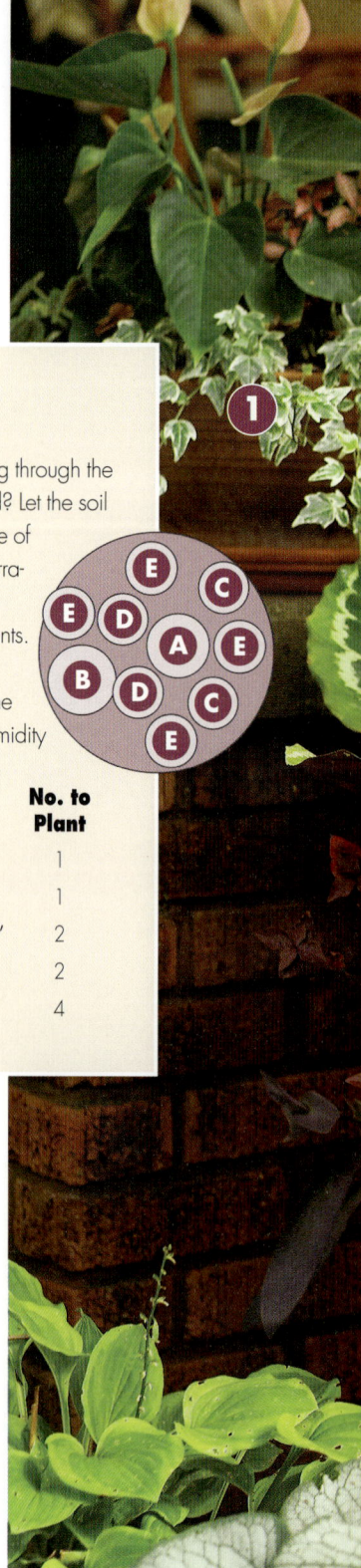

2 TROPICAL FEVER

To make an instant impact indoors or out, choose a large specimen like this peacock plant. Put it in moderate to bright light (but out of direct sun outside). I paired it with purple heart to play up its purple leaf markings and stems.

Grow a large plant in a lightweight plastic pot that you can slip into different decorative containers. Then it's a breeze to move outdoors when the weather warms. During the winter, this one lives in a pretty woven basket, topped with Spanish moss. In summer, I set the plastic pot inside a larger ceramic pot on the porch. A few annuals tucked around the edges give the container a temporary splash of pink for the summer. In fall, toss them on the compost when you bring the plastic pot back inside.

Place the plastic pot into a larger one. Add potting mix in the space between the containers and tuck in colorful annuals for the summer.

Code	Plant Name	No. to Plant
A	**Peacock plant** *Calathea roseopicta*	1
B	**Purple heart** *Tradescantia pallida*	4
C	**Impatiens** *Impatiens walleriana*	6
D	**Iresine** *Iresine herbstii* 'Purple Lady'	2

Grow these containers outdoors in the summer...

...and bring them inside for the winter months.

CONTAINERS | RECIPES

Bold deep-green leaves and splashes of red in a big metal container. Here's a combination that's hard to miss! And that's good — it has a lot to offer.

A great house plant, large-leafed philodendron also thrives in mostly sunny to part-shade spots outdoors, as well. Though it tolerates dry conditions, the thick, fleshy roots are shallow, so mulch the soil with a layer of pine bark to help keep it moist.

With veins of brilliant red, 'California' beefsteak plant echoes the burgundy tinge of the philodendron leaves. This colorful foliage plant is young here, but don't be fooled. You'll need to pinch back this vigorous grower, as well as the velvety leafed plectranthus in the middle of the pot, to keep them from taking over the container.

On the other hand, purple-flowered verbena and the lotus vine, with its needlelike leaves, are more shy, especially in a part-shade location. Encourage both to bloom by adding a small handful of balanced, slow-release fertilizer into the potting mix 4 to 6 inches down.

Any metal container can get deathly hot in summer sun. Be sure to place it where it'll get some shade during the hottest part of the day. Or line the inside of the pot with a couple layers of bubble wrap material before planting anything in it. That way you won't accidentally cook your plants in their big metal pot!

DARK AND DRAMATIC

Tips for care
- Part sun
- Moist, well-drained potting mix
- Feed monthly with half-strength 10-10-10 water-soluble plant food

Code	Plant Name	No. to Plant
A	Philodendron *Philodendron* 'Rojo Congo'	1
B	Beefsteak plant *Iresine herbstii* 'California'	2
C	Plectranthus *Plectranthus* 'Mona Lavender'	1
D	Verbena *Verbena* Babylon Carpet Blue®	3
E	Lotus vine *Lotus* 'Gold Flash'	3

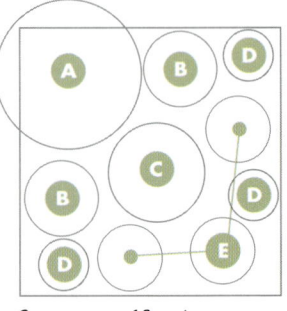

Container is 18 inches square.

A tip for brightening a shady garden bed is to use bright-colored containers or foliage. One look at this jewels of Opar in its gold pot shows you how well it works.

And part shade is exactly what this new plant from PanAmerican Seed™ needs. Full sun would cause the foliage to turn dark green, and full shade would tend to make the plant leggy. But a shady area with some morning sun will keep the leaves bright chartreuse and those delicate star-shaped blooms coming. After the flowers fade, seed pods, the even-smaller reddish "jewels" you see at right, hold on most of the summer.

I tucked in a bright little fuchsia, aptly named 'Electric Lights', another part-shade gem. The bigger plant behind the fragile fuchsia blooms protects them from damaging wind. A compact black mondo grass in the front of the pot adds color and leaf shape contrast. You may not even notice the tiny blue summer flowers and the black shiny berries that follow them. But that amazing black foliage shows well against the lighter leaves of the jewels of Opar as well as the glazed container.

A new color in the bacopa 'Blutopia' series, Blue can take full sun, but still produces plenty of the small flowers in a little shade. And like its companions, it will fill out nicely during the summer, but not so much that it needs cutting back. It won't crowd out its neighbors or ruin this gem of a container! ▢

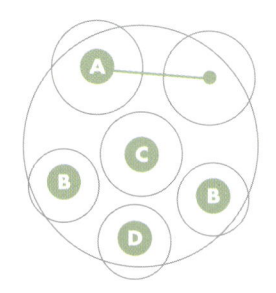

Tiny red "jewel" seed pods of the jewels of Opar last well into fall.

Container is 14 inches across.

GARDEN GEMS

Code	Plant Name	No. to Plant
A	**Jewels of Opar** *Talinum paniculatum* 'Limón'	2
B	**Bacopa** *Sutera cordata* 'Blutopia' Blue	2
C	**Fuchsia** *Fuchsia* 'Electric Lights'	1
D	**Mondo grass** *Ophiopogon planiscapus* 'Niger'	1

Tips for care

- Part shade
- Even soil moisture, let dry out between waterings
- Work some 13-13-13 slow-release fertilizer into the potting mix, and add ¼-strength balanced water-soluble fertilizer monthly

CONTAINERS | RECIPES

Check out these fantastic reader creations

First-Class Containers

It's no surprise that everybody likes container gardening. There are so many good reasons to grow plants in pots. Just think of the huge variety of plants to choose from. Plus, you can try a different bunch of plants the following year. The containers themselves come in a wide range of styles and sizes. And what better way to bring the garden up close to enjoy plant fragrance and textures?

Here at *Garden Gate*, we love container gardening and plant up dozens of pots each year. But we wanted to see what our readers are doing with containers. After all, sharing tips and planting ideas is what we're all about. So last summer we invited you to send us photos of your best containers. The response was great! You'll find our overall favorite, Editor's Choice, to the right. Following that are the best in each category of sun, shade and whimsy. Want to try one of these yourself? Take a look at the plan and plant list next to the photo.

Because there were so many wonderful containers, we included a few extras on p. 243. You can get those plans through our Web extra. Wondering what these lucky gardeners will be receiving for their efforts? Check out "Garden goods" below.

Now let's take a look at some great-looking reader-designed containers! □

— *Sherri Ribbey*

GARDEN GOODS

Hard work deserves a reward. Thanks to the generosity of the companies listed below, we're sending these gardeners some great stuff. The Editor's Choice, Melonie Ice, receives a Campania container, Dynamite™ plant food, Quench™ water crystals and a box filled with Simply Beautiful™ plants. The top pick for each category gets *P. Allen Smith's Container Gardens* book, along with a soil knife and sheath. We'll also mail all these gardeners our newest book, *Containers Made Easy: 101 Knockout Ideas*. Get your own online at www.GardenGateStore.com.

Editor's choice Melonie Ice, Michigan

Who says you need flowers to have a colorful planting? You can't miss the bright coleus in this part-shade container. It practically grabs you as you walk by. Contrasting shapes like the long slender New Zealand flax, round euphorbia and deeply cut sweet potato vine and fern keep this design lively.

Coleus and sweet potato vines both can be overly enthusiastic in a container. Pinch the stems back to a leaf node throughout the season to encourage branching, bushy plants. New Zealand flax doesn't usually grow fast enough in one season to look as good as this one, and it can be expensive. So take this tender perennial inside for the winter. Melonie uses a timer and keeps hers under lights for 12 hours a day. She waters it once or twice a month during winter but there's no need to fertilize.

This 16-in.-diameter container is made of concrete. To give it an aged, rustic appearance, Melonie applied spray paint in shades of green and brown to rags. Then she dabbed the fabric randomly over the surface. The soft colors blend into the background better than the original gray of the concrete.

- 1 **(A)** **Euphorbia** *Euphorbia continifolia* 'Burgundy Wine'
- 1 **(B)** **Coleus** *Solenostemon* 'Glennis'
- 1 **(C)** **New Zealand flax** *Phormium* 'Terracotta'
- 1 **(D)** **Sweet potato vine** *Ipomoea batatas* 'Sweet Caroline Bronze'
- 1 **(E)** **Autumn fern** *Dryopteris erythrosora* 'Brilliance'

Best sun container Mary Jo O'Conner, Illinois

If you want colorful flowers all summer long, plant annuals! Mary Jo got her planting off to a good start by filling this 16-in.-diameter urn with a well-drained potting mix and a dose of Osmocote® slow-release fertilizer. To keep the flowers coming, she added half-strength Miracle Gro® to the watering routine once every two weeks. But be careful not to water too much. None of these plants likes wet feet. You can find out if you need to water by inserting your index finger into the potting medium up to the first knuckle. If the soil is dry at your fingertip, it's time to water.

- 1 **(A)** **Purple fountain grass** *Pennisetum setaceum*
- 1 **(B)** **Sage** *Salvia farinacea* 'Victoria'
- 1 **(C)** **Begonia** *Begonia* Nonstop® Pink
- 1 **(D)** **Dahlia** *Dahlia* Godahlia™ Rose
- 1 **(E)** **Dahlia** *Dahlia* Godahlia™ Orange
- 2 **(F)** **Calibrachoa** *Calibrachoa* Superbells® Blue
- 1 **(G)** **Vinca** *Vinca major* 'Variegata'
- 1 **(H)** **Calibrachoa** *Calibrachoa* Spring Fling™ Lemon

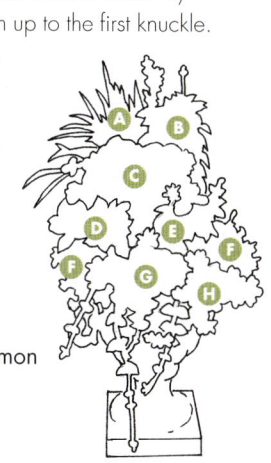

MORE CONTAINERS!

Best shade container Charlotte Watson, Ohio

Add sparkle to your shady patio with this bright pink combination. Make sure to wait until all danger of frost is past in spring before planting this container — both impatiens and caladium are sensitive to chilly temperatures. If an early frost threatens your container, cover the whole thing with a cotton sheet. Don't use plastic as a cover — wherever it touches the plant, the foliage will "burn" or turn crispy.

Charlotte has found that this 12-in. glazed ceramic pot holds moisture better than terra-cotta. In addition, she adds a layer of mulch on top of the potting mix. That way she only has to water once or twice a week even in the heat of summer.

- 1 **(A)** Caladium *Caladium* 'Pink Beauty'
- 1 **(B)** Impatiens *Impatiens* Swirl Raspberry
- 1 **(C)** Impatiens *Impatiens* Impulse™ Deep Pink
- 1 **(D)** Wishbone flower *Torenia* Duchess™ Pink

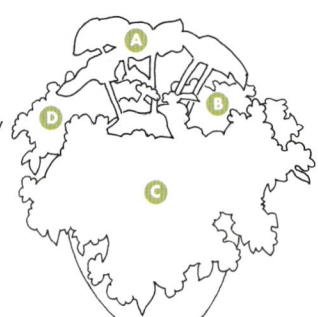

Best whimsical container Margie Reeves, Missouri

Margie's containers were the talk of the neighborhood last summer, and no wonder. What a surprise to find two of these "towers" framing the entry! Filled with colorful annuals, they put on a great show for visitors who came to her sunny front door.

This stack of pots is supported by a 55-in.-tall rebar post attached to a steel base. Starting at the bottom, the pots are 18, 14, 12 and 10 in. in diameter. To assemble, place the post in the bottom container and fill with potting mix. Level the soil out about 2 in. below the rim. Then slide the next pot onto the post. This one sits in the soil. Each additional pot will sit on the edge of the one below it. Add soil to each of these and they're ready for plants. Check out our Web extra to see how this "tower" is put together.

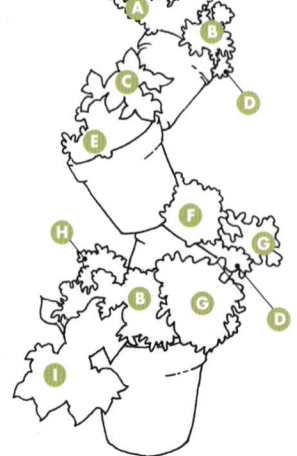

- 1 **(A)** Mexican heather *Cuphea hyssopifolia*
- 6 **(B)** Marigold *Tagetes* hybrid
- 3 **(C)** Coleus *Solenostemon scutellarioides* Wizard Mix
- 3 **(D)** Sweet alyssum *Lobularia maritima*
- 6 **(E)** Moss rose *Portulaca grandiflora*
- 1 **(F)** Melampodium *Melampodium divaricatum*
- 2 **(G)** Petunia *Petunia* Wave® Blue
- 3 **(H)** Coleus *Solenostemon* 'Black Dragon'
- 1 **(I)** Sweet potato vine *Ipomoea batatas* 'Margarita'

BONUS DESIGNS!

AS PROMISED, here are five more beautiful reader-designed containers. These folks will all receive a copy of our softcover book, *Containers Made Easy!*

A) Summer symphony
Andrew Grego, Ohio To keep this graceful full-sun container looking good, Andrew deadheads everything — including the fountain grass — so the flowers keep coming.

B) Color sensation
Rosemarie Calderon, New York Rosemarie grew these colorful coleus in part sun but they'll do just as well in the shade. She uses a liquid organic fertilizer, such as Neptune's Harvest, every week.

C) One person's trash…
Nan Taylor, California You never know what treasures you'll find at a flea market — Nan found railroad spikes and knitting needles. Once painted, they were ready to "plant."

D) Tropical dreams
Julie Amundson, Minnesota These tender perennials are the perfect way to liven up a shady spot. Julie saved herself some money by overwintering most of these plants in her basement.

E) Basket full of goodies
Patricia Evans, Kentucky Containers can be anything you want. This $20 basket was originally meant for storage. Pat added wheels to each corner to make it easy to move. Then she lined it with plastic, filled it with soil and plants and wheeled this beautiful basket into the sun.

WEB extra
Pot up some of your own containers just like these! Get the **plans** online.

CONTAINERS | RECIPES

It's intriguing how rich and lush the color green can look. This pot is a tiny tropical isle growing in the midst of its sedate surroundings.

Take a look at this plant combination. Do you wonder how the dry-loving variegated lantana can do so well in a pot with moisture-loving elephant ear and hibiscus? The secret's in the container — literally. This beautiful glazed container's slanting top edge creates the perfect conditions.

The small illustration below shows how the lantana is planted on the pot's high side, where the mix dries out more quickly, just what the shallow-rooted lantana likes. On the lower side, the mix stays more moist for the elephant ear tuber and the roots of the hibiscus. (Read more about hardy hibiscus on p. 32.)

In this east-facing spot, morning sun is enough to coax bright red blooms from the hibiscus, without scorching the elephant ear leaves.

This hibiscus will stay small enough for a container its first season. In fall, plant it out in the garden, where it'll eventually top out at 3½ to 4 feet tall. The roots won't have much time to get established, so protect the plant the first winter with 2 or 3 inches of compost or organic mulch.

When you move the hibiscus, take out the elephant ear, too. Lift the tuber and store it, or put the whole plant in a plastic pot so it's easy to bring inside for winter. By a sunny window, it'll make a dramatic house plant. Keep it moist, but don't fertilize until it's time to take it back outside when the soil warms up in spring. You can overwinter the lantana, too. Move it to its own pot and cut it back by half. Keep it on the dry side in a sunny window until spring. (You could just treat these plants as annuals and replace them in spring, too.)

Punch up *your* garden with this big, bold summertime look! □

Tips for care

- Part shade with morning sun
- Water deeply once or twice a week around the hibiscus and elephant ear through fall; less water around the lantana
- Feed weekly with a balanced, liquid, full-strength fertilizer

TROPICAL FLAIR

Code	Plant Name	No. to Plant
A	Elephant ear *Alocasia* 'Calidora'	1
B	Hardy hibiscus *Hibiscus moscheutos* 'Cinnamon Grappa'	2
C	Variegated lantana *Lantana camara* 'Samantha'	2

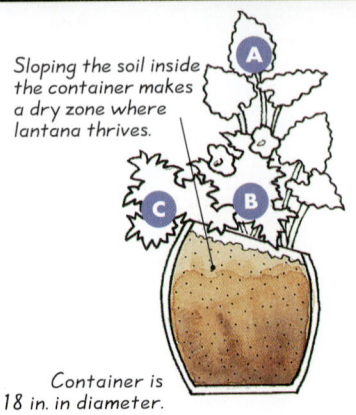

Sloping the soil inside the container makes a dry zone where lantana thrives.

Container is 18 in. in diameter.

If one container is good, two are better. But that doesn't mean they have to be exactly the same. While these are the same shape, the one on the right is actually black and a bit larger than the other one, which is red. Why use two different sizes? The red one is in a small corner, and doesn't have much room. The black one is against a large wall where a small pot would be dwarfed, and it has a bigger planting to match.

The part-sun black container planting has a mix of flowers, foliage plants and, unexpectedly, vegetables. Don't overlook edibles when you're building decorative containers. Many, such as oregano or this pepper, look as good as they taste. This planting looks bold and lush from June to frost with just a little TLC. Pinch back the coleus if it gets too leggy, and cut back the zinnias if they fade — they'll return later, looking fresh. □

BOLD COMBINATIONS

Code	Plant Name	No. to Plant
A	**Coleus** Solenostemon Solar™ Radiance	1
B	**Begonia** Begonia Dragon Wing™ Red	1
C	**Pepper** Capsicum annuum 'Golden Bell'	1
D	**Iresine** Iresine herbstii 'Aureoreticulata'	1
E	**Calibrachoa** Calibrachoa Superbells® Peach	1
F	**Zinnia** Zinnia 'Profusion® Deep Apricot'	1
G	**Hibiscus** Hibiscus moscheutos	1
H	**Variegated ginger** Alpinia zerumbet 'Samantha'	1

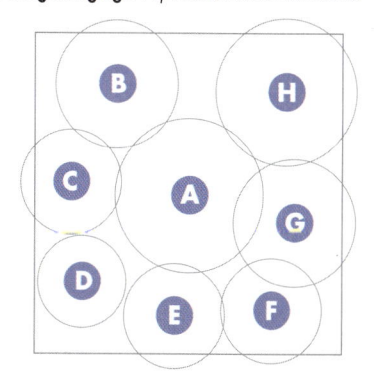

Container is 18 in. square.

www.GardenGateMagazine.com *the* YEAR IN GARDENING **245**

CONTAINERS | BASICS

Watering

DRINK UP Water is vital to plants' survival. Without it, they wilt and die. But with too much water, plants will rot. How do you find balance? Learn the "fingertip" test. Dig your pointer finger into the pot's soil, until it's buried to the first knuckle. Generally, if the soil's dry at your fingertip, then it's time to water. There are some exceptions, however. Drought-tolerant plants, such as cosmos and celosia, can get by on less water, whereas plants that like boggy soil, such as fiber optic grass and fuchsia, shouldn't ever have dry soil. And remember that plants in containers dry out quickly, so they'll need to be watered more frequently than their in-ground counterparts. The best time to water is in the morning — it's cooler then, so you won't lose a lot of water to evaporation, and the heat throughout the rest of the day will dry water from plants' foliage, preventing fungal diseases.

Whether you're using a hose, a watering wand or a watering can, you want to get the water source as close to the soil as you can. (You can see how we pull the plants aside to reach the soil.) To make sure your pot is getting enough liquid, keep pouring until water trickles out the bottom of the container.

FORGET TO WATER? Forgetting for a day or two isn't disastrous, but go much longer, and you may find that the soil in your container is dry and shrunken. In this case, you need to re-wet the soil. Just watering as normal won't do the trick — the water will run down the space between the dry soil and the container, and it won't reach plants' roots. To get the water to the plants, use a pencil, garden stake or small dowel to poke holes into the soil, then water as usual. You should see the soil begin to swell with moisture. As long as your container has a drainage hole in the bottom, you can also place the pot in a saucer filled with water. The soil will pull needed moisture up through the drainage hole, and the plants will quench their thirst.

POT FEET

These tiny accessories may look elegant tucked under a container, but they're also hard-working tools. Most containers have small drainage holes in their bases, so when it rains, your petunias don't drown. But when that drainage hole is flat against the ground, water can build up in the pot, or drain too slowly. Pot feet have small risers that hold containers up off the ground, so pots can drain properly. They also prevent those unsightly rings left when water and soil get trapped beneath a container. Pretty and functional — what could be better?

Pot feet are molded into dozens of shapes, from decorative scrolls to cute animals to actual feet.

EASY WATERING

Sometimes, a watering can alone just isn't enough. Here are four products that will make keeping your containers hydrated less, "Oh, do I have to?" and more, "Hey, that was easy!"

1 WATERING WANDS
Look for a wand with an extendable arm and a rotating head to make watering hanging baskets super simple. There's no need to grab a ladder or lift a heavy watering can — just attach the wand to the end of your hose, extend the arm and give your plants a drink.

2 SELF-WATERING CONTAINERS
Each of these containers has a reservoir in the base that holds up to a gallon of water, plus a perforated water-soil barrier that lets dry potting mix wick up the moisture it needs. Self-watering pots are great for keeping plants watered while you're away, or making moisture-loving tropicals and house plants happy.

3 MULCH
A layer of mulch over the top of your container slows the evaporation of moisture from the soil. Bark mulch is ideal for most situations, but you can also use decorative mulches, such as river stones.

4 CRYSTALS
These water-absorbing polymers suck up moisture when you water your container, and slowly release it back into the soil. Add a layer of them to your potting mix as you plant, and you can let more time pass between waterings.

Don't pour water down over plants' flowers and foliage. Not only can leaves funnel water away from the soil, but wet foliage is prone to fungal diseases. Instead, add water as close to the soil as you can.

CONTAINERS | RECIPES

Putting together a container planting? Don't forget about fall! We assembled this one in late summer, with the goal of fabulous fall color in mind. At the garden center, the vivid lavender-pink spring flowers of the 'PJM' rhododendron had long since gone by the wayside. But we chose the plant for its rich mahogany-red autumn leaves that really complement this rustic urn. Foliage hues of the two dwarf conifers also change as winter nears. The wispy, normally gold-green foliage of the cedar turns a warm bronze in cold weather and the gold new growth of the false cypress ages to a light green. These two plants will reach 4 to 6 feet in 10 years, but grow so slowly, that, with winter protection, they can be used in a container like this for several years.

A cut branch from a red-berried chokeberry, gold-green autumn leaves of the sedum and the burgundy hen and chicks add a nice color and texture contrast.

MOISTURE MATTERS For all the color this pot provides, it demands little care. Consistent moisture is the one crucial thing. It's important for everything but the hen and chicks (which does fine with a slightly dryer mix). And a layer of mulch over the tops of the individual pots helps hold in moisture.

WINTER CARE Though these plants are hardy to at least USDA zone 5, they won't survive in a container in cold-winter zones. That's why you simply take them all, still in the plastic pots they came in, and tuck them into the decorative urn. Once temps get down to about 40 degrees, move the smaller pots into an unheated garage or to holes in the garden in an area sheltered from wind. Water them in well and pile 3 inches of mulch or leaves on top to protect the roots. Check on them in winter, and water them lightly if they're dry. □

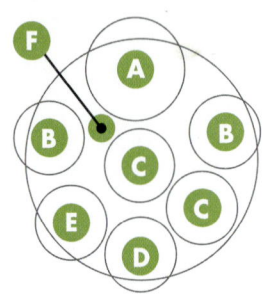

Tips for care

- Full sun to part shade
- Keep soil moist, but not wet. Do not allow it to dry out.

Container is 12 inches across.

GOLD RUSH

Code	Plant Name	No. of Plant
A	**Rhododendron** Rhododendron 'PJM'	1
B	**Gold Ellwood false cypress** Chamaecyparis lawsoniana 'Ellwood's Gold'	2
C	**Rheingold cedar** Thuja occidentalis 'Rheingold'	2
D	**Sedum** Sedum spurium 'Dragon's Blood'	1
E	**Hen and chicks** Sempervivum tectorum	1
F	**Chokeberry (cut stem)** Aronia arbutifolia berries	1

248 the YEAR IN GARDENING   www.GardenGateMagazine.com

Holiday colors of green, silver and red make the two containers above look like wrapped presents, ready for the giving. Many garden centers now carry evergreens, like this false cypress and white cedar, in small sizes. These tough, colorful beauties are perfect in cool-weather containers. Low temperatures and even a little snow don't bother them.

But if you garden in an area colder than USDA zone 7, leave the small evergreens in their plastic pots and tuck them into the larger container. Pre-dig a hole in the garden for each one while the weather's still good (and save the soil inside where it won't freeze), and you'll be able to move the plants into the ground when it gets really cold. The soil and a good 3-inch layer of mulch, like shredded bark or leaves, will protect them until spring. Or overwinter the plants in a basement or attached garage.

The fragrant thyme adds another flavor of green to this holiday treasure box. Snip a few of the variegated leaves to add a lemony taste to any dish. In contrast to the greens, the deep violet-red dianthus blooms add just the right zip. The 1¼-inch flowers are slightly fringed and have a light clove scent.

Finally, a trip to a craft store provides the perfect clear acrylic accents (used for floral arrangements) to complete these festive packages. These pieces echo the colors of the containers' edges.

But whether you give these containers away or enjoy them yourself, their cheerful personalities are sure to bring a smile to your face, holiday or no. □

HOLIDAY PACKAGES

Code	Plant Name	No. to Plant
A	**Dianthus** *Dianthus* 'Ideal Select Violet'	2
B	**Lemon thyme** *Thymus citriodorus*	1
C	**False cypress** *Chamaecyparis pisifera* 'Boulevard'	1
D	**White cedar** *Thuja occidentalis* 'Sunkist'	1

Tips for care

- Part sun or shade
- Tuck plants, pots and all, into container, top with a layer of mulch
- Shelter from harsh wind
- Transfer evergreens into the garden before the ground freezes

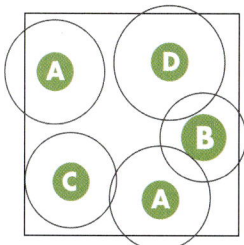

Containers are 8 inches square.

CONTAINERS | RECIPE

Condense Your Garden

IT'S A SMALL WORLD. Who wouldn't love having a bright, colorful, butterfly-attracting garden? Unfortunately, not everyone has the space or the energy to maintain a full-sized garden. But don't let that limit you! By planting up a container, you can still get the color, texture and life that make large gardens so attractive, but without all the space or upkeep requirements.

BIRDS AND BUTTERFLIES With its contrasting textures, bold colors and dynamic play on height, this garden is nothing short of spectacular. And its beauty is only enhanced by the winged creatures it attracts. But how do you translate all of that into a container? The key isn't to create an exact copy. You won't find a container big enough for a garden's worth of plants, and some of these choices just aren't right for a container. The trick is to try to replicate the general feel of the garden — shapes, colors and textures.

In our butterfly-attracting container, we did use some of the same plants as the garden: A canna and some coneflowers. But after that, we got creative. See the baby's breath in the center of this garden? White yarrow is a good container-friendly substitute. Bee balm wasn't in season for this late-summer container, but pink asters have the same mounding habit and star-shaped flowers. Red lantana stands in for the red nicotiana and dahlias down in front.

This container looks best in late summer and early autumn, and needs full sun and consistently moist soil to thrive. All of these plants will attract butterflies or hummingbirds, so place the container outside a window where you can see it from your favorite chair. And, if you live in a frost-free zone, leave your container out all winter (pull the canna tubers out and bring them inside so they'll survive the winter) so the birds can eat the coneflower seeds.

[the inspiration]

TAKE FLIGHT

Code	Plant Name	No. of Plant
A	**Russian sage** *Perovskia atriplicifolia*	2
B	**New York aster** *Aster novi-belgii* 'Loke Viking'	1
C	**Lantana** *Lantana camara* 'Dallas Red'	2
D	**Salvia** *Salvia xsylvestris* 'Mainacht' (May Night)	1
E	**Yarrow** *Achillea millefolium*	1
F	**Purple coneflower** *Echinacea purpurea* 'Magnus'	1
G	**Canna** *Canna* 'Striata'	1
H	**Black-eye Susan** *Rubeckia fulgida sullivantii* 'Goldstrum'	1

Container is 20 inch in diameter

did you know...

Pull the inner pot out to water plants. After it drains, replace it.

Anchor the float to the edge of the pond with fishing line.

Floating pots
Rosemary Jones, Pennsylvania

Have you ever thought of growing geraniums or lobelia in your pond instead of near it? Or how about the wax begonias and creeping Jenny in the floating pot above? You can, with Rosemary's floating pot support. She saw a similar product at a garden show but they were expensive, so she made her own for much less! It's a great way to dress up your pond for a party or garden tour.

All you need is a 1-inch-thick piece of plastic foam and a couple of lightweight plastic pots. A sheet of foam insulation from the hardware store works just fine or reuse packing material.

The size of the ring depends on the container. When we made one, we found that a 4-inch ring supported a gallon-sized container just fine. Cutting the interior hole ¼ to ½ inch smaller than the lip of the container kept it from slipping through the ring.

A lot of the plants you'll be using aren't meant to grow in water, so it's important to keep the roots from getting soggy. To prevent this, slip the outer pot into a plastic grocery bag before you put it into the foam ring. Trim off the top of the bag so just a few inches overlap the mouth of the pot. Then slip the planted pot inside. It will hold the bag in place and the bag will keep the water out. When that's all done, the whole thing is ready to go in the pond. If the float tips sideways, it's probably not heavy enough. Just add a few rocks inside the plastic-lined pot.

Turn a wine bottle into a waterer
Nancy Dolmanisth, MA

Don't you just hate slopping water on the floor when you water your house plants? Nancy found that inexpensive plastic wine pourers from the kitchen or liquor store are the perfect solution. And a brightly colored pourer looks good on top of a cobalt-blue wine bottle. The pourer fits snugly into the mouth of the bottle so there's no dripping. See how easily the slender spout slips through the densest foliage in the illustration below? With the small opening, water goes directly into the soil instead of onto the floor or the sensitive foliage of some plants.

Rather than hiding her new watering device under the kitchen sink, Nancy sets it on the plant stand as a colorful (and useful) ornament.

Wine pourer

The wine pourer directs water right where you want it.

Solid oak planter
Eda Fernandez, FL

Hurricane Katrina damaged two large live oak (*Quercus virginiana*) trees in Eda's yard so badly that they had to be removed. So Eda had her husband use his chainsaw to carve a 12-inch-deep bowl into the end of several of the sections of trunk. Then she added some potting mix and tucked in a variety of flowering plants, along with some Spanish moss to drape down the side. In her experience, even without drainage holes, the water seeps away so plants aren't sitting in a puddle. But you may want to drill a few holes or use moisture-loving plants to be safe.

Eda's new planters were 2 to 4 feet tall so she set them up on her patio near a bench. The beautiful flowers were a spot of color and an inspiration to everyone who saw them.

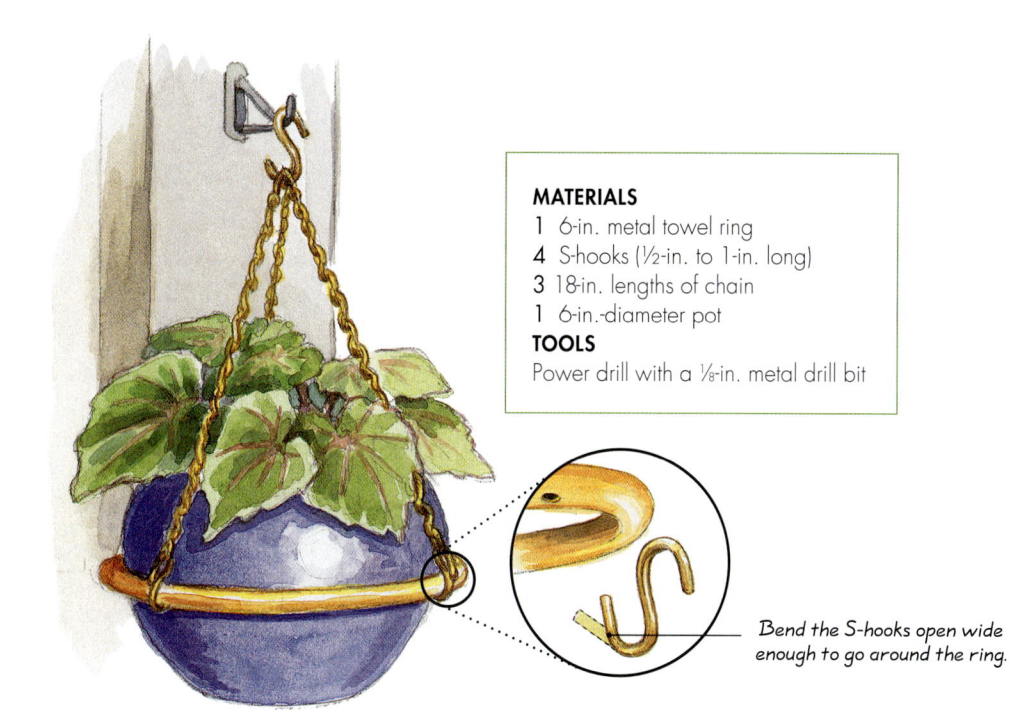

MATERIALS
- 1 6-in. metal towel ring
- 4 S-hooks (½-in. to 1-in. long)
- 3 18-in. lengths of chain
- 1 6-in.-diameter pot

TOOLS
Power drill with a ⅛-in. metal drill bit

Bend the S-hooks open wide enough to go around the ring.

Plant ring
Kevin Nash, Texas

Kevin came up with a quick and easy hanger for small containers. Would you believe it's made from an old brass towel ring he wasn't using anymore? You'll find everything you need to make your own in the list above.

First, take off the part of the towel ring that attaches to the wall. Then drill three evenly spaced holes around the towel ring, with a ⅛-inch drill bit. Don't drill all the way through.

Next, attach the chains to the S-hooks and crimp the ends of the hooks shut so the chains won't fall out. Then put one hook in each drilled hole. You can use any width of chain, but be sure it's strong enough to hold your container.

Use another S-hook to connect all three chains at the top and it's ready to hang!

---

product pick

Rice Hull Gardens

These aren't your average containers. Rice Hull Garden™ pots are made of rice hulls and organic pigments so they're easy on the environment. Durable enough to use indoors *or* out, these pots last about five years. You'll know it's time to toss one in the compost pile when it starts getting soft. Each 4-inch container includes a packet of one of three kinds of seeds. You can choose parsley, garlic chives or lemon basil. They're the perfect gift for your favorite gardener, and they even come with a bow!

Bottom line Made of a renewable resource in an ecologically friendly way — that's cool!
Source Potting Shed Creations at 800-505-7496 or www.pottingshedcreations.com; local garden centers
Price $15.50 each

did you know... (CONTINUED)

Stir the dye thoroughly into the concrete for even color.

product pick

Planter Feet concrete molds

Keep your container off the ground in style with your own handmade pot feet. Plastic molds come in seven different designs and you can even add color with concrete dye or paint. When we made the feet you see in the photo, we used a mortar mix without rock so the details of the mold would show. For best results, make the concrete the consistency of a brownie mix. Be sure to jiggle the molds to get rid of the air bubbles. The feet should dry in about 24 hours, depending on the weather.

Bottom line Pot feet are expensive. Planter Feet molds are reusable so you can make as many as you need for less.
Source GardenMolds at www.gardenmolds.com or call 800-588-7930
Price $7.50 per mold; one mold makes three pot feet at a time

Keep roots dry
Norma Ortiz, New York
Norma likes to use inexpensive clear plastic saucers under her bonsai trees like the one at right. But she noticed that the plants sometimes developed root problems if they sat in the saucer too long after a rain. Her solution? Drill a few holes in the side of the plastic saucer.

A layer of pebbles in the saucer provides extra humidity and better drainage. Norma starts by marking the holes just below the level of the rocks and a couple of inches apart. Then she uses a ⅛-inch drill bit to make small holes around the saucer. It's easier to drill the flexible plastic if you clamp a scrap of wood against the inside of the saucer where you're drilling. Now the saucer holds enough water to provide the needed humidity but not so much that it saturates the tree's roots.

Make sure the holes are just below the rock line.

Holiday hanging basket
Sandy Bostwick, WI

Don't put away your hanging baskets just because the weather gets cold. Do what Sandy does: Remove the annuals in fall but leave the soil inside and store the baskets where they won't freeze. In November, cut or buy evergreen branches, such as juniper and holly, and stick the stems in the soil. Add pinecones or an ornament if you want, too. Hang the baskets on your porch for a colorful garden accent, even in winter!

Explaining draining
Sharon Hocking, Illinois

Q *Does putting gravel into the bottom of a pot really make it drain better?*

A Actually, water in a container filled with just potting mix will drain quicker than water in a same-sized container with gravel in the bottom half.

Because there's more porous mix in the no-gravel pot, gravity will make the water drain out quickly. In the pot with gravel in the bottom, water will actually slow down as it passes from the finer-textured mix into the coarser-textured gravel. The result is the roots, which grow in the upper part of the mix, will stay wetter. This could be good or bad, depending on the plant.

But, for the best drainage, skip the gravel. Cover the drainage hole with a pot shard or piece of window screen and fill the pot up with just potting mix.

Gravel in the pot keeps the water around the plant roots.

Water drains quickly through potting mix.

---

product pick

Pots in the Garden

This new book by Ray Rogers helps you understand *why* a container planting looks good. Each chapter goes over principles of container design so you'll be able to create your own masterpiece containers every season. Sure, there's a section on techniques that tells you about the basics, such as fertilizer and soil. But what's really helpful are the mini-lessons in design with each photo. Ray may point out the contrasting colors in one photo and interesting texture in the next. When you're done reading, you'll be able to make great containers with whatever plants you find at the garden center.

Bottom line You don't have to be a garden designer to have beautiful containers. Just read this book.
Source Local or online bookstores or www.GardenGateStore.com
Price $29.95; hardcover; 248 pages

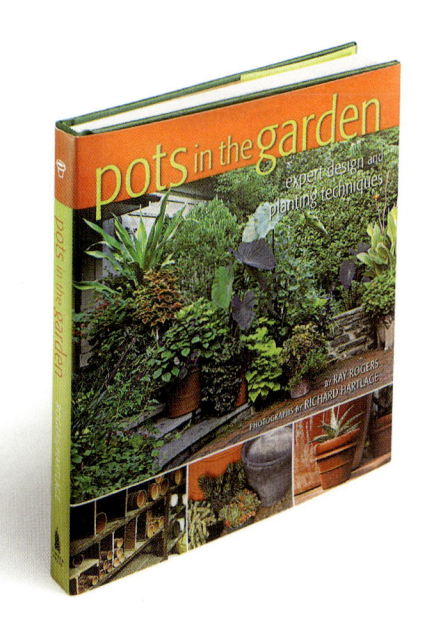

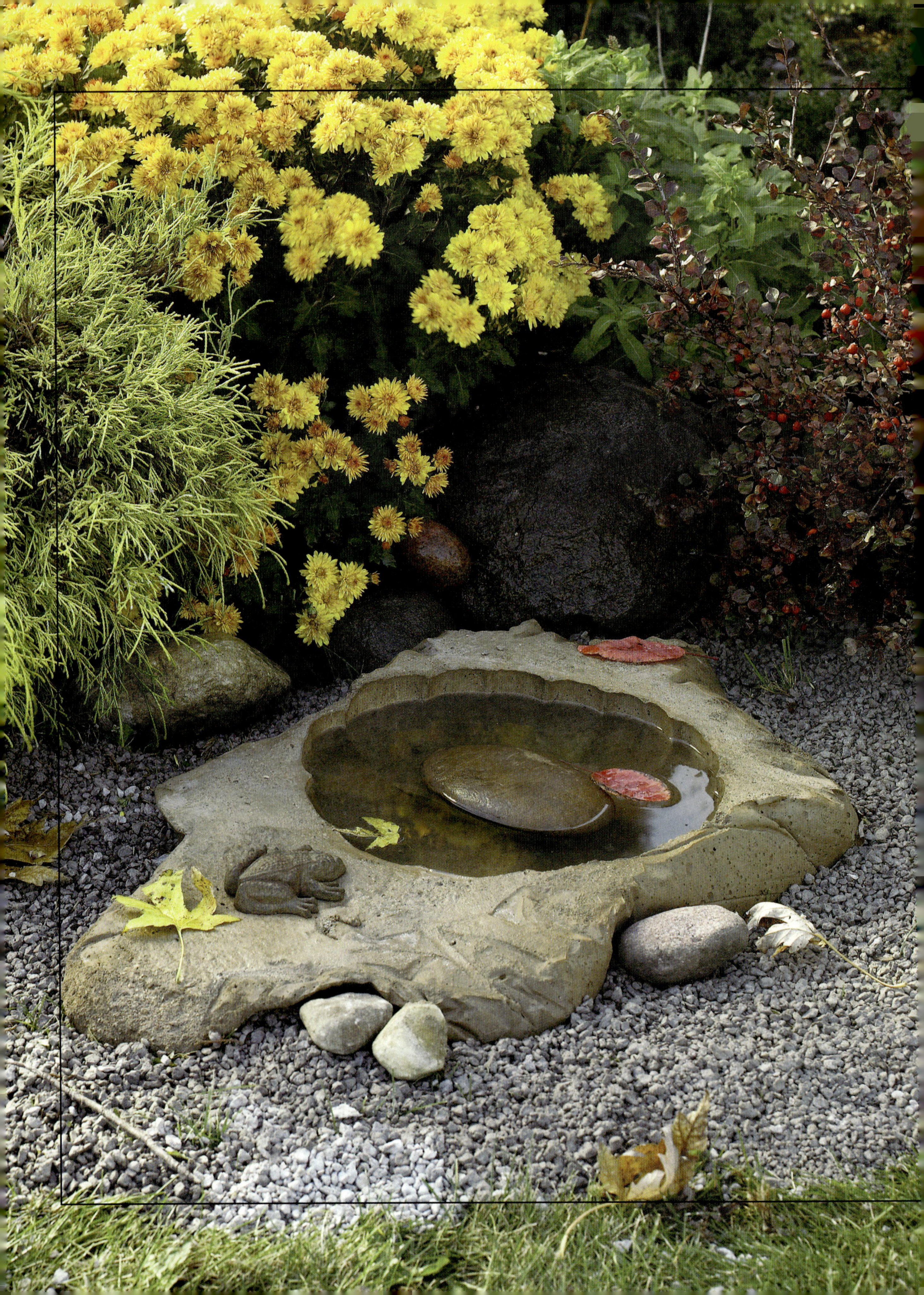

gardening basics

how to *grow* the garden you've always wanted

DIRTY GLOVES AND SORE MUSCLES are just part of gardening. So is the exhaustion and satisfaction you feel at the end of a great day of hard work. Want to know how to get the most out of your gardening efforts? You've come to the right place. For everything from composting to weeding, you'll find it here. Plus you'll get our best tips for environmentally friendly gardening this year.

Go Green!	258
Compost Q&A	260
Save Plants, Save Money	262
Garden Myths?	264
Seed-Starting Solutions	266
Woody Weeds	268
Fight Tough Weeds and Win (Eventually)	272
7 Common Diseases	274
Too Big? Time To Dig!	278
Must-Know Mail-Order Tips	280
How to Buy a Healthy Tree	282
Must-Have Garden Gadgets	284
Tool Trellis	286
Feed Birds What They Love	288
One-Of-A-Kind Birdbath	290
Did You Know	292
Beneficials You Should Know	304
Pests to Watch For	305
Weeds You Should Know	306
Know Your Zones	308

BASICS | SMART GARDENING

Go Green!

10 earth-friendly garden ideas you can use this year.

You see something about environmental issues in the news almost every day — it can be pretty discouraging. What better way to counter all those negatives than to tend a garden? It helps you feel better and makes the world a better place, too. But *how* you garden makes a big difference. Using natural resources carefully and avoiding chemicals as much as possible make your garden safer for you as well as the insects and wildlife that find food and shelter there.

Here are a few easy things you can do right now to help conserve resources and make your garden a beautiful place, too. Then take a look at our Web extra for more tips to help you "green" up your garden. □

— Sherri Ribbey

MULCH NEWS

Mulch is a great way to conserve water and keep weeds down without chemicals. But it's expensive if you have a big garden. You won't have to spread such a thick layer of mulch if you put down a two- to four-sheet layer of newspaper first. Most newspapers these days print with ecologically friendly soy ink. However, it's still a good idea to stick with the black and white pages. Colored ink sometimes contains heavy metals, so you can't trust those color ads that come along with your morning paper. Not sure what kind of ink your local paper uses? Call the newspaper office.

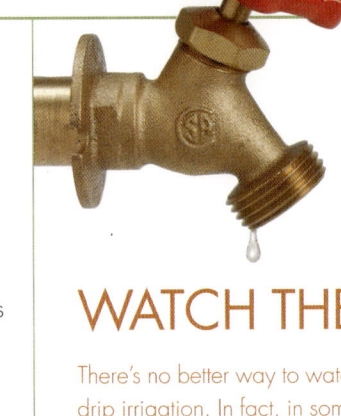

WATCH THE WATER

There's no better way to water efficiently than with drip irrigation. In fact, in some water-strapped states with regulations, it's the only way you can supply H_2O to thirsty plants regularly. Have a system installed or put one in yourself with components from the hardware store. To save even more water, get a programmable timer with a rain sensor. No more turning the faucet on and off or having the system come on when it rains. These handy gizmos can even be added to an existing system. Even more high tech is the "smart" controller. It communicates with area weather stations or satellites to supply the right amount of water for your garden based on current weather and rainfall. Get a controller just right for your garden from Rainbird at www.rainbird.com or local irrigation specialists.

Recycle those plastic pots

Gardeners use a lot of plastic pots. To keep them out of the landfill, check with your local nursery to see if it accepts its own nursery pots back. Or participate in a pot recycling program like the one at the Missouri Botanic Garden. Each year residents of the St. Louis area bring their pots to the botanic garden, where they're collected to be recycled into landscape timbers. If there's not a program in your area, urge local garden centers to start one. To see how the program works, go to www.mobot.org/hort/activ/plasticpots.shtml

A shade tree can help you save 15 to 50% on air-conditioning

Plant a shade tree off the southwest corner of your house for the most shade on hot summer afternoons.

WEB extra
Find 10 more *green tips* including lawn care for your region.

GREEN LAWNS

Many gardeners worry that lawns need too many chemicals to be environmentally friendly. But lawns filter pollutants, prevent erosion and add to your property value. Keeping a lawn doesn't have to come at the expense of the environment. There are more organic lawn care products, such as the Cockadoodle DOO® fertilizer and weed control program, out there these days. But remember, whether you use organic or inorganic fertilizer, more is not better. To avoid polluting ground water, read the label carefully and don't use more than the recommended rate. Be sure to sweep granules that fall on the sidewalk or driveway back into the lawn, not into the street.

How often do you really need to fertilize your lawns? Check out our Web extra to find lawn fertilizing tips for your region.

USING A REEL MOWER saves on gas and oil. If a regular reel mower is too hard for you to push, try this new battery-powered version from Mantis®.

QUICKER COMPOST

Trouble getting your compost to break down quickly? Try heating it up! Hot compost breaks down faster and kills weed seeds and many disease pathogens, as well. You'll get results in weeks, rather than months or even years. Here are some easy ways you can help heat up your compost pile.

- *Garden Gate* reader Terri Martin found that laying an old vinyl-coated pool cover over the top of her compost pile keeps in heat and moisture. If that's not handy, try a large plastic tarp.
- We've found that adding a layer of small tree branches — ½ in. diameter or less — to the middle of the pile provides oxygen, an important ingredient for quick-cooking compost.
- Cut up large pieces before adding them to the pile — small stuff breaks down more quickly.
- Large piles hold more heat, so make yours at least 3 ft. tall, wide and deep.

Easy fertilizer

It's not an organic fertilizer, but you only apply Dynamite™ once a year. That means there's less chance for this slow-release fertilizer to pollute ground water. Plus, the special coating releases the nitrogen inside more evenly than other brands.

Plants that filter the air

NASA scientists found that certain indoor plants filter contaminants from the air better than others. It takes 15 to 20 plants to clean a 1500-sq.-ft. area. Here are three of the best:

Boston fern *Nephrolepis exaltata*
Dracaena *Dracaena fragrans* 'Janet Craig'
Rubber plant (shown) *Ficus elastica*

ORGANIC FIRST AID

Ever wish you had a first aid kit for your plants? Keep these products on hand to treat and prevent many common garden problems. They're easy on wildlife but still protect plants against pests and disease.

INSECTICIDAL SOAP gets rid of soft-bodied insects like aphids.

POTASSIUM BICARBONATE takes care of powdery mildew.

LIQUID KELP/FISH FERTILIZER Used together, these two provide both the macro- and micronutrients that help plants thrive.

COMPOST TEA KIT Sprayed on foliage, compost tea helps fight foliar disease.

You'll find these products at your local garden center or Peaceful Valley Farm Supply at www.groworganic.com.

BASICS | SMART GARDENING

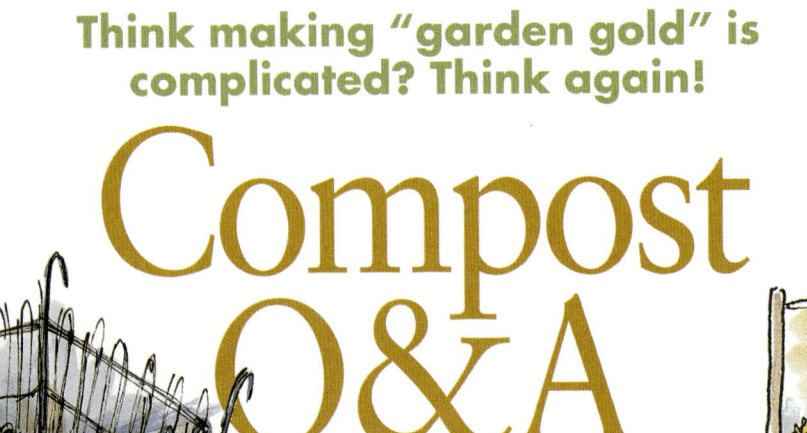

Think making "garden gold" is complicated? Think again!

Compost Q&A

To help you "break down" and streamline the process, I'll answer some compost questions so you can easily make your own or know what to look for the next time you buy a bag or two.

If you've been gardening for a while, you already know how great compost is. It improves the structure of the soil so it holds water and nutrients that plants need to thrive, and also allows air to get to the roots.

When making compost, you *can* follow recipes, keep turning schedules and track temperatures, but you don't have to. After all, any organic matter, given moisture and air, will break down in time. Composting just speeds it up.

What kinds of things can I use to make compost?

You can use almost anything organic you find around your home or garden. To make compost most quickly, keep a mix of about two parts "brown" stuff to one part "green." "Did you know…" below will tell you what kinds of things are brown and what are green. Too much brown slows down the composting action; too much green and the compost will be smelly and runny.

Sometimes a traditional compost pile's the answer; sometimes it isn't. In fall, all the leaves your trees drop are probably too much for any one pile. Not only will the sheer volume overwhelm you, those leaves just won't break down very quickly. Make quick work of them: Pile the leaves up and chop them with your lawn mower. Then either spread everything on top of your cleared vegetable bed and let it break down over the winter or use it as mulch on your perennial beds.

What do you do about twigs and branches? Well, if they're less than an inch in diameter, cut them into pieces shorter than 6 inches so they'll break down in a reasonable time. Go ahead and

---

Did you know… A good recipe for compost is two parts brown or woody to one part green, soft materials.

"BROWN" MATERIALS
Dead leaves
Wood chips
Plant debris
Paper and cardboard
Wood ash, straw or sawdust (in moderation)
Hair trimmings
Dust from vacuum cleaner
Shredded cotton or woolen cloth

"GREEN" MATERIALS
Kitchen scraps and coffee grounds
Grass clippings (but only in thin layers)
Pond sludge
Manure

LEAVE THESE OUT
Diseased or pesticide-treated plants
Weeds with seedheads
Meat, bones or dairy products
Human or pet waste

2 + 1 =

www.GardenGateMagazine.com

Pile fall leaves up and chop them with your lawn mower so they compost more quickly.

throw a few in the bin or on the pile. But you're probably better off shredding most of your woody debris and using it as mulch, which you *want* to break down slowly.

Is there any way to speed up compost?

Sure. As I've just mentioned, the smaller the pieces that go into the pile, the quicker they compost. Make sure your pile is moist but not overly wet — picture a wrung-out sponge. Don't bother with compost starter; just add garden soil or older compost, which has needed micro-organisms, to get things going. And turn the compost weekly with a garden fork to give the pile plenty of air.

Do you need more than one compost pile?

You might want two. Spring cleanup alone can be more than one pile can handle. With two, you'll have a second pile you can add to once the first pile is full. If you keep adding more to a single pile, it'll take longer for the whole thing to break down.

Should I consider buying a composter?

A ready-made compost tumbler might be the answer for folks who don't have room for full-blown piles in their gardens. There are lots of different styles to choose from, and most will make compost in just a few weeks. The downside is many models can cost $150 or more and don't have a huge capacity. Have more than a few small beds? You'd be better off using a pile or a bin. Check out www.GardenGateStore.com for a plan for a simple-to-build bin.

If you don't have a lot of stuff to compost and don't want to invest in a composter, save kitchen scraps in your freezer until you get enough to fill a garbage bag. Place the scraps (chopped into small pieces) in a black or opaque plastic garbage bag along with coffee grounds and a few cups of soil or compost and tie it securely.

(You can throw scraps in a bag as you get them, but the process will take longer.)

To keep critters out, set the bag inside a metal bucket or garbage can with a tight-fitting lid in a sunny space for a few weeks. Shake the bag once a day and open it for a few hours twice a week to let it breathe. Should the mix look wet and runny, add a little shredded paper or cardboard to the mix to absorb some of the excess moisture. You can make a small amount of compost this way in four to six weeks.

Is there a difference in quality between bagged composts?

Yes, the quality of compost depends on what was composted, for how long and the method being used. Before you buy, check to see if the bag feels overly heavy or compacted. If so, it may be wet or dense and claylike. When you open the bag, the compost should be dark-colored and fluffy and there shouldn't be any foul odor. Ideally it's dry enough that it won't hold its shape when you squeeze it in your hand, but instead crumbles. Composted manure should have a light smell. The smell of ammonia means the manure is still breaking down. Don't use it or you'll burn or even kill your plants. Instead, set it aside and let it finish breaking down. If you try bagged compost from a new source, ask to see it or buy a single bag to check the quality first. □

— *Deborah Gruca*

BUILD YOUR OWN COMPOST BIN

Visit us at www.GardenGateStore.com and find our plan for a great compost bin.

Don't want to invest in a composter? Compost kitchen scraps in a garbage bag.

BASICS | SMART GARDENING

Go from tiny to terrific in one season! Tender perennials, such as this spurge, above, may start out looking like dead twigs. But with some time, water and fertilizer you'll get a big, beautiful plant like this one.

Overwinter tender perennials
Save Plants, Save Money

Isn't that first spring trip to your favorite garden center exciting? I love bringing home new plants. In fall, those same plants look so good, I hate to toss them out. You can overwinter beauties like the tall burgundy-leafed spurge at left by treating them as house plants. But that takes up space that most of us don't have. However, that's not the only way to save your plants to grow them another year. Let's take a look at a method that works well without needing much room.

This technique won't work for *true* annuals. Plants such as marigolds and zinnias sprout, set seed and die each year. But other "annuals" are actually tender *perennials*, which means that they'll keep going for years if they don't freeze.

Now let's see how you can help your tender perennial live on and on. You'll see how the plant should look at each step of the process in "Start to finish" below.

BEAT THE FROST Several weeks before your average first frost, dig any plants you want to keep. For the last couple of years, I've dug this spurge and put it in a smaller pot. (You could leave it in the big container, but plastic nursery pots are easier to move.) Add fresh potting mix and water well.

This next step is hard, especially when the plant looks good, but you need to cut the stems back by about half. It would probably drop a lot of those leaves anyway, and cutting it back will get rid of a lot of potential insect hiding places. Now you're ready to bring the plant inside.

TAKE IT INSIDE Once inside, your plants need a cool, dry place to live for the winter — a spare room, an unheated basement, any place that doesn't freeze and where temperatures get no higher than 58 degrees. Don't worry about light — they won't need much. Place the nursery pots in a saucer filled with pebbles and water your plants about once a month.

SPRING IS HERE By early spring your plants may look as sad as the ones in the small photo at left. But that's OK. Set the plants outside in a shady spot as the weather warms — when it's 60 or 65 degrees during the day. Bring them back in it looks like temperatures are going to drop into the mid- to low 40s at night. Feed plants weekly with a half-strength all-purpose fertilizer. You should see new growth in a week or two, and you'll need to snip back some dead stems here and there.

Once the plants have filled out, they're ready to go into your summer containers. I do lose a plant or two some years but I've had success with the ones in "Save plants!" below and I'm able to enjoy them for another season! ☐

— *Sherri Ribbey*

Start to finish

Fall Cut the stems back by half. Place the pot in a pebble-filled saucer to hold it out of water. The extra water provides needed humidity.

Winter Don't worry if your plant loses most or all of its leaves. It's just going dormant and will start growing again in spring.

Early spring Put the plant outside in part shade. Water well and start fertilizing. Bring it back in for the night if temps dip into the 40s.

Spring As leaves grow, dead stems become obvious. Cut them back to new growth. In a few weeks you'll have a great-looking plant.

Save plants!
This technique works for plants that form woody stems where they're hardy. Here's a list of some you can overwinter. You'll be saving plants *and* cash, because you won't have to buy them again next year.

Cape fuchsia *Phygelius capensis*	**Flowering maple** *Abutilon* hybrid
Chenille plant *Acalypha hispida*	**Fuchsia** *Fuchsia* hybrid
Cigar plant *Cuphea ignea*	**Persian shield** *Strobilanthes dyeriana*
Spurge *Euphorbia cotinifolia*	**Salvia** *Salvia guaranitica* 'Black and Blue'

BASICS | SMART GARDENING

Garden Myths?

A lot of garden lore is passed along from person to person. But often something that "everybody knows" just isn't 100 percent accurate, so it pays to ask a few questions. Don't get me wrong — many garden "myths" (even some pretty strange-sounding ones) have at least a grain of truth in them. But there's almost always a little more to the story. Let's take a look at seven things you may have heard about gardening, and sift the true from the not-so-true. ◻

— *Marcia Leeper*

Don't "fall" for this

MAYBE YOU'VE HEARD
You should only plant perennials in the spring.

THE REAL STORY Although the heat of summer is a hard time to transplant anything, fall is actually a great time to plant perennials. September and October are good months to find bargains, and those purchases send out new root growth quickly in warm soil. Cooler temperatures and shorter days reduce the transplant shock often seen in late spring and summer. Insects are going dormant in the fall, so there's less chance of them damaging new plants or spreading disease. Just be sure to plant perennials several weeks before the ground freezes. They need time to get some new roots established before they go dormant for winter.

Give me a drink

MAYBE YOU'VE HEARD
If a plant is wilting, it needs water.

THE REAL STORY Although most of us reach for a watering can the minute we see a plant droop, it's a good idea to double-check before you start to pour.

On very warm, sunny days, plants, especially those with big leaves, may look wilted. That's because they're losing moisture from their leaves faster than it can be taken up by the roots. When the temperature cools down in the evening, the plant will perk up without any additional water. Overwatering can lead to root rot…which makes the plant droop as well! So before you water, push your finger into the soil around the roots. Water only if the soil is dry about an inch down.

If your plant continues to droop, you may need to investigate the roots. Mushy or rotten roots can inhibit water uptake. Unfortunately, root damage is usually irreversible, so you'll need to toss the plant. (And don't water its replacement too much!)

Too sweet for belief

MAYBE YOU'VE HEARD
Add sugar to the planting hole for sweeter tomatoes.

THE REAL STORY It probably does more harm than good. Added sugar can be turned into starch by the plant — and that leads to mealy tomatoes, not the juicy ones you want. Sugar can also ferment in the soil and rot the plant roots. Your best bet is to plant tomatoes in soil that's been amended with plenty of compost. Keep them evenly moist to avoid fruit cracking and blossom-end rot, and feed them with a tomato-specific fertilizer for big, juicy fruits.

Don't make this mis-"stake"

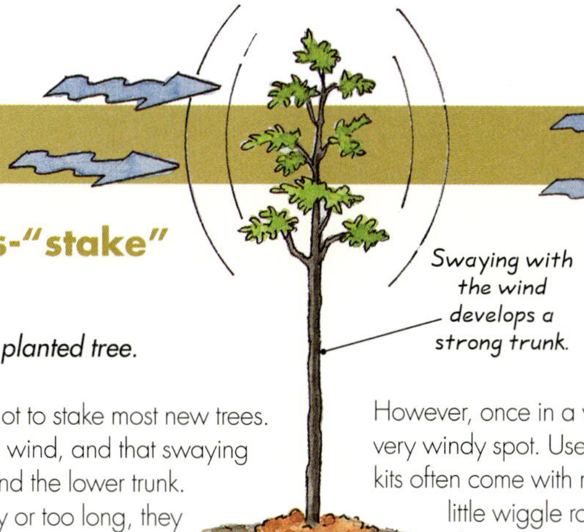

MAYBE YOU'VE HEARD
You should always stake a newly planted tree.

THE REAL STORY It's actually best not to stake most new trees. Unstaked, they'll sway slightly in the wind, and that swaying action strengthens the root system and the lower trunk.

When trees are staked too tightly or too long, they may snap off above the stakes. Or they may even topple over as soon as they're unstaked because they haven't developed strong root systems to anchor themselves.

However, once in a while it's necessary to stake a young tree in a very windy spot. Use a pliable material around the trunk (tree staking kits often come with rubber straps) and be sure the tree still has a little wiggle room. (But don't leave the strap so loose that it rubs against the bark.) One stake, placed to support the tree against the prevailing wind, may be all you really need. Don't leave the stakes in place more than a year.

Swaying with the wind develops a strong trunk.

Too-tight staking can cause trees to snap off in a strong wind.

Lighten up

MAYBE YOU'VE HEARD
Add sand to clay soil to improve drainage.

THE REAL STORY If you're not careful, you'll end up with something more like concrete than soil. Adding coarse sand will improve drainage, but add it *with* plenty of organic material, too. Work 3 or 4 in. of compost, chopped leaves or ground bark, plus 1 or 2 in. of sand, into the top 6 to 12 in. of soil. This will loosen the soil and make it more hospitable for plant roots. You'll need to add more compost for several years to get your soil into better condition.

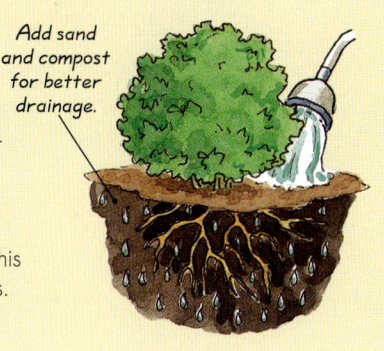

Sand alone will make clay soil even harder to work.

Add sand and compost for better drainage.

All dried up

MAYBE YOU'VE HEARD
Xeriscape plants don't need water.

THE REAL STORY All plants need water! It's true that xeriscape, or xeric, plants, those that have low water needs, can almost take care of themselves once they're established. But all new plants have small root systems that need sufficient moisture for the first year. For these dry-loving plants, a soaker hose is a good way to keep moisture at the root zone while the plant gets going, without getting the foliage too wet.

Can this "B" right?

MAYBE YOU'VE HEARD
Use vitamin B to prevent transplant shock.

THE REAL STORY A dose of vitamin B won't hurt your new tree or shrub, but it won't really help it, either. These products are often advertised as being able to stimulate growth of new root hairs and feeder roots. But actually, a healthy plant makes its own supply of vitamin B. The best thing you can do to encourage quick root growth is to settle your new plant into humus-rich soil, and keep it well watered as it gets established. An inch of water a week is a good rule of thumb.

www.GardenGateMagazine.com   *the* YEAR IN GARDENING   **265**

BASICS | PROBLEM SOLVER

Seed-Starting Solutions

Talk about a garden basic: Seeds are the starting point for just about anything you grow. And it's easy, right? Just stick them in the dirt and they sprout. Well, that's not always the case! Good old favorites like marigolds and zinnias really are that simple, but some seeds need a little extra effort. You may find yourself dealing with tiny seeds that are hard to handle, or seeds with hard coats or slow or patchy germination.

Let me walk you through some tips for dealing with these challenging seeds. It's worth the extra effort, because starting plants from seed is a great way to get lots of your favorites for very little cost. And I'll also share a list of perennials you can grow from seed — most of them will even bloom the first year. So gather up your potting mix and some containers, and let's get started. ◻
— *Marcia Leeper*

Seed spoons usually come in pairs, with different-sized depressions in each end.

Problem Very small seeds Well, the problem is obvious…even if the seeds aren't! Seeds this tiny are hard to handle, and when the seedlings come up, they're hair-thin and difficult to transplant.

Solution Pelleted seeds Look for pelleted seeds, like the ones on the saucer below, especially when you're buying impatiens, begonias and petunias. They're coated with a claylike substance to make them larger and easier to plant. Of course, even the pelleted seeds aren't very big, so I use the yellow seed spoon in the photo. It has small "dimples" on the ends that make it easy to pick up tiny seeds. You can buy these spoons at most garden centers or online garden retailers. These tools allow you to be pretty precise about planting, so you can tuck in just a few seeds per pot. That way, you won't need to thin or transplant the tiny seedlings until they're big enough to handle.

BEST FOR Begonia, impatiens, nemesia, nicotiana, petunia

Pelleted seeds still aren't huge, but they're big enough to handle.

WEB extra
Watch our seed-starting *video* for more tips.

266 *the* YEAR IN GARDENING   www.GardenGateMagazine.com

Problem Hard-coated seeds Some seeds have very hard coats. To help water penetrate these coats, you can scarify or presoak the seeds. Try a few seeds with each technique to see which works better for you.

Solution Scarification See how I've wrapped masking tape around the jaws of these needlenose pliers? That makes it easier to hold the seed. Using a knife or file, nick the coating, but don't go too deep. (If you see white, you've cut into the embryo and the seed probably won't germinate, so try another one.) This allows moisture to penetrate the hard coat for faster germination. For small hard-coated seeds, glue sandpaper onto the inside of a jar lid. Put your seeds in the jar, close the lid and shake them around.

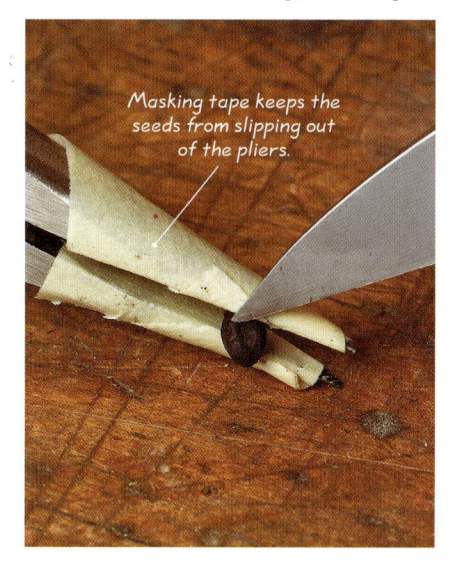

Masking tape keeps the seeds from slipping out of the pliers.

Presoaking Fill a small jar halfway with warm water and add the seeds. Soak seeds for 12 to 24 hours before planting. You must plant the seeds right away after soaking because they'll die if they dry out.

BEST FOR Beet, carrot, banana, canna, datura, false indigo, morning glory, sweet pea

Problem Slow to germinate Some seeds germinate slowly or unevenly. You can waste a lot of time and counter space trying to get them to sprout in potting mix.

Solution Presprouting This technique lets you plant individual seeds as they germinate. That way, all the seeds are getting the right amount of moisture, so the germinated seeds can't rot or dry out while you wait for the others to get started. You can also use presprouting to check viability and germination of older seeds.

Place seeds on a damp paper towel, then roll or fold the towel and put it in a plastic bag. Place the bag in a warm location out of direct sunlight. Check the seeds daily to see what's germinated. See how the dark seed coat on the two lupine seeds in front has started to split? Plant the presprouted seeds as soon as the seed coat has opened and before hair roots form. Just use tweezers to gently tuck the presprouted seeds into moist seed-starting mix. If the root has grown through the paper towel, just tear the paper off with the sprouted seed and plant. After you look at the seeds each day, roll the towel up again and put it back in the plastic bag to check later.

BEST FOR Beet, carrot, cucumber, squash, cardinal creeper, foxglove, hyacinth bean, lupine, Spanish flag, other climbing annuals

PHOTO: Douglas E. Smith

FIRST-YEAR PERENNIALS

As I mentioned earlier, it's pretty easy to start a lot of annuals from seed. But I bet you didn't realize that it's just as easy to start some perennials. Sometimes when I'm planning a new garden bed and count up how many perennials I need to create a really stunning drift, I'm just horrified. If I have to buy all those plants, I'm not going to be able to afford anything else for the garden!

But there are a few perennials you can start from seed and they'll even bloom that first year. Of course, they won't be at their full size for a year or two, but at least you'll have something happening in your garden while they're growing. Get these plants started in January and they'll bloom for you by July.

10 GREAT PERENNIALS FROM SEED

Agastache *Agastache* hybrids
Black-eyed Susan
  Rudbeckia hybrids
Blanket flower
  Gaillardia xgrandiflora
Coneflower *Echinacea purpurea*
Coreopsis *Coreopsis* hybrids
Hardy hibiscus
  Hibiscus moscheutos
Perennial bachelor's button
  Centaurea montana
Pinks *Dianthus* spp.
Salvia *Salvia* hybrids
Shasta daisy *Leucanthemum*
  x*superbum*

BASICS | PROBLEM SOLVER

9 pests you need to identify and get rid of now!
Woody Weeds

Weeds are weeds, right? Well, yes and no. Some can sneak up on you. The weeds I'll talk about here can grow into big shrubs or even full-size trees before you know it. Unlike many other weeds, if you let these grow, they become much more difficult, and sometimes expensive, to deal with. Which would you rather do: Pull out a small sprout, or pay to have a large tree cut down? I'll opt for dealing with these pests while they're still small. Plus, if you get rid of them when they're young, they won't have a chance to set seed and spread. And boy, can they spread! Seeds are eaten by birds, get caught on animal fur or carried by the wind into your garden, sometimes great distances.

Most trees and shrubs produce seeds. For example, oaks drop acorns, but you'd rarely refer to an oak as a weed. What's the difference? Weed plants not only drop large quantities of seed, but the seeds sprout easily wherever they land. And they're aggressive and grow fast, quickly shading or squeezing out plants you want to keep. As the plants mature, they start dropping more seeds, eventually taking over your garden.

Below, I'll show you four different control methods for woody weeds. All will work on these pests, but depending on the age of the weed, its location and the strength of your back, one will usually suit your needs and ability best. Let's take a look at nine woody weeds that you're likely to find in your hedge, shrub border or flower bed — maybe even in the cracks of your sidewalk! ❑

— *Jim Childs*

1 PULL SEEDLINGS If you spot them when they're young enough, woody weeds can be treated just like any other weed — simply pull them out. This is the best method in areas where you can't dig or spray, such as in ground cover beds. The common buckthorn in the photo above has fibrous roots, so it pulls easily. You may need to tug harder on a weed with a tap root, such as a mulberry.

2 SPRAY YOUNG SPROUTS Digging out weeds often turns up new weed seeds. But by spraying, especially in open, mulched areas, you won't have that problem. Even if you simply have too many weeds to pull or they're too entrenched to get easily, using nonselective herbicides, such as Roundup® Poison Ivy & Tough Brush Killer Plus, is easy. Always follow the label directions, but you usually apply these products to actively growing weeds in spring or summer.

3 DIG OUT SAPLINGS Cutting off a sapling at the soil line usually won't work long term. You need a shovel or spade to dig down deep enough to get most of the roots. Digging is the preferred method in beds where spraying a herbicide would be risky for the other plants. Plus, unlike spraying actively growing weeds, digging lets you get rid of these pests any time you can push the shovel into the soil.

4 CUT DOWN BIG ONES Once a woody weed gets too big to dig, you'll need to use a saw to remove it. Then dribble or brush on a systemic stump killer around the edges where the sap is flowing. It's absorbed into the wood and kills the roots. Be careful, it can kill any plant it gets on. You'll find these products at garden centers under several brand names. Many come with a dye mixed in so you can see which stumps you've treated.

Distinct leaf veins and a serrated edge help identify this pest.

American elder
Sambucus canadensis

QUICK WAY TO IDENTIFY Crush a stem or a few leaves and you'll get a disagreeable odor. Break or cut a mature stem and you'll discover a spongy white pith in the center. And last but not least, the creamy white flowers in spring and the dark purple fruits that follow are in large, flat-topped clusters.

WHY YOU WANT TO GET RID OF IT NOW! 10-ft.-tall, spreading shrub grows into a dense, messy thicket; birds eat the juicy berries in summer and spread seed; can also spread by stems that root wherever they touch the ground

WHERE DOES IT GROW BEST? Full sun to part shade in moist, fertile soil; tolerates moderately dry conditions

Common buckthorn
Rhamnus cathartica

QUICK WAY TO IDENTIFY If you scratch the bark and it's yellow underneath, you've found common buckthorn. Late in the fall you'll also notice that the foliage stays on this pest long after other leaves have fallen. And look closely at the leaves — there are usually three to five pairs of veins in each one.

WHY YOU WANT TO GET RID OF IT NOW! Grows quickly to a large shrub or small tree up to 20 ft. tall; ¼-in.-diameter messy black fruit in fall; birds eat and spread the seeds; sharp spines at tips of twigs can be dangerous as you walk through brushy areas

WHERE DOES IT GROW BEST? Part shade in moist to dry soil

Tatarian honeysuckle
Lonicera tatarica

QUICK WAY TO IDENTIFY The fragrant pink or white spring flowers are really quite pretty. Eventually they fade to yellow, and orange-red fruit sets on in summer. You can spot this pest easily in early spring because it's one of the first shrubs to leaf out.

WHY YOU WANT TO GET RID OF IT NOW! 10-ft.-tall and -wide shrub; birds eat and spread seeds; it grows into dense thickets that can force out other plants you want to keep

WHERE DOES IT GROW BEST? Sun or part shade; fertile, well-drained soil; tolerates almost any soil conditions except very dry areas

www.GardenGateMagazine.com   *the* YEAR IN GARDENING

MORE WOODY WEEDS!

Leaves can vary in size, but look for the deeply toothed edge.

White mulberry *Morus alba*

QUICK WAY TO IDENTIFY Break or crush a stem on a warm day and you'll spot a milky white sap bleeding from the wound. Or pull or dig a mulberry out of the ground and you'll see the long tap root is bright yellow-orange. Don't be confused by leaf shapes. Even on the same plant the leaves can be different shapes, with some of them lobed or shaped like a mitten.

WHY YOU WANT TO GET RID OF IT NOW! 30- to 50-ft.-tall shrubby tree; birds eat the messy purple fruit and spread seeds

WHERE DOES IT GROW BEST? Full sun to part shade; not tolerant of deep shade; grows in almost any kind of soil, from wet to dry

The yellow tap root is a good way to identify a white mulberry seedling.

Siberian elm *Ulmus pumila*

QUICK WAY TO IDENTIFY Remember American elms? The leaves of this weed look similar. However, they're usually smaller and riddled by insects. In spring, before the leaves even open, you'll spot clusters of pale-green flowers on the branches. Later, usually by early summer, small papery disclike seeds begin to fall.

WHY YOU WANT TO GET RID OF IT NOW! 50- to 70-ft.-tall, 30- to 50-ft.-wide tree; drops large quantities of seed that are spread by the wind; seeds sprout and grow very quickly; weak wood so you're constantly picking up twigs and branches under it

WHERE DOES IT GROW BEST? Full sun to part shade in moist to average soil

Box elder *Acer negundo*

QUICK WAY TO IDENTIFY Don't be confused — box elder leaves look similar to poison ivy. Both have three leaflets, but box elder leaves are not as pointed. And the stems are smooth green to dark red with a white waxy coating that you can rub off with your fingers.

WHY YOU WANT TO GET RID OF IT NOW! Up to 75-ft.-tall, single or multi-stemmed tree; winged seeds can sprout almost anywhere; new trees can also sprout from roots; weak wood breaks easily in storms; shallow roots make it hard to grow anything nearby

WHERE DOES IT GROW BEST? Full sun to part shade; rarely found in deep shade; prefers moist, even wet, areas but adapts to almost any soil except very dry

the YEAR IN GARDENING www.GardenGateMagazine.com

Tree of heaven *Ailanthus altissima*

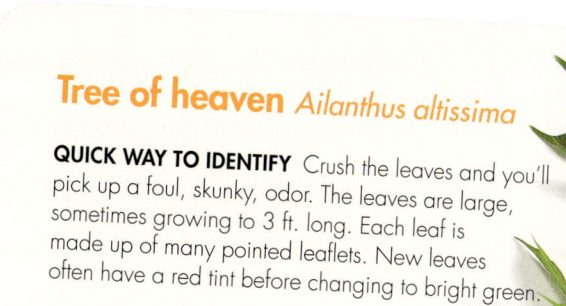

QUICK WAY TO IDENTIFY Crush the leaves and you'll pick up a foul, skunky, odor. The leaves are large, sometimes growing to 3 ft. long. Each leaf is made up of many pointed leaflets. New leaves often have a red tint before changing to bright green.

WHY YOU WANT TO GET RID OF IT NOW! Grows extremely fast up to 75 ft. tall with a 3-ft.-diameter trunk; wind-blown seeds sprout and grow anywhere, even in cracks in concrete; it's short-lived, averaging only 25 to 30 years; weak wood breaks easily in storms; toxin in the bark and leaves can keep seeds of other plants from sprouting

WHERE DOES IT GROW BEST? Sun or part shade in any type of soil, including rubble piles

Wild grape *Vitis* spp.

QUICK WAY TO IDENTIFY Long, twining vines wind their way into shrubs and trees. As the stems mature, the bark peels into narrow strips. Older vines produce clusters of small dark-purple fruit in late summer.

WHY YOU WANT TO GET RID OF IT NOW! Unlimited spread because vines root wherever they touch the soil; messy fruit eaten by birds helps spread this pest; thickets of vines can shade out or even kill mature shrubs and trees

WHERE DOES IT GROW BEST? Sun to part shade; any type of soil, moist or dry

Eastern red cedar
Juniperus virginiana

QUICK WAY TO IDENTIFY Prickly foliage is the quickest way to identify this evergreen. Crush a stem or some needles and they smell like a cedar closet. During the growing season you'll also spot blue berries along the branches of older trees.

WHY YOU WANT TO GET RID OF IT NOW! 15- to 40-ft.-tall, 8- to 20-ft.-wide tree; wood is slow to rot, so stumps of older trees are hard to remove; alternate host of cedar apple rust that affects plants in the apple family

WHERE DOES IT GROW BEST? Full sun to part shade in well-drained to dry and rocky soil

BASICS | PROBLEM SOLVER

Fight Tough Weeds and Win (Eventually)

Poison ivy

Nobody wants weeds, of course. Some of them aren't so bad — they're easy to pull and remove from your garden. But then there are the "Really Bad Weeds," plants that take root and just refuse to leave. Let's take a look at two of these pesky characters. You'll find them in lawns and gardens in most of the United States and Canada. There are no silver bullets — you'll have to work at getting rid of these weeds. But I'll share some techniques that work in our test garden, then you can get started weeding! ☐

— *Marcia A. Leeper*

Creeping Charlie

Creeping Charlie

How does this stuff move so fast? Creeping Charlie reseeds, but spreads even faster by rhizomes (underground stems) and stolons (above-ground shoots that root at every leaf node). It starts in shady spots where grass doesn't thrive, then creeps into your lawn and flower beds.

If you're one of those lucky gardeners with only small areas of creeping Charlie, you can keep it under control by pulling it and mulching the area. But what if it's invaded your lawn or larger areas? Let's take a look at a couple of options.

RAKE AND REMOVE Rather not use chemicals? A dethatching rake like the one I'm using here will cut and uproot the shallow-rooted plants. Then use a regular leaf rake to collect the pieces of the weed so they can't regrow. You may pull out some grass, too — grass will fill in a few small bare spots, but you'll need to sprinkle new seed over larger bare areas after you've raked.

Another annoying thing about creeping Charlie: Even if you get rid of your own, it's probably going to come creeping back from your neighbor's yard, even under a privacy fence. Metal edging or a barrier of concrete pavers won't stop the creeping Charlie, but it gives you a starting place to keep your eye out for invaders.

STERN STUFF If you have a lot of creeping Charlie in tight spots where you can't get to it with a rake, you'll probably need a broadleaf herbicide that contains triclopyr (such as Weed-B-Gon®) or 2,4-D (like Trimec®). Fall is the best time to treat creeping Charlie. But you can also treat it when it's growing vigorously and blooming in the spring, as it is in the photo. You may need to do two applications a few weeks apart. Take care around other plants.

Is your yard more creeping Charlie than grass? It may be best to kill everything with a glyphosate herbicide like Roundup® and start over.

Poison ivy

Just about every gardener's least favorite weed! Not only does poison ivy (*Toxicodendron radicans*) grow and spread rapidly, but it gives many people an itchy rash. And it's hard to kill, too — you'll need to outsmart it.

SUIT UP The most important step: Cover as much of your skin as possible, with long pants, long sleeves and gloves. I like to go a step farther — in the photo, you'll see how I use duct tape to tape my gloves to my sleeves and my pants legs to my boots so the poison ivy can't sneak into any gaps. And I "double-glove," with disposable gloves over my leather ones. That way, I don't get urushiol, the oil that causes the rash, on my leather gloves, but if the disposable glove rips, my hands aren't exposed. Safety glasses are also a good idea — you don't want a vine to snap back and hit you in the eye! Dispose of the vines in boxes or bags to protect everyone who comes in contact with it.

When I'm done working, I change clothes immediately. Urushiol can remain on clothing and tools for years, but it's water-soluble, so washing will remove it. Wash those clothes in a separate load. And no matter how careful I am, I wash my hands and arms with Tecnu® skin cleanser when I'm done working. If you use it within an hour or two of being exposed, you'll usually avoid getting a rash.

UP BY THE ROOTS Now, how do you actually get rid of this pest? Of course, the easiest fix is to pull new seedlings while they're small. But poison ivy often lurks under shrubs or near fences, so you don't find it until it's big. A systemic herbicide like Roundup® will work, but it's slow. I prefer to pull and cut the vines to get control quickly. You'll need to tug on the vines, as I'm doing in the photo, to see where they go. In addition to sending up new plants from seed, poison ivy can root along the ground for yards, and you'll need to detach it all along the vine to get rid of it.

Once you've pulled all the long, trailing vines free, you can cut the main vine. Dab or spray the cut end with a systemic brush killer (again, a herbicide that contains triclopyr is best).

Keep an eye on any areas where you've removed poison ivy. There will be a few suckers or seedlings popping up here and there for a couple of years. Get them while they're small, and you won't have a big patch to clean up again. Oh, and you could buy a goat. They like to eat poison ivy and have no reaction to it!

Two pairs of gloves protect my hands.

Duct tape closes the gap between boots and pants.

Is it, or isn't it?

Another sneaky thing about poison ivy: It has some lookalikes. You've probably heard the old saying, "Leaves of three, let it be." That's good advice — poison ivy doesn't really stand out in a crowd, but it always has three leaflets on each leaf, usually with red stems.

However, small boxelder (*Acer negundo*) seedlings look similar, and they tend to grow in the same places you'll find poison ivy — along the fence, behind the garage, and other places where you may not do a lot of cultivating. The clues? Boxelder stems aren't red, and often have a grayish "bloom" on them.

Another lookalike is Boston ivy (*Parthenocissus tricuspidata*), especially small, new growth. Unfortunately, it has a red stem, just like poison ivy, so it's a little harder to tell apart. Usually the leaf edges are a little more jagged, and the leaves are slightly smaller. But when in doubt, it's best to be careful!

Boxelder

Boston ivy

BASICS | PROBLEM SOLVER

7 Common Diseases
Break the cycle today!

It's easy to figure out how insects get from one plant to another. But fungal diseases? They don't have wings or legs. And plants don't sneeze or shake hands. So just how do these pests move through a garden so fast?

On these pages I've identified seven diseases that your plants may drag home from the nursery, catch on a wafting wind or pick up from a visiting bug. Keep in mind that some years you may have a serious problem with one of these diseases and other years it stays dormant, just waiting for the right conditions to help it grow.

But what causes these diseases to grow and spread? In the illustration at right you'll see that it takes three things. The important thing to remember is that if you can break the cycle by removing just one of these elements, your plants will stay healthy. ☐

— *Jim Childs*

Pathogen This is the organism that finds a susceptible plant and enters its system. It gets in through a pruning cut, an injury or simply through the leaves, stems or roots.

Environment Just the right weather conditions have to be present for the pathogen to grow and spread. It may need hot, cold, dry or humid weather — it depends on the disease.

Host The pathogen needs a susceptible plant to grow on. It may be a variety that's prone to the disease or simply a plant that's stressed.

Disease can only grow when all three of these factors are present.

Cedar-apple rust

BE ON THE LOOKOUT FOR: In fall, you'll spot hard brown galls on twigs of Eastern red cedar. In spring the galls swell, turn orange, as at left, and release spores. When those spores find the foliage of an apple tree in late spring, spots of orange rust, like the ones in the inset, grow on the leaves during the summer.

HOW IT SPREADS: Spores from galls are released in wet spring weather and travel by wind to infect new apple foliage. As they ripen, spores from the apple are then blown back to the cedar to continue the cycle next year.

CHECK THESE SUSCEPTIBLE PLANTS FIRST: Eastern red cedar, apples and crabapples

LONG-RANGE DIAGNOSIS: It's messy and unsightly.

Keep it under control: Don't plant Eastern red cedars and apple trees in the same garden; grow resistant apple cultivars. If you have susceptible apple trees, spray them with a fungicide as a preventative when the flower buds begin to open.

Infected apple leaves drop off in midsummer, leaving the tree unsightly.

Rust

BE ON THE LOOKOUT FOR: You'll spot powdery rusty-orange or brown spots, like these on a snapdragon, on either side of the leaf. It's most common in summer and fall, but can appear at any time.

HOW IT SPREADS: Spores are carried by wind and water to infect plants during humid conditions.

CHECK THESE SUSCEPTIBLE PLANTS FIRST: Geraniums, asters, mums, snapdragons and peonies; also check surrounding plants

LONG-RANGE DIAGNOSIS: Rust weakens the plant, reducing flower and fruit production.

Keep it under control: Remove and destroy infected leaves. Try to keep the foliage dry when you water and improve air circulation around the plant by removing dense vegetation nearby. Also, read descriptions to find resistant cultivars for your garden. If you still want to grow a susceptible plant, check with your local garden center for a fungicide you can spray in early summer as a preventative.

Rub the spots and they'll leave a rusty brown stain on your fingers.

Anthracnose

BE ON THE LOOKOUT FOR: Usually after a cool, wet spring, you'll find irregular dark blotches on leaves. Sometimes buds or small twigs will also be infected — symptoms vary with the host plant. Infected parts, especially leaves, eventually drop off.

HOW IT SPREADS: Spores overwinter on twigs, move through the air and begin to grow in cool, wet weather.

CHECK THESE SUSCEPTIBLE PLANTS FIRST: Mainly shade trees, such as sycamore, ash and maple; also some small ornamental trees, like the dogwood in this photo

LONG-RANGE DIAGNOSIS: Anthracnose rarely kills the tree, but repeated defoliation weakens the plant and makes it unsightly.

Keep it under control: Plant trees in sites with good air circulation and prune dense crowns to improve air movement. Keep trees fertilized and vigorous so they can grow new foliage quickly. When choosing a new tree, read tags or ask for resistant cultivars.

Irregular blotches spread across the leaves, including the veins.

IDENTIFY MORE DISEASES

Botrytis gray mold

BE ON THE LOOKOUT FOR: Small, wet-looking spots, usually in spring, appear on tender new flower buds and blossoms. But it can spread to leaves and stems, as it has on these tulips. Even fruits can be damaged during periods of cool, wet weather. The spots grow larger and are often covered with gray fuzz.

HOW IT SPREADS: Wind and rain spread the spores, which grow best in cool, wet weather.

CHECK THESE SUSCEPTIBLE PLANTS FIRST: Almost any plant can be stricken with botrytis gray mold.

LONG-RANGE DIAGNOSIS: Flower buds don't open, fruits are spoiled and the plant is weakened by this disease.

Keep it under control: Grow plants where air moves freely and don't wet flowers or foliage when you water. Bury infected plant parts 18 to 24 inches deep — don't put them in your compost pile. Several fungicides, including Maneb and Dicloran, are effective against this disease.

If the botrytis mold is severe, the entire plant can wither and rot.

Black spot

BE ON THE LOOKOUT FOR: Black spots on leaves and even occasionally on stems. The spots are small in spring but by summer they grow larger, then leaves turn yellow and eventually drop off.

HOW IT SPREADS: Fungus spores overwinter on infected leaves and stems left lying on the ground. Splashing water transfers the fungus to young leaves from spring through fall.

CHECK THESE SUSCEPTIBLE PLANTS FIRST: Roses

LONG-RANGE DIAGNOSIS: As old leaves drop off, new leaves sprout. Repeating this process weakens the plant, making it more susceptible to other diseases, insects and winter injury. Plus it's just plain unsightly.

Keep it under control: Search out resistant cultivars; grow roses where air is not blocked by surrounding plants; avoid wetting the leaves, especially late in the day; and remove infected leaves as you spot them. Fungicides from the garden center will help, but spray *before* you see symptoms.

Black spots look like soot on the leaves, but can't be rubbed off.

Powdery mildew

BE ON THE LOOKOUT FOR: The white granular patches look like dust on stems, the tops and bottoms of leaves and occasionally on flowers and fruit, and can be rubbed off with your fingers. You'll find powdery mildew any time during the growing season wherever susceptible plants are grown.

HOW IT SPREADS: Spores of powdery mildew move by air.

CHECK THESE SUSCEPTIBLE PLANTS FIRST: Phlox, lilac, bee balm, aster, rose, lungwort, zinnia, crabapple and many others

LONG-RANGE DIAGNOSIS: Powdery mildew won't kill a plant; it only affects the appearance.

Keep it under control: Plant resistant varieties. Keep plants healthy and well watered to avoid stress. Always provide good air circulation around susceptible plants. Apply potassium bicarbonate fungicides and horticultural oils before you find mildew or spay them to keep the problem from spreading to more leaves or other plants.

Powdery mildew is most common during mid- to late summer.

Crown rot

BE ON THE LOOKOUT FOR: Yellowing foliage and mushy stems appear just above the soil line. It can start any time during the growing season, but it's most prevalent during hot, humid periods. Once called Southern blight, this fatal rot is now spreading into much of North America.

HOW IT SPREADS: Crown rot organisms live near the surface of the soil, waiting to enter a plant and destroy the tissue.

CHECK THESE SUSCEPTIBLE PLANTS FIRST: Hosta, bleeding heart, phlox, daylily and many other perennials

LONG-RANGE DIAGNOSIS: It kills the plant if it's not stopped, and can become a permanent problem in your garden.

Keep it under control: Dig infected plants and remove the top 12 in. of soil. Bury everything in a hole several feet deep to keep the spores from spreading. Never add infected plants to your compost pile. One fungicide, Terrachlor®, may save infected plants if it's applied before the entire crown has rotted.

Look for these tiny spheres on stems and the surface of the soil.

BASICS | PROBLEM SOLVER

Too Big? Time To Dig!

We've all had this situation: A shrub that you chose and planted is just getting out of control. It won't play nicely with your other plants, and it makes your whole garden look unkempt. But even when you know the plant doesn't look that great, it's hard to make the decision to get rid of it. And the actual removal process isn't a piece of cake, either!

I deal with this problem sometimes in our test garden, as well as in my own yard. Often, the shrub in question is actually a great plant, but one that's just outgrown its space.

You'll probably notice a couple of specific problems. Maybe the shrub is shading out nearby perennials. Worse yet, if it's a shrub that spreads by suckers, like the fragrant sumac (*Rhus aromatica*) in the illustration, you're probably finding little shoots popping up in the middle of other plants. And maybe not just nearby plants — some shrubs can send out suckers several yards away, effectively taking over an entire garden bed.

Last, but by no means least on the list of problems, a large, overgrown shrub can harbor woody weeds. If you look closely at the illustration, you'll see that there's a mulberry sapling coming up in the middle. It looks untidy, and it's almost impossible to get the woody weed out without dealing with the overgrown shrub, too.

So is it time to take the plunge? Check out "Some tough questions" at left. Sound like your yard? Time to dig!

FIRST THINGS FIRST It's always good to have a plan in place before you make the first cut. Believe it or not, I've known people who replaced an overgrown shrub with exactly the same plant — just smaller. Even if you really like the plant, that isn't your best bet. In a couple of years, you'll be right back where you started.

Instead, give yourself a summer to think about what permanent plants you want in that place. I like to fill in the bare patch with some tall annuals. It gives me a chance to see how big a permanent replacement plant really needs to be to look good.

NO MORE SUCKERS It also helps to have a plan for the actual process. Although you may notice the problem shrub most when it's in full summer foliage, that's not really the easiest time to remove it. As you can see in the illustration above, waiting until most of the leaves are off in the fall makes it easier to see what you have to deal

You may have to dig and divide some perennials to get all the shrub roots out.

? SOME TOUGH QUESTIONS

If you answer yes to two or three of these, think hard about removing your shrub now, before it gets even bigger!

- ☐ Is the plant detracting from the general look of the garden?
- ☐ Do you find yourself apologizing for its appearance, either to visitors, a spouse or the next-door neighbor?
- ☐ Is the plant invading the growing space of other, better-behaved plants nearby? Or sending out suckers or reseeding in a nearby lawn area?
- ☐ Does it take more than a quick pruning every year to keep it within bounds?
- ☐ Take a look at it in the winter when the leaves are gone. Is it a "hiding place" for woody weed trees or shrubs?

Remove as many roots as possible so the shrub can't regrow.

QUICK TIP

A QUICK PULL This is a Weed Wrench™ (www.weedwrench.com), and it's just what you need to yank out unwanted trees and shrubs. It comes in several different sizes, to handle stems from 1 in. to 2½ in. in diameter.

with. You won't have as much debris to discard, either. Besides, you'll run less risk of crushing and damaging nearby plants.

OK, let's talk about those nearby plants for a minute. See how the sumac has sent up some suckers into the coneflowers to the left? How do you get rid of those invading sumac shoots? There are two approaches. If the perennials in question are easy to lift and divide, like these coneflowers, just dig up the whole clump, shrub sucker and all. Pull up on the cut end of the sucker to remove as much of it as you can, all the way to the base of the parent plant if possible. When you're done cleaning out the area, just split and replant the perennials as you normally would.

However, if you don't want to dig out whole clumps of perennials, cut off the sucker between the clump and the parent shrub. Carefully pull the sucker out of the middle of the perennials. Chances are, this method won't be so disruptive for the perennial, but the down side is that you may not get all the shrub roots, either.

And that brings up another point: Remember those annuals I suggested you plant for a summer? Not only do they give you a chance to try out some different heights and sizes in this space; planting annuals also gives you a summer to dig out any little suckers that may resprout, without having to disrupt more permanent plantings.

ROOTS AND ALL Once you've yanked out all the surrounding suckers, it's time to deal with the main plant. I like to cut back the top first, to make it easy to come to grips with the rootball. But I try to leave a "stump" about 18 inches tall so I have something to hold onto when I need to start pulling. Of course, you'll need a spade or shovel, because you want to get as many roots out of the ground as possible. (And take a look at the quick tip above for one of my favorite tools, one that makes jobs like this a lot easier!)

It's always tough to make big changes to your garden. But with a little planning, it goes much more smoothly. And just think of all your great new options! ☐

— *Marcia Leeper*

BASICS | SHOPPING

Must-Know Mail-Order Tips
with Dave Whitinger

Ordering plants from a list or a photo is an act of faith — you have to trust that the mail-order company will live up to its advertising. Many do. Some, however, don't. To help you avoid some of the pitfalls of shopping by mail, I spoke with Dave Whitinger, the "Dave" of the popular Web site Dave's Garden. He started the Web site so folks could share the triumphs and dilemmas they have in their gardens. He's also an avid mail-order gardener, so he had these tips to share.

1 READ THE CATALOG You don't want to pay a high price expecting a plant in a gallon-sized pot, only to open the package and find a plastic bag with a tiny dry root in it. Plant descriptions should list your choice as bare-root (BR) or by the size of the container. Sometimes you'll find trees or shrubs listed by height.

2 CHECK GUARANTEES, SUBSTITUTIONS AND REFUNDS Make sure that the company guarantees the plant to be true to name as well as healthy and viable when it arrives. Nurseries can't be responsible for the health of the plant once it's in your care. But if there are problems within the first 48 hours, most companies will work with you to correct the problem.

There's nothing worse than opening the box after ordering coral bells and getting daylilies. Most order forms ask you to list substitutions when you place your order. If not, call and ask what the policy is. You still have options even if you don't want a substitution. The nursery may hold your money and ship the plant later. Or it may offer a refund. I've found that ordering with a credit or debit card makes getting a refund much easier than waiting for a check.

3 SHIPPING TIMES Find out if you can request a shipping day, or at least a specific week. Keep in mind that orders often go out on Monday or Tuesday so plants won't sit in a truck or warehouse over a weekend. That means they'll usually arrive late in the week. And ask for the delivery to be left on a porch or other shady spot so the plants won't cook before you get home to unpack them.

4 PACKING TIPS Bare-root plants are easy to ship. But if you're buying container plants, that's a different matter. The last thing you want is your selection arriving with broken stems and bone-dry roots. In the photos at right I'll show you some things to look for in excellent packing, like individual compartments to keep plants held securely so they don't bounce around. Or tall, ridged sleeves, like the ones here, help keep stems from being crushed.

5 UNPACKING TIPS As you unpack, if something doesn't look quite right, you'll find a picture really is worth a thousand words. Have a camera handy and take a few snapshots as you open the box. Broken stems, exposed roots or dry

Garden Watchdog

Want to read mail-order experiences of other gardeners, or share your own? Go to www.davesgarden.com and click on the Garden Watchdog section. You'll find comments and ratings on more than 5,800 gardening vendors. To give you a sampling, below is a list of the 5 most highly rated and the 5 lowest rated major mail-order nurseries, as compiled by Dave's site.

THE TOP FIVE
Bluestone Perennials
Forestfarm
Lazy S'S Farm Nursery
High Country Gardens
Garden Crossings

THE BOTTOM FIVE
Michigan Bulb Co.
Wayside Gardens
Gardener's Choice
Direct Gardening
Four Seasons Nursery

Great packing

- Paper held in place with rubber bands keeps the soil in.
- Tall stems are protected by sturdy cardboard sleeves.
- Plants are kept separate and secure so they don't bump into each other during shipping.

Fair packing

- Have you ever opened a box like this outdoors on a windy day? Enough said!
- When you have to fish around blindly in the box of foam, plants can easily be damaged.

foliage can spell trouble. Even take a close-up of insects if you spot them crawling around.

No matter the condition of the order, don't ever assume anything is dead, even if it looks like it. After you take a few photos of plants that have been bounced out of the container, tuck them back into their pots, set them in a shaded spot and give them a good drink of water. Bare-root arrivals should be soaked in water for an hour or two and then planted directly into the garden or into a pot.

6 FIND THE BEST COMPANIES
What makes a good mail-order nursery? I know I've been seduced by colorful photos and descriptions in catalogs or on Web sites. But it's healthy plants and great service that draw me back for repeat business. So how do you know what you might be getting into before you order? Talk to friends who order plants. And check out the "Garden Watchdog" information at left. It's part of Dave's Web site, and it's a great way to read about other gardeners' experiences, good *and* bad.

Another way to find out how good a company is? If it's your first time ordering from it, don't place a huge order. I like to order just a plant or two until I see how a new nursery will perform. If it works out, you can always order more later.

All in all, shopping by mail can be easy and fun. But just like shopping in a store, problems can arise. Most quality companies have been around for a while and have learned how to solve those problems quickly. Keep these tips in mind as you order and you'll have a great plant shopping experience. □

— *Jim Childs*

BASICS | SHOPPING

How To Buy A Healthy Tree

Look for a main stem, or leader, that goes all the way to the top of the tree.

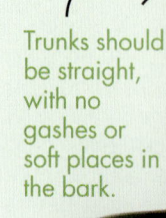

If you buy a few petunias and they don't work out, you throw them on the compost pile. But a tree is a bigger investment, so it's good to be sure you're getting just the right one.

So, you already know where the tree will go, and whether it should be a large shade tree or a small ornamental one. And you know which trees do well in your area and soil. It's time to go shopping. But how do you choose the one perfect tree?

I'm going to explain the process, step by step. First, let's assume that you'd like to save money by purchasing a younger, smaller tree, like the one at right. It won't have much impact right away, but young trees often catch up with older, bigger ones in a couple of years. That's because there's less "transplant shock" for younger trees. They can put out new roots and start growing more quickly.

But if you need a big tree *right now*, it's a good idea to look at larger trees, often sold balled and burlapped. I'll share some tips on buying these in "On the ball," below.

No matter what size tree you're buying, look closely at its leaves, trunk and roots. I'll show you what to look for and what to avoid in the photos at right. ◻

— Marcia Leeper

WEB extra
Come along as I shop for a tree in our online **video.**

ON THE BALL

Balled and burlapped (B&B) trees were grown in the ground to reach their current size, then dug up to sell. The burlap holds the soil to the roots, and a web of rope or a wire basket keeps everything secure. With all that soil, B&B trees are big and heavy, so you may need some help moving and planting them.

Look for a root ball that's solid and not squashed to one side.

Look for the same good leader and stem that you'd want on any tree. Then look at the root ball. Big trees like the one at left, with trunks that are 1½ to 3 in. in diameter, are dug with a tree spade. The root ball should be fairly flat on top, with tapering sides, and the burlap should be in good shape. That's a sign that the tree was dug recently, and hasn't been sitting for a long time. (If the tree's been out of the ground a while, the root ball may be sagging out of shape, with burlap that's starting to rot.)

When you plant, leave the burlap and the wire or rope on until the tree is in the hole. Then remove the rope or wire and as much burlap as possible, so they won't interfere with root growth.

Trunks should be straight, with no gashes or soft places in the bark.

the YEAR IN GARDENING   www.GardenGateMagazine.com

Take it from the top

WHO'S THE LEADER? First, I check to see if the tree has a leader, a main stem that develops into the trunk. Look closely at the tree in the photo at left, and you'll see that there's one main stem running all the way to the top. That's what you want on almost any tree. (Once in a while there's an exception: If you're looking for a weeping tree or a tree that develops unusual or contorted shapes as it grows, like some Japanese maples, you may not want a leader.) If the tree splits into two main stems right at the top, but the rest of the tree is perfect, it's OK to buy it. Just snip off one of the competing stems to let the other one take over. Keep an eye on the leader after you plant the tree — you may need to clip an extra one out a year or two later.

NO ONE'S IN CHARGE An injury to the trunk can cause multiple leaders, or even none at all. That's what you're seeing in photo A. You could snip off three of these stems and let one take over. But all of them are growing at odd angles, so you'd be better off looking for a different tree.

A Too many leaders! Look for a tree with only one main stem.

B A few tattered leaves are OK, but scorched leaves like these aren't a good sign.

LEAF ME OUT OF THIS Take a look at the foliage too, both the bottoms and the tops of the leaves. At the end of the summer, leaves may look a little tattered, but there shouldn't be any indication of insects or disease. Scorched leaf tips in photo B are a sign that the tree has root damage from being moved or that it got too dry at some point. It might snap out of it…but you'd better keep shopping.

In the middle of things

MOVING ON DOWN Next, look for a healthy trunk and branches. Most shade trees have a fairly straight trunk, like this pin oak at left, although some smaller ornamental trees may be a little more crooked. Don't worry too much if the branches aren't evenly spaced around the tree. You'll probably prune off most of the lower branches anyway in the next few years, to get them out of the way of foot traffic. (But don't remove them immediately. Let them contribute to the tree's growth until they're about an inch in diameter, then remove them.)

BARK OR BITE What shouldn't you buy? A tree with gashes, soft spots or other damage on the trunk, like the wound (C) on the photo. The trunk supports the tree, so you don't want a weak point here.

GRAFT AND CORRUPTION Many trees are grafted — you'll see a knobby place right down by the soil line. But the graft should be smoothly healed over, not sprouting new growth like this one (D).

C See soft spots or gashes on the trunk? Keep shopping.

D Graft unions should be smooth, not sprouting new growth.

The root of the matter

A SOLID FOUNDATION Of course a tree needs healthy roots, although they're a little harder to inspect than leaves or trunks. But usually you can lift a tree gently out of the pot to see what's down there. What are you looking for? The roots in photo E are growing fairly straight down into the container. You'll want to loosen them up a bit when you plant the tree, but they look healthy.

DON'T FORM A CIRCLE On the other hand, the roots in photo F indicate that this tree has probably been in the container too long. They're starting to circle, and circling roots may eventually kill the tree by girdling its trunk. (At the very least, the tree may not be anchored firmly and will tip over in a high wind.) You have two choices: Keep looking for another tree, or carefully disentangle and snip a few roots so that they're heading out into the soil, not around in a circle.

E Do buy a tree with roots that grow down into the pot.

F Don't buy a tree with circling roots like these.

BASICS | TOOLS

Must-Have Garden Gadgets
with Joe Lamp'l

Built-in knee pads move with you as you work.

Every time I pick up a garden catalog or magazine, there seems to be a new product claiming to make my gardening easier. But will it? Every year Joe Lamp'l, garden personality and creator of The joe gardener® Company, puts together a list of The Best of the Must-Haves™. You can find his favorite garden tools and lots of other garden tips at www.joegardener.com.

To evaluate all the products, Joe calls in a team of gardeners, from beginners to experts. The group looks over the products and tries them out. Eventually they narrowed the list down to the very best. If a tool or garden gadget passes this team of testers, it has to be good. To see if I agreed with their findings, I tried out 5 of Joe's recent picks, too. You can see my experiences in our online Web extra. But first, let's take a closer look at some of those must-have tools. ☐

— *Jim Childs*

IN THE KNOW

GOING GREEN Recently Joe found out that only about 3 percent of the insects in a garden damage plants. But most synthetic insecticides are non-selective, so they kill good *and* bad bugs. That's why he's switched to eco-friendly, selective pesticides, such as Bt (*Bacillus thuringiensis*) or Spinosad (spinosyn A and spinosyn D). They target only specific insect pests. Plus, they break down after use so they're less likely to harm the environment, beneficial insects or you. You'll find these insecticides at garden centers.

1) GREENJEANS™ I know why this is one of Joe's all-time favorite garden products. GreenJeans have great padding where every gardener needs it most, on the knees. The non-binding straps were well above and below my knee so they didn't cut off circulation like some knee pads do. I could easily stand and walk around while wearing these. And simple fasteners make them easy to put on. GreenJeans are washable — just hose them off when they get dirty. They come in four sizes so you can pick the one closest to your measurements and then adjust it with the straps to get a perfect fit.

Muscle and Arm Farm
800-443-2607
www.muscleandarmfarm.com
Suggested retail price $48

2) FISKARS™ 15-INCH POWER-LEVER® EASY REACH BYPASS PRUNER
If you've ever been scratched by a rose or a thorny shrub as you pruned, you can quickly see the advantage to this handy bypass pruner. The long handle let me reach further into a prickly plant without getting snagged. It also lets me reach higher if necessary. Don't have the strength in your hands that you used to? The patented handle mechanism lets you use both hands for more power and control. I was able to cut a ¾-in.-diameter branch with ease.

Check local retailers or Best Buds Garden Supply Company, Inc.
877-777-2837
www.bestbudsgarden.com
Suggested retail price $27.95

Use two hands for more power.

4) KOMBI GARDEN TOOL If you've ever tried to grub out a stand of brambles or other brush, you can imagine how the sharp teeth on this tool will cut through those tough roots. But it's also ideal for cultivating and edging beds or borders. I found it even did a good job raking rough soil to break up and smooth out dirt clods. This tool makes the job quick and easy.

There are five styles to choose from. Some, like this Kombi Jr., have D-handles, while others have long handles. And there are two blade widths to choose from, too. There's even a small trowel.

Kombi Gardening Tool
706-754-2875
Suggested retail price $7 to $48

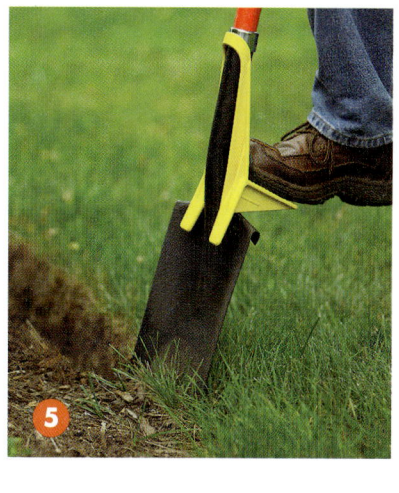

Sharp notches make cutting through soil or tough roots easy.

5) TRENCHFOOT™ Ever notice how you have to step on one side or the other of your spade or shovel as you dig? Seems a bit off balance, doesn't it? This heavy-duty, no-slip footpad replaces the narrow, off-center strip of rolled metal you usually use to push the blade into the soil. With the TrenchFoot you use the ball of your foot to push down, instead of the arch. And it's centered so you won't lose your balance as you dig.

This tool is easy to install, too. Simply slip it over the handle of your shovel and you're ready to dig. If you wish, slip it off one tool and use it on another. It'll fit either straight or D-handled tools.

TrenchFoot
888-468-8736
www.trenchfootinc.com
Or www.GardenGateStore.com
Suggested retail price $9 to $12

WEB extra
Watch me put all five tools to the test in our *video*.

3) DUAL-FLO™ This tool lets you choose the perfect water flow for any job. But the best part was the time and energy savings. I didn't have to walk back to the spigot, turn off the water, remove or switch nozzles, turn the water on and walk back to where I was working.

The Dual-Flo makes it easy to have a full stream for filling your watering can, as you see in photo A. Twist the side-mounted knob and you have the spray nozzle in photo B to mist those new seedlings. Like most pistol-grip nozzles, it has a full range of spray settings, too. Plus, when you need to reach that far corner of your garden, both nozzle ends are threaded so you can attach another hose without removing the Dual-Flo.

Choice Products, Inc.
800-473-6020
www.choiceproductsinc.com
Or www.GardenGateStore.com
Suggested retail price $19 to $25

Full stream of water

Rubber thread protector

Adjustable spray

www.GardenGateMagazine.com   the YEAR IN GARDENING   285

BASICS | TOOLS

Screws help reinforce trellis.

GET HOOKED Special pegboard hooks hold everything from shelves to tape measures.

Cork sheet

Pegboard

CEDAR'S PERFECT NATURALLY Or paint or stain your trellis to jazz it up with color.

TAKE YOUR CHOICE Substitute chalk board for the dry erase board, if you prefer.

MOUNTING THE TRELLIS

Once you've put this trellis together, it's time to attach it to the wall. Get a friend to hold the trellis in the right spot. Set a level across the top of it and adjust it up or down until it's level. Then draw a line on the wall along the bottom edge of the top horizontal piece. Set the trellis aside.

Next, line up the two 4-in. pieces of wood along and just below the line so the pieces are about 3 ft. apart. These will be brackets that the trellis will hang on. If you don't want them to show, place them so they'll be hidden behind the pegboard or other panels. Attach the brackets to the wall using two screws each (A). (If you're working on a drywall surface, use drywall anchors instead.)

Next, your helper places the trellis so the top horizontal piece is resting on the two wood brackets. Drill pilot holes and drive screws down through the horizontal piece of the trellis (B) into the brackets.

Side view

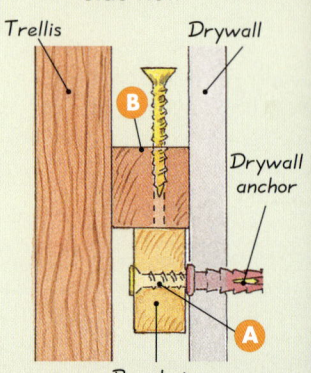

Trellis — Drywall — Drywall anchor — Bracket

286 *the* YEAR IN GARDENING www.GardenGateMagazine.com

This quick and easy organizer keeps tools right at your fingertips!

Tool Trellis

Spring is a busy time for gardeners. You have gardens to design, beds to dig and plants to buy. But there's one simple thing you can do first that will save time on all of your other tasks. What's that? Get organized!

I know, I can already hear you say, "But I don't have time to organize my tools!" Well, guess what? I bought a ready-made wooden trellis and a few other materials at a home improvement center, brought them home and had this organizer done by lunchtime. I figure the time it took more than made up for all the hours I'd have wasted searching for tools all season. Here's how to make it:

1 GATHER THE MATERIALS The simple cedar trellis used for this project measures 24x72 inches, but you can get whatever size works best for your situation. While you're at the home center, pick up the other materials and tools on the list at right.

2 MEASURE, CUT AND PAINT When you get home, measure the openings on the trellis where you want the pegboard and other panels to go. Add 1¼ inch to the width so the panel edges will overlap the trellis a bit on each side. Later, you'll drive screws through this overlapped area to attach the panels to the trellis. Cut the pegboard into four pieces the correct size, paint them and set them aside to dry. Measure and cut the white board into two pieces, each one wide enough to span two openings (again, plus 1¼ inch).

3 ASSEMBLE THE PIECES First of all, I found that a screw in each intersection made the trellis stiffer. I drilled ⅛-inch pilot holes and drove screws through the front of the trellis using the 1¼-inch screws, but if you don't want the screws to show, drive them in from the back instead.

Once the pegboard pieces are dry, place the trellis face down on the floor and screw the pieces of pegboard and dry erase board onto the back of the trellis using four of the shorter ¾-inch screws for each panel.

MATERIALS & TOOLS

- 1 24-x-72-in. cedar trellis
- 1 2-ft.-x-4-ft. piece of pegboard (or as needed)
- 1 2-ft.-x-2-ft. piece of white dry erase board (or as needed)
- 1 sheet of cork as needed
- 1¼-in. brass screws
- ¾-in. brass screws
- Pegboard hooks
- Latex paint
- Spray adhesive
- 4 drywall anchors (if needed)
- 2 4-in.-long ½-x-1-in. wood scraps

Drill, ⅛-, ¼-in. bits and screwdriver bit, pencil, tape measure, saw, level

Cut two pieces of cork to fit exactly into two of the openings. Use spray adhesive to attach them to the front side of the white dry erase board pieces.

4 CUSTOMIZE Of course, go ahead and customize your tool trellis however you'd like. If you want more pegboard space, for instance, you can even use one piece that runs the length of the trellis. Whatever the size of your pegboard, be sure to mount it to the trellis so there's at least a ½-inch space between it and the wall behind so you can easily slide the hooks into the pegboard. (You'll automatically have enough space if you mount the trellis as I did, with the vertical wood pieces facing out.) Check out "Mounting the trellis" at left to see how to attach it to the wall.

You can buy large packages of assorted hooks at hardware stores or home centers. But unless you need a lot of hooks, save money by just buying what you need, plus any special ones you want for your situation, like shelf brackets or special tool holders. With the trellis in place, attach some hooks to the pegboard, add a dry erase marker and hang your favorite tools. Voilà! You're ready to get to work! □

— *Deborah Gruca*

BASICS | WILDLIFE

Feed Birds What They Love with Sharon Dunn

Feeding birds is easy, fun and inexpensive. And nearly half of the households in North America provide some kind of food for wild birds.

Whether you're an old pro or new to bird feeding, check out these tips. Sharon Dunn, president of Duncraft, a company that specializes in bird feeding supplies, shared them.

Birds get about 75 percent of their food from wild sources. But if snow covers their food, they could use some help. Feeders filled with nutritious snacks are the way to go.

CHOOSE A LOCATION The best winter location for a feeder is on the south side of a structure, out of the wind. A few evergreens nearby provide extra perches for the birds waiting to eat and extra cover on those snowy days. But, by all means, place the feeder where you can enjoy watching the birds.

KEEP FOOD FRESH Store bird food in a spot that's cool and dry to keep oils in the seeds from turning rancid. Cool temperatures also prevent grain moth eggs from hatching (don't worry; they're not the same ones that eat your clothing). If you do find a few insects, freeze the seeds for five days to kill the bugs.

Seeds also attract four-legged pests, such as mice. Your best bet is to store seeds in something they can't chew through, such as metal or glass.

NO DIRTY DINING If your feeder looks dirty or smells like rancid oil, it's time to clean it. Scrub wooden feeders with a solution of one part bleach to nine parts water and set them in the sun to dry. Plastic or metal feeders can be emptied and washed with soap and hot water or the same bleach solution.

WHAT'S FOR DINNER? There are three basic feeder types. Learn more about how to use each one, what type of food to put in it and which birds it attracts, here. Finally, along with each type of food, you'll find a list of birds that will be attracted to the combination of feeder and seed. Choose one combination or try all of them, and it won't be long until you're enjoying loads of colorful visitors in your own back yard!

— *Jim Childs*

Mail-order source

Duncraft
www.duncraft.com
888-879-5095
Source for bird feeding supplies, including the outdoor birdseed ornaments in the photo above.

Hopper feeder This is one of the most popular feeders because it attracts a wide variety of birds, both large and small. A tray or platform on the base makes it easy for larger birds, like this female cardinal, to perch. The feeder may be made of wood, metal or plastic and hung or mounted on a pole. Below are three common seeds that work well in a hopper feeder. Unfortunately, squirrels also find these large feeders easy targets. Depending on the location of your feeder, place a baffle under or over it for protection, and use safflower seeds — squirrels don't like the taste.

SAFFLOWER
- Cardinals
- Titmice
- Chickadees
- Downy woodpeckers

BLACK SUNFLOWER
- Cardinals
- Blue jays
- Woodpeckers
- Goldfinches
- Purple finches
- Chickadees
- Titmice
- Nuthatcnes

CORN, MILO AND MILLET MIX
Attracts most birds, including "undesirables," such as
- Pigeons
- Grackles
- Starlings
- Sparrows

Seed tube Big birds often harass smaller birds, so seed tubes with short perches give small birds, like these goldfinches, a chance to eat in peace. Just don't add a tray to the base, or bigger birds will be able to land. This particular tube has small holes designed for Niger seed or chopped sunflower hearts — finch favorites. But you can also purchase tubes with larger openings to feed the same seeds you would serve from a hopper.

Tubes don't hold as much food as most hoppers, so you may need to fill them more often. They're small and lightweight so they can be hung almost anywhere. Don't have a tree branch handy? Use a shepherd's hook. Some tube feeders also have fittings so you can put them on a post if you prefer.

NIGER/NYGER/THISTLE SEED
- Goldfinches
- Purple finches
- Pine siskins
- Redpolls

CHOPPED SUNFLOWER
- Chickadees
- Nuthatches
- Painted buntings
- Titmice

Suet cage Birds that prefer feasting on insects, like this pileated woodpecker, are the first ones drawn to suet. It's fat that gives birds calories for warmth, especially in winter. And suet's a good spring and summer food for parents to take back to the nest for babies. Wire cages are the best way to serve suet — birds cling to the hanging cage and peck small portions out.

You can buy raw suet (beef fat) from a butcher shop and put it in the cage. However, most folks find it easier to pick up rendered suet cakes with seeds. The seeds add some extra protein. Raw suet goes rancid quickly, so unless you have lots of birds eating it, you're probably better off with the cakes. Want to make your own? Check out a recipe for suet cakes in the Web extra.

Raw beef suet

Rendered suet cakes

SUET
- Woodpeckers
- Chickadees
- Jays
- Titmice
- Catbirds
- Nuthatches

WEB extra Learn how to make your own suet cakes with our bird-tested *recipe*.

BASICS | WILDLIFE

One-of-a-Kind Birdbath

Make a birdbath this weekend... from a pumpkin(!?)

If you've never seen a concrete birdbath quite like this before, it's no wonder — there isn't one! I've made several of these birdbaths and each one is unique. But even better than that, this project is easy and quick to make. Once you've gathered everything you need, you can put it together in 20 minutes. And with just a few tools and ingredients, you won't get soaked buying the materials.

I'll show you the steps below, but here are the basics on how to make it: First, fold a 9-foot-by-12-foot piece of plastic sheeting or tarp in half twice to get a piece that's 4½ feet by 6 feet and four layers thick.

Pour the wet concrete onto the plastic, then press a pumpkin (or any curved object) into the concrete a couple of inches. Pull the edges of the plastic up and over the top and tape it into place. Once the concrete cures (in about 48 hours), you have a charming birdbath!

I suggest using a Cinderella pumpkin because the nice, deep ridges of that cultivar form an interesting impression in the basin of the birdbath. But you can use any pumpkin or round item to press into the concrete. A large exercise ball also works well, and, like the pumpkin, it removes easily when the concrete is dry. For the birdbath you see here, I used a mixture of black and red concrete dyes, but you can use other colors, or none at all, if you prefer. Want to make the outside contours more pronounced? The illustration shows how to push a few rocks up against the outside of the plastic after you've taped the edges up. Be sure to leave them in place until the concrete is dry.

This birdbath is so much fun to make that once I got my feet wet with the first one, I made loads of them, experimenting with colors and shapes. In fact, the hardest part is waiting until it's time to unwrap the finished product! □

— *Deborah Gruca*

MATERIALS & TOOLS

1 Cinderella pumpkin (often sold as 'Rouge Vif d'Etampes')
1 60-lb. bag of sand mix Portland cement
1 9x12-ft. 3-ml. plastic sheeting or tarp
1 roll duct tape
Concrete dye (optional)
Plastic mixing tub
Garden hoe for mixing
Small stones for shaping (optional)

1 MIX CEMENT AND WATER in a sturdy container — I used a plastic storage tote. (If you want to use dye, mix it into the water before pouring it into the dry cement.) The right consistency is soupy, with water pooling on the surface. Pour the mix onto the folded plastic.

After mixing, water should pool slightly along the edges of the container.

2 PRESS THE PUMPKIN firmly into the concrete and pull up and tape the edges of the plastic to the pumpkin in several places. Grasp the package by the top and jostle the whole thing for a few seconds to get air bubbles out of the mix. Then leave it on a flat surface outside to dry.

Tear off a few pieces of duct tape before you start wrapping the pumpkin.

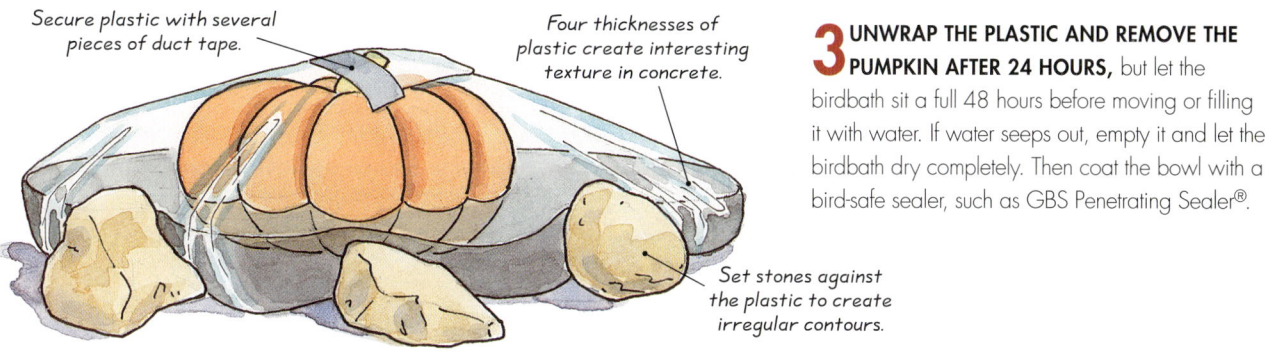

WEB extra
If you like this project, check out our sand-cast birdbath *video and plan!*

Set a stone in the deepest area to give the birds a safe place to land.

Secure plastic with several pieces of duct tape.

Four thicknesses of plastic create interesting texture in concrete.

Set stones against the plastic to create irregular contours.

3 UNWRAP THE PLASTIC AND REMOVE THE PUMPKIN AFTER 24 HOURS, but let the birdbath sit a full 48 hours before moving or filling it with water. If water seeps out, empty it and let the birdbath dry completely. Then coat the bowl with a bird-safe sealer, such as GBS Penetrating Sealer®.

www.GardenGateMagazine.com — *the* YEAR IN GARDENING — 291

did you know...

Make sure the clamp grips the faucet handle.

Provide support for the PVC pipe to avoid damaging the faucet.

Faucet extender
Alice and Bruce Roof, Iowa
Alice and Bruce's visually impaired neighbor had a raised bed that extended 5 feet out from the house, making it hard to reach the water faucet. So Bruce came up with the fix you see in the illustration above. Using a clamp, he attached a piece of straight 1⅞-inch-diameter radiator hose, found at automotive stores, to a length of 1½-inch PVC pipe that reaches the edge of the bed. If you can't find radiator hose, use a 1½-inch rubber coupling found in the plumbing department of the hardware store. Then he slipped the hose over the faucet handle and attached it with another clamp.

Bruce bent a piece of ⅜-inch rebar for a support to keep the PVC pipe from sagging. You can also use a "Y" stake, a notched board or even stacked bricks to keep the pipe level.

No more climbing into the raised bed to turn on the water. A simple twist of the PVC extension does the trick.

Is sewage sludge safe?
Stella Rand, Missouri

Q *What is sewage sludge fertilizer and is it safe to use it on my plants?*

A Sewage sludge (sometimes called "biosolids") is what's left after household and industrial wastes are treated at wastewater treatment plants. Milorganite® is an example of a sewage sludge fertilizer. It's great for your plants because it's an organic fertilizer that contains nutrients that they need. Organic fertilizers last longer in the soil than inorganic ones and encourage soil bacteria that help keep soil healthy.

You may have heard that sewage sludge fertilizer can contain harmful heavy metals and pathogens that can build up in soil. But the Environmental Protection Agency has set strict limits on these to make these fertilizers safe to use even on food crops.

If you prefer, you have other organic choices. Sea Rich™, a fish-based product, comes in a liquid form that can be sprayed on plants or watered into the soil. Seed meals, such as cottonseed meal, soybean meal and corn-byproduct-based fertilizers like Wow!® are also great organic fertilizers. Look for these and other organic products at www.gardensalive.com.

Easy leaf cleanup
Jeff Bruner, Maryland
Big leaves, such as sycamore and maple, mat down over the winter. This can kill grass and other plants. But those big leaves take up a lot of space in compost bins or leaf bags. Jeff rakes his leaves to the parking strip by the street. Then he runs over them with his lawn mower, and the shredded leaves shoot onto the sidewalk. The hard surface makes it easy to sweep up the fragments. If you're filling a lawn waste bag, you can get more leaves in each bag this way. And shredded leaves break down faster in a compost pile than unshredded ones do. You can even use the shredded leaves as mulch. If one pass with the mower isn't enough, rake the leaves back in the grass and go over them again with the mower before sweeping them up.

Shower cap bootie
Judy Wingfield, Illinois
Judy found that those complimentary hotel shower caps work just as well on your feet as on your head. Whenever she takes a break from gardening to come inside, she slips a shower cap over each shoe. They're just the right size and easy to put on and take off.

First year
Cut out dead or crossing branches.

Second year
Keep thinning out the oldest branches so light can reach the plant's center.

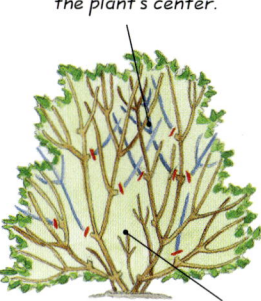

Third year
Remove old and crossing branches.

Cut ⅓ of the oldest branches.

New growth

Unshearing a shrub
Margaret White, Kansas

Q The forsythia hedge at my house has been pruned into a tight, boxy shape. Is there any way to "unshear" these plants for a more natural look?

A Sure. If you don't like the formal look or the work involved in maintaining it, it's simple to restore your forsythias to a more relaxed shape.

Because of all the dead branches on an older, established plant, sometimes it's best to just cut the plant to the ground and start over. Forsythia is tough, and will send out new stems from the base. It'll take three or four years for it to get as big as it was, but it'll start blooming again the year after you cut it back. But if you don't want the whole hedge cut down at once, the three illustrations above show how to simply remove some of the oldest stems each year for three years.

After flowering is done, use a bypass pruner, lopper or pruning saw to remove any dead or crossing branches from the plant. Then cut a few of the oldest stems as close to the ground as possible. This will loosen up the overall shape and allow light into the middle to encourage new growth there.

By year three your plants will have a much more natural shape.

Handling hardpan
Elizabeth Dresser, Connecticut

Q I found a hardpan about 3 inches underneath the surface of my small garden. What can I do with it?

A It depends on how thick this layer of hard, condensed soil is. You're lucky if it's only a few inches thick. In that case, you can break through it using a broadfork or a spade. Work in lots of compost, manure or peat to improve the drainage and soil structure and add nutrients. You'll need to continue amending your soil for several years to break it up.

You're more likely to have hardpan if your soil is acid or contains lots of clay. Some gardeners can have several feet of hardpan to contend with. In that case, you could amend the soil for years without much improvement.

Instead, build a raised bed above the hardpan. Then you can grow almost anything in your nice, well-drained soil.

product pick

Watering spout

With this new watering spout it's easy to have a watering can every place you need one. Just screw the spout onto an empty 1- or 2-liter bottle and you're ready to water. At first glance the bottle seemed awkward, but we found the arch of the handle and the length of the spout balanced out the heavy bottle just fine. The 13½-inch-long spout pours a steady stream without dripping and gets the water or liquid fertilizer just where you want it.

Bottom line Made of durable plastic, this spout makes watering a breeze.
Source Gardener's Supply at 888-833-1412 or www.gardeners.com
Price $14.95 for a set of 2 blue spouts

did you know... (CONTINUED)

Materials and tools
- 1 2-ft.-x-8-ft. wooden lattice panel
- 2 1¼-in. wood screws
- 2 2x2 24-in. stakes
- 2 8-ft. furring strips
- 12 ¾-in. wood screws
- Drill and ⅛-in. bit

Attach the trellis to the fascia under the gutter.

Place a ¾-in. screw about every 2 ft. to attach furring strips.

Easy pickings
Joe Kinderman, Indiana

Tomatoes grow like crazy on the south side of Joe's house. And the trellis he built, at left, helps him make the most of that sunny, tomato-friendly spot. It holds the vines away from the wall so they get more sun, and it prevents moisture damage to the siding. Plus, Joe found that if he places the trellis at an angle, there's more space behind it for him to reach his tomato harvest. The base of the trellis is about 1 foot further out than the top.

To make this trellis, you need the materials and tools in the box above left. Attach the lattice panel to the furring strips with ¾-inch wood screws. Predrilling the holes will make it easier to drive the screws in and keep the wood from splitting.

Attach the top of the trellis to the fascia of the roof with the 1¼-in. screws. Then pound the stakes into the ground to match the angle of the trellis. That way the trellis legs will be parallel to the stakes and easier to attach. You can tie or screw the stake and leg together. Now you're ready to grow tomatoes on a trellis, just as Joe does.

Portable shade
Donna Futrell, Montana

Too much time in the sun isn't good for Donna, as she's allergic to it. But that doesn't stop her from getting out and weeding her flower bed — she just brings along an umbrella. Donna's big canvas patio umbrella sits near her outdoor furniture in a cast-iron stand. When she wants to work in the garden, she tips the stand on its edge and rolls it, umbrella and all, over to the garden. The open umbrella creates a good-sized island of shade for her to work in. And if it's too windy to open the umbrella, she just weeds another day.

Banana soothie
Donna Ponce, Virginia

When bugs bite, go bananas! It may sound a little crazy, Donna says, but she rubs the inside of a fresh banana peel on mosquito bites and

---

Use this lumber for projects that come in direct contact with soil, such as posts or fences.

Lumber with this label is best for above-ground projects, such as railings and decks.

Veggie-safe lumber?
Sandy Palladino, Texas

Q *Are the new types of treated lumber safe to use in my vegetable garden?*

A Yes, the pressure-treated wood sold since 2004 is safe to use near your edible plants. The EPA banned the sale of the older CCA-treated lumber because of the arsenic it leached into surrounding soil. (It's still available for commercial use.) The new preservatives have no hazardous or carcinogenic ingredients. Because of their higher copper content, you can expect to pay 15 to 35 percent more for the new wood than for CCA-treated wood. Manufacturers produce wood with different levels of preservative for different uses. Labels like those above are stapled on the ends of boards to show their appropriate uses.

---

294 the YEAR IN GARDENING www.GardenGateMagazine.com

product pick

Smellkiller Zilosoap

Onions and garlic fresh from the garden taste great. But having their odor on your hands hours later isn't so good. Get rid of odors with this new product, the Smellkiller™ Zilosoap®. The metal disc, made of high-grade stainless steel, really did remove the smell of onion when we tried it. It works on any odor that might stay on your hands.

Use the nubby plastic case that surrounds the disc to scrub your dirty hands. And the little fingernail brush on the corner will spruce up your nails, too. Zilosoap comes in four colors: blue (shown), red, yellow and black.

Bottom line This device cleans and refreshes your hands — it's worth having around.
Source Frieling at 704-329-5100 or www.frieling.com; Garden Gate Store at www.GardenGateStore.com
Price $12

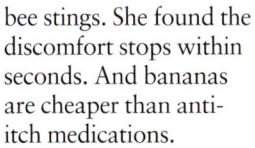

---

bee stings. She found the discomfort stops within seconds. And bananas are cheaper than anti-itch medications.

As with many folk remedies, no serious studies have been done. But we talked to Ara DerMarderosian, a researcher in pharmacognosy with the University of Rhode Island, and he says there is some science behind it. He's even used banana peels himself with success. Bananas contain polysaccharides (complex carbohydrates) and sugar. Polysaccharides soothe and the sugar has mild anti-microbial properties. So the next time you come in from the garden with a bug bite, wash the area first with soap and water, then rub it with a fresh banana peel.

Soothe sore muscles
Diane Johnson, Minnesota

It's not uncommon to get bumps and bruises out in the garden. Diane makes a homemade gel pack to help ease the pain. All you need is a couple of quart-sized zip-top bags, some water and the moisture crystals you add to your potting mix. Add one teaspoon of the crystals to the plastic bag. Then pour in two cups of cold water and seal the bag. In a few minutes you have a slushy pack for sore muscles. For a thicker consistency, use a tablespoon of crystals.

You can store the pack in the refrigerator. But first, slip another zip-top bag over the pack and seal it to avoid any leaking.

Feed veggies with manure
John Walker, Washington

Q *How far ahead of planting time should I work chicken manure into my vegetable beds?*
A Chicken manure is a great fertilizer for vegetable or flower gardens. Bagged manure products you find at the store probably have already been composted and are ready to use.

If you want to use fresh manure, you'll need to compost it for 1 to 3 months before adding it to the garden. Fresh manure can burn young seedlings and may contain disease organisms, plus it usually smells bad. Spread partly composted manure on the garden in fall. Then in spring, come back and work it into the soil.

Don't apply any kind of fresh manure to a vegetable garden within 60 days of harvesting the produce because it could have diseases like salmonella and *E. coli*. And, always wash fresh produce before you eat it.

Soften your hands while you work
Carolyn Neff, Texas

Gardening can be hard on your hands, but Carolyn has found a way to prevent them from getting dry and cracked after all that hard work. Before putting on her garden gloves, she rubs some hand cream on, especially around the cuticles. The hand cream softens her hands while she gardens. This works best if you're doing lighter chores like deadheading or pulling a few weeds — something that won't get much dirt or grit inside your gloves.

did you know... (CONTINUED)

Ticks don't wash out

Ticks are one of the hazards of working outside. Besides being unpleasant, some ticks carry Lyme disease. If you thought laundering your clothes would take care of any hitchhikers, think again. A scientist from the Agricultural Research Service recently found that ticks can make it through the wash cycle. His tests revealed that most lone star ticks (Amblyomma americanum) and deer ticks (Ixodes scapularis) survived various water temperatures and detergent types. They can even survive the "no heat" setting on the dryer. The good news is, after an hour tumbling on the high heat setting, all the ticks of both species died.

Millipede invasion!
Phyl Bates, Iowa

Q We've been seeing armies of millipedes trying to enter our house. How can we eliminate them?

A Unlike termites, millipedes don't eat any parts of buildings, so they're mainly just nuisance pests. They find their way into your house as they're looking for food and a place to hide. Millipedes eat rotting wood and plants and find damp, dark places to hide in.

To keep millipedes outdoors, seal cracks in your foundation with caulk and correct moisture problems in your home. Also, keep the area around your foundation clear of inviting places to hide, such as mulch, rocks, grass clippings and leaf litter. When you find millipedes in your house, vacuum or sweep them up and dispose of them.

If you feel you must, you can use residual insecticides, such as Ortho® Home Defense®, to protect your home from insect invaders. Spray outside around the foundation and entry points and inside around the baseboards. You'll need to spray these areas again in three months.

Do mothballs scare snakes?
Ken Kelnum, Oregon

Q I dislike snakes and heard that mothballs will keep them out of the garden. Is this a good idea?

A No, mothballs don't repel snakes. But even if they did, the chemical ingredient in mothballs, naphthalene, is very toxic to both people and animals. A few mothballs in your closet will keep moths away, but only use them according to the package instructions or you can sicken or kill pets and people.

Actually, snakes eat slugs and lots of other garden pests, so they're good to have around. But if you'd rather keep them away, try making your garden less appealing to them. (There really aren't any chemical snake repellents.) Keep the garden clear of logs, boards, rocks or tall, weedy plants. These areas make perfect hiding places for the reptiles.

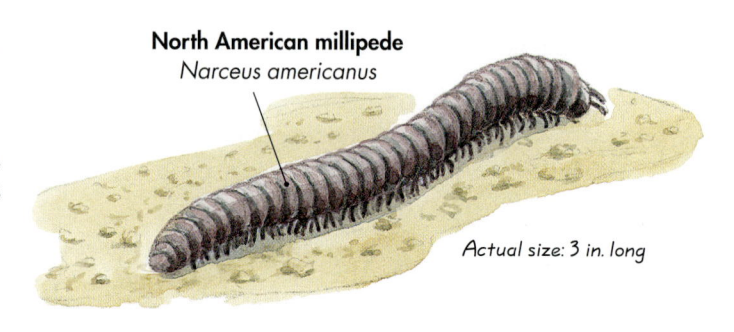

North American millipede
Narceus americanus

Actual size: 3 in. long

product pick

Mini circlehoe

Make weeding easier with the Mini circlehoe®. At 11 inches long, it's easy to handle and fits neatly into your pocket or garden tote. The 2-inch-diameter circular head is made of forged carbon steel and powder coated, so it won't rust. If you've tried the bigger version of this tool, you know it's sharpened on the inside of the circle. As you pull it toward you, it slices through the soil just below the surface like the one in the inset at left. It's great for getting into tight spaces without damaging the leaves, stems or roots of your favorite plants.

Bottom line It's a small tool that's a big help with weeding.
Source circlehoe at 800-735-4815 or www.circlehoe.com; or Gardening with Ease at 800-966-5119 or www.GardeningWithEase.com
Price $9.95

Attach a foam brush to the yardstick with tape or a rubber band.

Apply herbicide directly to weed leaves only.

Mind the moss!
Janice Ingram, North Carolina

Q I am cultivating a moss lawn. How can I kill the weeds and grass without hurting the moss?

A To save your moss, try applying an herbicide containing glyphosate, such as Roundup®, to just the weeds you want to kill. Instead of spraying it directly on the weeds, spray some on a 1-inch foam brush attached to a yardstick as in the illustration at left. Use a small amount on the brush so it doesn't accidentally drip on the moss. The yardstick lets you dab herbicide directly onto the grass and weed foliage without bending over.

in the news

Little beetles take a big bite
Salt cedar (*Tamarix* spp.) is a big problem in the west. Introduced in the 1800s for erosion control, this shrub escaped into the wild, where it out-competes native species along riverbanks and streams. But scientists with the Agricultural Research Service found a ¼-inch-long beetle from China that helps. Salt cedar leaf beetle (*Diorhabda elongata*), in both its larval and adult form, has chewed its way through hundreds of acres of this shrub in Colorado, Nevada, Utah, Wyoming and most recently, South Dakota. Research done before this insect's wild release showed it was no threat to other plants and so far, that's proven to be the case.

Catnip oil attracts lacewings
It's frustrating to buy beneficial insects, only to have them relocate down the block the minute you release them. You may soon be able to attract them to your yard with a lure. Scientists with the USDA found that a compound derived from catnip (*Nepeta* spp.) called *iridodial*, attracts lacewings (*Chrysopa* spp.) by the dozens. While adult lacewings only feed on pollen and nectar, their offspring are voracious predators of aphids, spider mites and other soft-bodied insects. Iridodial is so potent, a single lure will cover a large area — it takes only 25 milligrams to treat an acre of land. The product is in the final stages of development and should be available within a year.

Lumpy lawn
David Wolf, Wisconsin

Q Nightcrawler worms make small mounds all over my lawn. Is there any way to control them?

A In your lawn and garden, nightcrawlers are a sign of healthy soil, even though they're not native to North America. Their tunneling naturally aerates the soil and helps reduce the buildup of organic material. The small mounds of plant material, soil and castings they leave behind in your lawn are annoying, especially in the spring and fall when there is more rain. Over time, the mounds can make the lawn rough and difficult to mow. Try using a lightweight roller to flatten the lumps or a stiff rake to break them up. It's easier to break up the lumps if they're wet and not dried out. Don't use a roller too frequently because it does compact the soil, which can impact how well the grass grows. You could also use a power rake to break up the mounds in fall or early spring.

Mounds left by worms make the lawn lumpy.

did you know... (CONTINUED)

Foam pipe insulation keeps deer from rubbing tender bark.

Insulate trees from deer damage
Sy Brittma, New York

In early fall, male deer begin to grow new antlers, which are covered in a soft velvet. To get rid of the covering, they rub their antlers on young tree trunks and limbs, damaging the tree in the process.

Sy tried everything to keep the deer away. Finally, he found a solution: Pre-slit foam pipe insulation. It's easy to cut to whatever length you need. And the slit on the side lets you slip the insulation over the trunk, or even the lower branches as you see at left. This insulation comes in various sizes, so measure around your tree trunk before heading to the hardware store. You might want to secure the foam with a couple of pieces of duct tape to keep it from getting pulled off. Sy leaves the insulation on his trees all year to keep deer from nibbling at the bark, and his trees don't have any problems. But if deer are only a problem in your area from time to time, you might want to take the insulation off when it's not needed to prevent splitting, disease or insect problems.

Chipmunk trouble
Claudia Robertson, Ohio

Claudia was having trouble with chipmunks digging up her new plants. She came up with an easy way to keep her plants in the ground: rocks! Claudia uses large river rock, about 2 to 4 inches across. She lays them out in at least two circles around the new transplants like the ones below. The chipmunks stopped digging! Once the plants are established, she removes the stones to use on next year's new plants.

Nesting help
Marijean Hawks, California

With spring around the corner, it won't be long until birds start nesting. Marijean likes to help them out with some items that she'd normally just throw away. She puts dryer lint in one of those mesh bags onions or potatoes come in. To make it easier for birds to remove the lint, use bags with larger holes. Tie the bag shut with twine and leave some extra length so you can tie the bag to a branch or post. Marijean positions the lint bag near her already busy bird bath and feeders. Her feathered neighbors quickly take advantage of the fuzzy stuff to line their nests.

Easy dry gloves
Susie Marcy, Oregon

Gardening after a rainstorm can be pleasant, but it gets your garden gloves very wet. Susie knows just how to dry her gloves quickly — disposable cups! She removes the bottom of two tall plastic or waxed paper cups with scissors. Then she slips her gloves over the narrow top and sets them on a baking rack to air dry. Cutting a V-shaped notch at the mouth of the cup helps air circulate inside the gloves even more.

No more weeds from birdseed
Donna Napier, Arkansas

Tired of having to pull weeds that have sprouted from spilled seed under your birdfeeder? Try Donna's tip. She doesn't cry over spilled birdseed anymore — she microwaves it!

The process is simple: Donna fills a plastic bowl with fresh seed and then covers it with a paper towel so oil from the seeds won't splatter. She microwaves the seed for one minute per pound. When the seed is done "cooking," she lets it cool for several minutes. Then it's ready for the birds. Make sure you only heat the seed you're going to use right away. Microwaving softens the seed coat, making it more vulnerable to rot in storage.

You may have heard that microwaving affects the nutritional value of the seed. At this point, there's no proof that this is true.

Easy deer fence
Sylvina M. Powrie, Michigan

Deer can absolutely destroy a garden, but the fencing used to protect plants can ruin your view. Sylvina found that several green wire tri-fold tomato cages really help. She unfolds the panels to make a fence. The cages are cheaper than other fencing. Plus they're lightweight and easy to move. Two or three 4-foot-tall-by-4½-foot-wide panels are enough to surround her garden. The green wire blends in with the foliage and doesn't distract from the beauty of the flowers. She places the fencing about 3 feet out from the garden. You can even leave the cages out in the winter to protect shrubs. When her husband mows, Sylvina moves the fences but they're easy to put back in place before the deer arrive at dusk.

From shelf to greenhouse
Bill Barnard, NC

Ready-made mini greenhouses can be expensive. But you can make one like Bill's — for practically nothing.

He started with a plastic shelf unit that he wasn't using. Then he called a mattress store and got a twin-sized plastic bag for free. This size is perfect to fit over a 54x 36x18-inch shelf.

For additional space on top, Bill made an arch from flexible PVC. After cutting the 6-ft. sections in half, he attached one piece to the front leg, bent it over the top and attached it to the opposite leg. Then he did the same on the back. To get the bag over the shelf, he cut off one end of the bag. The excess could be anchored with bricks if it got windy. He also slit the side open for access to the plants and ventilation in warm weather.

The cutting done, Bill slipped the mattress bag over the top of the shelf and secured the side opening with spring clamps. See how he clamped it to the legs and along the opening? If you don't have any clamps, clothes pins work, too.

Since Bill is in North Carolina, he keeps plants outside all year round. Where temperatures get below freezing, the plastic isn't enough protection during the coldest months. But it's a great way to grow cool-weather crops, such as greens, and harden off new seedlings in spring.

Materials and tools
- 1 Plastic shelf unit with four shelves
- 1 Plastic bag from a mattress store
- 10 Spring clamps
- 4 Hose clamps
- 2 6-ft. sections of ½-in. flexible PVC pipe

Attach flexible PVC to the shelf with hose clamps.

On warm days, open this side vent so the greenhouse doesn't overheat.

Secure the mattress bag with spring clamps.

Iris-crunching raccoons
Anneke Hart, Ontario

Q *Raccoons dug up and chewed the foliage of my recently divided iris. They never bothered them before. What's going on?*

A Raccoons will eat lots of different insects, small animals and plants. They were probably attracted to the earthworms, grubs and insects that were brought up when you planted the iris. Raccoons have been known to tear up freshly laid sod for the same reason.

Did you feed your divisions with a fish-based fertilizer after planting? Raccoons love the smell and taste of these products. This would explain the chewed-up iris leaves.

The best raccoon repellents to try are radios, noise makers, lights and barking dogs. But raccoons are smart and quickly grow accustomed to things. If you use a live trap, first check with your local Department of Natural Resources office on the best way to go about it.

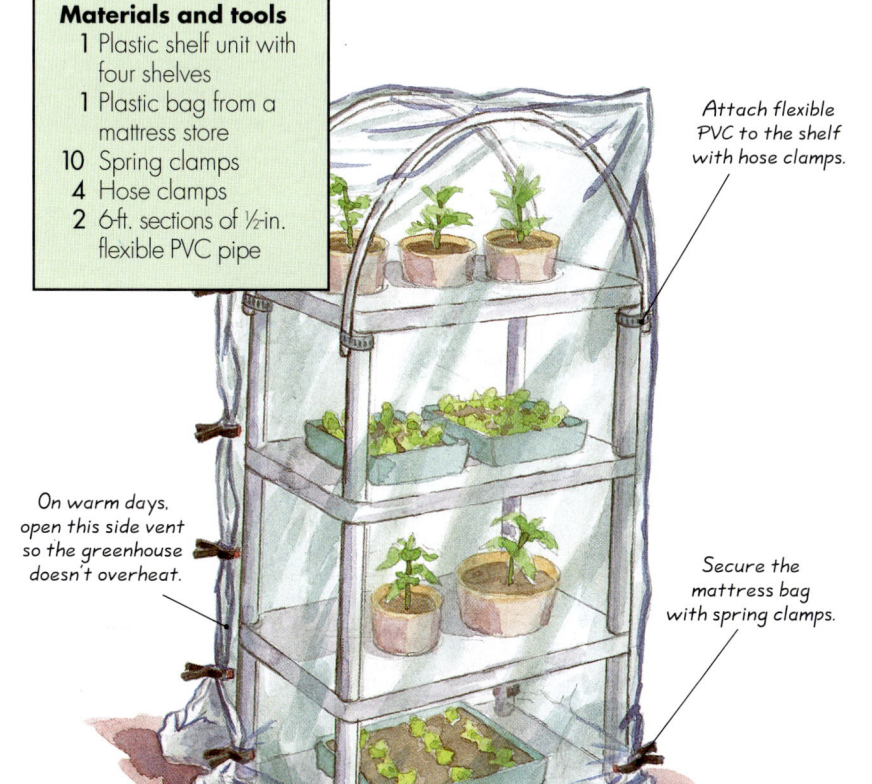

in the news

Are earthworms bad?
We've always thought of earthworms and compost worms as partners in gardening; these familiar friends are good for the soil. But most are introduced species that have become a real problem for our northern forests. Earthworms quickly devour the leaf litter that covers forest floors, depriving many creatures, from bacteria and fungi to small birds and amphibians, of food and shelter. Even native tree seedlings have difficulty germinating.

The most important thing you can do to help is to throw leftover bait worms in the trash when you're done fishing. For more information, visit Great Lakes Worm Watch online at www.greatlakesworm watch.org.

did you know... (CONTINUED)

Replace the avocado flesh with seed-starting medium.

Skin deep
Patricia Rice Jerez, Missouri

Instead of starting seeds in eggshells, Patricia uses avocado skins. They're easier to work with because they're bigger and easier to handle. After she's scooped out the flesh of each avocado, she saves the skins. When she's ready to start seeds, she takes the skin "bowl" and punches a few small holes in the bottom for drainage. She fills the skin with seed-starting mix. Then she adds a few of her favorite seeds and places the whole thing in a clear plastic "clam shell" container. Containers like these are usually found at a deli or sandwich shop. The containers above hold one or two avocados.

Holding pool
Rita Hosier, Iowa

Every so often Rita redesigns one of her perennial beds, and she needs a place to hold the plants for a few days while the work gets done. Her solution? A child-sized wading pool. Rita places the plastic pool in the shade and adds a little potting mix to the bottom. She adds water to the mix until it's moist but not soggy. As Rita digs plants from the border, she puts them in the pool, fills in around them with mix and waters again. Now she's free to work on the bed without worrying about losing her plants.

When the bed is ready, she puts the plants back in the ground. She's found her method keeps plants growing strong even when she's redoing a bed in midsummer.

Plant tie up
Dave Paquette, New Hampshire

Dave keeps floppy plants standing tall with a little help from other plants. He cuts a long daisy stem, removes the leaves and the flower and then ties the stem around leaning plants. For a big clump, you might have to tie a couple of stems together. This method works well for Dave's daisies and peonies. The green stems are supple enough to tie in a knot but strong enough to provide support. He's found that bindweed vine works well, too, and the stems are a lot longer. (You're pulling bindweed anyway — why not make it useful?) The green stems blend in with the foliage for a while, but as they turn brown, you may notice them more. Big foliage will cover the fading stems. Or throw the faded portion into the compost pile and replace it with another piece.

Jug of twine
Joyce Jones, Washington

Joyce was tired of her ball of twine unwinding while she worked in the garden, so she made an easy twine dispenser. On the side of a plastic quart-sized milk jug, she cut a square flap just big enough for the ball of twine to fit through. (You could use a gallon jug, too.) Then she stuffed the twine inside the milk jug.

To keep the end of the twine handy and prevent tangling, Joyce poked a hole in the jug cap with a nail. Then she threaded the twine through the hole and screwed on the cap.

The jug handle makes it easy to tote around or hang from a belt. And if Joyce forgets to take the twine inside, it won't get wet in the rain.

Punch the nail from the inside to make it easier to pull the twine through the hole.

Pull the flap open to put the twine inside.

A cluster of bamboo stakes adds height to a

Bamboo stake storage
Frank Bondzinski, Illinois

Like many gardeners, Frank has accumulated a large bundle of bamboo stakes. Instead of storing the unused stakes in the garage, Frank likes to form them into a garden ornament like the one above. His stakes fit nicely into a bare spot in his garden. But it's also an easy way to add height to a bed that needs it. Bamboo is perfect for Japanese-inspired gardens and works well with minimalist styles.

It's easier to poke the stakes into the ground if you loosen the soil with a shovel first. Frank criss-crosses his stakes but you can create your own designs. Variations in height make the arrangement look intentional. The added benefit is that whenever you need a stake, it's right there, saving you a trip to the garden shed.

Cutting corners
Helen Rodish, Iowa

Small seeds, like those of flowering tobacco or celosia, can be hard to handle. Getting the correct amount of seed in the right place is a challenge. Helen tried planting small seeds with tweezers, but that was too slow. After a little experimenting, she found a way to control the number and direction of the seed right from the packet. She cuts the top and side off the packet, creating a "trough." Notice the V-shape of the packet in the illustration below? This makes it easier to direct the flow. If seeds stick, tap the packet gently with your finger. When too many come out at once, Helen has a walnut pick handy. The sharp point is just right for pushing seeds where they need to go.

The open side makes it easier to see where the seed is going.

in the news

A formula to keep deer away
The U.S. Department of Agriculture Wildlife Services found that deer will walk right by plants that are coated with hydrolyzed casein, a milk protein, unless they're really desperate. You'll find this protein in powdered baby formulas, such as Nutramigen®, Alimentum® or Pregestimil®.

To try this yourself, add 1 to 2 tablespoons of white glue, such as Elmer's,® to one gallon of water and spray it on the plant. Then immediately sprinkle on the powdered formula. The glue holds the formula in place through the rain and lasts about a month.

What's with the hay?
If you use hay as mulch, be careful. Last summer an organic farmer in Virginia lost acres of veggies destined for the farmers' market. Turns out the hay he used to mulch his fields had been sprayed with a herbicide while it was growing. The residue proved toxic. So be sure to ask if the fields were sprayed before you take any hay home.

Much ado about mulch
A recent article in the *Journal of Environmental Horticulture* looked at years of mulch research to see what types work best. In a nutshell, for retaining moisture, moderating soil temperatures, suppressing weeds and disease and adding nutrients to soil, organic mulches worked better than plastics or landscape fabric. Bark, hay, manure, grass clippings, sawdust and others did the best job helping plants and soil stay healthy. When it comes to erosion control, ground covers work best, but if that's not possible, even a thin layer of organic mulch is better than landscape fabric.

did you know... (CONTINUED)

product picks

Noisebuster

Power equipment makes short work of tedious jobs like weeding or mowing, but those machines are noisy. Protect your hearing with the new Noisebuster® safety earmuffs. Put them on when you use lawn mowers, string trimmers, leaf blowers or any other noisy engine. They really make a difference. We tried them out with a lawn mower, and the earmuffs produced a sound like white noise, which is a lot easier on the ears than the roar of the engine. There's even a headphone jack so you can listen to your favorite tunes while you mow.

Bottom line Protecting your hearing is important, and these earmuffs really work.
Source Noisebuster at www.noisebuster.net or 877-226-1944; 21st Century Goods at www.21st-century-goods.com or 866-999-8422
Price $149

Simply Safe

When it comes to keeping outdoor furniture and hardscaping clean, you don't want something that might harm you, your plants or the environment. Try Simply Safe™ all-purpose cleaner. The formula is pH neutral, biodegradable and has no solvents, phosphates or bleach. This cedar tabletop was grimy until we scrubbed it with Simply Safe. It looked a lot better without the accumulated dirt and dust of the season. Plus, the fresh scent doesn't make you feel like grabbing a mask while you clean.

Bottom line This is a good buy. It's safe, smells nice and doesn't cost a fortune.
Source Local grocery or discount stores
Price $2 to $3 for a 32-oz. spray bottle

Add pipe insulation to the handle for a comfortable grip.

New life for an old can
Rita Bush-Anderson, Illinois
When the handle on her wheeled garbage can broke, Rita had an idea. With a little creative cutting, she turned the old garbage can into a "garden can." She takes her garden can with her while weeding and rolls it to the compost pile when she's done.

To remodel the can, Rita used a permanent marker to draw a line like the dotted one on the illustration above. She followed the lip edge at the back of the can. Then she dropped the line down about 8 inches along the side and front. For a handle, she drew a rectangle centered on the back. Rita used a utility knife to cut away the excess, following the lines she'd drawn. You could make the handles more comfortable by slipping on some slit pipe insulation.

No more lost plants
Carole Greenberg, Oregon
Do you forget where you've planted bulbs and slow-to-emerge perennials? Carole did, and she was tired of accidentally digging them up or stepping on the tender new growth. She tried marking plants with those white plastic tags but didn't like having white dots all over her garden.

Finally she thought of chopsticks. They're inexpensive, hold up well outside and are easy to find in a large package at the store.

To make the chopsticks decorative as well as functional, Carole dips them in latex paint to match the color of her outdoor furniture. Then she inserts the unpainted end into a foam block while the paint dries, and they're ready to go. When the plants are up, Carole often leaves the chopsticks in place. They last for several years even when she leaves them in the ground.

Mini-blind notes
Norma Musser, Pennsylvania
Your garden's at its peak and you notice a coreopsis needs dividing or a hosta should be moved. But that's not always the best time to do those chores. Norma makes notes on short pieces of old mini-blind so she won't forget what to do. Then she sticks the pieces in the ground near the plants needing attention, leaving just the edges showing.

Scum buster
Jim Franklin, California
Removing debris from ponds helps keep the water clean and clear. Jim recycled an old garden fork into a pond skimmer to make this job easier. To make one yourself, all you need is the garden fork, a few zip ties and ¼-inch hardware cloth.

A 12-inch-square piece of hardware cloth is big enough for a fork that's 9 inches wide and 12 inches long. You can adjust the size of the hardware cloth based on the size of your fork.

To assemble a strainer like the one below, lay the square of hardware cloth on top of the business end of the fork. Then thread a couple of zip ties through the mesh onto each tine. Keep the hardware cloth secure with an extra zip tie on either side of the handle on the fork shoulder. Now you're ready to clean the pond!

Next spring, the mini-blind sticking out of the soil is a reminder. Since the inked end was in the soil, it hasn't faded and Norma knows just what to do with her plant.

Secure the hardware cloth with two zip ties on each tine.

beneficials you should know

Actual size: 6 to 13 inches

Lady beetles

Seven-spotted lady beetle *Coccinella septempunctata*
Actual size: ⁵⁄₁₆ in. Found in most northeastern and north central states.

Convergent lady beetle *Hippodamia convergens*
Actual size: ¼ in. Found from southern Canada to South America.

Red-spotted black lady beetle *Chilocorus kuwanae*
Actual size: ⅛ in. Found in most states east of the Mississippi River.

IDENTIFICATION Next to butterflies, lady beetles are probably some of the most well-known insects. One of these hungry creatures can eat as many as 5,000 aphids over its lifetime, in both its larval and adult stages. So this is an insect you want in your garden! There are 450 species of lady beetles in North America. Most are red or red-orange with black spots, like the seven-spotted and convergent lady beetles at right. But you may also find some that are black or brown like the red-spotted black lady beetle.

Though many species dine primarily on aphids, some have a taste for scale, spider mites and other sap-feeding insects — pests you don't want in your garden.

Be careful if you handle lady beetles. They release a smelly fluid from their joints when frightened. It won't harm you, but it does smell bad.

LIFE CYCLE Female lady beetles lay clusters of tiny eggs in spring on plants near prey, like aphids. One female can lay up to 1,000 eggs in a season. The larvae that emerge look very different than their parents. With long bodies, bumpy skin and voracious appetites, they're sometimes compared to tiny alligators. After several molts, the larvae pupate and become adults. Adults live up to a year. They overwinter in leaf litter and under rocks and bark.

Some folks mail-order lady beetles to release in their gardens. But often the beetles fly away before finishing their job. Instead, try encouraging local populations to make your garden their home by avoiding insecticide use and leaving a little garden debris on the ground for overwintering sites. If that fails, try *wheast*, a mix of whey and yeast that's used as a food supplement by people who raise beneficial insects. Sprayed on plants, it provides additional nutrients to lady beetles when prey is hard to find. You can get this product from Planet Natural at 800-289-6656 or www.planetnatural.com. ☐

Tiger salamander *Ambystoma tigrinum*

IDENTIFICATION If you have salamanders around, you may never know it — they spend a lot of time in leaf litter and underground burrows. But every night they come out to devour slugs! They also eat snails, worms and other small insects. Adults are black to gray with yellow spots. Spot size and placement varies among individuals. At up to 13 in. long, the tiger salamander is one of the largest of its kind.

Tiger salamanders live anywhere there's a small body of water nearby for breeding. They're found throughout the central and eastern United States, southern Canada and central Mexico.

LIFE CYCLE In early spring, often before the ice has even melted, female salamanders lay 30 to 50 eggs in underwater vegetation. The young are born with gills and live in the water until summer when they metamorphose, or change, so they can live on land. Most adults overwinter in their burrows. Tiger salamanders can live up to 20 years.

When frightened, adults secrete a milky toxin from glands on their back and tail. Always wash your hands after handling a salamander because this toxin is slightly poisonous.

To attract tiger salamanders to your garden, provide undisturbed areas where they can dig burrows and some leaf litter for them to hide in. Leave a pile of dead leaves in the corner of your yard. It will provide shelter for salamanders and add nutrients to the soil as it breaks down. ☐

Spined assassin bug *Sinea diadema*

Actual size: ½ to ¾ in.

IDENTIFICATION Spined assassin bug may have a sinister-sounding name but it's actually one of the good guys. There are more than 100 species of assassin bug. Although some species are pests, this is one of the most common beneficials in the family. It's found in central and southern North America and Mexico. Adults are ½ to ¾ in. long, and brown with long legs, a broad flat abdomen and a narrow head with large eyes. The segmented beak is used to spear and inject venom into prey. When not in use, the beak folds away under the bug's body. As you might guess, the spined assassin bug does have spines. You'll see them on its head, thorax and front legs. This hungry predator eats a wide variety of pests, including aphids, caterpillars, leafhoppers and larvae of all kinds. These bugs are generally harmless to humans but if handled roughly, they can inflict a painful bite.

LIFE CYCLE Eggs of spined assassin bug that were laid in fall hatch as temperatures warm in spring. Nymphs, about ¼ in. long, look like miniature adults and start looking for something to eat right away. After several molts, the nymphs mature and mate, then females begin laying eggs. The first generation lives about two months and then dies. The second generation follows the same cycle, living until late fall. Eggs laid by these females will hatch next spring.

You may already have spined assassin bugs in your yard since they are fairly common. Give these hungry predators a variety of blooming plants to hide in and they'll help you out by hunting for insect prey. To be sure they stick around, avoid using pesticides. ☐

pests to watch

Look for black spots surrounded by yellow rings.

Groundhogs
Marmota monax

IDENTIFICATION Punxsutawney Phil may be cute, but a wild groundhog in your garden can be a problem. Though dandelion greens, clover and grasses are some of their favorites, garden vegetables and fruits often disappear when these furry pests are around. Their enthusiastic burrowing can cause nearby plants to suffer, too.

Sometimes called woodchucks, groundhogs are 16 to 27 in. long with dark red-brown hair, short, bushy tails and sharp teeth.

Widely distributed in North America, groundhogs are particularly common in the eastern United States up into northern Quebec and Ontario. In the West, they are found in Alaska and southern Yukon and Northwest Territories.

LIFE CYCLE Groundhogs can live up to 10 years However, the average life span in the wild is probably less since they are on the menu for coyotes, owls and hawks.

Each spring, females give birth to a litter of four to six helpless kits. They grow quickly and spend all summer binging on greens to put on weight for winter hibernation. Around October they retire to their dens and sleep until spring. But how do they know when to wake up? The groundhog's internal clock is affected by annual changes in daylight.

CONTROL To keep groundhogs from settling in your garden, clear areas with tall grass and remove brush piles, where they like to hide. Groundhogs are timid and can be frightened away by changes in their environment. If you already have groundhogs, try a repellent, such as Messina Wildlife Management's Groundhog Repellent. It smells and tastes bad to the groundhog. ☐

Groundhog

Tar spot
Rhytisma spp.

IDENTIFICATION When you think of fall, you also think of the rich red, yellow and orange leaves of maple trees. There's nothing more frustrating than having the beauty of that foliage marred by big black spots. If your maple tree looks like it's been splattered with black paint, it probably has tar spot, a fungal disease. There are several different species of this fungus, but the most common are *Rhytisma acerinum* and *R. punctatum*.

Tar spot starts out as ⅛-in.-diameter pale yellow spots in late spring to early summer. By mid- to late summer, you'll notice black spots inside the yellow ones. The "tar" is raised above the leaf surface, giving it a three-dimensional feel. Spots caused by *R. acerinum* grow to about an inch while spots caused by *R. punctatum* stay much smaller. Tar spot doesn't kill the tree, but it just doesn't look good, and heavy infestations can cause premature leaf drop.

CONTROL The fungus that causes tar spot overwinters on leaf debris, and spores are spread by the wind in spring. There are fungicides available but they're difficult to use and don't work very well. Your best bet for controlling this fungus is to rake up the fallen leaves in the fall and send them away in the yard waste. ☐

Maple leaves

Four-lined plant bug
Poecilocapsus lineatus

IDENTIFICATION The four-lined plant bug is one of the most common pests in the garden. It likes to feed on more than 250 species of ornamental, woody and edible plants. In urban areas the four-lined plant bug is usually found on perennials and shrubs.

Damage from this pest starts in late spring when plant foliage has emerged and eggs hatch. Nymphs look like tiny adults but are bright red to orange with black wing pads. Over a period of about six weeks and several molts, the four-lined plant bug gradually changes color. Adults are yellow to chartreuse with, you guessed it, four black lines running down the wing covers on their backs. Since mature bugs have wings, they move from plant to plant, feeding for about a month until they mate. After mating, the female cuts a small slit in a plant stem to make a winter home for her cluster of eggs. By midsummer most of the adults have died. There's just one generation of four-lined plant bugs each year.

DAMAGE You'll know four-lined plant bugs are around if you see tiny round sunken spots that are brown to translucent on the foliage of your plants. With heavy damage, the leaves might be distorted or curled.

Damage is often mistaken for leaf spot disease. But foliar disease spots from fungi or bacteria are irregular, and the marks left by the four-lined plant bugs are almost uniform in shape and size.

CONTROL What can you do to get rid of this hungry insect? Start checking your garden in spring for damage. Since the nymphs can't fly, their damage tends to be clustered in one area. And it's easier to get rid of them while they're less mobile. But whether you have nymphs or adults, the most environmentally friendly way to remove these unwelcome pests is with a few sprays of insecticidal soap. ☐

Actual size ¼ to ½ in. long

6 weeds to know

Velvetleaf
Abutilon theophrasti

IDENTIFICATION Velvetleaf, also called "Indian mallow" or "butter print," was introduced to North America from southern Asia in the 1700s — now you'll find it in all of the continental United States and well into Canada. This annual may grow 7 ft. tall or more. The stems and 2- to 6-in.-long heart-shaped leaves are covered with fine hairs. When you crush the leaves, they give off an unpleasant odor. Velvetleaf is so tall, with such large leaves, it shades out smaller plants around it. And the aggressive roots steal moisture and nutrients.

From July to October, five-petaled yellow-orange flowers bloom. They're replaced by the teacup-shaped seedpods you see in the illustration. One plant produces thousands of seeds that can remain viable for more than 50 years.

FAVORITE CONDITIONS Full sun is where you'll usually find velvetleaf growing, but it'll grow in part shade, too. Most often found in regularly cultivated areas like vegetable gardens, it's also at home in perennial beds, along roads and in waste areas.

CONTROL The simplest control is to hoe small seedlings out. It's easy to pull young velvetleaf plants. A taproot makes it harder to pull a mature velvetleaf, but you can just cut these big plants off at the soil line and they won't sprout again. No matter how you get rid of it, since this weed spreads by seed, make sure to remove it before any seeds ripen.

Most broadleaf herbicides will also kill velvetleaf. But you'll need to apply it several times over the growing season because seeds germinate all summer. That means you'll find seedlings from spring well into fall. ❑

Seedpods

Spotted knapweed
Centaurea maculosa

IDENTIFICATION From early July through August, spotted knapweed produces numerous pink and purple flowers. This weed gets its name from the black spots on the small leaves, or bracts, at the base of each flower. Spotted knapweed is an aggressive perennial that lives three to seven years. The first year, you'll spot a low rosette of leaves. In following years, it grows 2 to 4 ft. tall. Each mature plant can produce more than 1,000 seeds per year. These can remain viable in the soil at least five years.

FAVORITE CONDITIONS Found almost everywhere in North America except the Deep South, desert areas and the Rocky Mountains, this weed prefers spots that have been tilled and then left undisturbed. You'll find it in perennial beds, shrub borders and fencerows.

Ground ivy
Glechoma hederacea

IDENTIFICATION Ground ivy, also known as creeping Charlie, is a perennial that spreads by seeds and above-ground runners. Each runner can be several feet long, with many leaf nodes along the stem. Wherever these nodes touch the soil they take root quickly to form thick, dense mats.

In midspring to early summer, purple flowers completely cover the plant. The foliage is small with a scalloped edge and if crushed, it gives off a strong minty smell.

FAVORITE CONDITIONS You'll find ground ivy's at home in lawns or areas that are occasionally tilled. Moist, shaded spots are perfect for it, but it'll tolerate almost anything, from full sun to dry, compacted soil.

CONTROL In flower and vegetable gardens, pulling and hoeing are effective. Just make sure to pick up all of the pieces. Any part that's left behind can grow a new plant.

It spreads quickly in well-drained, light-textured soil and full sun or part shade.

CONTROL This plant is *allelopathic*, meaning it releases a toxin that inhibits the growth of nearby plants. So you definitely want to get rid of it. Remove small infestations by digging or pulling while the soil is moist. But make sure to remove the entire root or this pest will quickly grow back.

In areas where it's well established, you'll need to use an herbicide. Either a selective product, such as 2,4-D, or a non-selective one, such as Roundup®, can be used. After the initial treatment, monitor the area to control any missed plants or new seedlings. Since the seeds live in the soil for years, you'll have to pull occasional seedlings for quite a while. ❑

Once you get ground ivy under control, you'll want to keep it from creeping back into gardens from neighboring areas. It's a good idea to maintain a strip of bare soil around your garden where you can patrol occasionally and remove runners before they spread.

Since ground ivy can't grow as fast in tall grass, set your lawn mower blade high. You can also use selective herbicides that won't harm your lawn. Look for products containing dicamba, such as Acme Trimec® or Weed-B-Gon Lawn Weed Killer2®. Read the instructions, but in severe infestations you may need to make at least two applications about 10 to 14 days apart to get rid of ground ivy. ❑

First year rosette

Second year

Annual bluegrass
Poa annua

IDENTIFICATION Annual bluegrass is one of the first grassy weeds you'll spot in early spring. The seeds sprout in late summer or fall and can continue to grow through a mild winter. In cool regions where the soil stays moist, annual bluegrass grows all season. In hot and dry areas, it usually dies by midsummer. But the bright green tufts of grass are the most noticeable in spring or early summer. In flower or vegetable gardens, this pest can grow to be 6 to 8 in. tall. It'll be shorter in areas where you mow.

FAVORITE CONDITIONS The roots are shallow, so annual bluegrass grows best in damp areas. That means you'll often spot it growing in lawns, flower beds and other areas that stay moist or are irrigated. Although it prefers full sun, this weed can also grow in shade.

CONTROL Since annual bluegrass seeds are spread by mowing, foot traffic, birds and cultivating tools, the best control is preventing seed from spreading. And always clean your tools and mower before moving on to another area. Established plants are easy to pull or hoe out, so remove them before they go to seed.

Use at least a 2-in.-thick layer of mulch in borders and gardens to keep annual bluegrass from sprouting. In turf areas raise the mower height to around 2½ to 3 in. to keep your desirable grass tall. Weed seeds are less likely to germinate if they're kept in shade. ☐

Wild parsnip
Pastinaca sativa

IDENTIFICATION This invasive biennial is related to the edible parsnips you may grow in your vegetable garden. Like its cultivated cousin, wild parsnip has a long, white-yellow taproot that is edible. The first year, a rosette of leaves emerges and grows to about 1 ft. tall. Egg-shaped leaflets are in pairs along the stem and are deeply toothed or lobed. During the second year it sends up a thick, grooved flower stalk. Bright yellow flowers in flat clusters, like dill, appear from May to October. Flowering plants may grow as tall as 5 ft. Wild parsnip spreads by seed.

FAVORITE CONDITIONS Wild parsnip grows just about anywhere in North America in fields, ditches, prairies, bike paths, cultivated gardens and even your lawn. Although it prefers full sun and moist to wet soils, it will grow in shade and dry soils, too.

CONTROL Hand digging wild parsnip is the most effective control method. But the deep taproot can make it difficult. If possible, identify and dig up plants when they're in the rosette stage and the tap root is short and easier to dig. Cut or mow flower stalks on mature plants to prevent seeds from forming. Then dig up as much of the plant as you can. Herbicides that contain glyphosate, such as RoundUp®, can be an effective control. Follow label directions. Wear long sleeves, pants and gloves when handling wild parsnip because it exudes a chemical that causes photodermatitis blisters when your skin is exposed to sunlight. These can become very painful and may require medical attention. ☐

Yellow woodsorrel
Oxalis stricta

IDENTIFICATION It's the small, bright-yellow flowers, each with five petals, that are the first thing you notice about yellow woodsorrel. Later, when the petals drop, ¾-in.-long seed pods form. When the pointed pods ripen, they burst, shooting seeds up to 12 ft. away.

Weak, wiry stems grow from a single taproot. Wherever these stems touch the soil, they can take root, creating a dense tangle. Usually a small sprawling weed, yellow woodsorrel can grow to be 20 in. tall and wide if it is propped up by other plants.

Each leaf has three small leaflets that look similar to clover. However, if you examine them closely, each of the yellow woodsorrel leaflets is distinctly heart-shaped. Clover leaflets are much more rounded. And if you bite into a yellow woodsorrel leaf, you'll discover it has a tart taste. This is not a toxic plant, but the high acid content can make it dangerous to eat large quantities.

FAVORITE CONDITIONS This native perennial is found in USDA zones 2 to 11. It prefers lightly cultivated areas, such as perennial borders, but will also grow in lawns. Yellow woodsorrel grows in any type of soil, even the dry cracks in concrete. But you're just as likely to find it growing in potted plants you pick up at the garden center. While this common pest prefers part shade, it grows almost as well in full sun or heavy shade.

CONTROL A taproot makes yellow woodsorrel easy to pull. Or you can simply cut it off below ground with a hoe. And to prevent seeds from reaching the soil and sprouting, spread a 2- to 4-in.-thick layer of mulch around your shrubs and flowers.

Preemergent herbicides, such as Preen®, help prevent seeds from sprouting. Follow label directions and apply them in early spring. In lawns, broadleaf herbicides, such as 2,4-D, work well. For the best control, apply them when the weed is actively growing in spring and summer, before seeds form. ☐

www.GardenGateMagazine.com *the* YEAR IN GARDENING

know YOUR zone

WHAT'S A ZONE AND WHY DOES IT MATTER?

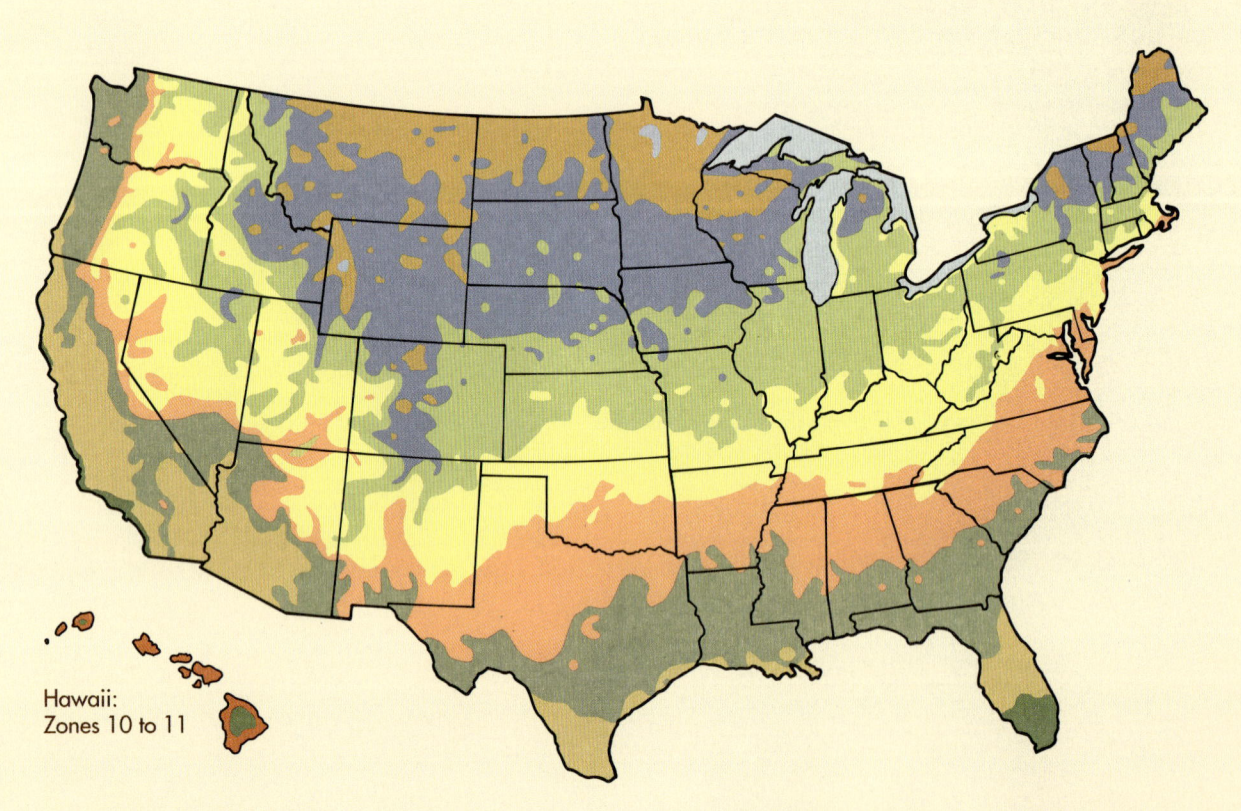

Alaska: Zones 1 to 7

Hawaii: Zones 10 to 11

COLD Hardiness

The USDA cold-hardiness map has long been the authority to help gardeners pick plants that will survive through the winter. It creates zones based on coldest average annual temperatures throughout the United States. A plant's cold-hardiness zone rating indicates where it's likely to survive the winter.

NOTE: For zones in Canada and Mexico, visit www.usna.usda.gov/Hardzone/ushzmap.html.

AVERAGE LOW TEMPERATURE	ZONE
Below -45	1
-40 to -45	2
-30 to -40	3
-20 to -30	4
-10 to -20	5
0 to -10	6

AVERAGE LOW TEMPERATURE	ZONE
10 to 0	7
20 to 10	8
30 to 20	9
40 to 30	10
Above 40	11

Alaska:
Zones 1 to 2

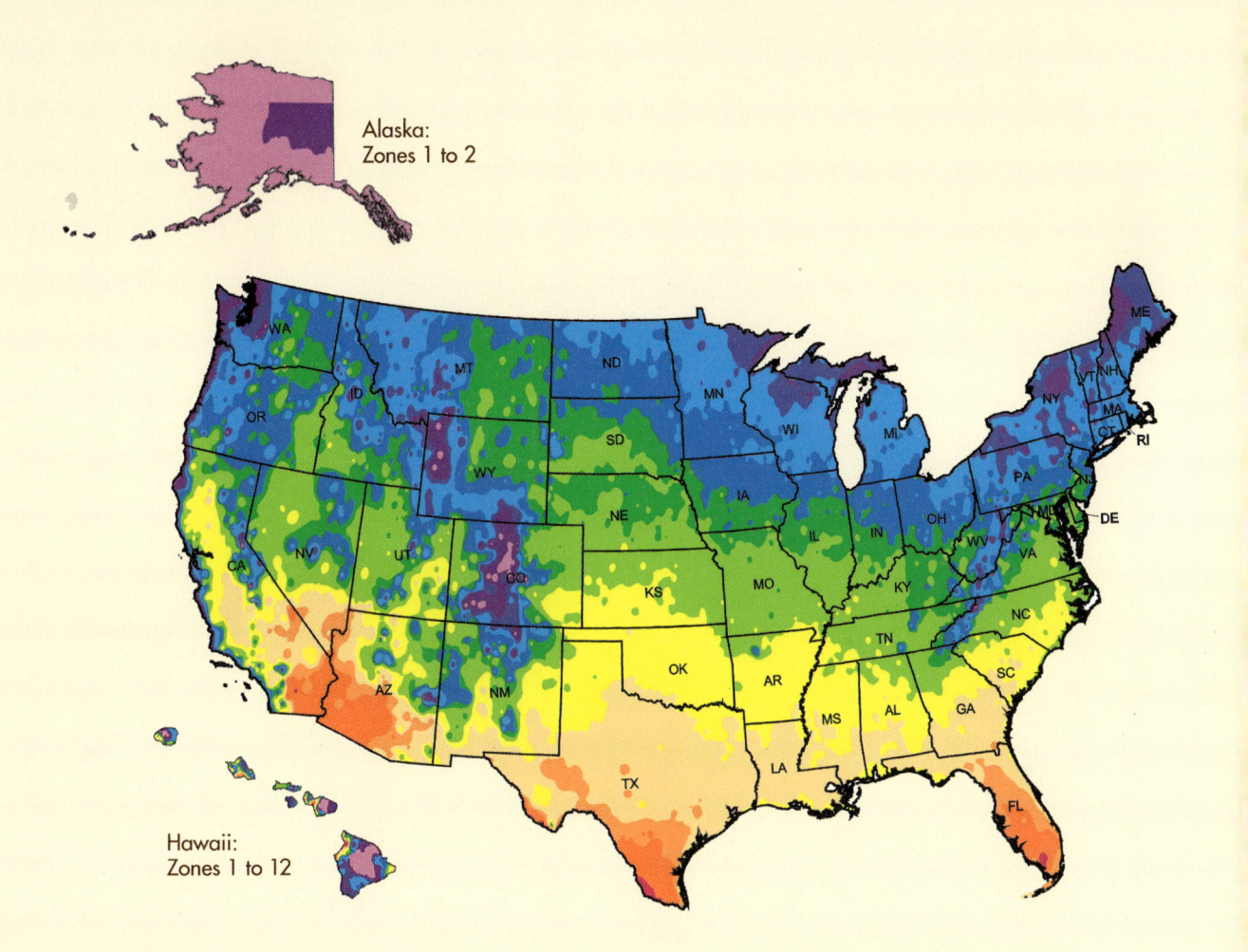

Hawaii:
Zones 1 to 12

DAYS ABOVE 86°	ZONE
Fewer than 1	1
1 to 7	2
7 to 14	3
14 to 30	4
30 to 45	5
45 to 60	6

DAYS ABOVE 86°	ZONE
60 to 90	7
90 to 120	8
120 to 150	9
150 to 180	10
180 to 210	11
More than 210	12

HEAT Tolerance

The American Horticultural Society's heat-zone map can help you determine how plants will cope with heat.

This map of the country is divided into 12 zones to indicate the average number of days in a year when the temperature goes above 86 degrees F. This is the temperature at which plants begin suffering and are unable to process water fast enough to maintain normal functions. Zone 1, the coldest zone, has less than one day. Zone 12, the hottest zone, has more than 210 days above 86 per year.

did you know...

Arbor Day Foundation changes zones

The National Arbor Day Foundation (NADF) has updated its hardiness zone map. Starting with the USDA zone map as a base, researchers examined 15 years of temperature information from the National Oceanic and Atmospheric Administration's 5,000 climatic data centers across the country. When everything was tabulated, the NADF decided to make some changes. Many areas of the country have moved up a full zone because of temperature changes over this time period. Check out www.arborday.org for the new cold-hardiness zone recommendations.

The YEAR IN GARDENING Volume 14 INDEX

Abutilon — *Calibrachoa*

Abutilon theophrasti
  weed watch, 306
Acer negundo
  woody weed, 270
Achillea
  filipendulina (fernleaf yarrow)
    seedheads in winter, 199(t)
  millefolium (common yarrow)
    and bulb combinations, 181(t)
Agastache mexicana
  'Kiegabi', 40
Ailanthus altissima
  woody weed, 271
air circulation, 157
Ajuga reptans
  top pick new perennial, 72
Alcea
  rosea (hollyhock)
    introduction, 56
  rugosa (Russian hollyhock)
    top pick back-of-the-border, 94
Amsonia
  hubrichtii
    seedheads in winter, 198(t)
  tabernaemontana (willow blue-star)
    seedheads in winter, 198(t)
Anemone
  blanda (Grecian windflower)
    and perennial combinations, 181(t)
  x*hybrida*
    seedheads in winter, 198(t)
Angelica gigas
  top pick back-of-the-border, 95
annuals
  combos for fall, 185
anthracnose, 275
apples, pest control on, 64

Aruncus
  and bulb combinations, 181(t)
Asclepias tuberosa
  seedheads in winter, 198(t)
assassin bugs, spined, 304
Aster novae-angliae
  top pick new perennial, 73
Astilbe
  x*arendsii*
    introduction, 57
  spp. (false spirea)
    and bulb combinations, 181(t)
    seedheads in winter, 198(t)
autumn, easy combinations for, 182
azalea *see Rhododendron*
baby's breath *see Gypsophila paniculata*
back yard gardens
  before & after, 110
bacteria as mood elevator, 64
Baptisia australis
  seedheads in winter, 198(t)
barrenwort *see Epimedium*
bee balm *see Monarda*
bee stings, 294
before & after
  color, color, color, 128
  midsummer makeover, 118
  neglected back yard, 110
  shade garden, 114
  starting from scratch, 106
  sunny side of street, 124
  water garden, 120
Belamcanda chinensis
  seedheads in winter, 198(t)
beneficial creatures, 304
bird baths
  ice-free, 203
  pumpkin, 290
bird feeders
  filling, 203
  hopper, 288
  No/No Feeders, 202
  seed tube, 289
  squirrel baffle, 202
  suet cage, 289
bird food
  Sharon Dunn on, 288
  Hot Meats™, 203
  no more weeds from birdseed, 298

birds
  container garden for, 250
  eBird database, 202
  lint bags for, 298
blackspot, 276
blossom-end rot, 63
bluebell, Spanish *see Hyacinthoides*
bluegrass *see Poa annua*
blue-star, willow *see Amsonia*
bonsai, 254
book reviews
  Down to Earth with Helen Dillon, 201
  Pots in the Garden, 255
  The Wildlife Gardener's Guide, 203
border gardens
  midsummer makeover, 118
  shade, 140
  top picks for back of, 92
borer, emerald ash, 64
botrytis gray mold, 276
Bougainvillea
  not blooming, 60
box elder *see Acer negundo*
buckthorn *see Rhamnus cathartica*
bugleweed *see Ajuga reptans*
bugs
  plant, 305
  spined assassin, 304
building projects
  bird bath, 290
  container hangers, 253
  greenhouse, 299
  steppers, 122
  string dispenser, 300
  tomato trellis, 294
  tool trellis, 286
  veggie-safe lumber, 294
bulbs
  combining with perennials, 180
  top pick new, 75
butterflies, container garden for, 250
butterfly weed *see Asclepias tuberosa*
calcium deficiency in tomato, 63
Calibrachoa x*hybrida*
  plant profile, 10

How to use your index

The index is divided by main topics with specific references following. All plants are referred to by botanical name.

For example, if you are looking for information about Jerusalem sage, the entry will look like this:
  sage, Jerusalem *see Phlomis*

Then turn to the reference for *Phlomis*, which looks like this:

Phlomis ← Main topic (in this case, genus name)
  russeliana (Jerusalem sage) ← Species reference
    seedheads in winter, 198(t) ← Page number / Information is in a table
  spp. (Jerusalem sage)
    top pick drought-tolerant plants, 87 ← Specific reference to topic

You also might come across a topic that gives you specific references as well as an idea of other places in the index to look for similar information. For example:
  containers
    see also garden plans
    blue, 189
    floating, 252

Camassia leichtlinii
  and perennial combinations, 181(t)
Camellia
  plant profile, 12
Campsis radicans
  moving, 60
Canna
  storing rhizomes, 58
cardinal flower *see Lobelia cardinalis*
cedar, eastern red *see Juniperus virginiana*
cedar, salt *see Tamarix*
cedar-apple rust, 274
Centaurea maculosa
  weed watch, 306
Ceratostigma plumbaginoides
  top pick drought-tolerant plant, 88
chia *see Salvia*
Chinese lantern *see Physalis alkekengi*
chipmunks, discouraging, 298
circlehoes, 296
Cistus
  top pick drought-tolerant plant, 87
cleaners *see* soap
Clematis
  growing from seed, 61
  seedheads in winter, 198(t)
  'Ville de Lyon', 16
clothing
  Greenjeans™, 284
Colchicum
  plant profile, 18
coleus *see Solenostemon*
Colocasia esculenta
  'Illustris', 28
color
  continuous blooming, 128
  element of design, 231
  layering, 130
  long-lasting, 190
  Kerry Mendez on season-long, 196
color themes
  blue, 186
  burgundy, 139
  gold, 138

compost and composting, 259, 260
compost bins, 261
coneflower, purple *see Echinacea purpurea*
coneflower, sweet *see Rudbeckia subtomentosa*
conifers, cleaning up, 59
containers
  see also garden plans
  blue, 189
  floating, 252
  gravel for drainage, 255
  growing vegetables in, 179
  hangers for, 253
  "pot feet", 246, 254
  recycle plastic pots, 258
  Rice Hull Garden™, 253
  types of, 234
  watering, 246
contrast as design element, 231
Convallaria majalis
  top pick for fragrance, 78
Cordyline
  top pick new perennial, 70
Coreopsis
  plant profile, 20
Cosmos
  plant profile, 24
crabapple *see Malus*

creeping Charlie *see Pilea nummularifolia*
Crocosmia
  top pick back-of-the-border, 95
crocus, autumn *see Colchicum*
crown rot, 277
Culver's root *see Veronicastrum virginicum*
daffodil *see Narcissus*
daffodil, Peruvian *see Hymenocallis* ×*festalis*
Dahlia
  top pick new perennial, 69
daisy, shasta *see Leucanthemum* ×*superbum*
daylily *see Hemerocallis*
decks
  create inviting spaces, 154
deer deterrents
  fences, 298
  foam pipe insulation, 298
  hydrolyzed casein, 301
Delphinium elatum
  top pick back-of-the-border, 93

design
  see also before & after; color; garden plans; pathways; *specific plant profiles; specific types of gardens*
  on a budget, 160
  combos for fall, 182
  elements of, 130, 231
  garden rooms, 142
  growing vegetables in perennial beds, 176
  island beds, 170
  landscape adds value to home, 201
  large scale, 164
  small spaces, 142, 183
  tiny gardens, 158
design challenge
  divide and disguise, 222
  island beds to block unsightly view, 226
  little house/big garden, 206
  privacy, 214
  rework bland bed, 210
  weedy to wonderful, 218
Dianthus
  top pick for fragrance, 78
Digitalis purpurea
  plant profile, 30

ILLUSTRATIONS: Mavis Augustine Torke

diseases, seven common, 274
dracaena *see Cordyline*
drip irrigation, 258
drought-tolerant plants, 86
earmuffs, 302
earthworms
  Great Lakes Worm Watch, 299
  lumpy lawn, 297
Echinacea purpurea
  seedheads in winter, 199(t)
edgers
  Kombi Gardening Tool, 285
elder, box *see Acer negundo*
elephant's ear *see Colocasia esculenta*
elm *see Ulmus pumila*
environmental issues
  earth-friendly gardening, 258
  veggie-safe lumber, 294
Epimedium
  top pick drought-tolerant plants, 91

Eryngium
  alpinum (alpine sea holly)
    top pick drought-tolerant plants, 89
  amethystinum (sea holly)
    seedheads in winter, 199(t)
Erythronium americanum
  and perennial combinations, 181(t)
Euphorbia
  polychroma (cushion spurge)
    top pick drought-tolerant plants, 90
  spp. (spurge)
    top pick new perennial, 71
false indigo *see Baptisia australis*
faucet extender, 292
fences
  camouflaging, 219
  deer, 298
  dressing up, 224
  for inviting spaces, 156
  for privacy, 215

fern, ostrich *see Matteuccia struthiopteris*
fertilizers
  chicken manure, 295
  lawn, 259
  sewage sludge, 292
  slow-release, 259
Festuca
  produce herbicide, 62
Filipendula rubra
  top pick back-of-the-border, 93
fire pits, 157
focal points
  element of design, 231
  ornaments as, 174
foliage color
  blue, 188
Forsythia ×*intermedia*
  top pick flowering shrub, 82
foundation gardens, long-lasting color for, 192, 194
fountain grass *see Pennisetum setaceum*
fountains, 157

foxglove *see Digitalis purpurea*
fragrance, top picks for, 76
Fritillaria meleagris
  and perennial combinations, 181(t)
front yard gardens and curb appeal, 150
furniture
  forest-friendly, 201
  for inviting spaces, 155
  ultimate lounger, 200
garages, dressing up, 97
garden myths, 264
garden plans
  border gardens
    fence dress-up, 224
    low-maintenance, 220
    summer color-filled, 108
  color-theme gardens
    orange and red, 224
    purple and red, 216
  container gardens
    bird/butterfly attracting, 250
    bold combo, 245
    bright-colored, 239
    dark and dramatic, 238
    gold rush, 248
    holiday, 249
    light and leafy, 236
    readers' favorites, 240
    shade, 242
    sunny, 241
    tropical, 237, 244
    whimsical, 242
    winter indoors, summer outdoors, 236
  corner gardens
    makeover, 212
  island beds
    getting started, 228
    going strong, 230
  patios and decks
    instead of lawn, 216
  regional gardens
    native plants, 42
  special situations
    garage dress-up, 97
  window boxes
    sunny, 208

gardeners
- Alan Branhagen, 42
- Sharon Dunn, 288
- Joe Lamp'l, 284
- Kerry Mendez, 196
- Jo Ellen Meyers Sharp, 180
- David Whitinger, 280

getaways, 134, 152

Glechoma hederacea
- weed watch, 306

gloves, drying, 298
goat's beard *see Aruncus*
goldenrod *see Solidago*
grape *see Vitis*
greenhouse, plastic covered shelf unit as, 299
ground cover, moss as, 297
groundhogs (pest watch), 305

Gypsophila paniculata
- Asiatic lilies as "stakes," 60

hanging baskets, holiday, 255
hardpan, 126, 293
hardscape
- glass blocks, 58
- large scale, 168
- softening, 146

health
- gardeners and lung cancer, 59
- homemade cold pack for sore muscles, 295
- soil bacteria as mood elevator, 64

hearing protection, 302

Helianthus
- top pick back-of-the-border, 96

Heliotropium arborescens
- top pick for fragrance, 77

Hemerocallis
- bumpy buds, flawed flowers, 65
- top pick new perennial, 71

herbicide from fescue, 62

Hibiscus
- *moscheutos* (rose mallow or hardy hibiscus)
  - plant profile, 32
- *syriacus* (rose of Sharon)
  - top pick flowering shrub, 85

hoes
- circlehoe, 296

hollyhock *see Alcea*
honeysuckle *see Lonicera tatarica*
hoses
- Dual-Flo™ nozzle, 285
- faucet extender, 292

Hosta
- hail damage, 64
- top pick new perennial, 73

house plants and pollution, 259
hyacinth, wood *see Hyacinthoides*

Hyacinthoides
- *hispanica* (Spanish bluebell) and perennial combinations, 181(t)
- *non-scripta* (wood hyacinth) and perennial combinations, 181(t)

Hyacinthus orientalis
- and perennial combinations, 181(t)
- top pick for fragrance, 79

Hydrangea
- *arborescens*
  - top pick flowering shrub, 85
- *macrophylla* (mop heads or snowballs)
  - plant profile, 36
- *paniculata*
  - top pick new shrub, 74

Hymenocallis ×*festalis*
- top pick for fragrance, 79

indigo, false *see Baptisia australis*
insect repellents, 201

Iris
- *sibirica* (Siberian iris)
  - plant profile, 52
  - seedheads in winter, 199(t)
- spp.
  - and bulb combinations, 181(t)
  - raccoons and, 299

irrigation, drip, 258
island beds
- to block unsightly view, 226
- designing, 170

ivy, ground *see Glechoma hederacea*
ivy, poison *see Rhus radicans*
Jacob's ladder *see Polemonium*

Juniperus virginiana
- woody weed, 271

knapweed, spotted *see Centaurea maculosa*
kneepads, 284
lacewings, luring with catnip oil, 297
ladybugs, 304
lamb's ears *see Stachys byzantina*
landscape design *see* design
lawns
- conversion from scratch, 106
- lumpy from nightcrawlers, 297

leaves, shredding, 292

Leucanthemum ×*superbum* 'Becky', 50

light
- shade types, 141

lighting, garden, 155

Ligularia
- and bulb combinations, 181(t)

lilac *see Syringa*

Lilium
- seedheads in winter, 199(t)
- top picks, 98

lily, blackberry *see Belamcanda chinensis*
lily, checkered *see Fritillaria meleagris*

lily, trout *see Erythronium americanum*
lily of the valley *see Convallaria majalis*
line as element of design, 231
Lobelia cardinalis
   and bulb combinations, 181(t)
   creating wet conditions for, 61
Lonicera tatarica
   woody weed, 269
lotions, 295
Lunaria annua
   seedheads in winter, 199(t)
lungwort *see Pulmonaria*
mail order
   David Whitinger's tips on, 280
Malus
   top pick new tree, 75
manure, chicken, 295
Matteuccia struthiopteris
   and bulb combinations, 181(t)

Matthiola incana
   top pick for fragrance, 77
meadow rue *see Thalictrum flavum glaucum*
mildew, powdery, 277
million bells *see Calibrachoa xhybrida*
millipedes, 296
Milorganite®, 292
mini-blinds, making garden notes with, 303
mockorange *see Philadelphus*
mold, botrytis gray, 276
Monarda
   top pick back-of-the-border, 94
money plant *see Lunaria annua*
mopheads *see Hydrangea*
Morus
   alba (white mulberry)
     woody weed, 270
   spp. (mulberry)
     pruning, 61

mosquitoes
   banana peels for bites, 294
   citronella incense coils, 201
moss as ground cover, 297
mulberry *see Morus*
mulches and mulching
   for containers, 247
   cypress, 63
   herbicide contaminated, 301
   newspaper, 258
   types of, 301
myths, gardening, 264
Narcissus
   color change, 59
   and perennial combinations, 181(t)
   top pick new bulb, 75
native plants
   Alan Branhagen on, 42
new plants for 2008, 68
nightcrawlers *see* earthworms
nurseries
   www.premiumplants.net (Hortech), 62

oregano *see Origanum*
Origanum
   top pick new perennial, 72
ornaments
   bamboo stake bundle, 301
   colored glass bottles, 200
   as design element, 174
   lighted holiday forms, 200
overwintering tender perennials, 262
Oxalis stricta
   weed watch, 307
Paeonia
   'Empress Wu's Yellow', 44
Panicum virgatum
   seedheads in winter, 199(t)
Papaver orientale
   seedheads in winter, 199(t)
parsnip, wild *see Pastinaca sativa*
Passiflora caerulea
   top pick for fragrance, 81
passion flower *see Passiflora caerulea*
Pastinaca sativa
   weed watch, 307
pathways
   large scale, 169
   plantings, 113
   stepping stones, 122
patios
   create inviting spaces, 154
   multi-level, 215
pavers, 156
Pennisetum setaceum
   dividing, 60
Penstemon pinifolius
   top pick drought-tolerant plants, 91
peony *see Paeonia*
peppers, drying, 62
perennials
   combining with bulbs, 180
   dwarf, 183
   first year bloomers, 267
   midsummer makeover, 118
   overwintering tender, 262
   temporary storage, 300
   timing of planting, 264
   top picks, 68, 86, 92
pergolas, 156
Perovskia atriplicifolia
   seedheads in winter, 199(t)

pests and pest control
  eco-friendly pesticide, 284
  organic first aid, 259
  pest to watch out for, 305
Petunia x*hybrida*
  top pick new perennial, 69
Philadelphus
  top pick for fragrance, 80
Phlomis
  russeliana (Jerusalem sage)
    seedheads in winter, 198(t)
  spp. (Jerusalem sage)
    top pick drought-tolerant plants, 87
Phlox paniculata
  eight new, 46
photography and seed sharing, 65
Physalis alkekengi
  seedheads in winter, 198(t)
Pilea nummularifolia
  tough weed, 272
pink *see Dianthus*
plant bugs *see* bugs
plant combinations
  burgundy, 139
  dramatic texture, 139
  fall splendor, 182
  golden, 138
  heat-defying, 112
  Jo Ellen Meyers Sharp on, 180
plant markers
  chopsticks, 303
  mini blind reminders, 303
plumbago *see Ceratostigma plumbaginoides*
Poa annua
  weed watch, 307
poison ivy *see Rhus radicans*
Polemonium
  spp. (Jacob's ladder)
    top pick new perennial, 70
  yezoense hidakanum
    introduction, 57
Polygonatum
  and bulb combinations, 181(t)
ponds
  floating pots, 252
  skimming, 303
  for sump pump overflow, 200

poppy, celandine *see Stylophorum diphyllum*
poppy, oriental *see Papaver orientale*
Primula sieboldii
  introduction, 57
privacy, design for reclaiming, 214
pruners, bypass
  Fiskars™ 15-inch power lever, 284
Pulmonaria
  spotty leaves, 65
queen-of-the-prairie *see Filipendula rubra*
raccoons eating iris, 299
raised beds, glass-block, 58
repetition as element of design, 231
Rhamnus cathartica
  woody weed, 269
Rhododendron
  top pick flowering shrub, 83
rhubarb, edible
  fertilizing, 63
Rhus radicans
  identifying, 273
  tough weed, 273
Rhytisma
  pest watch, 305
rock rose *see Cistus*

Rosa
  rose rosette disease, 58
  top pick new shrub, 74
rose, rock *see Cistus*
Rudbeckia subtomentosa
  plant profile, 48
rust
  cedar-apple, 274
  spread of, 275
sage *see Salvia*
sage, Jerusalem *see Phlomis*
sage, Russian *see Perovskia atriplicifolia*
salamanders, 304
salt cedar *see Tamarix*
Salvia
  greggii (autumn or woody sage)
    top pick drought-tolerant plants, 90
  hispanica (chia)
    edible seeds, 62
Sambucus canadensis
  woody weed, 269
scale (size) of ornaments, 174
screens to hide utilities, 146
sea holly *see Eryngium*
Sedum
  spp.
    seedheads in winter, 199(t)
  telephium (tall sedum)
    introduction, 56

seed sharing, 65
seed starting
  in avocado skins, 300
  hard-coated seeds, 267
  removing from packet, 301
  slow germination, 267
  small seeds, 266
sewage sludge, 292
shade, types of, 141
shade gardens
  before & after, 114
  borders, 140
  long-lasting color, 194
shape as element of design, 231
shoe covers, 292
shrubs
  overgrown, 278
  top picks, 74, 82
  unshearing, 293
slugs and ponds, 116
snakes and mothballs, 296
snowballs *see Hydrangea*
soap
  Simply Safe™, 302
  Smellkiller™ Zilosoap®, 295
soil amendments to lighten clay soil, 265
soil bacterium as mood enhancer, 64

Solenostemon
   top pick new perennial, 68
Solidago
   seedheads in winter, 198(t)
Solomon's seal *see Polygonatum*
sorrel *see Oxalis stricta*
sound, 157
spades
   Trenchfoot™, 285
speedwell *see Veronica spicata*
spurge *see Euphorbia*
Stachys byzantina
   and bulb combinations, 181(t)
stakes
   bamboo, 301
   daisy stems as ties, 300
   storage, 301
stepping stones, "floating," 122
stock *see Matthiola incana*
string dispensers, 300
stumps as planters, 253

Stylophorum diphyllum
   and bulb combinations, 181(t)
sunflower *see Helianthus*
switch grass *see Panicum virgatum*
Syringa
   meyeri (dwarf Korean lilac)
      top pick flowering shrub, 84
   vulgaris (common lilac)
      top pick for fragrance, 80
Tamarix
   combating, 297
tar spot *see Rhytisma*
texture
   dramatic, 139
   element of design, 231
Thalictrum flavum glaucum
   top pick back-of-the-border, 92
ticks, 296
tickseed *see Coreopsis*

tomatoes
   blossom-end rot, 63
   planting with sugar, 264
   types of, 63
tools and equipment
   circlehoe, 296
   Dual-Flo™ nozzle, 285
   earmuffs, 302
   faucet extender, 292
   glove dryer, 298
   Greenjeans™, 284
   Joe Lamp'l on, 284
   Kombi Gardening Tool, 285
   shoe covers, 292
   tool trellis, 286
   twine dispenser, 300
   Weed Wrench™, 279
transplanting and vitamin B, 265
tree of heaven *see Ailanthus altissima*

trees
   balled and burlapped, 282
   myths about staking, 265
   purchasing healthy, 282
   top pick new, 75
trellises
   tomato, 294
   for tools, 286
trumpet creeper *see Campsis radicans*
trumpet vine *see Campsis radicans*
Tulipa
   and perennial combinations, 181(t)
twine dispensers, 300
Ulmus pumila
   woody weed, 270
umbrellas
   for inviting spaces, 155
   for working in garden, 294
utilities, hiding in plain sight, 146
vegetables in perennial beds, 176
velvetleaf *see Abutilon theophrasti*
Veronica spicata
   top pick drought-tolerant plants, 89
Veronicastrum virginicum
   top pick back-of-the-border, 96
Viburnum carlesii
   top pick flowering shrub, 83
violet, dog's tooth *see Erythronium americanum*
Vitis
   woody weed, 271
walls, glass block, 58
water gardens
   before & after, 120
water-absorbing crystals, 247
watering
   containers, 246
   myths about, 264
watering cans
   spout for bottle, 293
   wine bottles with pourers, 252

weeds and weeding

weeds and weeding
  from birdseed, 298
  fighting tough, 272
  recycled garbage can for, 303
  Weed Wrench™, 279
  weeds to know, 306
  woody, 268
Weigela florida
  top pick flowering shrub, 84
wildlife
  see also birds; deer deterrents
  chipmunks, 298
  groundhogs, 305
  raccoons, 299
  snakes, 296
willow blue-star *see Amsonia*
wind as garden challenge, 126
windflower *see Anemone*
winter
  design with seedheads, 198
Wisteria floribunda
  top pick for fragrance, 81
xeriscape, watering, 265
yarrow *see Achillea*
Yucca filamentosa
  top pick drought-tolerant plants, 88

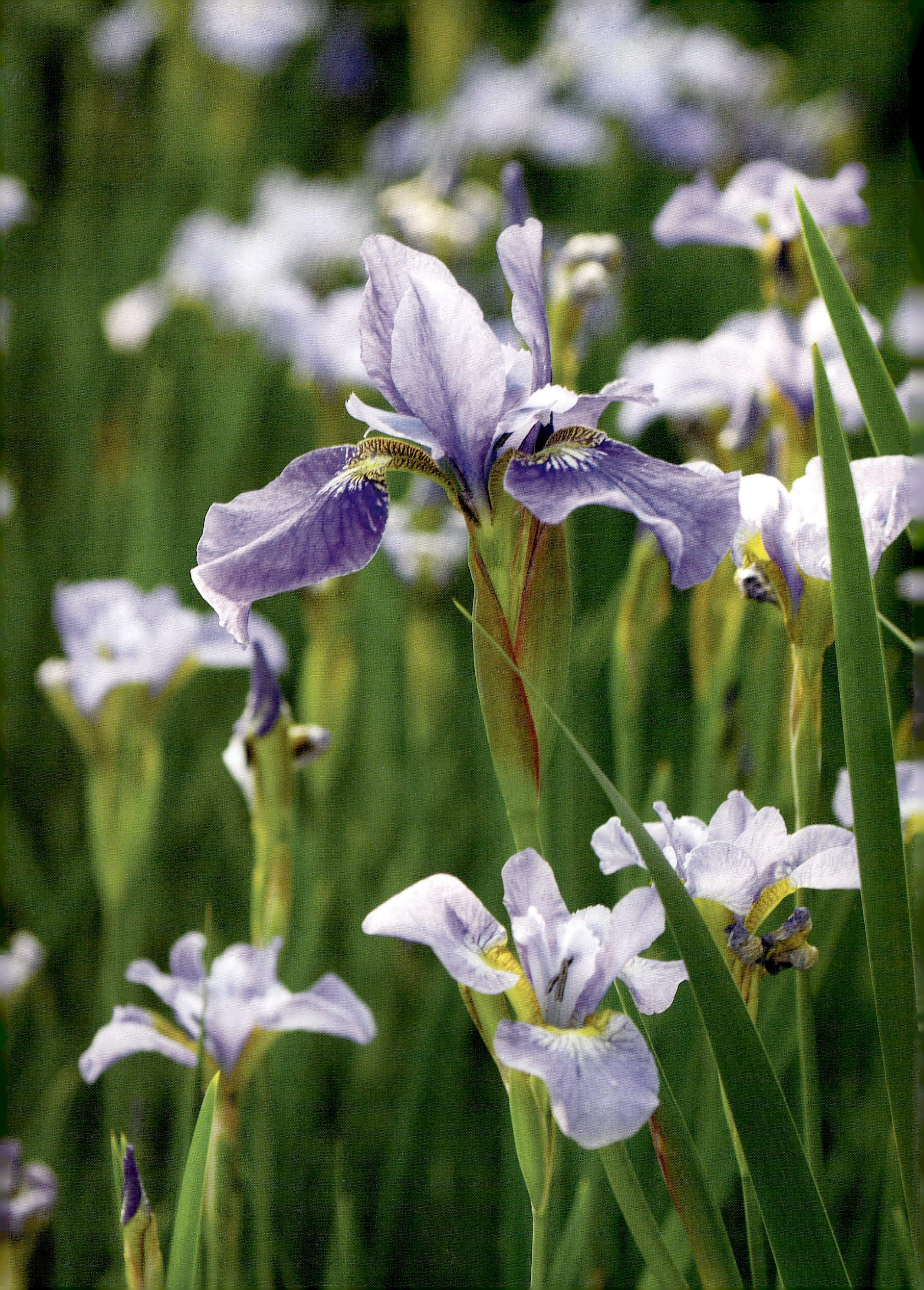

"And 'tis my faith that
*every flower
Enjoys the
air it breathes.*"

— William Wordsworth

Garden Gate
The YEAR IN GARDENING

www.GardenGateMagazine.com